A SHRINKING ISLAND

MODERNISM AND
NATIONAL CULTURE
IN ENGLAND

Jed Esty

PRINCETON UNIVERSITY PRESS

PRINCETON AND OXFORD

LIBRARY OF CONGRESS CATALOGING-IN-PUBLICATION DATA

ESTY, JOSHUA, 1967–

A SHRINKING ISLAND : MODERNISM AND NATIONAL CULTURE

IN ENGLAND / JOSHUA ESTY.

P. CM.

INCLUDES BIBLIOGRAPHICAL REFERENCES AND INDEX.

ISBN: 0-691-11548-6 (ALK. PAPER)

ISBN: 0-691-11549-4 (PBK. : ALK. PAPER)

1. ENGLISH LITERATURE—20TH CENTURY—HISTORY AND CRITICISM.

2. MODERNISM (LITERATURE)—ENGLAND. 3. LITERATURE AND

ANTHROPOLOGY—ENGLAND—HISTORY—20TH CENTURY.

4. LITERATURE AND SOCIETY—ENGLAND—HISTORY—20TH CENTURY.

5. ENGLAND—INTELLECTUAL LIFE—20TH CENTURY.

6. POSTCOLONIALISM IN LITERATURE. 7. IMPERIALISM IN LITERATURE.

8. NATIONALISM IN LITERATURE. I. TITLE.

PR478.M6E85 2003

820.9'112–DC21   2003043315

BRITISH LIBRARY CATALOGING-IN-PUBLICATION DATA IS AVAILABLE

THIS BOOK HAS BEEN COMPOSED IN SABON

PRINTED ON ACID-FREE PAPER. ∞

WWW.PUPRESS.PRINCETON.EDU

PRINTED IN THE UNITED STATES OF AMERICA

1 3 5 7 9 10 8 6 4 2

A SHRINKING ISLAND

For JCE and KCE

CONTENTS

ACKNOWLEDGMENTS

THE NAMES listed here testify to the large debt I owe to teachers, scholars, colleagues, and friends. The list, and the sense of gratitude that motivates it, extend well beyond those named here: to the writers who appear in my endnotes, and to many not named who have nevertheless contributed to the making of this book.

To begin with the teachers: Elliot Lilien of Concord-Carlisle High School lit up the big ideas and made historical explanation itself seem important. Mark Wollaeger and Joe Gordon were among my first mentors and have remained model academics even as they have become colleagues and friends. At Duke, I was fortunate to work with an astonishing variety of challenging and generous thinkers, especially Marianna Torgovnick, Fredric Jameson, Eve Sedgwick, and Susan Thorne. I owe a special debt to Michael Moses for intellectual support and friendship.

Many friends at Duke inspired me by the example of their own work and by their gracious responses to mine. I want especially to thank Nigel Alderman, Dan Blanton, Chris Cunningham, Carolyn Gerber, Heather Hicks, John Hunter, Joe McLaughlin, Katherine Stubbs, Maurice Wallace, and John Waters. Conversations with Ian Baucom have made this book—and the process of writing it—better.

I would also like to acknowledge a lively set of colleagues at Harvard, especially my closest readers in modern British literature, Nick Jenkins, Jesse Matz, and Jonah Siegel. Larry Buell, Phil Fisher, Stephen Greenblatt, Bill Handley, Graham Huggan, Shannon Jackson, Bob Kiely, Becky Krug, Jeff Masten, Peter Sacks, Elaine Scarry, Werner Sollors, and Helen Vendler all responded to my work at various stages, generating new ideas and clarifying old ones.

I spent a year working on this book at the Wesleyan Center for the Humanities, where I encountered a welcoming and vigorous cohort of scholars; I am especially grateful to David Weisberg, Sean McCann, Kach Tololyan, and of course Betsy Traube, for her intellectual leadership and institutional support. There are others from diverse times and places who have (perhaps without even knowing it) contributed ideas and suggestions or valuable advice and encouragement: Perry Anderson, David Bromwich, Jim Chandler, Laura Chrisman, Ed Comentale, Ashley Dawson, Jane Garrity, Michael Gorra, Lanny Hammer, Peter Kalliney, Tamar Katz, David Lloyd, Tim Mitchell, Michael Levenson, Jack Matthews, David McWhirter, Walter Benn Michaels, Peter Merrington, Franco Moretti, Gautam Premnath, Brian Richardson, John Paul Riquelme, Paul Saint-Amour, Sanford Schwartz, Robert von Hallberg, Michael Warren, Ayako

Yoshino-Miyaura, and the audiences to whom I presented work at Harvard, Northwestern, Chicago, Brown, Colby and Wesleyan.

Jim English, Anne Fernald, Doug Mao, Jesse Matz, Michael Tratner, and Mark Wollaeger all read sections along the way and offered invaluable and timely responses. I would also like to thank Eric Marler, Ansley Dalbo, and Emily Wong for diligent research and Praseeda Gopinath, for thoughtful assistance beyond the call of duty.

More recently, I have been welcomed by a group of true colleagues at the University of Illinois. My thanks to Janet Lyon, Jim Hurt, Zohreh Sullivan, Kwaku Korang, and Joe Valente, who gave me the opportunity to join them and who have always made me glad that I did. They—along with Matti Bunzl, Antoinette Burton, Tim Dean, Stephen Hartnett, Suvir Kaul, Ania Loomba, Bill Maxwell, and Julia Walker—read and responded to portions of the manuscript with remarkable intelligence and vision. Along with many other new friends, they have made the University of Illinois a humane and exciting place in which to live, work, think, and write.

There are several supporting institutions to thank for the time and resources I needed to research and write this book: Duke University for a graduate fellowship; the Lilly Library at Indiana University for an Everett Helm Visiting Fellowship; Harvard University for generous research support in many forms; the Center for the Humanities at Wesleyan University; the National Endowment for the Humanities for a 1999 research fellowship; and the English Department, the College of Liberal Arts and Sciences, and the Campus Research Board at the University of Illinois for release time and research assistance.

Mary Murrell at Princeton University Press has been a patient, efficient, and steadfast guide; I thank her, Sarah Green, and Vicky Wilson-Schwartz for their help in realizing the book. I cannot sufficiently thank Jim Buzard and his anonymous counterpart for their astonishingly learned, generous, and insightful readings of the manuscript.

Finally, to the kind of gratitude that extends way before and well beyond this occasion: I dedicate this book to my parents, John and Katharine Esty, who taught me to love words, to be curious about the world, and to finish what I started. And to Andrea, who has made writing the book—and everything else—worthwhile.

I am grateful to the Johns Hopkins University Press for permission to reprint portions of chapters 2, 3, and 4, which originally appeared in *ELH* 69.1 (2002), the *Yale Journal of Criticism* 16.1 (2003), and *Modernism/Modernity* 7.1 (2000).

A SHRINKING ISLAND

INTRODUCTION

LATE MODERNISM AND THE
ANTHROPOLOGICAL TURN

BOTH professional and lay readers in America seem to share an intuitive belief that English literature has suffered a steady decline in the twentieth century and, moreover, that the decline can be correlated to and even explained by the contraction of British power. Yet few would argue that geopolitical power corresponds in a predictable way to literary creativity. If anything, the evidence from the past century points to an inverse relation. We find celebrated literary booms in Revivalist Ireland and in Cold-War Latin America, classic instances of aesthetic experimentation in the semi-peripheral avant-gardes of Russian and Italian futurism, a high index of formal invention in the "minor literature" of Kafka and Beckett, and linguistic exuberance flowing out of the relative backwaters of Joyce's Liffey and Faulkner's Mississippi.[1] And yet the idea persists that postimperial English writing, in becoming provincial and ex-centric, also became stale and wan. This view is not restricted to outsiders; consider a fairly typical 1966 statement from the novelist Anthony Burgess:

> What subject-matter does England provide (or Wales or Scotland or Northern Ireland or the Channel Islands or the Isle of Man)? Not, I would say, the subject-matter of an expansive vision, which, whatever Americans may think, is there in America for the American writer's taking. Some of us got in just in time to record a dying, or heroically relinquished, empire. The transition from free society to welfare state provided material for a few novels, but the theme has lost all its vitality.[2]

Burgess's complaint reflects not, I think, a real relation between lost political and artistic power but the recurrent tendency of commentators on the English scene to metaphorize literary change as national decline. That metaphorical habit causes a great deal of critical haziness; it sustains myths of a fallen heritage in the land of Shakespeare, of an island's poetic sourcewaters run dry, of the death of the English (but not anglophone) novel. If we cast these myths aside, what precisely is the relationship between British imperial contraction and the shape of English literary culture?

Since elegists of English literature tend to date its decline to the eclipse of high modernism, we can restate this question in terms of modernism's original relationship to British hegemony: what accounts for the apparently coterminous lifespans of high modernism and high imperialism in the British sphere? How, in other words, was English modernism shaped and inflected, not just by the accumulation and concentration of economic, social, and cultural power in metropolitan London from 1880 to 1930, but by the relative diffusion of that power during the period from 1930 to 1960? The most widely held views about the end of modernism have tended to concentrate on causal factors associated with European politics (the rise of fascism and the dampening effects of World War II), economics (the depression that ran through the thirties), and culture (the growing threat to high art from mass media in the age of radio, cinema, and television). This study aims to extend those explanatory models by giving sustained consideration to the relationship between a fading imperialism and the putative death of English modernism (understood as the last major phase of English literature). Rather than describe the collapse of British power and the diminishment of English literature in terms of direct causality or—equally implausibly—in terms of mere coincidence, the chapters that follow concentrate on late modernism's indirect and mediated representations of imperial contraction in the form of an "anthropological turn" manifested in both cultural doctrine and literary style.

In this book, the anthropological turn names the discursive process by which English intellectuals translated the end of empire into a resurgent concept of national culture—one whose insular integrity seemed to mitigate some of modernism's characteristic social agonies while rendering obsolete some of modernism's defining aesthetic techniques. A *Shrinking Island* offers, in effect, a literary prehistory to the anthropological turn that Colin MacCabe, following a more conventional periodization, describes as having made postwar English culture into "an object of study like any other, privileged only by historical accident and not by some immanent qualities."[3] Defined against the assumptions of traditional English literary criticism, the anthropological turn more or less corresponds to the rise of "culturalism," that is, to an ethnographic and anti-elitist approach to symbolic practices whose classic institutional form is Birmingham-school Cultural Studies. By tracing this turn back to the thirties, we can see how canonical English writing of the prewar period established key tropes and concepts for the postwar reclamation of England's cultural integrity and authenticity.

From this perspective, it is possible to see that English modernists like T. S. Eliot, Virginia Woolf, and E. M. Forster did not (as is often assumed) resist the anthropological turn in a rearguard defense of the literary, but actively participated in the rise of an Anglocentric culture paradigm.[4] Taken together, their works of the thirties and forties begin to deemphasize the redemptive agency of *art*, which, because of its social autonomization, operates unmoored from any given national sphere, and to promote instead the redemptive agency of *culture*, which is restricted by national or ethnolinguistic borders. By tracing the anthropological turn through Eliot's late poetry, Woolf's last novel, and Forster's minor drama, this study describes the end-stage of a London-based modernism. It also points to that modernism's influence on broader cultural formations that have come to define postwar, postempire England. The key figures in this version of late modernism are canonical English writers who measured the passing of British hegemony not solely in terms of a vitiated imperial humanism but also in terms of a recovered cultural particularity that is, at least potentially, the basis for both social and aesthetic renewal. This small but central constellation of modernists in England actively manages the cultural transition between empire and welfare state. Their works reveal the inner logic and stylistic contours of a major literary culture caught in the act of becoming minor.

Since Anglo-American modernism is so famously a movement of opening salvoes, of bristling manifestoes and self-regarding innovations, it is now worthwhile to ask whether there are not also important closing statements that registered epochal change, just as the big blasts of 1914–22 had.[5] To press the historical case for modernism's end-stage requires a formational rather than formal account of the movement, one that brings into view the following familiar touchstones of the period 1890–1940: the rise of new mass transportation and communication technologies; the scientific paradigm shift crystallized by the theory of general relativity, the antipositivist and antihumanist philosophical turns flowing from (and in a sense against) Marx and Nietzsche, Darwin, and Freud; the broadly anti-Victorian social ethos of intellectuals, the galvanizing events of World War I and the Russian Revolution; and the role of new structures of patronage and dissemination endemic to literary circles in the early twentieth century.[6] In my view, the single term that best captures the multiple contextual dimensions needed to historicize modernist practice is Raymond Williams's "metropolitan perception," which has the additional virtue of situating modernism in the urban centers of Western power. Modernism, writes Williams, cannot properly be understood without an account of the metropolis as a place "beyond both city and nation in their older senses," which developed out of the "magnetic concentration of wealth and power in imperial capitals and the simultaneous cosmopolitan access to a wide variety of subordinate cultures."[7] Because it draws together the urban-imperial base and rich cultural superstructure of modernism, "metropolitan perception" will be a central term in this study, especially when paired with the useful (though unmelodious) term "demetropolitanization," meaning the retrenchment, in the thirties and forties, of all that metropolitan perception implies.

While many of the stylistic hallmarks of high modernism continued to appear in various experimental and nonmimetic literatures well after World War II, the broader cultural conditions of metropolitan modernism eroded rather sharply during the midcentury. Many of the generic and stylistic changes that characterize late modernism in this study could be ascribed to a kind of generational fatigue, especially since the canonical group of anglophone modernists seemed to enter into dogmatic middle age (Eliot, Pound, Lewis) or to expire (Yeats, Joyce, Woolf) with remarkable consistency sometime around 1940. But if we think in terms of generational exhaustion, we presume late modernism to be an aftereffect rather than a new historical phase requiring its own formal innovations. Moreover, if we interpolate the motif of exhaustion into the larger narrative of British culture, we only confirm an unreflective intuition about national decline without actually analyzing the nature of cultural change attendant on demetropolitanization. In taking up the question of late modernism and imperial contraction between 1930 and 1960, then, this study aims to address the blank space or interregnum between modernism and postmodernism, between empire and welfare state.[8]

While a tight canonical focus on English modernists like Forster, Woolf, and Eliot leaves out important experimental writing in the period, it has the advantage of directing attention to an established literary elite identified with London, the preeminent imperial metropole. That elite's response to imperial contraction brings out a crucial historical relationship between two processes that have not been fully theorized in relation to each other: decolonization and the rise of culturalism. Before proceeding with the elaboration of that intertwined history, though, it is worth addressing a preliminary question: was there in fact an *English* modernism? Or was there instead, as Terry Eagleton's *Exiles and Émigrés* (among other studies) has suggested, an international modernism briefly housed in England? Eagleton, like many leftist critics, considers a bourgeoisified English culture to have been proof against the incursions of the radical European avant-gardes.[9] Of course, the idea of English literature's resistance to aesthetic and political experimentation stems from the modernist period itself. Pound (no leftist!) offers a classic statement of the case in *How to Read* (1931):

> the Irish took over the business for a few years; Henry James led, or rather preceded, the novelists, and then the Britons resigned *en bloc*; the language is now in the keeping of the Irish (Yeats and Joyce); apart from Yeats, since the death of Hardy, poetry is being written by Americans. All the developments in English verse since 1910 are due almost wholly to Americans. In fact, there is no longer any reason to call it English verse, and there is no present reason to think of England at all.[10]

As Pound suggests, few of the radical innovators in British modernism were English-born, and, conversely, many of the English-born figures of the period (Forster and Lawrence, for instance) kept alive residual elements of Victorian realism and Edwardian pastoralism in their work. Many avant-gardists (Pound, Wyndham Lewis, Mina Loy) gave up on England as a place for radical innovation. It is probably fair to describe English modernism as a compromise formation, a semimodernized modernism. Nonetheless, English intellectuals like T. E. Hulme, F. M. Ford, Virginia Woolf, and Roger Fry did inject some of the excitement of continental thought and art (psychoanalysis, postimpressionism, Bergsonism) into the bloodstream of an otherwise conventional literary scene. To the extent that a cosmopolitan and experimental modernism posed itself against insular traditionalism throughout the second and third decades of the century, it is possible to measure in relative terms a subsequent Anglocentric turn in the 1930s and 1940s. By that point, the surviving modernists still living and writing in England had winnowed down to a smallish band, whose most canonical representatives are Forster, Woolf, and Eliot.[11]

It is precisely because of the politics of canonization and the institutionalized cultural power associated with, for example, *The Criterion* and the Bloomsbury group, that Eliot and Woolf (representing the established poetry and fiction of interwar English modernism) come to feature as the central figures in this book. Not only do Eliot and Woolf exemplify the last "major" generation of English writers but their late works offer some interesting and unexplored parallels, particularly insofar as both writers produce texts whose layered construction inscribes all the complexity of a massive historical transition in which metropolitan modernism gives way to the *petit recits* of national culture. In what follows, I read *Between the Acts* and *Four Quartets* as literary forms dedicated to accommodating the fading significance of English universalism to the emergent significance of English particularism. If these texts refer conspicuously to an English center of gravity, they do not simply reveal a latent, conservative, and artistically null nativism lurking underneath some liberatory and radical international modernism. By shifting the terms of debate from British decline to English revival, I do not propose to ignore the fact that English particularism has been the basis for a rearguard politics of ethnic identity in contemporary Britain and for an apparently provincial or insular literature. However, to grasp the late-imperial dialectic of lost universalism and restored particularity, we must be equally attentive to the ways in which nativism has been interwoven with the democratization of culture itself.

The first step in historicizing the Anglocentric turn as something other than a pretext for bad art (and bad politics) is to remember that, for some influential English writers, the end of empire entailed a metaphorical repair of the social divides that had conditioned modernism's aesthetics of failure and fragmentation. Working backward, then, we can identify imperialism's place in the modernist imaginary as both a floating symbol and a material predicate of lost cultural wholeness. This approach allows us to begin to fill in some of the theoretical gaps left in the project of reading anglophone modernism in the context of British imperial power. Although both modernism and imperialism reached a peak in the period from 1880 to 1945, we have very few general accounts of the relationship between them (particularly by comparison to Victorian colonial discourse studies or post-1945 postcolonial studies). Most colonial-discourse work in the modernist period tends to be limited to individual figures (Conrad, Forster) or to texts with obvious imperial settings or thematic content.[12] Two of the best recent books in this field, Ian Baucom's *Out of Place* and Simon Gikandi's *Maps of Englishness*, overcome the longstanding divide between domestic and imperial cultures. Like Gauri Viswanathan's *Masks of Conquest*, these books reconceptualize Englishness—even in its apparently insular manifestations—as shaped and haunted by forms of imperial experience and knowledge.[13] Their explorations across the nineteenth and twentieth centuries provide a critical backdrop for my own more period-intensive study of high and late modernism.

Baucom, Gikandi, and Viswanathan all affirm (implicitly or explicitly) Edward Said's foundational notion of the "cultural integrity of empire," reminding us that good theoretical or historical work cannot divorce the effects of imperialism in the colonies from its effects in the center, nor can it separate colonial power from European high culture. With this in mind, we must recognize imperialism as a significant context even for modernist works that seem insulated from imperial concerns. To do subtle justice to the cultural and literary aspects of metropolitan power in the English sphere, we must chart imperialism's presence not only as visible and narrative data but as unexpected formal encryptments and thematic outcroppings in ostensibly domestic texts. In *Howards End*, for example, Fredric Jameson has proposed that a figure of "placelessness" or spatial infinity marks the assimilation of the economic and political conditions of British imperialism into modernist narrative. In Jameson's view, the representation of the imperial-infinite remains politically unconscious, but emerges as an element of style. To make his case, Jameson argues that the modern colonial system created a meaning loss by relocating major elements of the British economy overseas. Once these aspects of production are beyond the view of those in the imperial center, they are no longer available for representation.[14]

Jameson's essay applies a Lukacsian notion of modernism as the literature par excellence of lost social totality to imperial England, described as a center that no longer possesses full knowledge of itself. I will return to this provocative claim in chapter 1, but it is worth mentioning here that Jameson's model corroborates, in an indirect way, the intellectual history of modern England proposed by Perry Anderson. In Anderson's influential analysis, the anthropological visibility and wholeness of tribal societies in the colonial periphery drew attention away from comprehensive sociological knowledge of England itself. As Anderson's colleague Tom Nairn puts the point, "Historically, the inward lack corresponded to an outward presence."[15] Thus, while the culture of imperial modernism represented itself as an expanding and synthesizing universalism *at the periphery* (where it encountered the putatively whole cultures of tribal premodernity), it registered an attenuated or absent totality *at the core*, where knowledge of the inside was mystified into the atomized but dazzling unreality of metropolitan perception.

If the metaphor of lost totality is one of the central deep structures of imperialism and modernism, it follows that the end of empire might be taken to augur a basic repair or reintegration of English culture itself. Such a turn of geopolitical events would therefore reinflect those aspects of modernist style that were based on lost social totality with a new—or newly imagined—sense of spatial and cultural consolidation. By this logic, the restored knowability of the home culture would seem to mitigate both the inner lack of Anderson's English intelligentsia and the fractured geography of Jameson's modernist elite. As it happens, most of the writers under consideration here have careers in which self-consciously metropolitan themes and techniques give way to Anglocentric representations of meaningful time and bounded space. Virginia Woolf, for example, wrote her first novel, *The Voyage Out* (1915), about a colonial journey and her last, *Between the Acts* (1941), about a country ritual; Eliot's multicultural metropolis in *The Waste Land* gave way to the sacred national sites of "Little Gidding"; Forster moved from the hot states of Italian and Indian culture in his major fiction to the delibidinalized insularity of his midcentury pageants and country rambles; and even the economist J. M. Keynes, their contemporary, followed (as described in chapter 4) a path from an early career in the India Office to the invention of a systemic, holistic British macroeconomics in his *General Theory* of 1936.[16]

As the more detailed readings of these writers will indicate, there are two kinds of argument at work in this book: the more strictly materialist claim that imperial contraction changed English writing through a series of symbolic mediations between social conditions and artistic production; and the claim that certain English intellectuals interpreted contraction as an opportunity for cultural repair. To put this another way: the fact of contraction certainly altered some of the social and institutional predicates of metropolitan perception, but it is even more clear that contraction gave modernists a master trope for projecting the end of what Keynes

called the "international but individualistic" era of European culture.[17] If
the Anderson-Nairn notion of an inner lack/outer presence characterizes
the high modernist era, with its primitivist art and colonial anthropology,
then late modernist work replaces a deep form of metropolitan presby-
opia with a new apprehension of a complete national life—an insular
romance of wholeness, or at least of layered social knowability. The relativization of England as one culture among many in the face of imperial
contraction seems to have entailed a relativization of literature as one
aspect of culture; together these discursive events constitute the anthropological turn of late modernism in particular and English culture in general
after 1930.

  With this initial hypothesis in place, we can reread the history of twentieth-century English literature in ways that substantially diverge from the
narrative proposed by Hugh Kenner in the book to which my title alludes,
A Sinking Island (1987). To shift emphasis from *sinking* to *shrinking* implies reworking Kenner's story of decline, posing a mixed history of contraction and consolidation against his one-directional humanist schema
of the exalted devolving into the petty-banal. Kenner sees the fragmentation of reading publics as the decisive factor in the demise of great modernist literature; England was simply the first territory to see its high aesthetic comprehensively undermined by an insurgent mass culture.[18] In
Kenner's narrative, as in many standard accounts of English modernism,
imperial decline and provincialism hover in the background as vague signs
of civilizational malaise or flaccidity. As I suggested at the start, this approach begs the question of how imperial decline does or does not relate
to the status of literary value in English culture. For this reason alone, it
is worth reconsidering the fact that the late modernist generation absorbed the potential energy of a contracting British state and converted it
into the language not of aesthetic decline but of cultural revival.

  As is no doubt apparent, I am not reading the entwined story of late
modernism and late imperialism through texts, like Evelyn Waugh's *Decline and Fall* or Graham Greene's *Brighton Rock*, that are overtly based
on the predicament of a provincial ex-empire. In contrast to literary histories of the thirties and forties centered on these "next generation" novelists or on the Auden circle of younger poets, this study addresses a residual
or late modernism. This generational restriction represents a literary-historical claim: that the end of British hegemony was a fait accompli to the
Auden-Greene generation and therefore not the occasion for searching
attempts to manage the transition between imperial universalism and national particularism. That generation's minor-chord lament stems in part
from not having come of age artistically during the days of imperial centrality; they inherited the cultural detritus and political guilt of empire
without the corresponding advantages of metropolitan perception. The

difference in historical experience between the modernist and Auden generations helps account for the former's interest in reviving English culture and the latter's interest in eulogizing it. Certainly, writers like Greene, Auden, and Larkin—whether they cultivated a satiric provincialism or an ironic cosmopolitanism—did not vest English culture itself with the kind of recuperative possibilities that one can see in the late modernist works analyzed in this study. Where Eliot and Woolf saw the end of British imperialism as an opportunity to forestall the depredations of modernity, the Auden generation interpreted it as yet another chapter in the unfolding of those same depredations.

Most of the writers conventionally taken to represent English literature in the midcentury—Greene, Waugh, Orwell, Auden, Larkin—remain committed to a literature of existential male antiheroism in a world of corrupt politics and culture. This constellation of writers became representative figures in part because their canonical-humanist conception of literary value, combined with their historical sense of pervasive national decline, seems to have accorded with the dominant assumptions of midcentury English criticism embodied in the figure of F. R. Leavis. By contrast to the aging modernists, their career trajectories tend to move further away from, not closer to, the ambiguous embrace of national identity or group politics. For this reason, I treat these writers only briefly and in the book's conclusion.

Modernism's nativist and culturalist turn represents the first part of a decolonizing dialectic in which the tropes and modes of colonial knowledge came home to roost at the end of empire. To capture the double movement of this dialectic, the book will trace a roughly chronological arc from the high modernism of the metropolitan era (summarized in chapter 1) to the late modernism and late imperialism of the thirties and forties (addressed with detailed critical readings in chapters 2 and 3), to postwar, postimperial English culture, particularly as it began to take shape in the 1950s (described in chapter 4). The imagined reintegration of a shrinking national culture connects late modernism to cultural formations in the fifties that projected England as the object of anthropological knowledge. The book follows its readings of modernist literature with close examinations of Keynesian economics, of English Cultural Studies, and of the first postwar generation of colonial migrant writing in England. It draws writers of the old liberal intelligentsia (Woolf, Keynes) and the modernist right (Eliot) into a single narrative with figures from the rise of cultural studies (Raymond Williams, Richard Hoggart); moreover, it links the literature of the dying empire (Forster) to the new writing of the multicultural England of the 1950s (Doris Lessing, George Lamming). These readings are organized in terms of the problematic of the anthropological turn and not strictly by the conventions of literary period or genre. While this may seem an eccentric trajectory, it has the specific virtue of accounting for changes in English culture that do not correspond to our unsatisfactory period markers—prewar/postwar and modernism/postmodernism—nor to the conventional story of imperial decline.

The redemptive discourse of Anglocentrism that I have begun to sketch may seem immediately explainable in terms of cultural responses to fascist aggression rather than to imperial contraction. But it is probably more accurate to place the rise of fascism and Hitler's war into the larger context of European political crisis that included the growing challenge to imperialism from within and without the metropolitan centers. War and imperial contraction were not just coincident in time but structurally interrelated, as most English intellectuals could see by the 1940s. If the familiar crises of the thirties and the coming war made national self-representation seem politically urgent, then it was in some sense the anthropological turn that made national self-representation seem conceptually *possible*. This was especially true for English intellectuals who were inclined to believe that an insular culture, but not a baggy multinational civilization, could unify its fragments. Imperial retrenchment thus yielded aesthetic solutions to the problem of England's social unknowability and its high/low cultural schism. The crisis of European cosmopolitanism did not simply force a retreat to insular culture; it also established the conditions for a potential transformation of that culture.[19] James Buzard describes this process in terms of a "metropolitan autoethnography," a kind of domestic epistemological romance in which "modern Western societies seek to know themselves as 'cultures,' " that is, as "self-sufficient entities possessing their own indigenous systems of meaning, essentially independent of their increasingly undeniable dependence upon 'the rest.' "[20]

Certainly the thirties witnessed a spike in authoethnographic discourses that projected England qua nation as newly representable in the holistic terms of anthropology. By transferring the holistic ethos (writing about "an entire way of life") from small-scale colonized societies to their own shrinking nation, English intellectuals found a distinctive way to respond to the imminent collapse of British hegemony. In the English midcentury and in some key late modernists texts, then, we find an overlooked chapter in the history of what George Marcus and Michael Fischer call the "repatriation" of anthropology. That repatriation is a crucial component in the midcentury reinvention of English culture. Where high modernism often emphasized the reification of social difference, the anthropologically inflected projects of the thirties afforded English intellectuals a new way to represent social difference within a dynamic, but knowable and bounded, social field, that is, within a totality corresponding to the idea of national culture.

The aging high modernists participated in the process of anthropological introversion by modifying some of their most distinctive stylistic and generic choices in the late thirties. For example, both Woolf and Eliot (to different degrees) inflect their own techniques for registering ego consciousness with a more powerful and more binding model of national tradition. Their cultural turn thus sheds retrospective light on the original relation between modernism's languages of subjectivity and its metropolitan habitat. To press this point is to affirm David Lloyd's powerful argument about the place of the archetypal subject in imperial cultures: "A major literature is established as such precisely by virtue of its claims to representative status, of its claims to realize the autonomy of the individual subject to such a degree that this individual subject becomes universally valid and archetypal."[21] In *Anomalous States*, Lloyd elaborates that argument into a cogent explanation of the relation between the end of empire, the challenge to high culture, and the critique of the sovereign subject. He points to an underlying link between "the erosion of the aesthetic domain and the demise of colonialism itself." Lloyd's narrative covers the general run of aesthetic culture from Goethe and Schiller through Arnold, culminating in an implicit account of the place of modernist aesthetics within the larger history of European humanism. The grand evolutionary culture-graph of modern Europe's anthropological imagination implies that metropolitan societies are closer to "normative humanity" than peripheral ones; moreover, it is the "ethical function" of aesthetics to "demonstrate the congruity of aesthetic works of increasing self-reflexive complexity with the preordained stages of humankind's development."[22] Modernism's virtuosity, in this sense, corresponds to European humanism's apex. In its historical dimension, Lloyd's point reformulates Sartre's well-known claim that European humanism has always depended on imperial power—an argument memorably captured in the introduction to Fanon's *Wretched of the Earth*.[23] Naturally then, as my readings of late Woolf and late Eliot will suggest, a crisis in imperialism provokes or exacerbates a crisis in humanism. In short, the political critique of colonialism and the philosophical critique of the subject—both gathering steam in the forties and fifties—can best be understood as coterminous in the history of ideas with the eclipse of historical or metropolitan modernism.

Lloyd's model of European imperial power and universal humanism reaching a kind of apotheosis in modernist complexity gives us a way to account for the actual historical relations—not just the intuitive affinities—between metropolitan perception and the literature of consciousness. Broadly speaking, high modernism, once understood as, among other things, an aesthetic devoted to or predicated on the autonomous value of "free-floating" subjects, has increasingly been rethought in terms of the social determinations that impinge on subjectivity. In my view, high modernism frames the conflict between the self-determining individual and the socially saturated individual as a polarizing opposition or inevitable double bind.[24] More specifically, the double bind of modernist subjectivity conforms to Keynes's description of an "international but individualistic" era, when both art and the soul seemed more thrillingly free from traditional communities, but more harrowingly prey to the laws of the market. By contrast, the language of Anglocentric revival (including Keynes's own work in the thirties) projects a cultural arena more tethered to national tradition, but correspondingly less vulnerable to an atomizing and homogenizing global capitalism. The anthropological turn allows English modernists to imagine the rescue of socially marginalized art within a whole culture sponsored by the ascendant corporate nationalism of the welfare state.[25]

The irony of late modernism in England is that the cultural turn tended to render obsolete certain aspects of modernist literary practice by fulfilling certain aspects of modernist social doctrine. Subsuming the twin crises of art's autonomization and lost organic community into the reactivated notion of cultural totality, modernists presided over a self-obsolescing aesthetic. As we will see, their work in the late thirties defines the dialectical switchpoint where English modernism, projecting the reintegration of art and culture, becomes something else altogether. These tectonic shifts confirm, by retrospect, the originally divided aesthetic ideology of high modernism, which was predicated on the nonfulfillment of its own ideals. It depended, for example, on the tension between a doctrine of impersonality and the development of highly idiosyncratic styles. Likewise, it tended to express nostalgia for organic communities while engaging in an aesthetic embrace of the fragmented metropolis. When, in the demetropolitanizing phase, modernists begin to connect aesthetic impersonality less to ingenious stylistic invention (which could always be assimilated back to the notion of the idiosyncratic mind) and more directly to shared rituals and traditions, the equation shifts. Eliot and Woolf, for example, each mined their English heritage in the 1930s in order to modernize, yet again, their representation of transpersonal agency or communal voice, thereby generating new solutions to the old problem of literary impersonality.

Although I have suggested that the personal/impersonal antinomy of English high modernism reaches a new resolution via the supervening doctrine of anthropological holism, I do not read (as Lukács does) modernist representations of consciousness as a cosmopolitan indulgence subsequently corrected when the return to national concerns enforces a properly sociohistorical aesthetic. Modernist representations of the subject were always, as Adorno insisted, shaped by (not detached from) specific and objective social conditions. Indeed, a genuinely critical or negative art required (more than ever) the language of subjectivity in order to avoid simply reproducing the real world in a naive attempt at mimetic objectivity or social realism.[26] This Adornean model of "objective subjectivity" as the key to modernist technique seems to have come under pressure in the midcentury, at least in practice, for English writers like Eliot and Woolf. The classic high modernist texts of the twenties (say *The Waste Land* or *Mrs. Dalloway*) sought to inscribe historical experience into virtuoso forms and to mediate between idealist patterns (myth) and materialist details (history) through a capacious, inventive new language of consciousness. By contrast, the texts of late modernism (say *Four Quartets* or *Between the Acts*) seem to posit an inherited cultural legacy as the agent required to mediate between totality and particularity, between unity and fragmentation, or between the collective and the individual. The anthropological turn refers to this *relative* shift away from the mediating symbolic and social power of artistic forms and individual minds.

If we recall Lloyd's point that the formation of archetypal ethical subjects and of formal complexity stems from the apex of a certain historical (and eventually imperial) European aesthetic culture, we can see that modernism represents in a sense both the high-water mark and the crumbling point of that formation. Its charged antinomy between formal and subjective virtuosity on the one hand and increasingly rationalized social conditions on the other reflects neither ideological escape from modernity (Lukács) nor its pure negation (Adorno), but precisely the impossible oscillation between the two. In a sense, the joint demise of aesthetic culture and colonial power makes space for a new dispensation, a new representation of the subject/object problem—one that is not necessarily better or worse, not necessarily more or less political or historical. Certainly the texts of late modernism in England suggest a linked erosion of modernist aesthetics and colonial power, displacing the humanist/antihumanist and liberal/antiliberal polarities of high modernism with emergent culturalisms of both the left and the right.

The cultural turn—with its integrative and tribal promises—had obvious appeal for modernists struggling to reconcile the heroic dissidence and social marginality of high art in the age of avant-gardism. But it also carried all the predictable burdens of any cultural particularism or restrictive nationalism: the danger of false unity, cloying nostalgia, creative claustrophobia, and narrowed horizons of meaning. Naturally, then, the surviving London modernists maintained several degrees of suspicion about the nativist premises entailed in the anthropologization of English writing. As a transitional generation, they cut their Anglocentrism with international ideas: Eliot's investment in the unity of European Christendom, Keynes's commitment to global monetary regulation, and Woolf's and Forster's persistent liberal cosmopolitanism (combined with sexual and gender dissidence from official forms of national culture). But what is perhaps even more historically important—and interpretively challenging—than these *explicit* disavowals of nationalism is the fact that their late works *implicitly* reinscribe universalism into the language of English particularism.

Indeed the anthropological turn of 1930–60 consolidates a second-order universalism based on English cultural integrity. If the primary universalism of the metropolitan era turned on the sovereign subject of a border-crossing, myth-making imperial humanism, then this new secondary universalism turns on the representative status of a bounded culture. The afterlife of British hegemony is written into this new language of cultural exemplarity, so that Englishness represents not just a type, but the very archetype, of modern nationalism, of deep and integral shared traditions emanating from within the prototypical industrial class society. Within this trajectory, the late modernists of the contracting English center, with their self-conscious and balky reintegration into insular culture, stand as a kind of paradigm of the historical fate of European universalism in its classic form.

The anthropological turn describes the decisive assimilation of a restrictive cultural nationalism back into an English canon that had, during the Arnoldian phase of imperial humanism, projected both the blessings and the limitations of cultural nationalism onto its own provinces, fringes, and colonies. In a 1940 essay, Eliot notes that while the young symbolist W. B. Yeats had an expropriative, anglicized relationship to Irish culture, the later Yeats developed a more fully nativist mode of expression and that "in becoming more Irish . . . he became at the same time universal."[27] Here Eliot emphasizes the roots of universalism in the collective life of a representative *people* rather than in the psychic contours of a representative *person*. Both the timing of the essay and the example of Yeats are historically apposite, since Eliot and his London contemporaries were beginning to borrow the logic of cultural nationalism back from the colonies, adapting it for a belated brand of Anglocentric revivalism. Such borrowings situate late modernism in England within a broader history of twentieth-century decolonization movements, in which the universalist forms of imperial nationalism were both exposed as, and transformed into, ethnolinguistic nationalism.

Modernist works like *Between the Act* and *Four Quartets* thus not only register the aesthetic changes of demetropolitanization but also offer valuable conceptual resources for coming to terms with the problem of universalism. From its banishment in the discourse of identity politics, universalism has recently resurfaced to trouble cultural theory—particularly studies of nationalism and the new cosmopolitanism. Insofar as the aesthetic formulations of late modernist Anglocentrism strike a separate and uneasy peace between universalist and particularist concepts of nationhood, they shed new light on the unresolved theoretical opposition between civic and ethnic nationalism.[28] The chapters that follow suggest a specific literary-historical context for this basic divide, which has structured any number of major theoretical statements on the problem of national culture in recent years. Consider, for example, Homi Bhabha's exploration of the split subject of national discourse. In Bhabha's model, the nation, when it is no longer defined against its "Other or Outside," finds itself foundering on its own internal contradictions, since there can be no effective, positive, or final signification of the people. Bhabha's poststructuralist and psychoanalytic idiom recasts the Marxist problematic of structural antagonism into the crisis of the crumbling sign and the "narcissistic neuroses of the national discourse." At this point, the "nation reveals, in its ambivalent and vacillating representation, an ethnography of its own claim to being *the* norm of social contemporaneity."[29] If we set this model into the case of late modernism's anthropological turn—undertaken precisely at the point when Englishness can no longer be defined against its imperial Outside—we can see it gain historical flesh and dialectical motion. The attempt on the part of English writers to reinscribe universal status into the particularist language of home anthropology defines the transition from imperial to postimperial Englishness. It stands as a living version of Bhabha's ethnography of normative power that does not merely dissolve itself once it relativizes its own claims but continues to exert political influence and to take on new guises in contemporary U.K. culture. Of course, the fact that England is frequently the actual historical referent of Bhabha's general statements about colonial and postcolonial culture only underscores the point that the history of England's demetropolitanization continues to be taken as paradigmatic. This accords quite precisely with the logic of second-order universalism that I have described above as a "post-British" effect.

I BEGAN THIS introduction with skepticism about the entwined narrative of geopolitical and aesthetic decline that so often displaces analysis of English literature after 1930. By no means do I intend to pose a progressivist narrative against that familiar logic of devolution, nor will I be offering a moral-political brief either for or against Anglocentrism. Instead, *A Shrinking Island* attempts two main analytical tasks: (1) to trace the relationship between shifting concepts of English culture and shifting aesthetic practices of canonical modernist writers; and (2) to describe the influential afterlife of late modernism's anthropological turn in the making of English identity after empire. Chapters 2 and 3 emphasize literary analysis of canonical figures whereas chapters 1 and 4 emphasize material causes, cultural movements, and intellectual formations. In this sense, the book's structure reflects its subject: the process by which the canonical authority of high modernism was first concentrated in a small band of heroic artists during the metropolitan era, then diffused and challenged by the reorganization of national culture in the postmetropolitan era. The importance of national ritual and national allegory in texts that thematize imperial contraction occupies the center of attention in chapters 2 and 3, which are anchored respectively by readings of *Between the Act* and *Four Quartets*. These are modernist texts that reward rereading and fresh interpretation because they render an especially dense kind of artistic justice to their world; their language not only reflects and refracts events but has sporadic power to negate, to ignore, and even to change the course of events. To put it another way, I tack between context and text in order to tell a story about intellectuals and artists who both shape and are shaped by historical forces.

Chapter 1 addresses the preeminence and subsequent attenuation of metropolitan perception as a feature of English modernism. It begins by considering the early fiction of E. M. Forster in terms of a symbolic geography that reflects the tension between pastoral English values and the sprawling British economy. Forster's fiction repeatedly plots or maps the relation of anterior core and modern metropolis as overlapping in space but incommensurate in values, condensing any number of social contradictions (democracy and privilege, aesthetic culture and industrial materialism, personal liberty and sexual stricture) into his signature trope of a dwindling English essence suspended in a thrilling, but disorienting, metropolitan contact zone. The motor of Forsterian narrative in this way turns on the symbolic and reciprocal relationship between the privileged epistemology and threatened ontology of imperial Englishness. Williams's "metropolitan perception" identifies just this combination of cultural capital and social atomization as the basis of high modernism. Chapter 1 explores a specifically English model of metropolitan perception, providing the basis for subsequent analyses of demetropolitanization as a modernist endstage that trades lost civilizational reach for restored cultural integrity.

To establish a convincing framework for the larger historical claim that English intellectuals began seriously to reckon with imperial contraction a generation before the decolonization movements of the 1960s, chapter 1 also surveys the legislative, diplomatic, and cultural markers of imperial contraction in the thirties and forties. Its final two sections explore intellectual and artistic responses to British retrenchment, tracking the homeward migration of a whole range of tropes, genres, and discursive forms previously associated with the colonies. With the engines of imperial (and industrial) expansion sputtering in the thirties, England was recoded, or seen to metamorphose, from a Hegelian subject of world-historical development to a Herderian object of its own insular history. One cultural index of this broader change is the boom in historical self-consumption in England, where the leisure classes turned to insular sources of rural mystique and chthonic myth. At the same time, English writing—ranging from Orwell's urban fiction to the "home anthropology" of the Mass-Observation movement—increasingly made the nation into an object of documentary observation, a knowable unit of cultural and social relations rather than a fractured metropole. As the evidence will suggest, both of these strands of Anglocentrism borrowed cultural authenticity from the colonies and gained authority from the participation of canonical modernists.

In chapter 2, I trace the odd career of a neotraditional subgenre, the pageant-play, in English modernist writing of the thirties (including the "minor" modernism of writers like J. C. Powys and Charles Williams). Eliot and Forster experimented with the production of pageant-plays, while Woolf's final novel, *Between the Acts*, takes a village pageant as its central subject. Few critics have taken account of this antiquarian, distinctly unmodernist genre, but its sudden prominence points up key dimensions of English modernism's closing chapter. Modernist interest in folk-dramatic forms no doubt reflects at some level the need to establish alternative public ceremonies to the corporatist rituals of fascist Europe (and to mass cultural forms at home), but this renewed interest in native and Anglocentric rituals also takes shape within the broader logic of the anthropological turn. For the modernists in the 1930s, appropriation of the genre's tribal solidarity provides an occasion to explore English cultural integrity at the end of empire.

The modernist pageant texts confront a national history increasingly cut free from its moorings in colonial modernity. In these texts—which number among the least read of Forster's and Eliot's works, and the least understood of Woolf's—we can see the transition that directs emphasis away from the myths, symbols, and epiphanies of a universally significant but privately rendered mind and toward the public performance of civic rituals. Chapter 2 concludes with a sustained reinterpretation of Woolf's *Between the Acts* because that novel stages a fascinating contest between narration and performance and because it continues to be, in my view, too easily assimilated back to Woolf's famously resistant politics of privacy rather than read in light of a reluctant turn to cultural solidarity. For Woolf, the political crises of the time compelled intellectuals to think nationally, but also shifted the real terms of national identity away from aggressive Britishness, toward humane Englishness.

As I suggest in concluding chapter 2, *Between the Acts* offers a kind of valediction to both modernism and imperialism, confirming Jameson's reading of the relationship between the two. In the novel, the reorientation of the spatial referent from imperial-infinite to deep-insular coincides with the demystification of—or at least a notable revision of—Woolf's intrasubjective style. In other words, the political and imperial unconscious of English modernism breaks the crust of Woolf's last novel in a way that defines demetropolitanization's aesthetic effects. In a strikingly similar fashion, T. S. Eliot's last major poem, *Four Quartets*, manages a kind of epic revaluation of time and space in what seems an unavoidably Anglocentric—though not bluntly nationalist—way. The poem's invocation of the insular core culture anchors time to space in order to free it from history; it attracts the filaments and fragments of metropolitan consciousness, shaping them into an allegory that restores meaning reciprocally to the poet and his national culture.

In chapter 3, I read *Four Quartets* as a late modernist form that powerfully transvalues England itself, converting it into a significant cultural totality rather than a merely negative and even generic embodiment of European modernity (as in *The Waste Land*). Of course, as in Woolf, the formal shifts are relative, based on revisionary impulses and changing emphases, not on an outright revolution in either values or style. Despite the structural importance of demetropolitanization to their changing literary practice, Woolf and Eliot (and Forster) consciously moderate xenophobic nationalism: even in their later works, raw nativism is still etherialized into "the literary tradition," dissolved into "Christian community," or rendered as an intensely private, anticorporatist experience. More to the point, though, their late works revise or unsettle a modernist aesthetic predicated on social fragmentation; they recalibrate the modernist ratios, often subordinating the lament over a lost common culture to the imagined restoration of its conditions of possibility. Although Eliot's notion of cultural repair represents a fantasy projection of Englishness, the fantasy is both licensed and galvanized by a real history of imperial contraction and failed cosmopolitanism in the 1930s.

Eliot's centrality in chapter 3 stems from his culturally authoritative articulation of the possibility that an epochal change in European history might discredit the progressive time of secular modernity in a way that the eloquent protests of high modernism never could.[30] Eliot's *Quartets* makes a new attempt to pose meaningful, shaped, or eschatological time against mere chronology—an attempt that attaches timeless value not to an intercultural canon of great art but to a recrudescent concept of cultural unity. In this view, the end of empire "repairs" a fragmented English society, obviating the vocation of the heroic modernist in a broken culture. With the arrival of a limited kind of European apocalypse circa 1940, history itself begins to have an incarnate form, so there is no longer the pressing need to use form against a meaningless, merely chronological history. This proposition becomes, in a sense, the central hypothesis of my reading of Eliot. *Four Quartets*, with its prodigious complexity, both registers and enacts the turn from cosmopolitan aesthetics to national culture by which the high phase of English modernism came to its end. Chapter 3 thus takes Eliot to be the canonical instance of a broader culture of retrenchment featuring minor writers like Mary Butts, J.R.R. Tolkien, and Charles Williams. Butts's spiky pastoralism, Tolkien's archive fever, and Williams's pulp-fiction mythopoetics all represent a countermodernism gaining visibility and currency in the thirties as the fate of metropolitan modernity itself—especially in England—seems to hang in the balance.

Although I read Woolf and Eliot as participants in the same Anglocentric turn, it is important not to blur distinctions between these two writers. Despite their sustained friendship, they represented opposing wings of the literary establishment. Eliot, for all his doctrinal changes in the interwar years, still cleaved to the Hulmean, classical, and antihumanist modernism that emerged in the ferment of the London avant-garde during World War I. Woolf, by contrast, represented the liberal-humanist values of Bloomsbury, with cultural and literary authority vested largely in the free-thinking and eccentric soul. The anthropological concept of a whole culture, galvanized by British contraction, seems to have appealed to Woolf and Eliot from almost opposite directions, closing the distance between their respectively affiliative and filiative notions of national belonging. The notion of tribal bonds lying underneath modernist anomie seems to have driven Eliot to embrace cultural rather than aesthetic authority while causing Woolf, the wary individualist, to confront her own organicist and Anglocentric premises. My readings therefore suggest, not ideological unity between Woolf and Eliot, but converging paths inflected by a similar sense of British crisis and English opportunity.

I take this limited model of convergence to exemplify the structural force of demetropolitanization in England of the thirties and forties, both in high and low cultural registers. Political differences (imperialism versus anti-imperialism, for example) and philosophical differences (humanism versus antihumanism, for example) among English intellectuals were substantially mitigated by the burgeoning power of the culture concept under the sign of the shrinking island. The anthropological turn identifies a deep historical effect, but not an utterly deterministic one. The end of empire cannot be neatly and discretely mapped onto the exact decades in question, nor can it be said to explain in any final way the shape of something so elusive and multiply determined as a poem or novel. When, for example, I argue that *Four Quartets* registers an epochal shift, I mean both that the poem uses a lapidary design to address England's changing status and that its form assimilates history in ways that outstrip Eliot's conscious intentions. For this reason, we can take Eliot's writing—despite its obvious political partiality—as significant in the broader cultural history of English modernism and not just within the restricted domain of the Tory dreamscape. With varying degrees of self-consciousness, English intellectuals of the thirties took the impress of national retrenchment both in their most delicate turns of phrase and in their most obdurate ideological principles.

In chapter 4, I turn to the economist J. M. Keynes precisely because he mediates between the high-cultural and deep-structural elements of demetropolitanization. Keynes's lifespan (1883–1946) covers the beginning, peak, and decline of both modernism and imperialism in Britain. He combines Bloomsbury liberalism with Burkean organicism, embodying the ideological blend that carried English destiny from imperial center to welfare state. As I argue in the first section of chapter 4, Keynesian thought allows us to see the modernist generation's crucial role in the dialectical motion of devolution. Despite their often conservative invocation of the folk against the masses—indeed, because of that invocation and its pastoralist and tribal dimensions—the modernists define the initial return of anthropological knowledge to England after empire. Seeking to avoid the twin dangers of the old Benthamite individualism and the new totalitarian conformism, Keynes found the necessary conceptual and rhetorical resources in the softer half of that political hybrid "the nation-state"; that is, he invoked the nation as defined by English cultural traditions rather than the state as defined by British imperial power.[31] Just as English modernists shifted orientation from the free-flowing anomie of artistic coteries in European capitals to the everyday life of a more integrated insular culture, so too did Keynes shift orientation from a classical international capitalism to a restructured macroeconomy based on the formalization of collective interest in the state. Keynes's *General Theory*, published almost contemporaneously with *Between the Acts* and *Four Quartets*, thus replicates in economic terms the recuperation of social totality that his literary contemporaries began to imagine in cultural terms. Moreover, Keynes's ability to see the national economy at home in "total" or "macro" terms derives in part from his own transfer of a holistic sociocultural knowledge from the colonial periphery back to the atomized center.

When we read Keynes alongside his literary contemporaries, we can see late modernism as the dialectical precursor to Cultural Studies in England. If, in its late and Anglocentric phase, modernist writing tried to realign art and culture, then Cultural Studies, in its early and Anglocentric phase, tried to realign culture and society. Chapter 4 turns from Keynes to the pioneering work of E. P. Thompson, Richard Hoggart, and Raymond Williams, which attempted, in part, to displace rarefied (modernist) aesthetics with a more socially comprehensive and populist view of English culture. As many observers have noted, their innovative analyses of a total way of life relied on a latently organic notion of Englishness. But Cultural Studies nativism has not been fully contextualized as a postimperial effect, nor as the fulfillment of a latemodernist domestication of anthropology. As my readings will suggest, early Cultural Studies echoes the demetropolitanizing logic by which England becomes the archetype of cultural particularism. This second-order universalism surfaces in the recurrent claim that England bears an exemplary relation to modernity: the country where industrial, imperial capitalism hit first and hit hardest is also the country first out the other side; it is the very paradigm of demodernization. Even with (indeed, I suspect because of) its residual Anglocentrism, though, Cultural Studies managed to unsettle the canonical status of cosmopolitan modernism and to democratize culture in an anthropological frame.[32]

The point in chapter 4, then, is not to flog the nationalist "flaw" of Cultural Studies, but to address the historical symmetry between high modernism's presbyopic view of cultural totality (i.e., fuzzy at home, vivid overseas) and early Cultural Studies corresponding myopia when it came to matters of race, gender, and empire in its reconstruction of cultural totality at home. The Anglocentric logic of early Cultural Studies should, in other words, be read in terms of the limits imposed by postimperial conditions in England rather than in terms of humanist failings on the part of certain native intellectuals. Cultural Studies emerges in the fifties with a historical vocation to translate the language of British universalism into the language of English particularism. During the same period, postwar colonial-immigrant writing about England took up a similar task: not to hail multiculturalism, but to insist that the ethnolinguistic restrictiveness of English culture be seen for what it was, the parochial heart underneath the promises of universal British subjecthood. Chapter 4 juxtaposes the "home anthropology" of English cultural studies to the "reverse ethnography" of colonial writers like Doris Lessing, Sam Selvon, and George Lamming, arguing that both projects aim to objectify Englishness, to consolidate and identify its sources of integrity and rediscover its local color. Both projects redress an Arnoldian legacy in which England plays the role of secular modern center—a blank metaculture tethered by British power to an array of colorful subordinate cultural nationalisms. Like the Anglocentrism of the late modernists, then, these fifties representations of Englishness aim not so much to fetishize national tradition as to recognize and come to terms with its limitations. Of course, to insist on a particularist definition of Englishness after empire is to flirt with a romanticized and absolutist national identity (à la Enoch Powell). However, it is also to perform an ideological critique of universalist imperialism. This double effect challenges both English and postcolonial writing about England.

The narrative of reverse colonization and reverse ethnography attached to postcolonial immigration in the fifties brings forth the grand historical irony, always hovering at the edge of this study, that England seems finally to be both beneficiary of, *and subject to*, the knowledge/power structures of British imperialism. As Stuart Hall (among others) has pointed out,

English intellectuals, like their counterparts in ex-colonies, have been involved in an attempt to "recover an alternative set of cultural origins not contaminated by the colonising experience."[33] Despite obvious distinctions between the history of the center and its colonies, it is worth noting how important the motif of reverse colonization has been—particularly in an era of U.S. cultural hegemony—to the reconstruction of England as a minor culture. This book reads reverse colonization back into the heart of high modernism, where writers like Woolf and Eliot had begun to absorb the decolonizing force of cultural nationalism at the center. Such an itinerary provides a genuine prehistory to contemporary English literature, now often read according to the paradigms of (postcolonial or multicultural) minority discourse, but also read as a minor culture in itself.[34] As Sean Golden puts the matter: "The term 'native,' once condescendingly assigned to the colonised, is now clung to and honoured by English writers in their steeply declining present circumstances." Seamus Heaney makes a similar point in describing a process of contraction and decentering that "began to speed up in the 1920s, 1930s, and 1940s" and that removed England's sense of "entitlement" to "world culture."[35] In that process, the shrinking island becomes the governing figure for a paradigmatically English end to the triumph of European civilization. It stands not just for contracting spatial hegemony but for a faltering in the temporal concept of modernity itself—a faltering from which no modernism could emerge untransformed.

ONE

MODERNISM AND METROPOLITAN
PERCEPTION IN ENGLAND

The Other Side of the Hedge

THE UNNAMED protagonist in E. M. Forster's 1904 fable "The Other Side of the Hedge" confronts a bifurcated world. As the story begins, he is walking on a gray, featureless, and apparently endless Road, bounded on one side by a thick hedge. The protagonist, who has always walked the Road and knows no other world, suddenly slips and crashes through the hedge. Once on his feet, he finds himself in a green and pleasant land cozily encircled by the hedge—a land whose citizens are unaware of the great gray road beyond. Although he develops a quick affinity for the soothing pastoral existence of the inner zone, he is troubled by the curiously static nature of his newfound Eden. Living inside the hedge, in a land without time, progress, or science, the protagonist comes to appreciate the virtues of life on the Road: "We are always learning, expanding, developing. Why, even in my short life, I have seen a great deal of advance—the Transvaal War, the Fiscal Question, Christian Science, Radium."[1] He cannot imagine himself removed from the great round of wars and discoveries, from the forward march of humanity (though the pathway of the Road around the circular hedge seems, from his new perspective, to be circular as well). Although his attachment to the wheel of progress falters, it is held together by habit, obligation, and a lingering suspicion that the Road cannot be escaped.

But when the protagonist attempts to return to the Road of modernity, to heed what he calls the "destiny of our race," his body recoils from the gate, unable or unwilling to break back through the hedge. Reeling, he sinks into a pastoral reverie in which he perceives only "the magic song of nightingales, and the odour of invisible hay, and stars piercing the falling sky."[2] As he loses consciousness, enfolded in the ground of the inner zone, the protagonist recognizes the face of a long-lost brother, another refugee from the Road. With the promise of fraternal reunion, life inside the hedge takes on a delirious uncertainty and gauzy fragility. The fragility stems in part from the narrator's own sense of obligation toward the Road, his sense that life inside the hedge—especially in its disengagement from the expanding world of science and politics—is fantastical, fleeting, too good to be true. The story's inward plunge expresses a fond wish to enter (or reenter, for the inner zone is uncannily familiar) a bounded world, to abandon the gray Road of modernity and enjoy the fraternal embrace of the greensward.[3]

With its almost diagrammatic clarity, oriented (as the title suggests) to fabular setting rather than realistic plotting or characterization, this story maps out the spatial and symbolic logic of metropole-core relations in England circa 1900. The hedge literalizes the divide between an insular pastoral nation—increasingly a figment of the literary imagination—and the vast metropolitan routes that connect the core culture to every corner of the globe through British political, economic, and technological power. During the most active years of Forster's career as a novelist (1905–25), his fictions repeatedly stage the conflict of values implied by these two national incarnations. In *Howards End* (1910), for example, the central encounter between the Schlegels and the Wilcoxes takes place within a representational scheme that pits the old humanist core of English culture against the modernizing strain of British imperialism. Here, in "The Other Side of the Hedge," Forster codes the Road as the location of a constantly expanding and entropic culture, one that pushes back epistemological and political boundaries (the discovery of Radium; the Transvaal War).[4] By contrast, the centripetal forces of the inner world impel the protagonist into the static embrace of ahistorical belonging, a pleasurable, if fantastic, sensation for a soul caught in the clutches of modernity. The central spatial figure of the hedge divides the two worlds, but also defines and maintains them in a suspended, agonizing adjacency. In this fantastic split map, the green zone of the nation remains embedded and intact within modernity, receding, but not disappearing, from the view of the wistful cosmopolitan.

Forster's tale epitomizes modernism's defining tension between tradition and modernity, expressed as a bifocal aesthetic equally attuned to the erosion of traditional communities and to the expansion of modern political and economic forces. Many of the central works of modernism evince a deep dissatisfaction with life in the bourgeois metropolis and an impossible yearning for the coherence of traditional societies (Forster's old England, Yeats's romantic Ireland, Pound's Confucian China, Conrad's tribal Patusan, Lawrence's mystical Mexico—we could easily multiply these examples). The stylistic experiments, linguistic dislocations, and urban alienation of modernist texts register this central conflict between older, imagined communities and the unimaginable or unknowable spaces of metropolitan Europe. Modernist forms—mythic, ironic, experimental, or fabular—make layered maps from incommensurable local and supralocal zones in countries that are checkered by uneven development and continually reorganized by capitalism. They embed their ideals of tribal, pastoral, or traditional community *within* the representation of modernity, creating not just a sad allegory of the other side of the hedge but a critical and dialectical juxtaposition of tradition and modernity.

In the case of Forster, nostalgia for an insular and pastoral state competes with the compensatory epistemological and intercultural privileges of dwelling at the center of expansive industrial and imperial power. After all, Forster finds the green spaces and long traditions of his native culture nourishing, but also unfulfilling and overfamiliar.[5] His narratives, like the protagonists within them, require the symbolic crunch and frisson of cultural difference provided by metropolitan perception as well as the lingering allure of insular landscapes. They require, in other words, the coexistence of British hegemony and Anglocentric idealism. The political language for Forster's elegiac tenderness toward a vanishing cultural integrity at the core of a multinational British empire is Little Englandism; it finds classic expression in a work nearly contemporaneous with Forster's tale, J. A. Hobson's *Imperialism* (1902).

Hobson, like Forster, wrote in the aftermath of the Berlin Conference (1884) and the Boer War (1899–1902)—two events that defined the vast scope of European imperialism in theory and revealed its strategic shakiness as a practice. Hobson roundly criticized the Great Powers for their conduct of global empire building. He called for Britain to abandon Joseph Chamberlain's expansionist policy in favor of a more genuinely internationalist federation. Hobson's *Imperialism* has become a well-known text in the history of British colonial and anticolonial *cultural* debate, in part because Hobson—chiefly an economist—describes imperialism's bad spiritual and aesthetic consequences. He proposes that higher matters of culture and civilization would receive more attention in England if the imperial-acquisitive drive were to be rechanneled. This view emerges within a somewhat quirky but influential theory of social "drives" analogous to the psychoanalytic model of a libidinal economy:

> Regarded from the standpoint of economy of energy, the same "choice of life" confronts the nation as the individual. An individual may expend all his energy in acquiring external possessions, adding field to field, barn to barn, factory to factory—may "spread himself" over the widest area of property, amassing material wealth which is in some sense "himself" . . .He does this by specialising upon the lower acquisitive plane of interest at the cost of neglecting the cultivation of the higher qualities . . . of his nature.[6]

Hobson wishes England to concentrate less on external acquisition and colonial expansion, more on cultivating its own internal resources, both economic and cultural. He describes imperialism as a mutant form of nationalism that has overflown its "natural banks" and warped national feeling from a "cohesive, pacific, internal" force into an "exclusive, hostile" force.[7] Hobson's work poses the baggy and boundless empire against "the burning vitality of compact, independent nations, the strong heart in the small body."[8] This imagery establishes the keynote of Edwardian Little Englandism, a rhetoric that would, over the next several decades, be transformed from a specialized anti-imperial politics into the major resource for postimperial conceptions of England by intellectuals of various political stripes.[9]

Although Forster and Hobson emphasized the attenuation of an older English way of life by the depredations of British imperialism, many historians have argued that imperialism (despite its obvious modernizing force in both the metropole and the periphery) acted as a political brake on—or anachronistic back-eddy within—the general process of modernization, prolonging the viability of aristocratic and pastoral values in industrial England. Tom Nairn, for example, has suggested that imperialism tended, by and large, to block or at least retard the modernization of English politics, preventing the formation of a genuinely popular nationalism. Similarly, Perry Anderson accounts for imperialism as a force not of modernity but of traditionalism in English culture: "it was this ostensible apotheosis of British capitalism which gave its characteristic style to that society, consecrating and fossilizing to this day its interior space, its ideological horizons, its intimate sensibility."[10] Anderson's consecrated inner space reminds us of the fundamental point that imperialism and pastoral idealism were in fact ideologically compatible. As many critics have noted, in fact, pastoral nostalgia was a crucial element within imperialist rhetoric: England's agrarian heart served as the inspiration for, justification for, and central beneficiary of colonial expansion.[11]

Nevertheless, from the point of view of cultural history, and modernist-era English writing in particular, British expansion tended symbolically to affirm the material triumphs of an industrialized, enterprising, and forward-looking middle-class society. Imperialism, in other words, may always have signified a crisis within industrial capitalism and may have had mixed and even anachronistic political effects in England, but culturally it was an index of progress and therefore of the disintegrating effects of global modernity on local cultures both at home and abroad. If empire hallowed Englishness by virtue of its projection to (and invention for) the colonies, it also hollowed Englishness by splitting its being into core and periphery—a structural divide condensed into the figure of Forster's hedge. Hobson figures the split through a psychological analogy: imperialism disrupts English self-possession by incorporating territories that are only "in some sense" identical with itself. Leaving aside the question of whether modern English culture, even *without* an empire, could have been in any meaningful sense self-identical, it is nonetheless important to track the cultural currency of the idea that imperialism both determined and symbolized a fracturing of English society.[12]

One of the more fascinating accounts of England's lost insular whole-ness in the course of British expansion emerges in Gertrude Stein's 1934 lecture "What Is English Literature." For Stein, the great historical achievement of English writing was its harmonious and insular empiri-cism: "English literature when it is directly and completely describing the daily island life beginning with Chaucer and going on to now did have this complete quality of completeness."[13] However, with the expansion of an island nation into a world empire, Stein proposes, English writing lost its gift for lyric mimesis, becoming preoccupied with the problem of mediating the national inside and the colonial outside: "you have to ex-plain the inside to the inside and the owning of the outside to the inside that has to be explained to the inside life and the owning of the outside has to be explained to the outside."[14] Stein's lecture not only describes the fissure in English identity as an imperial event but proposes an idio-syncratic theory about the modal and stylistic shifts associated with the new literature of imperial explanation.[15] In the end, Stein suggests, a liter-ature leached of its original raison d'être and bred for inside-outside ex-planation loses that vocation too: "As the time went on to the end of the nineteenth century and Victoria was over and the Boer war it began to be a little different in England. The daily island life was less daily and the owning everything outside was less owning, and, and this should be remembered, there were a great many writing but the writing was not so good."[16] Stein describes a lost aesthetic of insular completeness in the middle of British expansion, followed by a further attenuation at the end of British expansion.

Fredric Jameson has developed Stein's central insight into a theoretical account of the absent totality of English modernism, the proper aesthetic for an insular culture dissolved and diffused by the forces of imperial modernity. As I noted in the introduction, Jameson hypothesizes that modernism—in the form of Forster's fiction, for example—registers a "meaning loss" attendant on the colonial mode of production (in which those at the center can no longer grasp a complete and "daily" island life, because vital economic and social aspects of that life transpire and are determined elsewhere). With structures of production and distribution operating increasingly beyond the view of those in the imperial center, they were increasingly unavailable for representation. The task of appre-hending and describing the complete daily life of the society was thus even less possible in early twentieth-century Britain than it had been in the mid-Victorian heyday of industrial capitalism. For Jameson, Forster's *How-ards End* encodes this problem into a symbolic geography in which a gray, open-ended placelessness or infinity (much like that of the entropic Road in the fable of the hedge) is associated with imperialism.[17]

The value of Jameson's method is precisely that it captures Forster's narrative form not just as a self-conscious device for criticizing British imperialism but also as a politically unconscious mode of writing that registers its place within the horizons of empire.[18] Jameson's model provides a specifically English account of metropolitan perception as both an ontological problem and an aesthetic solution.[19] In Forster's major fiction, including *Howards End*, the narrative dynamism of the English/not-English split—its resistance to synthesis in symbolic terms—produces intercultural plots and tender ironies. This prototypically metropolitan aesthetic culminates in *A Passage to India*, with its failed colonial romance. Forster's later career represents an attempt to recover artistically from the aftermath of that failed romance. During the collapse of British hegemony, his writing loses the friction and narrative tension attendant on core/periphery incommensurability; it features the attenuation of those alien infinities (such as the Marabar Caves) that had provided such productive antitheses to pastoral knowability in the major fiction. Once disembedded from the context of British power and metropolitan irony, then, Forster's Anglocentrism comes to exemplify the formal recession of late modernism. If metropolitan perception—as a constitutive category of Forster's modernism—both projected Englishness as a precious vanishing core and dissolved it as a meaningful category of identity, demetropolitanization seeks to reconcile the over- and underdetermined nature of Englishness by reviving an anthropological concept of national integrity restored by imperial contraction.

"A Planet Full of Scraps"

The foregoing discussion suggests that imperialism both consolidated (and indeed generated) certain myths of Englishness but also had a disintegrative effect on the knowability or completeness of English culture. In other words, metropolitan perception subsumes the lost value of territorial coherence while registering the epistemological privilege associated with modernity's borderless spaces. The meaningful traditions of the old European nations had given way to massive multicultural empires. For E. M. Forster, writing in 1920, history itself had become "a dead object fallen across the page, which no historical arts can arrange, and which bewilders us as much by its shapelessness as by its size." It had become, in other words, "a planet full of scraps."[20]

The mixed cultural effects of imperialism in the modernist era were further complicated by the uncertain historical status of empire itself. The problem of "meaning loss" at the core reaches its crisis point during high modernism in part because the already epistemologically unstable metropole/periphery relation was becoming, in the years after 1900, more and more *politically* unstable. By the turn of the century, British imperialism was near its territorial peak but had already started to lose momentum, to fissure internally, and to meet serious resistance from nationalist movements in the colonies.[21] During the 1890s, Britain's sphere of influence and informal power had met new challenges from Russia (in Turkey and Persia) and the United States (in Latin America and the Caribbean). The Boer War (1899–1902), in which the mighty British barely defeated a ragtag opponent, undermined imperial confidence. Meanwhile, within the first dozen years of the new century, the epoch of European expansion and discovery reached its terrestrial end with the arrival of the Norwegian (not British) flag at the South Pole. In 1917, Lenin pointed out that the Great Powers had "*completed* the seizure of the unoccupied territories on our planet. For the first time the world is completely divided up, so that in the future *only* redivision is possible."[22] At the same time, the massive upheavals of World War I and the Russian revolution coincided with the crisis of Irish Home Rule, throwing into serious question British power in the dominions.

With all of this in mind, some cultural historians have argued that high modernism corresponds not to the moment of metropolitan concentration of power but to its ebb and diffusion. Edward Said, for example, claims that modernism was, from the beginning, animated by an awareness that imperialism was corrupt or weakening or both.[23] Kumkum Sangari suggests that modernist writing expressed a defensive awareness of imperial vulnerability all along: "Modernism is a major act of cultural self-definition, made at a time when colonial territories are being reparceled and emergent nationalisms are beginning to present the early outlines of decolonization."[24] On the other hand, these were still the *early* outlines of decolonization. London in 1900 or 1920 could still count itself a true world city, a capital of economic, political, military and cultural power with substantial influence on the course of events in an almost unimaginably disparate empire. High modernism is not, then, the literature simply of imperial crisis but of a complex moment involving inherited centrality and growing vulnerability.[25]

The problem of periodizing modernism and imperialism raises some further questions about their historical relation to each other—questions that have, in effect, two basic answers. The first view identifies in literary modernism an implicit critique of, or an explicit counterdiscourse to, imperialism. Benita Parry, for example, makes the point that "stylistic modernism" disrupts the "moral confidence" of European imperialism.[26] Similarly, Edward Said has suggested that modernism's "pervasive irony" and social skepticism tend to cut against the triumphalism of the imperial European bourgeoisie.[27] On the other hand, as Said goes on to suggest, several of modernism's aesthetic hallmarks—including that same pervasive irony—can be understood as formal correlates to high imperialism. This second view deemphasizes modernism's sporadic rhetorical or critical engagements with the question of empire in favor of a set of hypotheses about imperialism's indirect impact on modernist form.

As I have suggested, both Fredric Jameson's account of Forster's stylistic infinities and Raymond Williams's concept of "metropolitan perception" represent key formulations of this second premise, in which epistemological privilege in the metropolis enables certain characteristic forms of modernist thought and expression. Metropolitan perception names a distinctive feature of modernist art in the urban centers where European artists had free access to each other's work and to cultural materials from all over the world. Stephen Slemon, too, points out the importance of conceiving European modernism in terms of its "wholesale appropriation and refiguration of non-Western artistic and cultural practices."[28] This model of cosmopolitan privilege accounts for modernism's general capacity to rise above, while incorporating, the local materials of any given cultural tradition, as well as for the more specific appropriative practices of modernist primitivism. Imperial sciences like geography and anthropology produced vast amounts of new information, including works such as J. G. Frazer's encyclopedic mythography, *The Golden Bough* (a famous source text for both Eliot and Lawrence). A stream of people, ideas, objects, and aesthetics was flowing from the exotic fringes toward the metropolis, shaping and inflecting modernist form. Along these lines, Kumkum Sangari suggests this summary of metropolitan culture: "the freewheeling appropriations of modernism also coincide with and are dependent on the rigorous documentation, inventory, and reclassification of 'Third World' cultural products by the museum/library archive. Modernism as it exists is inconceivable without the archive and the archive as it exists is inconceivable without the political and economic relations of colonialism."[29] This view, in which modernism and imperialism are linked less as discursive antagonists than as a compatible base/superstructure dyad, has been the operating premise of a great deal of scholarship in the dozen years or so since the appearance of James Clifford's *The Predicament of Culture*. In that time the study of Euro-American modernism has been enlivened and expanded by attention to the intersections between anthropological knowledge, primitivist thinking, and modernist art.[30] Most new readings of this kind are underpinned by a model of epistemological privilege in the metropolis, according to which cultural materials from the colonial periphery were collected, circulated, curated, absorbed, and imitated by European arts and sciences.

The burgeoning anthropological archive offered living models of organic community to metropolitan intellectuals suffering the apparent loss of their own local sense of gemeinschaft. The privileges of geopolitical centrality operated in a more abstract way, too, tending to reinforce the idea that modernist art could access universal human realms of psyche and myth. Dramatizing its own location in broken and atomized societies, modernism (in its more heroic vein) offered back images of aesthetic wholeness. Although Said proposes that modernism's interest in autonomous total forms compensates for the already crumbling "synthesis" of the European empires,[31] imperialism (as a discourse) and empire (as a material fact of history) continue to support and underwrite British modernist culture into the "high" moment of the 1920s, when such landmarks of metropolitan modernism as *The Waste Land, Mrs. Dalloway,* and *A Passage to India* were published. These texts exemplify the overlapping power of two spatiotemporal logics associated with metropolitan perception. In them, modernism's epistemological reach across space and time complements its mystification of the here and now, its depiction of the metropole itself as a blind spot or absent totality.

Englishness as/vs. Modernity

In its high metropolitan phase, England seems to epitomize industrial and imperial modernity.[32] Yet its abbreviated avant-garde episode and vaunted social stability make English artistic life seem remarkably unmodern at the same time. To explain this apparent contradiction from the point of view of intellectual or cultural history, we have to bear in mind the problem of imperialism's dual effect, its hallowing and hollowing of English national culture. For Perry Anderson, as I noted in the introduction, England's half-modernized artistic life corresponds to the inner lack/outer presence of a fundamentally imperial and anthropological intelligentsia. Imperialism, exploding and exporting Englishness, defines Englishness in terms of its metacultural or universalist capacity to absorb and transcend the local and thus sets the conditions for an abiding high humanism. Perhaps the most famous comment on the humanism-imperialism link comes from Sartre's preface to Fanon's *Wretched of the Earth*:

> there is nothing more consistent than a racist humanism since the European has only been able to become a man through creating slaves and monsters. While there was a native population somewhere this imposture was not shown up; in the notion of the human race we found an abstract assumption of universality which served as cover for the most realistic practices. On the

other side of the ocean there was a race of less-than-humans who, thanks to us, might reach our status a thousand years hence.[33]

Such abstract assumptions of universalism depended, as Said has noted, on the silence of the non-Western world.[34] It also had unintended consequences for English intellectuals who discovered that the colonial encounter—which projected the colonizing subject as the prototype of upwardly mobile humanity—tended to exacerbate their own nostalgia for the vanishing cultural authenticity of English life. Imperialism only confirmed the lost gemeinschaft of the older European nations, whose artistic souls were then constrained to supplement metropolitan anomie with expropriated shards of those putatively more complete, more tribal, or more traditional societies overseas.[35]

Since England was arguably the most modernized and most imperially marked European metropole, it best exemplifies the logic of imperial universalism construed as a humanist transcendence of national culture. As Tom Nairn puts it, "the greater nations remain grandly unaware of their narrowness, because their culture, or their imagined centrality makes them identify with Humanity or Progress *tout court.*"[36] English humanism framed as both an imperial privilege and a national lack has its classic expression in the writing of Matthew Arnold. Arnold's *On the Study of Celtic Literature,* for example, fixes the relationship between center and satellite into a pattern that carries over from Victorian into modernist-era Britain. Early in the text, Arnold finds that he can only define England with coy evasiveness, because he believes that political and economic success have drained his nation of cultural vigor. He writes: "Our language is the loosest, the most analytic of all European languages. And we, then, what are we? what is England[?]. I will not answer, A vast obscure Cymric basis with a vast visible Teutonic superstructure; but I will say that the answer sometimes suggests itself, at any rate,—sometimes knocks at our mind's door for admission; and we begin to cast about and see whether it be let in."[37] He never does answer, except to imply that England is a mobile composite of other types of national geniuses; it is essentially without essence. The English difference, for Arnold, is precisely its resistance to typification or stereotype: "we [English] strike people as odd and singular, not to be referred to any known type, and like nothing but ourselves."[38] Arnold also circulates the idea that England's assimilative national identity represents an evolved blend of European tribalisms, which becomes the mythic basis for England's ability to absorb and to govern subordinate cultures overseas.[39]

The Arnoldian legacy, like Forster's fiction of the hedge, indicates the attenuation of English self-knowledge and self-possession during the era of British hegemony and its replacement by a clichéd stock of national myths from both home and abroad. As the essays collected in Hobsbawm and Ranger's *The Invention of Tradition* have shown, sub-British cultures, from Scottish to Zulu to Sikh, were encouraged to develop their distinctive and quaint cultural heritages as compensation for political subalternity. Imperial agents overseas performed two tasks that were only superficially paradoxical: the identification of peripheral cultures as still traditional or organic and the remaking of those cultures into modernized, specialized, and disenchanted societies. This contradictory process accords quite precisely with the structure of feeling described by Renato Rosaldo as "imperialist nostalgia."[40] England, meanwhile, became (or was cast as) the secularized and rationalized center of modernity to the point where its intellectuals could only engage in a perennial lament about its cultural vacuity. Tom Nairn vividly describes this phenomenon:

> Unlike their Celtic fringe, the English are too vague and mixed-up to fit a nationalist stereotype. Nobody knows what an "Englishman" is, in that sense. . . . Too internally differentiated for the vulgar measurements of nationalism, the English then spread themselves too far externally. Empire diluted the imponderable essence even farther, to the point where recapture has become impossible. This is why there is no national dress, an obscure and unresurrected folklore, and a faltering iconography.[41]

Where other nationalities, like Scotland's and Ireland's, were "easily summed up in typifying commonplaces," imperial England laid claim to the notion that there were no limiting or particularist versions of its own national culture.[42]

If English humanism represented a limited transcendence of ethnic or territorial bounds in keeping with the logic of universal British subjecthood, so too did metropolitan modernism imply a metacultural or cosmopolitan perspective, an aesthetic based on comparing, mixing, and incorporating an array of local traditions. This is a broad claim whose obvious canonical examples are *Ulysses, The Waste Land* and *The Cantos*. Its value here is that it allows for a comparative framing of modernist and humanist universalism, which crucially overlap in the British sphere. Perhaps the best way to describe modernism's capacity to address and to activate transcultural signifiers, mobile subjects, linguistic compendia, and mythic collocations is to return to Georg Simmel's classic description of the modernist city—one of the key sources for Raymond Williams's version of metropolitan perception. In Simmel's metropolis,

> the broadest and the most general contents and forms of life are intimately bound up with the most individual ones. Both have a common prehistory and also common enemies in the narrow formations and groupings, whose striving for self-preservation set them in conflict with the broad and general

on the outside, as well as the freely mobile and individual on the inside. . . .
It is not only the immediate size of the area and population which, on the
basis of world-historical correlation between the increase in the size of the
social unit and the degree of personal inner and outer freedom, makes the
metropolis the locus of this condition. It is rather in transcending this purely
tangible extensiveness that the metropolis also becomes the seat of cosmopolitanism. . . . The most significant aspect of the metropolis lies in this functional magnitude beyond its actual physical boundaries.[43]

This metropolis is not only, as Williams says, "beyond city and nation"
in its physical magnitude, it is also the preeminent site of a cosmopolitan
subjectivity cut free from the moorings of "narrow formations" like the
nation or the region, the clan or the family, the church or the guild (though
not, of course, free from any and all objective social conditions). This
experience of selfhood in what Keynes called an "international but individualistic" era provides one basis for what we generally take to be the
most innovative and typical forms of modernist writing. In this model,
metropolitan modernism is not cultural but metacultural and synthetic;
its irony is by nature cosmopolitan.[44] Such a modernism is universalist in
its self-conception and in its implied dedication to what Simmel calls the
"broad and general on the outside" and the "freely mobile and individual
on the inside."

English modernism thus represents the confluence of two types of self-
universalizing discourse: Englishness (the politically normative type for
an expanding liberal, capitalist, democratic order) and modernism (the
aesthetically normative type for high literature in the twentieth century).
Both international modernism and imperial Englishness tend to subsume
national, ethnic, or regional particularisms. As Edward Said observes:
"There is a convergence between the great geographical scope of the empires, especially the British one, and universalizing cultural discourses."[45]
Similarly, in describing "English imperialist culture," Tom Nairn writes:
"[England] possessed so much, and had dominated so much of the world
for so long, that its power could not help looking 'universal.' "[46] Said and
Nairn are describing the same metropolitan culture, the one that emerged
in the years conventionally taken to define modernism (1870–1940). With
the massive but "politically unconscious" (in the manner of Jameson's
Forster) context of imperial centrality in place, English modernism found
that it could conceive of its literary representations as plagued by national
lack but, correspondingly, buoyed up by freedom from the local, the particular, and the merely insular.

Why then, given this convergence of universalist discourses, was English modernism relatively insular and traditionalist by comparison not
only to the continental avant-gardes but also to the Irish and American

elements of Anglophone modernism? Why, in other words, if metropolitan perception accrues in the center, were so many modernisms eccentric or provincial? The simple answer is no doubt that there are many ways to resist or transgress national literary traditions and that not all of them depend either on an artist's birthplace or on an artist's location inside or outside the metropolis—particularly in view of the fact that modernists artists were themselves so mobile. Nevertheless, there is a reasonable case to be made that modernism was, as Robert Crawford puts it, an "essentially provincial phenomenon . . . aiming to outflank the Anglocentricity of established Englishness through a combination of the demotic and the multicultural."[47] Crawford's argument accords with Sean Golden's polemic about English literary nativism as a "nostalgic" movement, an "anti-Modernism" that "constitutes a reactionary trend."[48] These two critics, speaking from the perspectives of Scottish and Irish literary history, make the case that something specific keeps English modernism inside the hedge.[49]

The claim that English culture repels or marginalizes modernism because of its insularity conforms with an older understanding going back to Eagleton (*Exiles*), to Kenner, and to the modernists themselves.[50] But this claim has a dialectical counterpart, less remarked upon: if English culture was too national for a thriving intercultural modernism, it was *also not national enough*. This buried element of the problem becomes visible when we reread English modernism in terms of the imperial hollowing-out of national culture. From this perspective, English culture does not engender a radical modernism because it is *already* universalist and metacultural. The Arnoldian absence of national essence makes the ground unripe for the kind of dramatic clash between the national and the international that marks high modernist aesthetics. In short, with its transcultural languages already framed by the model of imperial humanism and its implied distance from the restrictions of a given culture, England stands as a paradigm of modernization, but not of modernism.[51]

The case of modernism in Britain/England is therefore a strange one. Although London was for a brief time host to the buzzing modernism of the Vortex and of *BLAST*, it subsequently became the repudiated headquarters of bourgeois life and the house of various domesticated or "establishment" modernisms. Competing models of modernism, as a literature of transcultural privilege/imperial centrality and as a literature of provincial insurgency/imperial degeneracy, can perhaps be reconciled by defining modernism more loosely, through its equipoise between universalist and localist claims—an equipoise that corresponds to the simultaneously expanding and contracting quality of imperialism in the period from 1890 to 1930.

This description brings us to the threshold of the shrinking island both historically and conceptually. For if high modernism offered a *cosmopolitan-aesthetic* mediation of universal perspectives and their local antitheses, then late modernism represents a new *national-cultural* mediation of the universal and the local. With the shift in geopolitical gravity during the 1930s and 40s, English intellectuals had increasingly to develop a language of cultural particularity disembedded from the Manichean logic of empire. In other words, as the historical conditions of possibility for metropolitan modernism began to erode, the latent nativism of Forster, Woolf, and Eliot came to the surface. Their works of the 1935–45 period manage the partial assimilation of cosmopolitan writing into a nativist lineage (running from Hardy and Housman to Davie and Larkin) that had always been modernism's middlebrow antagonist. The persistence of an insular tradition, combined with the broad reaches of imperial English humanism itself, doubly outflanked high modernism and set the stage for demetropolitanization. Because modernism in England never fully modernized, it was able rapidly to decommission itself into a politically ambiguous and culturally holistic Anglocentrism. On the one hand, that Anglocentrism contained conservative and hierarchical elements of false national unity, forestalling the momentum of mass culture and social dissensus in the thirties. On the other, it also contained the potential for a more democratic cultural retotalization, one that partially fulfills the thwarted and radical avant-gardist ambition of reintegrating art into a more capacious concept of culture.

Autoethnography and the Romance of Retrenchment

Although the specter of national decline emerged in earlier decades, it was not until the thirties that the converging crises of economic disaster, imperial overextension, and totalitarian threat pointed to the inevitability of British contraction. While anticolonial nationalisms gathered force on the periphery, doubts about the survival of empire penetrated both critics and defenders of British colonialism, so that a range of intellectual and artistic projects from the thirties seem not so much *pro*empire or *anti*empire as incipiently, anticipatorily *post*empire. Imperial retrenchment and national defense began not only to influence English cultural production in a reciprocally reinforcing way but to trump some of the social antagonisms and political debates of the previous decades. As Francis Mulhern points out in his analysis of radical English thought in the late thirties, there was "an unprecedented political and ideological fusion of 'the social question' and 'the national interest.' "[52] In such a moment, war patriotism of course generated the effect of English unity and in some sense prescribed its language, but that more conspicuous effect intersects with a variety of late imperial discursive turns that helped transform the methods for representing English unity—indeed, to transform the meaning of Englishness itself on the eve of a postimperial future.

It was by no means an act of civilizational prophecy for writers like Forster, Woolf, and Eliot—or for their contemporaries in other fields—to register an awareness of English culture's shifting status during this sea change in the history of British power. Indeed, as a brief historical sketch will suggest, English culture during the 1930s and 40s is littered with the signs of British imperial contraction both as an anticipated crisis and a burgeoning historical reality. The purpose of this sketch is not to enter into the historiographical debates on the undecidable question of when the decisive "end" or "beginning of the end" of British imperialism occurred but to set the broader context of cultural change that defines the anthropological turn both in and around late modernist literature. The culture of retrenchment takes identifiable shape and gathers momentum in the thirties, is intertwined with but not fully defined by World War II, and persists into the postwar era that we tend to associate with formal and global-scale decolonization.[53]

Although English leaders and English public opinion in the late 1930s might not have predicted the "remarkably sudden and complete" decolonization that occurred in the postwar years, it was already becoming clear that England's global domain would not grow any further and that, if anything, it would shrink.[54] The most important structural changes in the contraction of London's imperial ambit took place long before the official retreat of British imperialism in the 1960s. Although victory in World War I did increase the size of the British empire (by adding German holdings in Africa and the Pacific), the Irish Home Rule crisis of 1912–16 signaled the beginning of twentieth-century decolonization. The dominions—Canada, South Africa, Australia, New Zealand—began to seek autonomy from British authority and went on to gain important concessions at the 1923 Imperial Conference. By the end of World War I, nationalism and separatism had become potent forces in the rest of the empire as well, especially in Egypt and India. In the 1919 Government of India Act, London ceded control of the Indian provinces to local governments; three years later a degree of constitutional independence was granted to Egypt.[55]

Still, events of the 1920s neither utterly destroyed the imperial "illusion of permanence" nor fully roused England to alarm about its shrinking domain. In Paul Kennedy's view, "colonial unrest" did not become especially important for Britain until the 1930s, when the military challenges in Europe began seriously to divert resources away from the empire.[56] It was also in the 1930s that Britain's strategic vulnerability was exacerbated by severe economic depression. In 1931, Britain was forced to go off the gold standard and the pound's value was drastically and suddenly reduced. London had ceased to be the "only centre" of world trade and capital flows.[57] The contracting domestic economy suggested to political leaders that England might no longer have the resources to hold together its empire. Although die-hard imperialists still argued (probably mistakenly) for the necessity of the colonies as a source of wealth, the years between 1931 and 1945 were a time not so much for imperial consolidation as for the reconception of England's shrinking economy.[58]

Prolonged economic crisis made the colonies seem a drain on England's spare resources. This attitude, combined with increasingly independent-minded governments in Canada, South Africa, and the Irish Free State, caused London to cede more constitutional power to the overseas dominions over the course of the thirties. The 1931 Statute of Westminster granted constitutional equality to the dominions, severing their ties from London's parliament. Ireland continued on the path of constitutional separation from Britain during the 1930s, and by the end of the decade dominion separatism had demolished the "'organic unity' of the British empire."[59] Meanwhile, the anticolonial nationalisms of the Asian and African empire intensified during the interwar period. In 1935, the India Congress Party, growing in influence, secured an agreement that promised the eventual self-government of India.[60]

Thus, by the time the threat of European war became immediate, England (with Wales and Scotland still in tow) was already on its way to an insular status it had not experienced in hundreds of years. The temporary loss of Malaya and Burma to Japan in 1942 prefigured the more permanent breakup of the Asian empire that occurred after the war. World War II exposed the cracks and patches in Britain's imperial structure with a kind of historical finality, precipitating (despite the Allied victory) the formal process of decolonization.[61] The war's temporary suspension of cultural exchange between England and Europe exacerbated the more comprehensive and permanent (if less acute) crisis created by the end of colonial expansion and the imminent loss of the empire. For T. S. Eliot, as for most of his English contemporaries, the European conflict was tightly interwoven with broader historical phenomena; World War II was just the acute tip of a deeper catastrophe.[62] In her fateful diary entry of 23 September 1939, Virginia Woolf succinctly captures an English response to continental war in the form of a generalized sense of contraction and crisis: "Civilisation has shrunk."[63]

Woolf's sense of isolation and contraction were, however, tempered by a redemptive version of insularity, in which humane English values represented a sane alternative to the barbarism of Hitler, but only insofar as those values could be separated from the imperial aggression that had become a hallmark of British power. The confrontation with an expansionist, racist Germany provided English intellectuals with an unflattering reflection of their own imperial system. Leonard Woolf suggested that Britain could only stand up to Hitler by addressing its own "economic barbarism."[64] Similarly, in the 1941 essay "Tolerance," E. M. Forster notes that Nazism should lead to awareness of the "racial prejudice in the British Empire."[65] Like many writers at the time, Forster was seeking ways to redefine England as a coherent community without tripping into ethnic absolutism. The invocation of inherited, rather than state-produced, unity became a crucial element of Anglocentric discourse on both the right and left. Such a logic seems to have inspired Eliot's investment in English culture as a defensible, historically integral unit; in this cause Eliot invoked a Coleridgean ethic of organic and territorial unity, urging that England should find a way to make itself (again) a vital and "compact body like Germany." To reclaim territorial and cultural integrity for English culture was to disavow the history of British expansionism while assimilating the anthropological (and colonial) notion of solidarity back to the core. Both the conservative Eliot and the liberal-left Bloomsbury intellectuals proposed to define national community in terms of the cohesion of shared habits (immemorial Englishness) rather than the cohesion of shared goals (imperial Britishness).

While it is probably inaccurate to suggest that Englishness represented, for these modernists (particularly Virginia Woolf), an unproblematic haven from the nightmare of European history, it is nonetheless worth taking stock of the redemptive elements in their national thinking. When imperial decline became an imminent prospect, critics of modernity—including most modernists—suddenly had an opportunity to imagine England outside the stream of worldwide modernization, detached from the headlong "progress" of the British state. This appealed to Woolf as a feminist Outsider and to Eliot as an antisecular Tory. Shrinking back to its original island center, England would no longer be a world-historical nation, but it might recapture the humanist, aesthetic, and pastoralist values that had been eroded or degraded by imperial capitalism.[66]

Both popular writers and established modernists participated in the inward reorientation (or deorientalizing) of English culture during the thirties and forties. Yet the midcentury movement that I am describing should not be understood in terms of a simple shift from "outward-looking" to "inward-looking."[67] What does change in deep and permanent ways is that England becomes less firmly situated within a colonial system based on dualisms like home/abroad, modern/primitive, or metropolis/ periphery. For centuries, these imperial dualisms informed definitions of the English homeland and of English historical experience. England had been, for example, the ordered green space at the center of a chaotic tropical empire or, conversely, the sick, gray city removed from vital colonial action. Now, however, such representations would have to be reworked to make sense of England in its own terms, as a center without a periphery. As Hobson's Edwardian ideal of the "cohesive and internal" nation became more of an immediate historical fact, politicians and economists were beginning to ask whether the island could be self-sufficient without the raw materials and resources so long supplied by the colonies. The question has an important analogue in cultural terms: could the resources of Englishness suffice after centuries of appropriation and exchange? What symbolic functions did the overseas colonies serve, and which of those functions, if any, could be served by England itself? Would the new insularity change or superannuate literary techniques that were developed in the context of metropolitan power? The literature of the 1930s and '40s, when understood in the context of England's conversion from imperial hub to small European nation, invites us to consider these questions.

If, as I suggested in the previous section, recent scholarship has comprehensively rethought modernist art in terms of its relationship to anthropological knowledge and primitivist resources, it is perhaps worthwhile now to reconsider the period between 1930 and 1960 in terms of the introversion and repatriation of anthropological thinking. In English culture, that introversion did not simply winnow down the possibilities for imaginative writing; it also created new genres and stories adapted to the needs of a late imperial welfare state and generated new romances about the folk, about the working class, about the countryside, about national character.[68] Fascism's rise in Europe not only isolated England politically and culturally but signaled the power of *völkisch* national thinking in an era of mass politics—a double-whammy that galvanized intellectual interest in the language of cultural solidarity on the shrinking island. In the culture of retrenchment, then, the political challenge of the time—the need to generate a counterfascist version of national solidarity without sacrificing the institutions of English tradition and liberal politics—intersected with an intellectual quest for revitalized sources of local authenticity, of folk consciousness, of chthonic identity. In several different textual and cultural locations during the period from 1930 to 1950, England was refigured as the object of its own imperial discourse, its own touristic imagination, its own historical affections, its own documentary gaze, its own primitivizing fantasies, its own ritual pageantry, its own economic theories, and its own myths of origin.

This broad domestication of imperial discourses in midcentury England can be divided into two (sometimes overlapping) tendencies: the romantic and the documentary. If, as Edward Said suggests, the period from 1880 to 1930 witnessed the transplantation of romance genres to the empire, then the midcentury witnesses something of a comeback for the domestic romance. Instead of projecting the irrational and the primitive onto the colonial periphery, English intellectuals had to rediscover magic and mystery in the center.[69] Of course, English writers had been using the language of imperialism to describe England well back into the Victorian era; Conrad's famous description of London as "one of the dark places of the earth" comes immediately to mind as an example.[70] However, the literary reimportation of colonial tropes to the English sphere became more urgent and widespread in the 1930s. By the midcentury, the colonies (which were fast becoming the "new nations" of the postcolonial world) could no longer serve as a fantastic source or haven for nonbourgeois values and nonrational mysteries. John McClure argues that English modernists like Conrad and Forster used the romance formula to project mystery and magic onto colonies that were rapidly losing their exotic aura through westernization.[71] Such literature performs what McClure describes as a belated reenchantment of the colonies. For similar reasons, English writers in the 1930s used a variety of literary techniques and narratives to bring about the reenchantment of England itself. Perhaps the best way to describe this phenomenon is to call it the reimportation to England of the "surplus of neo-traditional capital" that had been, in Terence Ranger's influential formulation, exported to the colonies over the previous decades.[72]

One crucial aspect of this broader (re)substitution of England's own fetishized or primitivized past for the vanishing pleasures of colonial exoticism was the relocation of cultural origins on the island itself. Colonial discourse of the nineteenth and early twentieth centuries tended to view colonized territories as the originary locations of modern European civilization. According to this rhetoric, thoroughly documented by Edward Said in *Orientalism*, modern Europe had reconnected, through conquest, with the primary sites of its Judeo-Christian, Indo-European, Greco-Roman heritage. At the point of imperial decline, however, a newly insular English culture reinvests in its own autochthonous origin stories. Where orientalist discourse had located civilizational origins in the colonies (Egyptian monuments, Indian languages, Palestinian religions), the new discourse of historical self-consumption uncovers the roots of contemporary life in the native English soil (Druidic monuments, Anglo-Saxon languages, Arthurian legends). Country houses and medieval heraldry replace Elgin Marbles and Egyptology.[73] Woolf's *Between the Acts* somewhat parodically reflects this Anglocentric romance of origins: in the novel, Lucy Swithin's Outline of History begins not in Egypt or Mesopotamia but with the bubbling primeval murk of ancient England.

In British folklore studies, similarly, the end of empire required a redirection of energies toward the "discovery" of British and English objects of study. Richard Dorson recounts the changes in a discipline which, during the Victorian era, had become almost entirely focused on life outside

Britain. However, "with the gradual shrinkage of Empire, the splendid colonial laboratory of folklore dwindled."[74] At this point, Celtic sources became particularly important in British folklore studies; as Dorson recounts, "the English seekers came to learn that fountains of oral folklore bubbled at their very doorstep."[75] And when even the Celtic sources of Ireland were "lopped off from the British trunk," the folklorists had to find sources within England itself.[76]

Not surprisingly, the isolation of England due to both continental and imperial events produced a thirties boom in domestic tourism.[77] The romance of retrenchment was, above all, ruralist in its orientation, dwelling in the green and pleasant land of Chaucerian, Shakespearian, and Wordsworthian stereotype. Best-selling Batsford guidebooks pointed domestic travelers of the 1930s toward the architectural landmarks of old England, while a wave of new amateur-naturalist books directed them to nationally sacred landscapes.[78] H.V. Morton's *In Search of England* (1927) initiated a publishing trend that ran through to the early 1940s, with dozens of popular books dedicated to the quest for authentic rural life in England.[79] T. S. Eliot's *Criterion* was, among other things, the site of an unabashed school of nostalgic ruralists (including John Betjeman and T. F. Powys) who idealized the old green and sceptered isle.[80] Many writers promised the possibility of rustic adventure in the home islands, with titles like *Gone Rustic, Southshire Pilgrimage*, or *This Unknown Island*.[81]

With its increasing cultural isolation in the 1930s, then, England was becoming self-consciously historical, even antiquarian. As English culture moved from expanding imperial modernity to preservationist national past, the island itself became one large museum—a repository of history whose acquisition-and-collection phase was over (by dint of geopolitical circumstance), leaving only the task of obsessive curatorship. Visiting England in the years just before World War II, Malcolm Cowley described the effect of "England under glass," a nation becoming its own museum: "Even the people sometimes looked like wax figures dressed in authentic costumes."[82] Raphael Samuel's prodigious work in this area suggests a boom in local, domestic, and unofficial forms of memory making, not just an elitist appeal to Heritage. What Samuel calls the broad "historicist turn in national life" corresponds closely in both content and timing to what I have been calling the anthropological turn.[83] Many cultural historians have noted the domestic tourism boom, but fewer have pursued the connections between the reburgeoning languages of English "self-discovery" (epitomized by J. B. Priestley's 1934 *English Journey*) and the fading languages of imperial exploration and travel. Such a connection, in which England begins to function as a symbolic replacement for its colonies, becomes even clearer when we move beyond the soft-focus "country ramble" mode of tourism to the scientifically inflected mode of documentary and ethnography.

The various strands of domestic romance, pastoral idealism, and Anglocentric preservation described above reached a new pitch in the 1930s. If the imperial-Arnoldian legacy had, as I have suggested, hollowed out the core of Englishness by making it a mobile, composite, metaculture, then the challenge was to restore the positive content of the national imago (thereby inverting Tom Nairn's formula of the English intelligentsia's inner lack/outward presence). The thirties craze for "discovering England" included a host of new literary and ethnographic projects designed to reveal the real daily life of the nation, most of which self-consciously posed themselves against elite literature. For example, the documentary novel—one of the genres most commonly associated with the thirties—took as its premise the idea that English society was an unknown quantity. Convinced that traditional literary genres had ignored class and regional difference, documentarians sought to address the situation with new forms of reportage, fiction, and film. Southern suburbanites could now satisfy their taste for new knowledge and exotic customs by learning about the "real life" of the northern urban masses. George Orwell's fictional itinerary during the decade is a case in point: he moves from describing a corrupt colonialism in Asia with *Burmese Days* (1934) to exploring what he considers the unknown territories of English life in works like *The Road to Wigan Pier* (1937).[84] Moreover Orwell's career, blending documentary or social realism with intense pastoral longing for English essence, exemplifies not just the dual nature of the anthropological turn but the inter-implication of its romantic and realistic aspects.

Both the romantic and autoethnographic elements of late-imperial Anglocentrism turned on a domesticated rhetoric of cultural salvage.[85] Indeed, it is the motif of salvage—not elegy—that marks one of the subtle but unmistakable shifts from metropolitan pastoralism to late-imperial pastoralism: the idea that cultural wholeness and essence could be restored to England rather than simply mourned at the core and projected onto the colonies. In Mary Louise Pratt's usage, the term autoethnography signifies a rhetorical strategy by which colonized peoples began to represent themselves while borrowing and adapting European "fieldwork" techniques.[86] I use autoethnography here to describe English intellectual appropriations of colonial-anthropological techniques to reclaim English vitality and cultural coherence from its dissolution into modern, atomized culturelessness.

Viewed against a long history of Anglocentric cultural-salvage operations, the nativism of the 1930s era is distinct in its self-conscious replacement of mimetic primitivism (based on an idealization of the alien tribe) with an insular primitivism (based on an idealization of the domestic folk).[87] This is not simply a voluntary decision on the part of metropolitan intellectuals but a way of managing both the practical force of insularization in the thirties and the growing resistance of colonized societies. The cultural shifts unfolding in England during the 1930s and '40s are, of course, part of a larger twentieth-century phenomenon in which European centrality has been challenged by non-Western cultures. Indeed, the reversal and repatriation of anthropology marks this midcentury phase of contraction in the European empires more generally, when non-European intellectuals began to challenge the universalist assumptions of imperial humanism across the board.[88] In England in particular, as Paul Rich observes, there was "an academic revolution in anthropology in which the colonial periphery rebelled against the metropolitan centre, a revolution which led to innovatory work in social theory, especially of the inner mechanics of culture, by the end of the Second World War."[89]

One of the most visible signs of the fact that the anthropological eye of British intellectual life began during the 1930s to train its gaze back onto England after years of colonial fieldwork was Mass-Observation, a movement of leftist intellectuals who set out to perform a "home anthropology" for England. One of its founders, Tom Harrisson, had written an ethnographic work called *Savage Civilisation* about life in the New Hebrides (Melanesia) and was eager to bring fieldwork home to industrial England. Harrisson and his group established a network of observers to record, describe, and make known the habits and beliefs of the English people. Like the documentary writers, these domestic ethnographers were motivated by the impulse to "discover the unknown" within their own culture.[90] The Mass-Observers even secured the disciplinary imprimatur of Bronislaw Malinowski, the leading practitioner of tropical fieldwork and functionalist anthropology. Endorsing the new school of English autoethnography, Malinowski writes: "from the start of my own fieldwork, it has been my deepest and strongest conviction that we must finish by studying ourselves through the same methods and with the same mental attitude with which we approach exotic tribes."[91]

In a suggestive essay juxtaposing Mass-Observation with the high modernist "day book," James Buzard isolates the crucial question facing both modernist form and autoethnographic technique, namely, whether British culture "was something amenable to—even longing for—totalization, or something anathema to it."[92] As an anthropological effort to capture the whole national culture, Mass-Observation offered an alternative to modernism's artistic projection of totality. Its methods signal the specifically anthropological displacement of modernist aesthetics as the preeminent language of mediation between the particulars of daily life in a complex society and the abstract ideal of national identity. Indeed, Buzard points out elsewhere that the rise of autoethnographic discourse in England tends to correspond to the eclipse of high modernism.[93] But of course, as Buzard also notes, modernism itself had changed in the years between, say, *The Waste Land* and *Four Quartets*, precisely insofar as it executed its own anthropological/Anglocentric turn and, at least in some quarters, "made its peace with nationalism."[94] Like the later works of Eliot and Woolf, the reports of the Mass-Observers imagined that a kind of cultural totality, somehow immanent in what Gertrude Stein would have called "daily island life" could be represented anew in the thirties. The domesticated language of ethnography finessed the problem of national totality by assuming its presence. We should note as well that Mass-Observation's attempt at a radically democratic and decentralized representational apparatus (what was "Mass" about the project was not just the observed but the observers) ended up becoming normative and even statist in its effects. The centralizing effect of Mass Observation, particularly with the onset of World War II, took the litany of shared Englishness on a short trip from radical intentions to conservative organicism. That trip reveals the deep ties between national romance and ethnographic realism in this period and their shared debt to an ideal of cultural authenticity borrowed back from the colonies.

Thus, the key feature of anthropological turn was its ability, not to divide romance from realism, but to combine them under the sign of the shrinking island. The documentary and autoethnographic elements of the new Anglocentrism proposed to know the reality—including the social difference and antagonisms—of the entire nation. But even when set against elite or nostalgic constructions of the English folk, these more "realist" projects were built on an epistemological romance whose inner logic assumed the restored knowability of English culture at the moment of its insularization. Domesticated anthropology yielded a compromise totality, in which the national essence and the fractured present could be brought together not by the obscure midwifery of metropolitan modernism but by the increasing cultural power of relativist, particularist, and realist beliefs about English boundedness and knowability. Home anthropology becomes the language of reconciliation between a potentially transformative epistemology of English class society and an apparently conservative ontology of Englishness. The culture concept has a relativist agenda because it entails the proposition that all ways of life are distinct and integral in themselves, but, as James Clifford has noted, it almost always has an organicist premise.[95]

We are now in a position to identify with greater precision what distinguishes the anthropological turn of the thirties from earlier (and later) forms of autoethnography in England and, more to the point, what marks its historical relationship to British contraction. One need only glance through the essays collected by Robert Colls and Philip Dodd in their study of Englishness from 1880 to 1920 to see that several of the strands I have analyzed in this chapter—organicism, ruralism, domestic tourism, autoethnography—emerged in English culture well before the 1930s. However, these discursive movements took on new kinds of historical and literary significance at the moment of national crisis and neorevivalism in the mid-twentieth century.[96] To be more precise, where earlier forms of home anthropology located cultural essence or cultural authenticity in subpockets of the national culture—in those "others" distanced by class or region from the metropole—this version of home anthropology attempts to represent the nation as the seat of authentic cultural totality. The reabsorption of anthropological holism to English culture in the thirties located authenticity at the level of national culture.[97] From the larger historical perspective, it is possible to understand the period from 1930 to 1960 as the moment when England (re)attained the status of a culturally meaningful unit in the face not only of British contraction but of the ongoing globalization of capitalism. Given England's relative provincialization and territorial contraction within the world economy of the mid-twentieth century, it became newly possible for intellectuals of all kinds to conceive of England as possessing the kind of cultural boundedness, unity, and knowability previously restricted to peripheral regions like Hardy's Wessex or to subject nations like Yeats's Ireland.[98]

Modernist Valedictions circa 1940

For Eliot, Woolf, and Forster, the English nation of the thirties was thrown into historical relief as the actual embodiment—or at least the symbol—of a living and integrated culture rather than as the metropolitan seat from which a rational cosmopolitanism could stand apart from any given culture. Their Anglocentric turn implicitly reversed the Arnoldian legacy in, which England featured as a culturally etiolated center. This is a modernist question, because modernism had not only enshrined the split map of Forster's hedge but absorbed the Arnoldian legacy in its anthropological cultivation of peripheral cultures and its mystification of its own society as hopelessly reified, dazzlingly atomized: unknowable or unreal. If metropolitan anthropology had shown Europe that there still existed what Eliot calls "living total cultures" elsewhere in the world; empire's *end* allowed for the possibility of recreating such a culture in England, *as* England. In concluding chapter 1, I want to consider some of the literary-historical consequences of this possibility by asking how modernist writers participated in the culture of retrenchment that I have outlined above.[99]

As a cultural phenomenon, demetropolitanization depended not on an absolute or sudden shift in British power but on the short-lived belief among both popular and canonical English writers that the contraction of the British state might represent an interruption in the gathering power of global capitalism and thus a partial remediation of the social atomization attendant on metropolitan modernity. The moment of imperial contraction seemed to be a back-eddy in the course of modernity, a pause long enough for artists to stop mourning the loss of cultural wholeness and to concentrate on its remaining traces in contemporary England. If metropolitan perception had conferred on modernists a privileged intercultural epistemology, paid for in the coin of art's social segregation, then demetropolitanization implied a tighter link between artist and society, paid for in the coin of a more limited or nationalized social referent.

Contraction was both a material predicate and an available metaphor for the revival of cultural integrity in midcentury England. Jameson's account of imperialism and modernism as lost totality begins to explain, by historical extension, the importance of insularity as a master trope for cultural completeness. If expansion had exacerbated (or simply symbolized) the fundamental unknowability of English society as a totality, then contraction mitigated (or was taken symbolically to repair) that unknowability. Likewise, if modernist metaphoric and stylistic registers captured the "meaning loss" of an England that was and was not identical to itself during the metropolitan era, then a counterpart set of metaphors and stylistic devices in later modernist texts might be understood to capture a new phase of apparent or incipient self-identity in demetropolitanizing England. As historical events seemed to superannuate the split map of Forster's metropole, the values of cultural integrity moved from their marginal symbolic position inside the hedge to define a newly insular national destiny. No longer conceived as the central node of a widening British state, England had to become a self-sufficient symbolic system, replacing or displacing the empire rather than coexisting with it either as its green and inviolate core *or* as its lost inner essence.

The end of empire thus *activated* and *nationalized* certain modernist concepts of community that had been the vain wishes and half-buried utopian kernels of an essentially postlapsarian and cosmopolitan modernism. Eliot, for example, participated in the thirties romance of retrenchment by proposing that a domesticated primitivism should be cultivated in place of the older modernist habit of chasing after tribal vitality in the tropics. In *The Idea of a Christian Society*, he suggests that, rather than imitate savages, English intellectuals should uncover the local roots of an integrated culture based on native Christianity (native, that is, since the Roman conquest). For Eliot, to undo the Arnoldian legacy means to demystify the idea of liberal progress (which events on the darkening continent seemed to be achieving without any help from poets and literary critics). But it also means bringing to light the essentially religious root structure of English cultural integrity, still lying underneath a superficially rationalist and pluralist society. The waning of imperialism aids Eliot not only as brute political fact but also insofar as the image of England drained of its spiritual essence was an illusion generated by unfavorable Arnoldian comparisons to the colonized folk. In the distorting mirror of empire, England appears to epitomize secular modernity. But in the moment of imperial contraction, England can catch sight of its own cultural authenticity and vitality. For Eliot, and as I will argue in what follows, for Forster and Woolf and Keynes (though they are somewhat trickier cases), England's detachment from imperialism thus mitigates its rationalized and culturally depleted status.[100]

The central claim that a new and redemptive form of thirties Anglocentrism activated and renationalized certain dissident or marginal modernist values explains, not incidentally, the absence of D. H. Lawrence (a canonical English modernist) from this study. Dead by 1930, Lawrence, simply put, did not live to see the antimodern values of so much English modernism revived by the apparent flagging of British industry and empire and by the failure of internationalism in the decade after his death. Lawrence's novels of the two preceding decades contained some powerful, but vexed and premature, attempts to reenchant England by tapping the odd sexual, animal, vegetable, or vitalist vein. But at a systemic level, Lawrence became convinced that the revitalization of industrialized, rationalized England was, by and large, a lost cause; he then moved his search for the authentic life to the peripheral zones of Australia and North America. Unlike Eliot, who increasingly sought to relocate cultural vitality in the core, Lawrence remained within the classic paradigm of modernist primitivism.[101] As Raymond Williams has observed, "the tragedy of Lawrence . . . is that he did not live to come home."[102] To the end Lawrence remained pessimistic about the loss of organic community, rural mystery, and human vitality in a Europe desiccated and sickened by modernity.

As the case of Lawrence makes clear, my argument about English modernism depends on a subtle but definite shift in the tone of pastoral Anglocentrism, from nostalgic or elegiac in the era of high modernism to revivalist in the era of imperial contraction. This shift in tone distinguishes, for example, Lawrence's representations of a dying England in the second decade of the century from J. C. Powys's thirties revivalism or, in fact, early Forster from late Forster. In chapter 2, I will return to Forster at some length, but here we can briefly clarify the historical distance this chapter has traveled from the metropolitan logic of the Hedge to late-imperial Anglocentrism. If late Forster rewrites—or at least shifts the emphasis of—early Forster, moving from composed and nostalgic irony to urgent sincerity, it is not Forster's abiding pastoral and humanist values that have changed but the context for, and form of, their literary expression. Forster's original circle-and-road geography worked because it defined an irrevocable and extrinsic tension between Englishness and modernity in an expansive British state. When that world-state contracts, the bounded pastoral zone begins to detach from the dynamic Road outside the Hedge, and Forster's narrative and ideological tensions become attenuated. This point can only really be made by considering the *forms* into which pastoral values are inscribed by Forster—by addressing, that is, the genre shift in Forster's career from the novels of the major period to the nonnarrative writing (essays, pageants, stories, memoirs, reviews) of the thirties and forties. The pastoral elements of these latter genres operate relatively unfettered by the metropolitan irony that drives the major fiction. An England imaginarily broken off from metropolitan perception turns out not to provide the necessary friction and political desire to sustain full-scale narrative momentum, complication, and resolution. While the novels have beautiful strains of pastoral idealism, their narrative logic emphasizes modernity's inevitable (sometimes thrilling) threat to the inner green core. What the modernist Forster could only represent as an ideal encapsulated in ironic and layered metropolitan narratives, the Forster of the later period could imagine embodied and performed in the pageant-plays of Little England.

In Forster's pageants, as in the broader discourse of native culturalism, the importance of place as a sign of cultural unity trumps social differences such as class, race, region, religion, or gender. This is why spatial figures and geographical referents—from metropolitan to insular—are of such central concern in this argument.[103] As Raphael Samuel has observed, the success of Anglocentric heritage movements has always depended precisely on the displacement of class antagonism by social affiliation to place. Moreover, Samuel notes, this process should not be too easily dismissed as a ruse of conservative nationalism. When read within the framework of literary history and compared to high modernism's representation of social atomization, the Anglocentric investment in national culture seems to allow for a more democratic, or at least more systematic, view of the cultural system. For example, Eliot's attempt to marry the conservative religious recovery of Anglican community with the anthropological and relativist neutrality of a student of culture may be a rhetorical pose at one level, but it proceeds alongside and enables an important attempt on his part to reconceive the alienated cosmopolitan Artist as the local mediator of a vital national culture. The Anglocentric turn of aging modernists was predicated on the idea that the British crisis could be withstood, not just by defending England, but also by reimagining it as a less patriarchal (Woolf), less atomized (Eliot), or less laissez-faire (Keynes) society.

Late modernist forms are crucial to understanding the culture of retrenchment because they register the historical supersession, not the desirability or undesirability, of imperialism. In formal terms, that supersession implies a new kind of shaped temporality and bounded spatiality, as against the open-ended time and infinite placelessness of metropolitan perception. Where high modernist works posed various kinds of occult or apocalyptic temporalities against mere mechanical time, late modernist works by Forster, Woolf, and Eliot extract a notion of shaped time from the resources of national culture. In *Between the Acts*, for example, Woolf manages to fuse the day-book unity of *Mrs. Dalloway* and the historical dilation of *Orlando*, symbolically condensing the wide-open past into the frame of a single day through an appeal to national tradition. In a suggestive commentary, Gillian Beer has observed that Woolf's sense of "prehistory" in *Between the Acts* echoes Eliot's temporal concerts in *Four Quartets*.[104] Beer emphasizes the vast geological and Darwinian time frame that animates both texts. But it is equally noteworthy, I think, that both writers use a distinctively national history to mediate between vast temporal scales and subjective apprehensions of time.

The recoding of national time and space into bounded or meaningful wholes by English intellectuals can be read as implying both a dangerously false national totality (one that ignores or obscures real social differences) and a potentially transformative national totality (one that challenges an entrenched and crippling ideology of social fragmentation). Of course the modernists themselves, as cosmopolitan and dissident intellectuals, were sensitive to the danger of national unity as false consciousness. Forster, Woolf, and Eliot all maintained distance from nationalism throughout the thirties and forties by invoking international and individualist values against Englishness. Nevertheless, at the moment of retrenchment, they each seemed to demystify aesthetic autonomy within a newly conceived system of anthropological/national culture.

The schematic model of metropolitan modernism (1890–1930) adduced earlier in this chapter suggests that social totality, ungraspable in the metropole itself, tended to move not just *out* to the colonial periphery but *up* into the realms of aesthetic completion and mediation. With demetropolitanization, then, the concept of totality is simultaneously domesticated and democratized; after 1930 it is referred decisively back to the category of national culture. In what follows, this study gives serious consideration to the idea that modernist intellectuals themselves reimagined social wholeness in cultural rather than aesthetic terms. The relativist/organicist ambiguity built into the discourse of cultural particularism allowed modernists like Eliot and Woolf to adapt their own literary practices to the compromise between aesthetic and anthropological representation of social wholeness. Ambitious modernists had, of course, always wished to "represent the social totality—while at the same time *addressing it*. To be innovative and popular, complex and simple, esoteric and direct: to heal the great fracture between avant-garde exploration and mass culture."[105] In the end-stage of English modernism, that wish (split between political despair and political compromise) took on startling new forms in the context of a potentially repaired insular culture.

Indeed, the assimilation of anthropological holism to England provided modernists with a response to the avant-garde imperative—increasingly urgent in the thirties—to reunify art and life. That decade featured a number of attempted solutions to (and abandonments of) the problem of art's autonomization; among these the late or countermodernism of Forster, Woolf, and Eliot represents a compromise with nativism that gestures, provisionally, to the reintegration of art and culture.[106] Despite its demodernizing content, their compromise answers to the same historical pressures registered in the avant-gardist program of anti-art or the literary left's commitment to political art.[107] Its vision of art's deeper integration into insular culture was enabled but also defanged by its deference to anthropological holism and to the emergent discourse of welfare-state corporate nationalism.[108]

Late modernism's anthropological turn does not, then, constitute a revolutionary antiaesthetic, just a shifting emphasis from aesthetic to cultural totality under the specific aegis of Anglocentrism. In this sense, Forster, Woolf, and Eliot represent only an initial phase in the midcentury particularization of English identity. Susan Hegeman has suggested that the transition from an evolutionary-hierarchical model of culture (à la Arnold or Frazer) to a relativist and functionalist view was coincident with and bound up in modernism all along.[109] Modernism, in this view (which is also that of James Clifford), reflects the coexistence and competing claims of two equally strong positions on culture (aesthetic and anthropological) and two equally strong anthropological *epistemes* (evolutionary and functionalist). It is only when the anthropological and functionalist positions come to the fore and are assimilated to Western cultures (in accord with the crisis of European imperialism and humanism) that we have the end-stage of English modernism. If, as Said broadly argues, colonial resistance and imperial decline unsettled and discredited the *grands récits* of modern Europe, then the late works of Eliot, Woolf, and Forster (and Keynes) stand not only as residual formations of high modernism but as transitional documents of a midcentury turn of thought that relativizes British power into English particularity and relocates aesthetic autonomy into a devalorized or functionalist anthropology of culture.[110]

Events of the thirties, both continental and colonial, challenged the universalist and cosmopolitan tenets of metropolitan intellectuals, forcing them into the embrace of ethnically and nationally specific little worlds. In this moment of demetropolitanization, imperial Britain (abstract, infinite, expanding, diluting, schismatic) gives way to empirical England (concrete, bounded, insular, consolidated, integral). In a sense, modernism and fascism represent two sometimes opposed and sometimes overlapping versions of a deterritorialized Enlightenment rationalism converting itself—dialectically and, as it were, instantaneously—into a territorially restrictive appeal to national belonging. With fascism haunting the conversion of the universal into the particular and haunting the space of reconciliation between social totality and national organicism, the anthropological turn becomes a vital, if compromised, Anglocentric via media between the atomized, but sometimes thrilling, freedom of metropolitan perception and the stark conformism of totalitarian politics. Autoethnography and domestic romance gave Anglocentrism its cultural flesh and blood—its long-lost Arnoldian essence or positivity—and secured additional cultural prestige from the participation of modernist writers like Woolf, Eliot, and Forster. Adapting their own cosmopolitan habits to new national imperatives and opportunities, these modernists also began to convert self-consciously border-crossing literary practices into artistically mediated expressions of a whole culture. At this point, as the next several chapters will demonstrate in detail, Forster, Eliot, and Woolf explored the diffusion of metropolitan and modernist textual authority in their encounter with a more spontaneous, communal, and ritualized brand of English art.

A final word of methodological clarification is in order here before moving onto the critical readings of chapter 2. High modernism is sometimes thought by its detractors to have been ahistorical in its flights of aestheticism, mythicism, or subjectivism. In this view, the thirties are commonly understood as the decade in which History or Politics invaded the cloistered realm of Art and won the field.[111] But thirties modernism, as defined here, like even the more conspicuously engagé kinds of thirties writing, always entails aesthetic experimentation; likewise, high modernist experimentalism was always an attempt to come to terms with contemporary history. In this sense, there is no such thing as an "ahistorical" literary aesthetic, just different languages and techniques for addressing history. This book tries to take note of subtle shifts in historical consciousness among English modernists against the backdrop of demetropolitanization. Consider, for example, The Years, in which Woolf attempted to "do history" by narrating generational and social change together over time, but found that even in the quasi-epic form of the family saga there was a missing dimension of group ritual or public symbolism. With that absence in mind, Woolf represents history in Between the Acts through the neotraditional protocols of the village pageant and manages more fully to engage the question of art's collective effects. These two Woolf novels suggest an almost insuperable problem that also clarifies a subtle difference between high and late modernism as defined in this book. That is, *The Years* depicts a series of determinate social changes, but only by filtering them through the relatively small or private unit of the bourgeois family and its interiorized subjects. *Between the Acts* manages to depict a familiar and shared ritual cutting *across* social classes, but only by condensing history into an essential and abstract Englishness.

Similarly, Eliot's *Four Quartets*, though sometimes mistaken as a retreat from history's nightmare into religious dogmatism, trades in abstract national symbols in order to generate a profound meditation on historical time. By contrast, high modernist texts like *The Waste Land* tended to reflect a direct and unpalliated engagement with the brute facts of global modernization and its shapeless temporality. High modernism's heroic streak lies precisely in its avowedly hopeless struggle with modernity, but real history also includes the invented traditions, especially nationalism, that have been invoked collectively and subjectively to give shape to the passage of time. Late modernist Anglocentrism indulges in nativist or organicist concepts of national experience, but thereby finds some new points of engagement with collective and cultural expression. To state the point briefly: high modernism was more historically engaged with the uncut facts of ceaseless modernization but in a socially limited way, whereas late modernism is more socially and anthropologically engaged but has a more limited (i.e., national and organicist) concept of history.

TWO

INSULAR RITES: VIRGINIA WOOLF

AND THE LATE

MODERNIST PAGEANT-PLAY

I HAVE SO FAR proposed a general account of thirties literary tropes and intellectual projects that domesticated the anthropological paradigms of the metropolitan era. The reorientation of anthropological thinking to problems of national self-representation provided the method for English intellectuals to channel the potential energy of a contracting British civilization into a resurgent discourse of national particularism. Virginia Woolf and T. S. Eliot, two writers with apparently divergent ideological profiles and a common position at the institutional center of English modernism, both participated in an anthropological turn that sharpened the autocritical aspects of their own modernist practice. Attuned to the failure of interwar cosmopolitanism and to art's increasing social marginality, Eliot and Woolf turned their attention to the possibilities embodied in shared national traditions and public rituals.

Of course, the conflict between modernism's elite reception and its broad social ambitions had been a central feature of the movement all along. Modernist writers expressed frustration at their marginality in a number of ways. Woolf, for example, developed a rich and generous body of criticism dedicated to preserving English literature for the "common reader." Eliot, for his part, had always idealized ritual expression as the organic root of modern art. Thus, when Woolf and Eliot step up their interest in the collective production or consumption of art, it does not represent a revolution (or even an evolution) of *values*, but it does reflect their belief in new and greater *opportunities* to integrate aesthetic and social power. What was once a cultural ideal projected backward into literary history or outward onto primitive tribes could now become a vital part of a demetropolitanized English culture; what had been an unrealized tenet of modernist doctrine could now become a more direct part of modernist practice.

Woolf and Eliot participated in an Anglocentric revival that redirected attention from tribal and tropical rituals to homespun and folkloric ones and that shaped a number of important features of literary culture in the thirties. One way to trace that revival's implications for English modernism is to reconsider the strange and largely unexamined career of an exotic subgenre, the pageant-play. Whether as a dramatic form or a subject for fiction, the village pageant drew the attention of several major English writers during the 1930s. Woolf made a pageant-play the subject of her last novel, *Between the Acts*, choosing her plot partly in response to a pageant written by her Bloomsbury contemporary, E. M. Forster. Eliot, too, experimented with the genre during the 1930s (as did other well-known writers, such as John Cowper Powys and Charles Williams). What accounts for the recirculation of this odd, anachronistic genre? Why did the pageant-play, with its dubious promise of rank amateurism, costumed set pieces, hackneyed nationalism, and potted history, appeal to Forster and Eliot (as a dramatic form), to Woolf (as a narrative device), and to their contemporaries during the decade of documentary realism and political poetry? To answer those questions requires an historical detour into the Edwardian fields where modern pageantry was born and then an unusual itinerary through the thirties, one that runs from Powys's monumental novel *A Glastonbury Romance* (1932) to Eliot's flawed but fascinating pageant *The Rock* (1934) to Forster's *Abinger Pageant* (1934) and *England's Pleasant Land* (published 1940), concluding with Woolf's *Between the Acts* (1941), a text that both exemplifies and complicates the midcentury transition from textual privacy to public performance.

The cultural changes reflected in these pageant-play texts seem to be readily explained by the menacing context of European fascism. The success of Nazi theater and spectacle no doubt turned the attention of English writers to matters of national community and public art. But this familiar explanation takes on new shades of meaning when considered alongside the self-anthropologizing dimensions of national representation in late imperial England. The pageant-play experiments in question aimed not just to rehearse the tropes of Merrie Englande but to gauge the vitality of native rituals. As a village rite, the pageant could produce a pastoral, apolitical, and doughtily cohesive version of national identity. It seemed to be a vessel of inherited folk consciousness, the midsummer day's dream of an entire community. Moreover, it was perfectly suited to the tenets of English civic nationalism, likely to promote and express just enough collective spirit to bind citizens together but not to trip over into the frightening power of fascist mob fever. At a time when the masses began to assert themselves on both the literary and political stages of Europe, the English pageant-play was refitted to perform insular and interclass harmony.

If the pageant-play experiments of Eliot, Forster, and Woolf appear to make sense in terms of thirties cultural politics, they nonetheless required some fairly sharp departures from the conventions and assumptions of metropolitan modernism and, for that matter, from the burgeoning genres of political theater.[1] Pageantry's amateur and participatory ideals, for example, were somewhat alien to the realities of the modernist marketplace, which tended to be dominated by small sects of urban bohemians. Pageants were rural, not metropolitan; they were organized by stable, inherited traditions rather than by a modern dialectic of urban chaos and symbolic order. Neotraditional pageantry asked writers to consider themselves in direct exchange with an audience, at once answering to the modernist desire for social relevance and destabilizing a modernist aesthetic based on the attenuation of art's social relevance. By tracing the encounter between cosmopolitan artists and insular traditions in the following chapters, we can begin to see the pageant-novels and pageant-plays of the thirties as opportunities for metropolitan modernists to reflect elegiacally on the eclipse of their movement.

Amnesia in Fancy Dress: Pageants for a New Century

> A Pageant is a Festival of Thanksgiving, in which a great city
> or a little hamlet celebrates its glorious past, its prosperous
> present, and its hopes and aspirations for the future. It is a
> Commemoration of Local Worthies. It is also a great Festival
> of Brotherhood; in which all distinctions of whatever kind are
> sunk in a common effort. It is, therefore, entirely undenomina-
> tional and non-political. It calls together all the scattered
> kindred from all parts of the world. It reminds the old of the
> history of their home and shows the young what
> treasures are in their keeping. It is the great incentive
> to the right kind of patriotism: love of hearth; love of town;
> love of country; love of England.
> —Louis Napoleon Parker, *Several of My Lives*[2]

Both popular and scholarly histories cite pageantry as one of the ur-genres of English literature, as a folk practice from which subsequent literary forms descend. For Woolf, as for Eliot, the genre also had distinct associations with the Elizabethan era, a premodern golden age before English culture suffered from what Woolf understood as a rift between artist and audience and what Eliot understood as the dissociation of sensibility. Modernist appropriations of the pageant form were, in this sense, motivated by a deeply antiquarian impulse to recover the primal outdoor scene of English literature. But the pageant experiments of Woolf, Eliot, and their contemporaries in the 1930s had a more immediate precursor as well: the Edwardian pageant-play.

Indeed the modern pageant-play is unusual among genres in having a clear starting point, 1905, and a canonical founder, the portentously named Louis Napoleon Parker. Parker, a playwright, part-time composer, and all-around impresario, launched the boom with his 1905 Sherbourne Pageant, which he dubbed an "historical folk-play."[3] Although the dramatic form that Parker created and popularized did incorporate elements from the passion play, the court masque, and the Lord Mayor's show, it claimed to be, and indeed was, a distinctively new twentieth-century genre.[4] The Parkerian pageant emerged from a milieu of late-Victorian preservationist movements. William Morris's Arts and Crafts movement, for example, had generated fresh interest in authentic village culture, while John Ruskin championed traditional English pageantry in 1882. Parker combined these nineteenth-century revivalist impulses with an enthusiasm for Wagnerian opera and German folk festivals. The result was an Edwardian pageant boom in which popular dramatic productions turned local history into massive outdoor spectacle.

The Parkerian pageant-plays were generally staged over several days, in an outdoor setting—usually in a field near a major historical monument or ruin (just as Ruskin would have wanted it), with large casts of amateur actors and well-drilled squads of local writers, composers, musicians, builders, painters, and seamstresses. In structure, the pageants resembled chronicle plays, but the hero of the piece was a provincial town instead of a celebrated saint.[5] Each pageant presented a series of historical episodes linked by prologues and epilogues, narrative and dramatic choruses, musical interludes, dances, and parades. In the finale, the choruses and cast would assemble in the staging fields for a final triumphant scene before marching past the audience, who would join in for the singing of "God Save the King."

Despite—or probably more accurately, because of—the pageant-play's particular combination of rote patriotism, recycled literary materials, and often clumsy theatrical amateurism, these productions became widely popular in Britain (and the United States).[6] Their popularity should come as no surprise: they were the Hollywood epics of their day, complete with ornate special effects, the proverbial cast of thousands, and the stock figure of an eccentric, dictatorial director. The scale of the casts was such that the ratio of performers to spectators often approached 1:1.[7] Ambitious "pageant-masters" of the Parker school constructed elaborate sets and huge temporary grandstands for pageant week. At Parker's own Colchester pageant, a sixty-by-thirty-foot Roman temple was constructed for a scene showing the labor of British slaves. The props at Colchester included "hundreds of suits of armour, thousands of weapons, shields, etc., thrones, biers, chariots, triumphal cars, and a thousand and one items which only the patriotic work of the ladies and gentlemen of the Committee could furnish."[8]

It would be stretching accuracy to describe these plays as a literary form. Although much effort went into the dramatic and poetic composition of the text, the pageants functioned in practice as visual and aural spectacle more than verbal exchange. The pageant-plays observed no Aristotelian unities of time and action and had no commitment to dramatic or psychological realism. Instead, the form was dedicated to the continuous history and glorious legends, to the genius loci and chthonic pretensions, of a particular English place. At its worst, the pageantry movement traded in the boosterist prose of chamber-of-commerce brochures, gussied up in flowery couplets. In the 1909 Colchester Pageant, for example, the local oysters feature heavily; the text begins inauspiciously by informing the audience that the Romans were first "attracted by your delicious bivalves."[9] Given the unignorable presence of this kind of wretched material, what can be learned from these invented Edwardian traditions that will help us understand their subsequent revival among modernist writers?

The most striking feature of pageantry is its communitarian ethos; broad participation was integral to the genre's self-definition and to its cultural success both as an Edwardian practice and as an object of thirties revivalism. Despite their autocratic title, the Edwardian pageant-masters always defined the town itself as the artistic agent of a pageant production.[10] Local artists collaborated with hired professionals on the musical and textual composition; in Harry Irvine's Chelsea Pageant of 1908, for example, there were seven separate authors for ten historical episodes. Parker's rule of thumb for selecting actors was: "nobody is too good to be in a Pageant and almost everybody is good enough."[11] Often as many as a third of the town's residents would act in its pageant. This fact goes some way to justifying the earl of Darnley's boast that the pageant movement had "enlarged enormously the sum-total of the world's artists."[12] Pageantry's claims for democratic art were no doubt partial and self-congratulatory—such claims became a fat target for Woolf's irony in *Between the Acts*—but they should not be dismissed (nor does Woolf simply dismiss them). Certainly the participatory ethic helps account for the genre's recirculation in the thirties: despite its rather complacent investment in civic unity, pageantry not only answers to the political left's desire for more popular forms of art, but it jibes with the avant-gardist ambition of making everyone—and thus no one—into an artist.

The pageant movement's original popularity stemmed largely from its claims to local authenticity. Pageant-masters all over England used the generic formula developed by Parker with great success by adapting it to the demands of local legend and sanctified history. One pageant organizer from Rochester describes the effect of pageant preparation on the town: "We were discovering that it was an exciting thing to live in our city. . . . Once again the city was becoming Saxon, medieval, Dickensian: there was only a thin veneer of modernism disguising it."[13] Parker himself is the most effective spokesman for the genre's ambitions: "Scenes in a Pageant convey

a thrill no stage can produce when they are represented on the very ground
where they took place in real life; especially when they are played, as often
happens, by descendants of the historical protagonists, speaking a verba-
tim reproduction of the actual words used by them."[14] In a sense, the *ubi
sunt* logic ("Here it was . . .") of the historical pageant tries, finally, to
replace representation (symbolization, substitution, condensation) with
literal, territorial, and even genetic reenactment. When we combine this
vision of historical authenticity with the fact of massive amateur participation, we can see that the pageant-play form aspires to representational
adequacy in two ways—that is, toward the kind of aesthetic and political
representation whose respective ideals are mimesis and democracy.

It is a curious, but recognizable, feature of the English political landscape that pageantry's cultural populism could be married to a broadly
royalist sensibility. During the pageant-play's heyday, its historical scheme
remained surprisingly consistent and formulaic. The typical pageant
would run from Roman times to the Revolution, culminating in a final
scene where the besieged and glorious townsfolk resist the Cromwellian
usurper. In fact, in order to remain innocent of class division or political
sectarianism, Parker made it a generic prescription that no scene represent
an historical era closer to the present than the mid-seventeenth century.
A "properly conducted pageant" he wrote, should be "designed to kill"
the "modernising spirit."[15] The typical pageant managed to represent
hundreds of years of English history by suggesting that all the important
things had stayed the same. The key to the genre, then, is that it displays
a series of chronological episodes in order to project the absence of
change. The pageant-play dissolves history into the seductive symbolic
continuity of rural folkways and national traditions; here, in the manner
described by Patrick Wright, history is displaced by heritage and reduced
to "amnesia in fancy dress."[16]

Although Edwardian pageantry flourished as an overt and direct celebration of *local* heritage, it was always part of the genre's formula to
represent local attachments as the basis for more expansive kinds of patriotism.[17] As the epigraph from Parker suggests, pageants were designed to
make the local past play an inspirational role for both centrifugal, colonial action and centripetal, nostalgic memory. What Parker has in mind
is a distinctly English and Edwardian kind of political love that unites the
"scattered kindred" on five continents during a period of post–Boer War
imperial anxiety. In a fairly typical celebration of pageantry's significance,
Sir Herbert Austin echoes Parker: "the future of humanity depends primarily upon the virile spirit of the Anglo-Saxon peoples. To sever the
traditions which whisper to every Englishman that he has a heritage of
greatness would be a disaster not national only, but international. It is on
pageantry that we rely in a very large degree for the perpetuation of the

tradition of greatness the British people have earned."[18] The riches of English tradition are, in this view, both the motivation *for* and the exported good *of* imperialism. The international ambitions of pageantry typically surfaced in the final patriotic speeches and in one of the genre's obligatory closing devices, the recognition of the town's colonial "daughter-cities." In the final scene at Dover, for instance, dozens of actresses appeared as embodiments of the original Dover and its forty-four "American and Colonial" namesakes: "Look up and behold a wondrous thing! / For these her daughters from overseas, / That follow in Dover's company."[19] The closing processions of Edwardian pageants, with their happy overseas Yorks and Dovers and Colchesters, projected a lucid and legible—if corny—family relation that managed to link the English center to the Asian, African, Australian, and American peripheries.

The Edwardian pageant movement can be seen as an English counterpart to the kinds of invented traditions described by Hobsbawm and Ranger for the colonial periphery and the Celtic semi-periphery.[20] In the Hobsbawm/Ranger model of imperial multiculturalism, the nationalisms of various imperial territories were not only tolerated but encouraged by the administrators of imperial rule. So long as political and economic matters remained more or less subordinate to Pax Britannica, colonies were free to have their national cultures collected, commemorated, displayed, invented, and translated under the governing tropes of local color and the "vanishing way of life." For the imperial English, by contrast, national culture seemed to remain immanent in the local. The Edwardian pageant-play's short circuit from the local/provincial to the international/ imperial creates an odd exclusion of the intermediate term, the national itself. It is, of course, ultimately a nationalist formula that links England's green core to its colonial territories, but it is worth pausing over the curiously hollow quality of English nationhood in the pageant-play version of locally produced yet internationally disseminated values. As represented in the pageant movement, cultural Englishness meant a particular relationship between regional myth and colonial ambition, but it did not rest on any limiting or typifying representation of the national *as such*.

This kind of asymmetry between English nationalism and other cultural nationalisms of the British empire is confirmed by the fact that both Scotland (1908) and Wales (1909) held national pageants during the period when local, town-based pageants flourished in England.[21] The Scots and Welsh pageants were celebrations of local color, performed in ways that presented their cultures as enriching subsets of the United Kingdom. Where those nations were understood as sites of cultural essence, England (qua nation) was understood as a modern metaculture. Thus York and

Colchester and Dover—but not England—staged their identities in the form of historical folk drama.

When, however, writers of the 1930s rekindled interest in pageantry, they began to take England itself as the direct object of local-color discourses. Indeed, the 1930s pageant-plays and pageant-novels revise the Edwardian logic that linked the local to the imperial while bypassing the positive, identifying content of Englishness. By the time Forster writes *England's Pleasant Land* or Woolf's Miss La Trobe stages the village pageant as "our island history," the idea of an explicitly national pageant had come to the fore. In fact, one of the most striking shared features of the pageant experiments by Eliot and Forster and Woolf is their insistence on establishing—or, more accurately, reestablishing—England's insular contours in the face of British decline. For them, the folkloric aspects of pageantry were not for tropical dissemination; the rehearsal of island history was, instead, a beginning and an end in itself. The shifting orientation of pageantry—its reappropriation from imperial occasions and purposes to incipiently postimperial ones—marks the moment when English culture began to assume, in a new way, the provincial status previously associated with its colonial satellites.

Within the nativist cultural turn of the thirties, the belated pageantry texts of Eliot, Forster, and Woolf serve as explorations of primitive English forms. The recovery of such forms marks an important departure from modernist primitivism; rather than model art (or life) on ethnographic data collected from the colonies, these English intellectuals increasingly sought inspiration in the island's own imagined past. The return to the center of anthropological paradigms gave them new resources for describing English culture as a thing-in-itself. At the same time, forms of ritual consciousness that had been thematized in modernist texts were becoming available for more direct and dramatic expression.[22] In their pageant experiments, they substantially revised Parker's historical scheme by incorporating episodes from the immediate past and from the present. Even Eliot, who might well have appreciated the Parkerian idea of stopping English history in the seventeenth century, moved pageant episodes right up to the present day. However, what is more surprising is the way that the original logic of the genre—history popularized as amnesia in fancy dress—resisted revision. Despite recoding pageantry's imperial orientation in order to fit a later moment of national retrenchment, thirties writers manage to preserve several key elements of pageantry's original appeal: its function as a modern folk ritual, its technical demand for collective or choral voices, and its tight unity of place coupled with an almost magical dilation of historical time.

"A Little Nucleus of Eternity":
J. C. Powys's *A Glastonbury Romance*

The antiquarian impulses that gave rise to Edwardian historical pageantry took on new forms of expression during the 1930s under the pressure not only of economic depression and European fascism but of imperial uncertainty. By contrast to an Edwardian rhetoric of imperial defense (triggered in part by Pyrrhic victory in the Boer War), the thirties' rhetoric of imperial twilight admitted graver doubts about the future of overseas rule; indeed, colonial withdrawal—once a partisan goal—was becoming a historical reality. In this moment of retrenchment, invocations of national heritage began to displace rather than to advance worldly ambition. But the revival of Anglocentrism in certain literary and intellectual quarters of the period did not, as is often suggested, translate simply into the muffling of artistic creativity by the moribund forces of nativism. If modernist writing begins to converge—or seems in historical retrospect to converge—with varieties of literary traditionalism in the 1930s, we should not simply mourn the death of cosmopolitan vitality but rather consider the mixed and often creative results of new literary and cultural relationships then forming in England. By taking up a largely rural and neotraditional genre like the pageant-play, modernists like Eliot and Woolf are not just revealing the latent nativism that stunted English modernism all along but acting a dynamic part in the larger historical transformation of modernism itself.

This kind of approach to English modernism's "cultural turn" in the 1930s gives us a new way to come to grips with one of the most underread major books of the era: John Cowper Powys's *A Glastonbury Romance* (1932). It would be difficult to imagine a novel more comprehensively dedicated to reviving and celebrating chthonic Englishness than Powys's opus. Generally read as a local colorist or a prolix Thomas Hardy, Powys nonetheless stands out as a monumental "minor" writer of the period. *A Glastonbury Romance* has achieved the unusual status of a hidden masterpiece: its massive size (1,120 pages in the new Overlook Press edition) and weakness for metaphysical claptrap have kept it out of the canon (especially in the United States), but the spiritual ambition and sheer energy of Powys's prose has captured the attention of many distinguished and devoted readers.[23] It is a book poised between grandeur and elephantiasis, by turns bloated and brilliant, turgid and lucid, self-indulgent and worldly, ersatz and inventive. It does not make generic choices so much as generic accumulations, so that it is a Hardyesque novel of rural England, but also a Lawrentian plunge into erotic subcurrents, a Dostoyev-

skian excavation of profound moral uncertainty, a Proustian study in per-
fumed memory, and a Dickensian comedy featuring two dozen and more
"flat" characters, not to mention more than a dozen fully rounded ones. It
combines infinitely detailed realism with an intensely animated mysticism,
making a picturesque English landscape bristle with supercharged meaning. As a specimen of 1930s literature, it tempers its rural mysticism with
both leftist politics and sexual dissidence. More to the point, *A Glastonbury Romance* captures many of the key historical and aesthetic transitions of the period in a grand narrative whose climactic central episode is
the performance of a pageant-play.[24]

Readers trained in naturalist and modernist fiction are hard-pressed to
know what to make of a novel that begins with these words:

> At the striking of noon on a certain fifth of March, there occurred within a
> causal radius of Brandon railway station and yet beyond the deepest pools
> of emptiness between the uttermost stellar systems one of those infinitesimal
> ripples in the creative silence of the First Cause which always occur when an
> exceptional stir of heightened consciousness agitates any living organism in
> this astronomical universe.[25]

Powys's taste for grand adjectives and his irrepressible thirst for Significance might not inspire confidence, but the book quickly turns to a more
concrete and inviting evocation of character and landscape. Although the
book falls recognizably within the provincial English tradition of Hardy
and Lawrence, Powys's attitudes should nonetheless be distinguished
from the rural nostalgia of those writers. Where Hardy and Lawrence
lament the passing of an older way of life, Powys tends to insist on the
indestructible vitality of the land and its mysteries. As a confident chroni-
cler of the life, not death, of an old island country, he evinces a robust
antimodernism.[26]

In order to keep our attention fixed on primordial powers associated
with the country, Powys introduces a protagonist, John Crow, who will
be spiritually reeducated and made more responsive to the English genius
of place. The plot of *A Glastonbury Romance* begins when Crow, a
Frenchified and thoroughly modernized (and modernist) artist, returns to
England for the reading of a will. It is to Crow's dim and desensitized
consciousness that the novel's opening "infinitesimal ripple" is directed.
At this early stage, the intellectual cynic Crow cannot really apprehend
the "complicated superhuman vibrations" that thrum and twang in the
novel's teeming air; those vibrations, in fact, "had more connexion with
the feelings of certain primitive tribes of men in the heart of Africa" (21).
As the story of a cosmopolitan artist who learns, rather belatedly, to grasp
the rich invisible life of his native soil, this novel makes a fairly clear plot
out of modernism's turn to Anglocentric revivalism.[27] Powys does not

underestimate the work required to shift his protagonist's attention from
continental aesthetics to a properly local brand of soulful receptiveness:
after all, Crow's education, which begins on the road, continues for more
than a thousand pages in Glastonbury itself. As in a Parkerian pageant,
the town itself is the hero of this text; at every turn, Powys is at pains to
show how place determines plot. He refers to the townsfolk as "natives"
or "aboriginals" or "autocthones." Although Powys frequently (in this
novel and others) draws on Welsh/Celtic sources in describing premodern
and sacred places, he does not pose Celtic mysticism against English rationalism. In fact, what the novel aims to reveal, I think, is a properly and
natively English form of primitive resistance to modernity.

The antimodern and antimodernist strains in Powys's writing converge
in *A Glastonbury Romance*, where both modern institutions *and* the prevailing artistic representations of those institutions are thrown into contest with the unseen powers of an enchanted town. Powys not only
schools the modernist John Crow but satirizes another would-be modernist, Ned Athling. Athling, a local poet, casts his lot with the aesthetic
innovators of his time: "New forms are coming into art, drawn from
inventions and machinery . . . and drawn too, anyone can see, from the
life of people in masses, working people in masses; and I sometimes feel
as if there were something babyish in going on with the old country
themes, with the old love and death themes" (528). But the dim-witted
Athling has been duped by the makers of the new. Like John Crow, he
will be educated away from modernist art and toward a revitalized connection to "the old country themes." His lover, the aristocratic Rachel
Zoyland, rejects the aesthetic of machines and masses. The irony of their
lover's aesthetic quarrel—in which the farmboy-poet longs for modernity,
while the Paris-educated sophisticate longs for the old strong currents of
rural England—colors the entire novel.

Powys's willful affirmation of rural life sets him apart even from those
modernists (like Lawrence or Eliot) whose nostalgic laments about lost
organic community represent a direct engagement with modernity's
power to destroy the traditional world. However, the distinction between
Powys's rural traditionalism and the more canonical, urban varieties of
antimodern modernism was, as I have suggested, eroding in the 1930s.
Certainly Powys's lust for organic community and his interest in occult
meaning align him with identifiably high modernist ideas and techniques.[28] In *A Glastonbury Romance*, Powys adapted the heroic and encyclopedic modernist ambitions represented by Joyce's *Ulysses*: "A Great
Modern Novel," wrote Powys, "consists of and ought to include Just
Everything."[29] Powys's novel shares with *Ulysses* an intense localism;
however, while Joyce (following in the comic tradition of Dickens and
Thackeray) multiplies social spaces and styles, using the differentiated

languages of the modern city, Powys remains within a circumscribed pocket of English provincial life.

A *Glastonbury Romance* dilates local-color narrative into epic length. It would be impossible to summarize the novel's many subplots, but the central plot turns on the conflict between a spiritualist, John Geard, and an industrialist, Philip Crow (cousin to the intellectual John Crow). The Geard-Crow conflict puts Powys's idiosyncratic system of creative/destructive antinomies into narrative form. Geard, a puffy and vaguely alcoholic "open-air preacher," represents the spiritual revival of Glastonbury. A charlatan and saint in equal parts, Geard plans to remake Glastonbury (the legendary home of Merlin and a sacred site for both pagan and Christian England) into an English Mecca: "Why shouldn't the Lord have chosen me . . . to bring back an Age of Faith to our Western World? The way I am doing it will seem heresy to some, blasphemy to others, pure hocuspocus to most" (286). Geard's chief antagonist, Philip Crow, represents the forces of energetic and entrepreneurial industry. As the figure of modernization itself, Crow directly attacks Glastonbury's magical touristic heritage: "I'll electrify the caves of the Druids" (51). Indeed, Crow takes it as his mission to destroy the local legends and "monkish mummery" of the town: "He would conquer it, this effeminate flower-garden of pretty-pretty superstitions and medieval abracadabra! He would plant factory upon factory in it, dynamo upon dynamo! He would have mines beneath it, railways across it, airlines above it!" (230). The Geard-Crow conflict captures the fundamental alternatives for English cultural identity in the midcentury: the celebration of an essentially rural and premodern heritage or an even fuller embrace of rational modernization and technological progress.

Geard's Glastonbury revival mixes antique enthusiasms with modern marketing, creating a contemporary brand of heritage production laced with evangelism. Geard's movement, thus, has no problem joining forces strategically with the other major ideological camp in the novel, the communists, in common cause against Philip Crow's dominant industrial capitalism. Powys describes an alliance of the traditionalist folk (galvanized by the revival of Glastonbury's spiritual past) and the politicized masses (galvanized by the rhetoric of Marxist change)—an alliance that threatens both the shallow rationalism and classic liberal individualism of Crow. In the rising action of the novel's first half, the combined forces of communal politics and spiritual revival chip away at Crow's empire. Each of these three camps comes in for fairly conspicuous satire in the novel, though Powys is least ironic about Geard and his dull, dogged connection to the land's mysteries.

The novel presents local politics as an intricate surface drama, underneath which we are encouraged to imagine a fundamental and universal battle of good and evil. As the local antiquary puts it: "this place is charged and soaked with a desperate invisible struggle" (350). *A Glastonbury Romance* becomes an Anglicized version of the Grail quest, a massive fictional effort to recode gray, industrial England as a *paysage moralisé*. Unlike Eliot's mediated, allusive version of the quest romance in *The Waste Land*, Powys's romance literalizes the presence of the Grail in England. Powys's dialogue with the anthropological Eliot is quite self-conscious; when Philip Crow bests John Geard in an impromptu debate between industry and spirit, the crowd reacts in this way: "There was a feeling among them all as they went off as if they had stretched out their arms to grasp a Golden Bough and had been rewarded for their pains with a handful of dust" (342). Powys alludes to the Frazerian *Waste Land*, but he also offers a narrative formulation of the key concept in late Eliot: the co-presence of time and the timeless. Several characters glimpse this potential intersection of the incommensurable: "What Mr. Geard kept his mind steadily upon, all this while, was that crack, that cranny, that slit in Time through which the Timeless . . . had broken the laws of Nature!" (708). For Powys, as for the Eliot of *Four Quartets*, the intersection of temporal and eternal orders takes place within a bounded and resacralized English landscape.

The meeting of time and the timeless in Glastonbury depends, of course, on the town's status as a taxidermied village where an otherwise vanishing rural life is preserved. The ruins and hollows of the town harbor prehistorical spirits: "No sacred pool, in Rome, or Jerusalem, or Mecca, or Thibet, has gathered such an historic continuum of psycho-chemical forces about it as this spot contained then, and contains still" (708). With this kind of profound continuity in place, it comes as no surprise to discover that the climactic episode of the novel will be a Midsummer pageant-play. In this novel's representation of pageantry, as in the pageant movement itself, tradition displaces history. The mystical mayor Geard, eager to make Glastonbury a bulwark against modern rationalism, imagines that a pageant will advance his cause, because pageantry makes a literalized performance out of local heritage. John Crow, the cynical bohemian, agrees to produce Geard's pageant in order to amuse himself and to debunk Geard's spiritual excesses. But the pivotal irony is that Crow himself is at least half-converted; his continental sophistication pales next to the social and spiritual power of Geard's archaic nativism.

Crow organizes his pageant along Parkerian lines: it is staged in a large open field at the base of a ruined tower and features a series of massive, costumed tableaux depicting historical and legendary events. With its central location in the plot of *A Glastonbury Romance*, the pageant serves Powys as a collective ritual or spectacle whose social meaning remains highly ambiguous, both for the spectators in the novel and for readers of

the novel. Powys creates ironic counterpoint by narrating the performance of a ritual; the Glastonbury pageant is subject to all the errors,
miscues, and contingencies of amateur theater. Missing props and forgotten speeches leave hordes of actors bewildered, huddled in tents and hidden behind hedgerows, unsure of where, if anywhere, the performance
is heading (565). Meanwhile, the audience must contend with dramatic
speeches whose words are lost, "blown away upon the wind." The accidents of community drama unsettle the meaning of this summer rite—a
possibility that Virginia Woolf exploits to similar effect in *Between the
Acts*. Still, for Powys (as for Woolf) the pageant's social significance remains, even—perhaps especially—when its exact meaning is unclear.

As the turning point of this mammoth novel, the Glastonbury pageant
brings together a sprawling cast of characters and activates the ideological
conflicts among the various camps in Glastonbury. The pageant includes
Christian and Arthurian episodes along with other bits of local legend
from Roman and medieval times. It peels back layers of modern acculturation to uncover the most pagan and prehistoric versions of life on the
patch of soil called Glastonbury. Even the Welsh-blooded characters—
who as "true aboriginals" already have a kind of Druidic sensitivity—are
given new access to ancestral memories that are "pre-Celtic" (756).

Although the Glastonbury pageant is an English ritual, John Crow hires
a group from Dublin to help organize the pageant, as if Celts have a special knack for reviving the past, and Irish revivals could thus lead the way
for English ones. The imported Dubliners manage to reach back into deep,
chthonic England, acting as dramaturgical shamans for the town. In fitting tribute to the Victorian champions of village pageantry, Ruskin and
Morris, Powys's fictionalized pageant kindles a revival of local arts and
crafts. At this point, Geard and his communist allies begin to gain the
upper hand over the industrialist Philip Crow by seizing the means of
production. They form a factory commune in Glastonbury dedicated to
the production of religious handicrafts and Arthurian souvenirs for Glastonbury's burgeoning tourist economy: "there began to spring up—out
of the void as it almost seemed—a very exciting and most original school
of Glastonbury design, genuinely indigenous and wherein the roughnesses
and crudities of drawing, colouring and perspective, and their variation
too under so many different hands, possessed the imaginative freshness
and childlike appeal of an authentically primitive art, an art which the
whole western world seemed especially to thirst for" (923). Rather than
attempt to enact or even thematize a *primitivist* aesthetic based on metropolitan appropriations, Powys imagines the transformed means of production that could give rise to authentically local and *primitive* crafts.

The anthropological dimensions of Powys's English romance become
most pronounced during the pageant scene, which unfolds as the descrip-

tion of a social ritual that gives climactic resolution to more than five hundred pages of rising action. At this point, the reader begins to understand (and even forgive) the novel's length. The scene's power stems from the tension between the pageant's myths of collective heritage and the novel's closely observed taxonomy of social and libidinal conflict. For here Powys arranges all the major and minor characters in one scene, displaying with elaborate skill the complex webs of social rank, ideological affiliation, and emotional bond in Glastonbury. Suddenly the many narrative strands take the form of an organized, if multifarious, social calculus; the pageant audience itself becomes a narrative *tableau vivant* facing the dramatic *tableaux vivants* of the show. With almost Wagnerian ambition, Powys presents the pageant as a moment of reckoning.

Shortly after the spectators and actors are assembled, the equipoise between theatrical unity and social conflict erupts into action. The audience becomes susceptible to a "cumulative wave of crowd-hypnosis," and the pageant turns into a riot of sorts. When the pageant attempts to invoke local tradition, the crowd lurches in the direction of class vengeance: "Like an animal organism that has taken an emetic, Glastonbury now disembogued from the obscurest recesses of its complex being all manner of queer chemical substances. . . . the real People of Glastonbury emerged and asserted itself" (561). After an instant, though, the rising masses become, once again, the depoliticized folk. Powys's preoccupation with the primitive and pre-political nature of the struggle trumps the superficially modern allegiances of class: "in these violent upheavals of class against class, there is something far deeper than principle or opinion at stake. Skin against skin . . . blood against blood . . . nerves against nerves . . . rise up from incalculable depths" (569). Having represented the crowd's action as a periodic, animal venting of aggressive impulses, Powys returns to his titular commitment and proceeds to narrate a romance of unity among the people of Glastonbury.

The pageant scene is not only a narrative turning point, it also gives Powys a chance to explore and refine what is arguably the most important formal feature of the novel, its experiment in perspective. Throughout the novel, Powys diffuses omniscient perspective into a set of semidivine "invisible watchers" of Glastonbury. For Powys, this device represented a technical advance over his previous novel *Wolf Solent* and a move away from the Jamesian center of consciousness: "It [his new method] is more objective & does not strain the whole business through one single character as that did but jumps about boldly and shamelessly from one person's thoughts to another's, using the old-fashioned privilege of the ubiquitous author-god."[30] In the text, Powys does flit quickly from mind to mind, registering consciousness in free indirect discourse. However, what is even more apparent is that Powys seems eager to refine, and in some ways to outflank, the novel of consciousness. He uses psychological realism (in a recognizably modernist vein) to point out that the details of an individual consciousness are far less important and interesting than its debt to a collective unconscious. In the novel's first chapter, for example, Powys records the inner experience of four different characters in compelling psychological detail, but quickly notes: "Such were the thoughts of four human skulls at that moment; but only to one mood out of all these did the great maternal soul of the Earth respond" (30). This "but" signals the beginning of a typical Powysian swerve out of individual consciousness and toward the mythic, chthonic roots of meaning. Powys wants to establish a place-based model of characterization. Just as the novel relentlessly antiques social incident, turning class conflict into folk drama, it demodernizes psychological incidents, turning flickering sensory impressions and sexual passion alike into the diffuse epiphenomena of ancient, primordial forces. As a result, the individual psyche becomes an accidental conduit, not the fundamental unit, of thought.

The novel's attempt to disperse and revise the Jamesian center of consciousness reaches fulfillment in the pageant-play scene, because it is there that Powys manages to diffuse narrative perspective in the direction of a genuinely transindividual or collective consciousness. Powys uses mobile shifts of perspective not (just) to show the fragmentary and perspectival quality of social perception but to indicate the presence of a deeper communal viewpoint. In this way, Powys anticipates Virginia Woolf's experiment in narrated ritual, where a village pageant becomes the occasion for a finely pitched struggle between consciousness and community.

In *A Glastonbury Romance*, as in Woolf's *Between the Acts*, the pageant scene cannot be sustained; it gives way to an anticlimactic dispersal of community. In the novel's second half, the Grail itself makes an appearance, but no one is able to understand its presence. After this second of two major spiritual anticlimaxes in Glastonbury (the chaotic pageant and the unremarked Grail), the novel ends—like so many ambitious provincial fictions—with a flood. Powys's rather labored deus ex machina wipes away the infrastructure of both Geard's mystical tourism and Crow's rabid modernizing, leaving no clear victory for either side. The town seems destined to sink back into degraded versions of both Crow's and Geard's visions, with a decaying industrial apparatus (uninvigorated by the dynamic entrepreneur) and an ersatz tourist economy (unredeemed by the mystic preacher).

Powys's decision to make a pageant the central event in this massive condition-of-England novel indicates the pageant-play's social and symbolic function in a wider discourse of insular revivalism. More specifically, the novel's urgent attention to spiritual themes lying beneath political struggles brings Powys's work into close thematic and ideological convergence with T. S. Eliot's writing of the same period. Powys's representation of Glastonbury as "a little nucleus of Eternity" anticipates Eliot's own quest in *Four Quartets* to locate sacred English places where time and the timeless briefly intersect. Moreover, although Eliot's success as a poet and critic were well established by the early 1930s, he himself was beginning to experiment with the possibilities of verse drama and pageantry.

Rebuilding the Ruined House: T. S. Eliot's *The Rock*

In 1934, the London director Martin Browne, working on behalf of a charitable organization called the Forty-Five Churches Fund, recruited T. S. Eliot to participate in the composition of a pageant-play. To the chagrin of many admirers then and since, the great poetic experimenter agreed to work within the conventions of this neotraditional, collaborative, and rather unliterary genre. As he set to work on *The Rock*, Eliot was "puzzled by the problem of how to create an interesting form while retaining the pageant-elements demanded."[31] Like the Edwardian pageant-masters, Eliot understood himself to be balancing civic and aesthetic responsibility. Writing for the benefit of a church-building fund, Eliot eschewed the persona of alienated urban modernist and began gathering resources for the restoration of a common culture in England.

The pageant-play experiment gave Eliot an opportunity to write for a live audience. For the coterie poet who wrote with envy about music-hall singer Marie Lloyd, *The Rock* meant a chance to connect more directly to the public by using a popular and traditional English form.[32] When *The Rock* was performed at Sadler's Wells Theatre during the summer of 1934, it met with modest public success and general critical dismay. Eliot's pageant broke from the established Parkerian convention in that it was urban and indoor but resembled the original model in scale (hundreds of actors in elaborate costume) and in form (a sequence of historical episodes interlarded with narrative and dramatic choruses). The pageant's urban setting and indebtedness to music-hall revue made it rather different from the rural and municipal orientation of the Edwardian pageant-plays, but *The Rock* was designed to capitalize on the lingering popularity of open-air pageantry in England. Where Powys before him and Woolf and Forster after him use the pageant-play in a more recognizably rural guise, Eliot's urban-Christian showcase nonetheless serves a classically pastoral function: it activates an amnesiac and socially cohesive idea of English heritage.

Eliot organizes the play's action around three workmen (Ethelbert, Alfred, and Edwin), who remain on stage, building a new church, during the course of the performance. An Agitator arrives to pose questions about the civic value of church building in a time of widespread secularism and economic scarcity. As if in response, a series of historical apparitions—including Saxon bands, a reformed medieval jester, Sir Christopher Wren, and a Victorian Bishop—materialize on stage in order to affirm the cultural importance of English Christianity. At intervals, a chorus (actors were wrapped in coarse cloth and half-covered by white masks at the original performances) offers dramatic and oracular commentary in verse. As a longtime advocate for the revival of verse drama, Eliot considered this part of the text the most important; the ten choruses were the only part of *The Rock* that he wanted to preserve and reissue.

Because of its topical and occasional nature and the aesthetic compromises that Eliot made in its production, *The Rock* is now rarely read, taught, or performed. The text features a rather motley assortment of styles, ranging from some recognizably elegant and hieratic modernist poetry to some embarrassingly crude dramatic scenes in prose. To read the book of words today is to encounter a fascinating mixture of high and low cultural registers from the 1930s; Eliot manages to combine stock pageantry devices with popular ballet, pantomime, music-hall ditties, radical oratory, Latin liturgy, and Brechtian chants. The dialogue is generally uninspired, particularly when carried by Ethelbert, an improbably over-informed bricklayer who no doubt annoyed audiences with his cockney-fied disquisitions on matters like the Social Credit movement. From most perspectives, *The Rock* is an interesting but failed artistic experiment.[33]

Despite its manifest formal shortcomings, though, *The Rock* marks a key transition both for Eliot and for the demetropolitanization of English literature in the 1930s. In 1927, Eliot entered the Anglican Church and assumed English citizenship. These acts of affiliation (or would-be filiation) formalized Eliot's growing commitment to the idea of a revived, coherent Anglo-Christian community, but they also inaugurated a period of artistic crisis and literary reinvention, during which he attempted to surmount two major limitations of modernist poetry: its isolated production and elite reception. As a version of popular and collaborative drama, the pageant-play allowed Eliot to experiment with entirely new kinds of literary and social meaning.[34] The power of pageantry to embody and reanimate a particular cultural heritage depends, of course, on an audience—a community—that already recognizes and values that heritage. In other words, Eliot's shift in form proceeds alongside, and relies on, his estimation that there was, after all, a core English public that would be receptive to the traditions of verse drama, stylized historical pageantry, and Christian community.

When we read the admittedly awkward scenes at the center of *The Rock*, we can see how strained Eliot's writing became as he tried to shift emphasis from exquisite bourgeois lament about a broken society to more concrete definitions of meaningful community. In the early scenes and choruses, we can still recognize the London of *The Waste Land*—a spiritually empty urban shell that inspires the poet's most sharply rendered and satirically turned details:

> In the land of lobelias and tennis flannels
> The rabbit shall burrow and the thorn revisit,
> The nettle shall flourish on the gravel court[35]

Rather than persist as an exquisite connoisseur of the city's degraded charms, though, the Eliot of *The Rock* gradually turns his choruses to more austere and prophetic utterances. Both the dramatic scenes and verse choruses try to expose the modern city as host to a series of false reports about human progress. Here Eliot's antimodern sensibility reaches an almost expository clarity. The third chorus expresses contempt for "schemes of human greatness now thoroughly discredited" and for a culture whose energies have been devoted to such banal material ends as "devising the perfect refrigerator" (31). The text plays several variations on this theme, seeking to demystify the claims of human progress made by self-congratulatory secular, liberal, and democratic institutions.

Although the stakes of social redemption in *The Rock* are overtly Christian and universalist, Eliot represents them through his particular interest in London, the bloated metropolis whose river is choked with "foreign flotations" and whose soul has been diverted by material invention and expansion (7). Of course, the conversion of London from ghastly metropolis into organic community was Eliot's desideratum all along. What marks a shift in his writing during the 1930s is not simply the petrification of youthful agony into middle-aged dogmatism but a growing sense that organic community might possibly be achieved, or at least adumbrated, in a new way. Pointing the way out of the waste land, Eliot's chorus identifies a newly apparent faltering of the entire modern enterprise. The historical conditions for Eliot's more pragmatic interest in the revival of Anglo-Christian community can be glimpsed in the second chorus of *The Rock*, which recapitulates British national history in this way:

> When your fathers fixed the place of GOD,
> And settled all the inconvenient saints,
> Apostles, martyrs, in a kind of Whipsnade,
> Then they could set about imperial expansion
> Accompanied by industrial development.
> Exporting iron, coal and cotton goods
> And intellectual enlightenment
> And everything, including capital

And several versions of the Word of GOD
The British race assured of a mission
Performed it, but left much at home unsure.   (20)

The chorus identifies an unfortunate and prolonged dilution of Anglo-Christian culture by British racial ambitions but also moves imperial expansion safely into the past tense: that secular mission *has been performed*. And if the age of empire building has drawn to a close, the moment is ripe for the renewal of the nation's spiritual health. Observing that Britain's expanding power falsely confirmed the rightness of its values, Eliot heralds the end of empire as an opportunity to expose the wrongheadedness of secular, liberal notions of progress. For those who saw overseas colonialism as an index of Western triumph and progress, its incipient end signified an ebb in Britain's fortunes and powers. For Eliot, however, the end of Pax Britannica augured the beginning of England's recovery. In an island nation no longer dedicated to expansion, Eliot's vision of a rebuilt organic culture might come to fruition.

In Eliot's view, the imperial enterprise created problems not only by spreading the disorder of liberal modernity from Europe to other societies with previously intact traditions but also by reinforcing the idea that England itself was irremediably modernized. In other words, imperialist discourses like anthropology tended to confirm the loss of traditional sources of meaning and harmony in industrial Europe, creating a spiritual and cultural anomie that could only be palliated by imperfect imitations of alien primitive cultures. Eliot, for his part, eschewed the mimetic primitivism of modernist art and social theory in favor of a more dedicated program of reviving what he considered the most successful (if not, strictly speaking, the most ancient) version of authentic English culture: a premodern, agricultural, Christian society. In *The Rock*, he advances the notion that the English can and should be revitalized through a recovery of their own Christian and tribal identity, as a people still capable of close obedience to God and nature: "We are children quickly tired . . . controlled by the rhythm of the blood and the day and the night and the seasons" (85). This vision of a reawakened primitive*ness* in place of a merely compensatory and derivative primitiv*ism*, is one mark of Eliot's departure from metropolitan modernism.

Like *A Glastonbury Romance*, *The Rock* peels back layers of modern enterprise and material distraction to reveal a local version of the primordial struggle between good and evil. In a gray, modern London, habituated to what Eliot sees as the moral vacuum of secular liberalism, the revival of the culture depends on locating grand Manichean challenges in the here and now:

The desert is not remote in southern tropics,
The desert is not only around the corner,
The desert is squeezed in the tube-train next to you   (9)

While these stern exhortations enjoin the audience to understand its place
in an awful struggle, they also perform a reenchantment of daily life: the
dwindling theological stakes of life in the modern city are replaced by a
vital and organic spiritual quest.

But to inspire a popular reconception of prevailing assumptions about
modernity was no easy task in 1930s London. The cultural ambition of
Eliot's pageant leads, perhaps not surprisingly, to obvious strains in his
writing. Consider, for example, this awkward ventriloquized philosophy,
mouthed by the bricklayer Bert: "There's some new notion about time,
what says that the past—what's be'ind you—is what's goin' to 'appen in
the future, bein' as the future 'as already 'appened" (15–16). Eliot's attempt to revive eschatological time in a culture thoroughly adapted to
secular-historical time reappears, to somewhat better effect, in *Four Quartets*. But *The Rock* pursues the point in all of its scholastic thorniness:

Then came, at a predetermined moment, a moment in
   time and of time,
A moment not out of time, but in time, in what we call
   history; transecting, bisecting the world of time, a
   moment in time but not like a moment of time,
A moment in time but time was made through that
   moment: for without the meaning there is not time,
   and that moment of time gave the meaning   (50)

This passage from the seventh chorus (one of the more admired sections
of the play) tries to frame the paradox whereby an eternal order that is
"out of time" nonetheless "makes time." This conceptual problem—how
to express the intersection of time and the timeless—becomes the organizing theme of *Four Quartets*, but here Eliot tries to capture it for a live
audience. While it may strike us now as unpromising material for the
revival of verse drama, this theological conundrum—with its embedded
critique of historicism—fits the ahistorical, amnesiac logic of pageantry.

Eliot was not the only one to experiment with pageantry in an intertwined effort to reenact the national past and revive Christian faith. In
order to grasp the symbolic currency of the pageant-play in thirties England, we can briefly turn to another neotraditional experimenter, Charles
Williams, who wrote both the 1937 pageant-novel *Descent into Hell* (a
roman à clef whose protagonist bears a strong resemblance to T. S. Eliot)
and the 1939 pageant-play *Judgment at Chelmsford* (which, like *The
Rock*, stages the history of the Anglican Church). Perhaps even more mar-

ginal to today's modernist canon then J. C. Powys, Williams was a well-known literary figure in his time, a close associate not only of Eliot but also of the so-called Oxford Christians J.R.R. Tolkien and C. S. Lewis. Like Tolkien and Lewis, Williams made his career by grafting Christian materials onto popular fiction. In *Descent into Hell*, Williams fuses a ghost story onto a realistic novel plot organized around the performance of an open-air pageant in the new suburb of Battle Hill. The ghost story and the pageant plot are fully entwined: the play both enacts the town's past and calls forth its ghosts. This double and intensely localized logic of the living dead determines the shape of the novel: "simultaneity approached the Hill, the experience of its inhabitants had there become coeval; propinquity no longer depended upon sequence."[36] Propinquity trumps sequence: as in the Parkerian pageant, the territorial unity and continuity of the town erases temporal distinctions, even those separating the living and the dead. Williams's "spiritual shocker" literalizes the magical invocations of the *ubi sunt*; its interpolated pageant dissolves historical time into rooted identity. The resulting literary effect is not gothic horror but an austere and thrilling encounter with the eternal meant to shock the townsfolk (and the reader) into a recognition of God in ways that Eliot would certainly have endorsed.

Williams uses pageantry to re-Christianize and reterritorialize the ghost story, giving a readable plot to Eliot's cherished proposition about the copresence of historical and eternal time. Moreover, he uses the pageant-novel form to comment on the effort (shared by himself and Eliot and others in the 1930s) to reinvent a classical choral function for modern drama. The novel's protagonist, Peter Stanhope (the pseudonym used by Williams himself when publishing poetry), has an Eliotic ambition to overthrow the naturalist bourgeois drama and has "even imposed modern plays in verse on the London theater" (10). Stanhope uses the community pageant-play to restore antique dramatic conventions to the living stage. But the encounter between Stanhope and his public is frequently absurd. He must contend, for example, with the officious Mrs. Parry, a local would-be dramaturge who proposes to turn his impersonal Greek chorus into garlanded wood nymphs. And, if not wood nymphs, perhaps they could be dryads from Watteau? Despite Mrs. Parry's attempts to assimilate the chorus to banal and picturesque conventions, however, a grim Stanhope insists on a classical choral function. The role of this chorus is to offer something other than humanist or pastoral color, it is to express the temporal depth of the piece by voicing Stanhope's words in the guise of a transpersonal agent—a moral authority that is anything but human and whose theological notion of timelessness exceeds even the Parkerian ethos of costumed amnesia.

The ideal of a transpersonal, or choral, poetic speaker is thus the most important device in the pageant-play form for both the fictional Peter Stanhope and the real T. S. Eliot.[37] It is the choral function that naturalized and made possible the dramatic utterance of verse, an experimentally classical form that Eliot wished to restore to prominence in the hope that it would reintegrate cultural, religious, and literary functions divorced from each other in the course of modern literary history. The Eliotic ideal surfaces in the climactic scene of *Descent into Hell*, as Pauline Anstruther (Stanhope's disciple) has an epiphany during the performance of the pageant:

> They were in the groups of the last royal declamations, and swept aside, and the mighty stage was clear. Suddenly again, from somewhere in that great abyss of clarity, a trumpet sounded, and then a great uproar, and then a single voice. It was the beginning of the end; the judgment of mortality was there. She was standing aside, and she heard the voice and knew it; from the edge of eternity the poets were speaking to the world, and two modes of experience were mingled in that sole utterance. (186)

By narrating Pauline's ideal absorption of dramatic verse, Williams can stage-manage the effects (and affects) of a reassociated sensibility. The pageant's power to revive the dead produces a "fanfare of recovered identities" in the middle of a drab suburb (203). It combines local legend and dramatic verse to reanimate the ritual consciousness that Eliot devoutly wished to remake for Christian England: "The realism of the ordinary stage is something to which we can no longer respond, because to us it is no longer realistic. We know that the gesture of daily existence is inadequate for the stage; instead of pretending that the stage's gesture is a copy of reality, let us adopt a literary untruth, a thorough-going convention, a ritual. For the stage—not only in its remote origins, but always—is a ritual, and the failure of the contemporary stage to satisfy the craving for ritual is one of the reasons why it is not a living art."[38] What Williams narrates is what Eliot attempts in *The Rock*: the recovery of primitive sources in the English literary tradition and the revival of a ritual consciousness that could only be represented in etiolated form in *The Waste Land*.

"Innocent Island": E. M. Forster's Passage to England

In the summer of 1934, while *The Rock* played at Sadler's Wells, E. M. Forster's "Abinger Pageant" was performed in the fields of Surrey. Like Eliot, Forster wrote his pageant, and a later one entitled *England's Pleasant Land*, for specific charitable purposes.[39] But Forster's pageant texts are nonetheless revealing about some larger shifts both in his career and in midcentury English literature. By the 1930s, Forster had stopped writing and publishing novels, despite the success of *A Passage to India* in 1924 and despite the faithful encouragement of friends and admirers. Although Forster continued writing and publishing in other genres for decades after *Passage*, his career as a novelist came to what many saw as a premature end. The most useful and most accepted account of Forster's abandonment of the novel is that he at last found the inherited conventions of heterosexual courtship and marriage plots both stifling and dishonest.[40] There is, I think, an additional and complementary layer of explanation to be found in Forster's participation in the revival of Anglocentric pastoral idealism in the 1930s. Forster had always, of course, expressed Anglocentric pastoral ideals, but his Edwardian novels (like *Howards End*) embed those ideals in a symbolic geography featuring images of separation from a lost nativist Eden. Forster's novels depend, in fact, on the tension between pastoral England and metropolitan modernity, whereas his writing of the 1930s and 1940s dissolves that tension into a wish-fulfilling (and non-narrative) evocation of insular tradition.

As a modern novelist, Forster addresses the recurring conflict between, on the one hand, a pastoral English core of humanist and aesthetic values and, on the other, the world of industry and empire, of crass commercial values and diminished spirituality. As I suggested in chapter 1, intercultural and interclass encounters drive the machinery of Forsterian narrative: plot takes place on the boundary of two cultures—even if, as in *The Longest Journey* or *Howards End*, the two cultures are nominally English. Whether the key encounter takes place between national types (Gino and the Herritons in *Where Angels Fear to Tread*), class representatives (Wilcoxes and Schlegels in *Howards End*), or racialized subjects (Fielding and Aziz in *A Passage to India*), the novels stage conflicts that depend on the cosmopolitan/imperial economy. That is, metropolitan conditions bring the English gentry into social contact with Italian suitors, imperial rubber merchants, and Indian doctors. The novels convey a postlapsarian sadness about a certain lost England, but they also recognize the value of cosmopolitanism in creating a necessary spark from cultural friction. Libidinalized encounters between cultural strangers provide narrative incident and momentum in Forster novels. In the end, the reconciliation of a feminized, Anglo-sphere of culture and a masculinized, metropolitan sphere of action is generally thwarted, muted, or confined to the symbolic gesture of the "next generation." Forster's pastoral idealism, which seeks to reconcile sympathetic, progressive liberalism with remorseless capitalism, remains unfulfilled in the novels.

As long as the bifurcated geography of metropolitan life obtained, intellectuals like Forster had to come to terms with the contending mythologies of the old English core and the expanding English "engine of modernity." Forster's narratives both reflect that ideological divide as a condition of England and use it in a figurative language that encodes the impossibility of idealized sexual and personal relations. In other words, the symbolic geography of a divided (i.e., metropolitan) England has two functions in Forster's novels: it acts as a trigger for plot incidents (intercultural encounter), and it supplies an indirect language for unfulfilled personal relations, which in turn represent a failed synthesis of the contradictions of an England that was both liberal and imperial. Within Forster's modernist symbolic style, boundless or unknowable spaces tend to represent mysterious, extra-English elements. In Fredric Jameson's reading of *Howards End*, the figure of "placelessness" or spatial infinity marks the assimilation of the economic and political conditions of British imperialism into modernist narrative. In Jameson's view, the representation of the imperial-infinite remains politically unconscious in *Howards End* but emerges as an element of style.[41]

Dangerous (but aesthetically compelling) infinities reappear in Forster's description of the Marabar Caves in *A Passage to India*. In that novel, Forster moves the action to the colonies while retaining his central thematic encounter between an alluring but disorienting alienness and a knowable but historically enervated Englishness. What Forster describes as "muddle" lies at the heart of the English experience in *Passage*; English characters regularly cast the unknowability of Indian landscape against the familiar green core of England.[42] Meanwhile, the Aziz-Fielding plot describes a thwarted or postponed union between men. The novel ultimately concludes with skepticism about "transcultural male bonding."[43] There is no final reconciliation of Aziz with Fielding, of English sensibility with Indian life, of exoticized pleasure with liberal anti-imperialism. In *Passage*, then, Forster records the epistemological obstacles of imperialism that lead to muffled fantasies and thwarted romance. Here spatial infinity does not operate as a crypto-imperialist figure (Jameson's "leak to infinity" that destabilizes the English setting of *Howards End*), but instead breaks the surface of the novel's political unconscious at Marabar, becoming an unignorable thematic element that exposes metropolitan perception as an imperial problem. In other words, Forster's cosmopolitan nostalgia about etiolated English community is, in this later fiction, represented explicitly as a systemic problem linked to *colonial* space. This metropolitan political dynamic, so crucial to Forsterian plot and imagery all along, becomes manifest in *Passage*.

After 1924, Forster's work registers the increasingly untenable status of imperial romance and metropolitan perception, taking account both directly and indirectly of the accelerating instability, so well documented by *Passage*, of Britain's overseas rule.[44] If *Passage* marks Forster's greatest success both as an observer of British imperialism and as a writer of modernist fiction, his work of the 1930s registers not only England's development toward postimperial cultural status but also English literature's departure from modernist aesthetics. These changes are particularly interesting when understood according to the shifting status of Forster's symbolic geography. With the erosion of the trope of imperial infinity, Forster imagined the possibility of reclaiming England as a spatially finite and knowable community. Having illustrated the epistemological limits of imperialism in the 1920s, he turned to the green insular core of Anglocentric fantasy in the 1930s, no longer framing England as one part of a charged domestic/alien dyad but rather as the self-sufficient object of pastoral romance. Taking up the nonnarrative genres of essay, short story, and pageant-play, Forster evokes a vision of Englishness into which he dissolves the political and cultural conflicts that drove his novels. Insular rites displace metropolitan fictions.[45]

Shifting from multicultural plots to monocultural tableaux, Forster finds new literary resources during the thirties, including, of course, the pageant-play. The final item in Forster's collection *Abinger Harvest* is the "Abinger Pageant," a history of his home village and a tribute to old rural England. In the original volume, the pageant follows a series of essays on India and empire; this editorial sequence, moving readers from meditations on imperial twilight to pastoral invocations of the old country, recapitulates the larger relationship between British decline and Anglocentric revival during the thirties. The essay "My Wood" (1926), written shortly after the publication of *A Passage to India*, makes that connection pragmatic and explicit. Forster purchased his wood with the royalties from *Passage*, a fact that neatly literalizes his reinvestment in English territory. Here Forster muses on his chunk of the native landscape, tripping into a flight of fancy about the joys of geographical possession: "Happy Canute! Happier Alexander! And after all, why should even the world be the limit of possession? A rocket containing a Union Jack, will, it is hoped, be shortly fired at the moon. Mars. Sirius. Beyond which . . . But these immensities ended by saddening me. I could not suppose that my wood was the destined nucleus of universal dominion—it is so very small and contains no mineral wealth beyond the blackberries."[46] In a characteristic swerve, the essay moves from inflated expansionism to sad provincialism, but the blackberries slyly reveal Forster's proprietary contentment with a narrow yet fruitful plot of ground. Like many other English intellectuals, Forster turns to domestic delectation at a point when external historical events seemed to be making the repossession of an ideal England both more necessary and more plausible. The essays in *Abinger Harvest* frequently recur to a cherished Burkean vision of England as "a world that shall be small and fruitful and clean" (*AH* 285). The pageant-plays, too, recapture what Margaret Schlegel wanted all along and could only half-have: "the sense of space, which is the basis of all earthly beauty." To recapture that sense of proportionate and insular space was "to realize England."[47] While that desire could not be fulfilled and sustained in the metropolitan geography of Forsterian narrative, it could be performed and celebrated in the knowable space of the pageant-play.

Forster's pageant-plays are spectacles of Englishness, fueled by the 1930s notion that England was becoming "historical," as opposed to "modern." To reinhabit the pastoral Anglocentric core meant becoming a communicant with what Patrick Wright aptly calls "Deep England."[48] However, because communion with Deep England depended on native status, on an organic link to the land, it could easily be converted into the kind of patriotism that Forster abhorred: a xenophobic passion that was exclusionary with regard to region, class, gender, and sexuality. Like so many other liberal intellectuals coming to terms with patriotism in the late 1930s, Forster addressed himself to the problem of finding a nourishing, but not choking, version of English nativism. As the decade wore on, fascist aggression made fervent nationalism both increasingly unappealing and increasingly necessary. Forster summarizes the problem: "if Fascism wins we are done for, and . . . we must become Fascist to win."[49] His solution was to focus on the ways in which national unity flows automatically from the recognition of a "common language, a common religion, a common culture."[50] Forster works to represent Englishness as a slow and natural historical efflux rather than an artificially invented tradition: "In England our culture is not governmental. It is national: it springs naturally out of our way of looking at things, and out of the way we have looked at things in the past. It has developed slowly, easily, lazily; The English love of freedom, the English countryside, English prudishness and hypocrisy, English freakishness, our mild idealism. . . ."[51] This organic view of an essential and natural "English way" depends on seeing national life as something utterly familiar and knowable, yet also charmed. Making a cultural virtue out of a political necessity, Forster took up the pageant in order to identify England's antique sources of identity and vitality.

Forster's pageant texts thus revive England by ritually invoking it as a knowable and archaic place. They mitigate the potentially exclusionary nature of national tradition with their ethic of spontaneous and communal performance. Moreover, they represent a version of traditional community (symbolized most often by male bonding across class lines) that is not, as in Forster's novels, remote and unattainable. Forster thus reenchants English politics and revives the time-honored function of the pastoral: the dissolution of class conflict, or as William Empson puts it, the implication of a "beautiful relation between rich and poor."[52]

The "Abinger Pageant" presents six scenes based on the history of the village from the Roman to the Victorian period. It preserves the standard episodic chronology, but, as Forster's introduction points out: "It is rural rather than historical and tries to show the continuity of country life" (*AH* 350). The opposition between the rural and the historical implies that change does not really happen in the countryside. Such a claim—and the dramatic apparatus that illustrates it—recapitulate the basic logic of Edwardian pageantry: local history performed in order to suggest that history has not really happened in and to this place. The play's narrator describes surviving local artifacts of the Roman, Saxon, and Norman periods, converting a temporal sequence into a natural tableau, so that the landscape/stage embodies the same logic as the pageant itself. It is a living diorama of a durable English "way of life." Similarly, in Forster's second pageant, *England's Pleasant Land*:

> The action covers a period of nearly one thousand years.
> The scene of the play is the English countryside, close to a village and to a manor house, which have grown up together during the centuries.
> The play is not about any particular person. It is about the land, and the characters should be thought of as types who are connected in various ways with rural England.[53]

The codes of rural England here will depend, once again, on abiding essences rather than historical changes. Perhaps the most active phrase in this flat and modest prose is "grown up together": the pageant tells English history as a story of gradually formed symbioses, between nature and culture, Saxon and Norman, villager and lord. The liberal-conservative version of English history borne by those words presents an organic bond between gentry and peasant that covers a multitude of social conflicts in its celebration of the "natural."

In both of his pageant-plays of the 1930s, then, Forster emphasizes the continuities of country life. In staging this rural order, Forster calls the roll of local names and places: "Listen for a moment to some of our local names, the names of our fields and woods and roads: The nine acres, the ten acres . . . the old twenty acres, Shoulder of Mutton Field, Hogs Ham . . . Roundabouts and Upper Chalks, Frogberry Lane, Stane Street and Friday Street, Hackhurst, The Shiffolds . . . Great Spleck, Fillebar, Middle Maggots . . ." (*AH* 352). This coarse Anglo-Saxon poetry of village life proposes a logic of tribal tautology: Englishness inheres in the village and the land; the landscape's meaning inheres in the texture of the English language—hence a mystified nexus of culture and identity based in England's pleasant land.[54] The pageant enacts what the modernist novel could only describe and mourn: an undisturbed and spontaneous sense of native belonging, attached to what Forster predictably identifies as "the genius of place." Here Forster traffics in all the clichés of Merrie England: Chaucer and blacksmiths, bonfires and hunting horns, village fairs and visiting bishops. The text is conspicuously verbless: it uses nouns without predicates, making litanies and incantations whose very grammar seems to dissolve the connective tissue of narrative. With this kind of device in operation, the nation emerges in mystical and perpetual self-identity based on juxtaposed elements rather than on complex narratives and contradictory histories.

This Englishness built of folksy, rural emanations thus holds the rhetorical allure of the accidental and the natural. In contrast to prescriptive "top-down" nationalisms, the pageant-play seeks to perform rather than to narrate or impose national identity. As Simon Featherstone points out, one of the pastoral's most subtle generic ruses is the casting of local or "personal truths" as the "truths of popular, national, but not state experience."[55] The pageant's eclectic brand of Englishness—made up of legendary objects, venerable monuments, well-loved vignettes, and sacred memories—appears to offer an open promise of national belonging but is marked by familiar regional (and associated class) particularities of the southern suburbs.

England's Pleasant Land has a somewhat more complete historical picture of rural England than the "Abinger Pageant." Like the earlier pageant, it describes successive and successful accommodations that have kept the rural order of England secure for seven hundred years, from the Norman Conquest to the Industrial Age. But history really begins in 1760, with the enclosures of common land and the destruction of the yeoman economy by large protocapitalist landholders (*EPL* 21). As that economic systems fades, of course, so too does the central myth of rural English identity. At this point in Forster's pageant, a running conflict between two squires carries the theme of England's division between inward and outward orientation: Squire Jeremiah argues that enclosure leads to more efficient farming—a necessary revenue boost for England's wars and external ambitions (*EPL* 32–33)—while Squire George counters with a conservative pastoralism in which local considerations outweigh foreign demands. The scene dramatizes a historical choice between agricultural modernization and the yeoman life. Quoting a passage from Goldsmith's "The Deserted Village," the text makes it clear that the romanticized peasantry had already substantially disappeared by the end of the eighteenth century. Of course, romantic invocations of a lost agricultural society follow rhythms quite separate from the realities of economic and social history.

Despite conflict over land ownership, Forster manages to represent interclass communion (always a cherished vision for the author of *Howards End*). Squire George, the local landlord, seeks to heal the wounds of a peasant revolt by reciting the most shopworn routine in the English pastoral repertoire: Shakespeare's "This blessed plot" speech (*EPL* 64). Old George's gentry idealism provides the cue for his son to strike a deal with

Jack, the villagers' spokesman. Following instincts that were more carefully and problematically explored in his novels, Forster imagines a
golden moment of cooperation between rich and poor for the sake of
rural England. In a moment of spontaneous affinity between young men
of different backgrounds, George and Jack shake hands, agreeing to abandon the cruelty of the past and the snobbishness of the present (*EPL* 66).
Thus, despite the earlier rift caused by the enclosures and revolts, and
despite the advent of industrialism, the pageant's narrator is able to open
act 2 in 1899 with the observation that "the countryside still looks as it
did in the days of the Enclosures—unspoiled, pleasant and green. But a
change is at hand" (*EPL* 51). Each time history appears to pierce the
pastoral continuity evoked in the pageant, the ever-renewable resources
of English country life appear to perdure.

Readers of Forster's novels are trained to expect a finely poised irony
hovering over the romantic pastoralism, but it is strangely absent throughout these texts. The historical insipidness of Forster's pageant is especially
remarkable in light of his own critical commentary on "the fatuities of
pageantry in England—Druids, Drake, the Lady Mary receiving the keys
of the city in all her dowdiness. A pageant requires not only splendour,
but a touch of the grotesque, which should lurk like onion in a salad"
(*AH* 55). And there is, after all, a bit of onion in this salad. The pageant-
play's submersion of class tension and historical change into a timeless
pastoral vision is broken for a moment, when the peasants give Squire
George a clock, representing the "gift of history" (*EPL* 62). Their gift
is revealed as "hideous": in a rare symbolic eruption, the unexpressed
historical time of modernity asserts itself. This hideous clock measures the
repressed mechanical time that the pageant-play is otherwise calculated to
displace and disguise. As a figure for lost history, the clock also signals
the erosion of narrative, its displacement by timeless rural essences and
frozen tableaux.

The closing scenes of *England's Pleasant Land*, like those of the "Abinger Pageant," address the problem of suburbanization. The chorus chants
ominously, "Ripe, ripe for Development is England's Pleasant Land,"
while the stage directions call for the appearance of little bungalows, followed by "motor cars, motor bikes, motor buses, paper and empty tins"
(*EPL* 77–79). The only relief from this "Pageant of Horrors" is an urgent
plea to preserve England's "green and pleasant land."[56] Although the pageant ends with the forces of modernization poised for incursion into rural
England, the pageant never seriously questions the value of the latter. Such
pastoral idealism is a feature of both the Edwardian Forster and the reluctant patriot of the 1930s. Where Forster's metropolitan fictions represented an attempted synthesis of democratic humanism and antimodern
nostalgia, the writing of the 1930s and '40s tends to arrange those senti-

ments in separate, incompatible packages. Although the pageant-plays work toward a version of the symbolic encounter between males representing different classes, they do so with unignorable aesthetic enervation.

Lacking in linguistic complexity and figurative depth, the pageant represents an ideal of village craft rather than professional art. Read as texts, Forster's plays only offer a weak synthesis of the ideological and libidinal elements that were alive in his earlier fiction.[57] As participatory village rituals, though, they have the appeal of a communal and spontaneous representation of an entire, cherished way of life. The neotraditional strain of late modernist writing that appropriated pageantry in the 1930s had visions of community stripped of aesthetic rarefaction and class privilege. If, in an earlier moment, the pleasures of metropolitan centrality compensated for the lost magic of rural English life, then, in the midcentury, the vanished pleasures of pastoral belonging are revived to compensate for the erosion of metropolitan perception.

Forster's liberal traditionalism inclined him to this particular version of community drama in the 1930s because it seemed to represent the shared memories of a community, not the propagandizing and didactic weight of other forms of political art and theater then circulating in Britain. To Forster, pageantry derived from a popular and spontaneous form of national attachment rather than from statist and xenophobic ideology. However, the pageant-play also had a nostalgic belief in heritage, in the mystified communion between *topos* and *ethnos*, that could very easily be recoded not just as magical and irrational but, even more dangerously, as fascist.[58] As a community drama, the pageant-play makes a certain kind of sense in the 1930s, the decade of engaged literature and new forms of political theater. But its rural, mystical, and nostalgic depiction of English life were no doubt bland—if not downright offensive—to the tastes of the literary left, including those, like Auden, who were interested in more urban and modernizing and politicizing forms of group theater.[59] The ritualistic and communal nature of the pageant-play distinguishes it from the more familiar 1930s notions of public or political art (such as the documentary novel, the radio play, or the Spanish Civil War poem). Yet, like those other forms, the pageant play expresses two desires that signal a late modernist transition: (1) the desire to mount a more participatory model of art production (as against the aesthetic virtuosity of high modernism), and (2) the desire to connect more directly with a public of art consumers (as against the cloistered alienation of high modernism).

Forster's pageants express a strong interest in the recuperation of a native heritage but also testify to the problems that arise in the conversion of a metropolitan to an insular aesthetic. Despite his reinvestment of cultural value in local traditions, Forster cannot help but experience and express ambivalence about the narrowing of England's cultural horizons in the 1930s and '40s. In keeping with his lifelong (and literarily success-ful) commitment to a cosmopolitan orientation, Forster finds that the re-sources of a putatively self-sufficient island culture have substantial limi-tations. On the one hand, England's pastoral core had always been a source of cultural value—a real and imaginary homeland. On the other hand, the homeland's value always depended on the possibility of escape, of travel and of intercultural encounter. To be ensconced within the island brings both the epistemological comfort of a bounded space and the cul-tural claustrophobia of narrowed horizons. While striving to replace the fruitful cultural dissonances of his modernist-era writing with an Anglo-centric neopastoralism, Forster nonetheless evinces a clear ambivalence about the lost privileges of metropolitan perception. Such an ambivalence also characterizes the writing of Virginia Woolf, who shared Forster's interest in the village pageant-play as a device for negotiating the political and aesthetic predicaments of English modernism during the late 1930s.

Island Stories and Modernist Ends in *Between the Acts*

Like her contemporaries Forster and Eliot, Virginia Woolf faced questions about the nature and status of public art during the 1930s. In *The Years* (1937) she tried to reinvent herself, to extend her form in response to increasing demands for social engagement. But she was discouraged by the results: "[w]hat I meant I think was to give a picture of society as a whole; give characters from every side; turn them towards society, not private life; exhibit the effect of ceremonies; Keep one toe on the ground by means of dates, facts; envelop the whole in a changing temporal atmo-sphere; Compose into one vast many-sided group at the end; and then shift the stress from present to future. . . . Of course I completely failed."[60] Woolf seems to reflect on *The Years* as a work that did not transform her method, but simply extended it thematically by covering the life of the large Pargiter clan over several decades and three generations. The new novel Woolf had in mind in the late 1930s would not simply enlarge cer-tain themes, it would renovate novelistic form. And more: it would ex-plore the relation of writer and audience, allowing Woolf to make more direct contact with popular taste and contemporary social referents. But how could the difficult and sometimes private idioms of high modernism be accommodated to the desire (now felt by both Woolf and her engagé critics) for a more public or communal art?

So far, my presentation of Woolf recalls a familiar figure of the thirties literary landscape: the modernist aesthete disciplined away from exqui-site treatments of bourgeois consciousness by the imperatives of social crisis. In the final years of the decade, this test of modernist commitments was intensified and complicated by an urgent political problem: how could Woolf, an intellectual pacifist, respond to the growing menace of fascism? More to the point: what stance could a lifelong Outsider—a woman artist who cherished her idiosyncratic and dissenting freedoms— take in relation to the wagon-circling patriotism of the late 1930s? Woolf had always been suspicious of British nationalism (linked as it was to patriarchy, imperialism, and xenophobia), yet in the end she wanted to find palatable ways to express her affinity for England and to assert the value of English traditions.

The problem of social engagement and the problem of nationalism converge in Woolf's final novel, *Between the Acts*, where Woolf makes the performance of a village pageant the central device in her exploration of community art and English history. Although Woolf missed the 1938 performances of Forster's *England's Pleasant Land* (later published in book form by Woolf's own Hogarth Press), his attempt to forge a meaningfully shaped communal history using the pageant form clearly struck a chord. It was at that time that Woolf's ideas for her new novel began to crystallize; by organizing the narrative around a pageant, she would be able to "exhibit the effect of ceremonies" and to break narrative momentum with poetic and choral structures. Woolf, like Forster, was becoming impatient with the limits of narrative itself. Although *The Years* had represented a shift toward a more encompassing social form, Woolf still felt hampered by certain generic limitations particular to the novel. The problem was the forward momentum of narrative: "thats [sic] the horror to me of the novel." But, she wrote to Stephen Spender, "I am very anxious to develop it further; and almost tried a poetry section in this book; wanted to get some chorus; some quite different level."[61] Although *Between the Acts* has sometimes been read as an addendum to Woolf's major novels or as a work bedeviled and finally swamped by Woolf's sense of artistic impotence and political despair, it is also an innovative and daring attempt by Woolf to bring her fiction to that "different level." Where *The Years* aimed for historical extension, *Between the Acts* returns Woolf to the temporal economy of the modernist day book, unspooling itself in the space of a single summer day. At Pointz Hall, in the "heart of the country," villagers and gentry have gathered to perform and watch a pageant-play that rehearses English history from the birth of the nation to the present time. By comparison to the Parkerian model, Woolf's pageant is smaller in scale and less formulaic in dramatic structure. It proceeds from the powerful dissenting vision of its balky director, Miss La Trobe, an outsider marked by whispered implications of queerness and foreignness. Through Miss La Trobe's show, the text registers the political and aesthetic impulses that motivated Forster's turn to pageantry but renders them in highly self-conscious and self-interrogating form. The interpolated genre of the pageant allows Woolf to combine public ritual and modernist narrative and to investigate the social currency of England's "island history."

For Woolf, as for Powys, Eliot, and Forster, pageantry was a dramatic genre that could allow for the emergence of a choral voice, giving form to communal values rather than to individual impressions or divisive ideologies. The desirability of a collective or impersonal voice had become an urgent political as well as aesthetic matter in the period. The pageant-in-novel design allowed Woolf to introduce a folkloric choral element (that "quite different level") without relinquishing the familiar techniques of her distinctive narrative style.[62] Despite the flexible generic structure of *Between The Acts*, however, Woolf's confrontation with national community creates obvious strains in her writing. Several times in the novel, Woolf reverses course between collective and recuperative ideas of Englishness and her fundamental wariness (as both artist and woman) about any kind of national or collective participation. The pageant's retelling of English cultural history is continuously challenged by the intersubjective and intrapsychic dramas that occur "between the acts." And yet, in the course of Woolf's narration, the modernist novel of consciousness begins to look like something new altogether.

Ubi Sunt

Woolf's prickly rapprochement with national heritage is apparent from the outset of *Between The Acts*, when she describes her setting: "Pointz Hall was seen in the light of an early summer morning to be a middle-sized house. It did not rank among the houses that are mentioned in guide books. It was too homely."[63] By describing a place untouched by the domestic tourism industry, Woolf suggests that we are approaching authentic, not official, England. But that description of Pointz Hall is soon contradicted by another: "The ground sloped up, so that to quote Figgis's Guide Book (1833), 'it commanded a fine view of the surrounding country. . . . The spire of Bolney Minster, Rough Norton woods, and on an eminence rather to the left, Hogben's Folly, so called because . . .' The Guide Book still told the truth. 1830 was true in 1939" (52). This narrative equivocation indicates Woolf's desire to avoid antiquarian nationalism, but it also establishes her surprisingly unironic appreciation of the unchanging English country.[64] "1830 was true in 1939": this terse formula collapses more than a century of modern history, while the brief list of place names—which recalls Forster's local catalogs—temporarily forestalls narrative momentum. Woolf begins the novel with descriptions that make history visible in spatial form, in the landscape around Pointz Hall: "you could still see, plainly marked, the scars made by the Britons; by the Romans; by the Elizabethan manor house; and by the plough, when they

ploughed the hill to grow wheat in the Napoleonic wars" (4). The absorption of historical sequence into a single sentence and a single glimpse anticipates the logic of living history that the pageant-play later performs.

In fact, *Between the Acts* doubles and redoubles its telling of the national story even before the pageant begins. Early on, Lucy Swithin, the
aging spirit of domesticity at Pointz Hall, reads an "Outline of History."
Like the pageant, the outline organizes itself around the intensely local
logic of the *ubi sunt*, seducing Lucy Swithin with stories of what happened
on this very spot of soil in the dim past.[65] The outline begins with the
geological creation myth of England: the moment when the island calved
off from the great Eurasian landmass. Its text inspires Swithin to envision
her England as a prehistoric swamp writhing with iguanadons. But the
outline also serves as the starting point for a comforting narrative about
the birth of culture as an island story.[66] The outline thus establishes two
competing fantasies of historical reversion that structure the novel: in the
first, modernity collapses back into destructive barbarism; in the second,
modernity is salvaged by the presence of immemorial folkways. Taken as
a primer for reading the pageant, the outline draws our attention to a
contest between redemptive tradition and barbaric regress.

This same opposition is represented characterologically in the frame
narrative, which features two anglicized, domestic women and two metropolitan, aggressive men. The elder siblings at Pointz Hall, Lucy Swithin
and Bart Oliver (an old India hand), represent competing versions of Englishness: one pastoral and insular, one barbaric and expansive. Early in
the novel, old Oliver dozes in a chair, dreaming of "a bullock maggot-
eaten in the sun; and in the shadow of the rock, savages; and in his hand
a gun. The dream hand clenched; the real hand lay on the chair arm, the
veins swollen but only with a brownish fluid now" (17). This dream of
violent imperial power, like the old man having it, is moribund but not
quite dead. The decaying bullock (or castrated bull) seems a fitting emblem for the dying empire, an incarnation of John Bull with his masculine
sap running dry. Although the retired empire man is something of a stock
figure for Woolf (and indeed in much English fiction of the period), Bart
Oliver is certainly more senescent and obsolescent than, for example,
Peter Walsh in *Mrs. Dalloway*.[67] By the end of the novel, the ex-imperial
warrior is merely "spectral," a ghostly gasping sign of fading Britannia
(218). Lucy Swithin (whose surname echoes "within" and signals interiority) is the presiding figure of insular domesticity. Her native and naive
Englishness contrasts sharply with her brother's unregenerate (if creaky)
imperialism. A flighty but sympathetic older woman, Lucy, like Mrs.
Ramsay in *To The Lighthouse* or Mrs. Wilcox in Forster's *Howards End*,
fixes value to the long, slow accumulations of insular culture.

The elder Olivers are caught in an unresolved dialectic: "[w]hat she saw he didn't; what he saw she didn't—and so on, *ad infinitum*" (26). Bart's aggressive imperialism threatens the peace of Lucy's insular humanism, just as Lucy's batty devotion to pastoral and aesthetic values rankles Bart's crusty utilitarianism. In the language of the novel—one that Forster would have understood—she connects, he divides. With these characters in view, Maria DiBattista has suggested that a dialectic of unification and separation (love and hate) structures the novel.[68] Within that very broad dialectic, the novel also makes particular symbolic assignments that correspond to competing versions of English national destiny.

In a sense, the elder Olivers represent defunct ways both of unifying and separating; the potential symbolic resolution lies in the next generation, where Giles and Isa Oliver repeat the terms of the Bart/Lucy pairing. Giles, a London stockbroker, represents the modern British forces of empire and finance, and he acts as a conduit, bringing the specter of war into the sheltered pastoral scene at Pointz Hall. Woolf uses Giles to suggest links between capitalism, imperialism, and patriarchal aggression. By contrast, Isa (like Lucy) is a figure of beleaguered domesticity. When Bart Oliver lies dreaming of imperial romance, Isa interrupts, "destroying youth and India" (18). At moments like this, the symbolic antagonism between domestic and imperial versions of England comes to the fore.[69] However, although the transfer of these terms from aged siblings to a younger couple makes for a more direct allegorical encounter, the trajectory of the Giles-Isa marriage plot remains indistinct and unresolved in the novel.

Thus the frozen or unresolved quality of the dialectic established by Bart and Lucy gets more or less replayed in the next generation, where Woolf does not offer a figurative resolution to the struggle between two models of English history. But Woolf does introduce two further characters into this rather static pattern of gendered associations. The unexpected arrival of Mrs. Manresa and William Dodge at Pointz Hall on pageant day gives Woolf a way not only to reinforce the symbolic economy described above but to kick the settled English gentry into unpredictable motion. Manresa, the brash Philistine, captivates the Oliver men, while Dodge, the feminized artist, establishes a quick rapport with both Isa and Lucy. Where Dodge understands culture and heritage, Manresa eats, flirts, and recoils whenever she "scents culture." Where he sublimates, she desublimates, converting verbal exchanges into libidinal ones, turning attention from art to appetite (50). As a trigger for sexual and aggressive impulses, Manresa rekindles "youth and empire" in Bart and inspires awkward violence in Giles (her "sulky hero"). It is no surprise, then, to discover that Manresa comes from outside the Anglocentric sphere of the country house: she is not only a gate-crasher, but a Tasmanian-born parvenu (39). Carnal and colonial, Manresa disrupts the peaceable domestic spirit that dwells in Pointz Hall. While the pageant draws attention to the values of insular culture, Manresa threatens it by rechanneling libidinal currents in the direction of sex and violence. Thus Dodge and Manresa repeat the novel's basic symbolic antagonism between genteel insular culture and destructive imperial libido, while reversing the previous association of the former with femininity, the latter with masculinity.

In this way, the frame narrative repeatedly lays down a figurative divide between an England whose values are feminine, pastoral, literary and an England whose values are masculine, industrial, expansive.[70] Like many other English intellectuals in the 1930s, Woolf seems interested in trying to reclaim English tradition—what DiBattista rightly describes as an "adversary, anterior culture"—from an imperial Britishness that had appropriated the national past.[71] The novel does not paper over the long entanglement of peaceable, humanist tradition and aggressive, expansive modernization. In fact, the novel's political tension is driven precisely by Woolf's awareness that she might not be able to prize apart these two nationalisms, that it might not be possible to celebrate the right kind of English civilization without fueling the wrong kind of British patriotism. Like Eliot and Forster, Woolf experiments with pageantry in an effort to reestablish the nationalism of shared experiences (pastoral memory) as against the nationalism of shared goals (imperial mission). But the interpolation of ritual into narrative gives Woolf a new symbolic purchase on this familiar problem. The novel uses the pageant, with its evocations of rural continuity, against the frame narrative, with its inevitable progression through cycles of creation and destruction. History's tragic motion repeats itself through the narrative, but the village ritual interrupts and suspends the narrative motion, freezing history into Englishness.

Deep Play

Woolf introduces the Pointz Hall pageant as a potentially unofficial version of national discourse. Both the food and the decorations are left over from a coronation celebration, as if to suggest that the village, having purged itself of official ceremony, can now engage in a more spontaneous and authentic ritual.[72] With the townsfolk gathered on the lawn, the pageant begins. Enter a village girl swathed in pink, who announces, "*England am I*," then cues a teenage actor ("*England's grown a girl now*"), who is quickly replaced on stage by "Eliza Clark, licensed to sell tobacco," personifying the Elizabethan age (76–83). In quick succession and with a gently spoofing touch, Woolf presents both the pageant's audience and the novel's readers with the conventional figure of the female-embodied nation. From this point, the pageant unfolds as a history not of politics or society but of literature. Skipping such major events as the Magna Carta and the Revolution, the pageant condenses English history down to four scenes: Elizabethan drama, Restoration comedy, Victorian melodrama, and the present day.

Woolf parodies the various phases of English literature and devotes her wit to laying bare the symbolic ruses of pageantry. In the midst of the Restoration comedy pastiche, a chorus of villagers moves on and off the open-field stage: "*Digging and delving*, the villagers sang passing in single file in and out between the trees, *for the earth is always the same, summer and winter and spring; and spring and winter again; ploughing and sowing, eating and growing; time passes . . .*" (125). Woolf ends the passage with an ellipsis and an abrupt, ironic echo of the famous middle section of *To The Lighthouse*: time passes. Or does it, if "the earth is always the same"? Here time is measured by cycles of pastoral repetition, not, as in *To The Lighthouse*, by the irreversible and disturbing aftereffects of a modern world war. At this point, Woolf picks up the third-person narration to draw further attention to the tight relations between the pageant's pastoral conventions and its outdoor setting. The very landscape around Pointz Hall apparently echoes the tune in the pageant. Moreover: "[t]he cows, making a step forward, then standing still, were saying the same thing to perfection" (134). Since Woolf has been gleefully parodying the rural clichés of pageantry, the echoing cows would seem to underscore the pageant's rote quality. This is cultural expression so ancient and so familiar that it barely counts as culture at all: even the local animals know the tune. With culture barely extending beyond natural reflection, we can take Woolf's point as an aesthetic criticism of an enervated rural idiom, but also as the description of an organic village art form.[73]

In the next scene, Woolf takes obvious delight in exposing the social and literary conventions of Victorian life. Moral earnestness, routine courtship comedies, missionary zeal, superficial materiality, stiff and prudish etiquette, and invidious class consciousness are all satirized briskly in an antic penny-opera. The earnest hero and pious heroine breathlessly vow to spend "*a lifetime in the African desert among the heathens*" (166). The plodding inevitability of Victorian marriage plots is spoofed by a chorus in top hats and side whiskers, who repeatedly ask the musical question: "*O has Mr. Sibthorp a wife? / O has Mr. Sibthorp a wife?*" (169). But the most important figure in the scene is its narrator, a Victorian constable, who stands (we are to imagine) at Hyde Park Corner, "*directing the traffic of 'Er Majesty's Empire. The Shah of Persia; Sultan of Morocco; or it may be 'Er Majesty in person; or Cook's tourists; black men; white men; sailors; soldiers; crossing the ocean; to proclaim her Empire; all of 'em Obey the Rule of my truncheon*" (161–62). Caricaturing the busy busy world of Anglo-imperial manhood, Woolf also underscores a darker point about the connections between colonial authority and domestic politics. The policeman declares: *"The ruler of an Empire must keep his eye on the cot; spy too in the kitchen; drawing room; library"* (162–63). By satirizing the masculine types through whom she connects violent overseas power to domestic patriarchal power, Woolf not only exposes one of the key ideological conventions of Edwardian pageantry (the rural heart that justifies British manifest destiny but also initiates the symbolic and political reorganization of that convention with a dissenting version of the island story. The mutually supportive institutions of empire and patriarchy come in for familiarly barbed treatment by Woolf. But their Victorian placement in the pageant has the effect of shunting them backward into the quaint past. A key turn in Woolf's thinking is registered here: empire is no longer seen as a political error of the British establishment but as a dated and outmoded enterprise belonging to an earlier, rather foolish era. Like Eliot's *The Rock*, the text situates itself on the historical threshold of the postimperial age, a gesture that makes it possible for Woolf to delink insular affinities from aggressive politics and therefore to explore the potential virtues of a nationally coded investment in group ritual.

Nonetheless, in narrating the pageant's performance of English history, Woolf's tone is undeniably critical and ironic. While mining the resources of the insular literary tradition, she takes obvious delight in parodying its conventions. Given the pious and fraternal rhetoric of pageantry in Woolf's time, it is hard to imagine her responding with anything short of a gag reflex to the typical pageant's promises of triumphant Englishness. In Woolf's text, the accidents and indignities of amateur theater—missed cues, muffed lines, ragtag costumes—undercut the patriotic rhetoric. Woolf parodies not only the pageant and its vulgar archive of civic materials but also the pat, inattentive responses of the pageant's audience. For these reasons, the critical consensus on *Between the Acts* has been that Woolf uses the pageant to deflate nationalism and deflect political commitment. It is true in this pageant-novel that myths and traditions are *put on* in both senses of the phrase: they are donned as historical fancy dress, and they are spoofed. And yet there are moments of communal longing and national sentiment that run against that grain. The travesties of literary convention *in* the pageant do not add up to a parodic reduction *of* the pageant. To read the text this way is to assign the pageant some symbolic weight and purpose beyond its function as a mere object of Woolfian irony and distrust of patriotism. While she may doubt the value of the pageant's conventionalized content, Woolf has a genuine interest in the power of the pageant's form, or to be more precise, in its ritual occasion.

As I hope is becoming clear, my reading is not meant as the latest round in the game of interpretive ping-pong about Woolf and nationalism in *Between the Acts*; it seems clear that the novel is designed precisely to express both antinationalist and nationalist sentiments, to reflect both authoritarian and antiauthoritarian possibilities in group ritual. The novel's irony reflects Woolf's interest in redefining, not eschewing, national tradition. Its revisionary relationship to "our island history" defines a nativist turn whose aesthetic and cultural effects are not simply (as often assumed) reductive or conservative. Indeed, Woolf's hybrid pageant-novel exemplifies a kind of experimental writing of the thirties that reflects on national ideology with the anthropological self-consciousness proper to a postmetropolitan era.

Narrative and/as Ritual

As I have proposed, a number of wartime intellectual projects began to turn ethnographic devices acquired in the colonies to the task of representing the home culture. With this in mind, we might understand the pageant device in Woolf's novel as a way to shift emphasis from the professional irony of modernist narrative to the inherent liminality of patriotic ritual.[74] Seeking to express a troubled half-love for England, Woolf presents an *uncertain performance* of—rather than either a thorough ironization of or a complete identification with—nationalism. By sketching the performance, she exerts control over the delicate politics of her communal attachments, dividing the pageant's meaning almost equally between inherited national cliché, La Trobe's dissident sensibility, and the accidental quality of spontaneous outdoor art. The function of Woolf's narrated ritual becomes especially clear in the pageant's final scene, when the director, Miss La Trobe, proposes to represent the present day. Here Woolf and her authorial surrogate confront a representational crisis that is both *in* and *of* the novel: the problem of rendering the community to the community, of performing an anthropology of the here and now. The viewers immediately understand the problem when they read the pageant program: " 'Ourselves. . .' They returned to the programme. But what could she know about ourselves? The Elizabethans, yes; the Victorians, perhaps; but ourselves; sitting here on a June day in 1939—it was ridiculous" (178–79). Miss La Trobe's ambition is to "expose them, as it were, to douche them, with present-time reality" (178–79). But the audience cannot absorb a representation of itself. At this point, nature intervenes in the form of a rain shower, a universal "douching" that immediately unites the audience, which then engages in a collective and primitive shudder at the power of the gods. Such evanescent rites of summer suggest that a ritualized relation to nature can make a collective where art cannot or should not. Woolf uses the scene to represent a spontaneous and tempo-rary cultural unity, as against the authoritarian (or authorial) imposition of social unity. It is easy to understand that fascism might make an English writer of the 1930s keen to explore the problem of national art or of how to represent the community to itself. But that problematic emerges in the text not only because the war makes national representation newly urgent but also because the anthropological turn makes it newly possible.

This reading of the late modernist moment in England integrates a rela-tively underexamined story about the discursive effects of imperial re-trenchment with the usual narrative about the political and aesthetic cri-ses of the late thirties. If we think of the years around World War II as a period of historical transition, fraught with beginnings as well as endings, we can perhaps better appreciate thirties texts that have sometimes been read as extreme, rigidified, or broken-down versions of twenties master-pieces. *Between the Acts* thematizes the problem of community self-repre-sentation more directly than earlier Woolf texts in part because it registers a new opportunity for the revival and redefinition of a broad national tradition. If the rituals invoked here are more nostalgic and Anglocentric than the corresponding myths of cosmopolitan high modernism, they are also more popular and communal. The fading of Pax Britannica opened the way for a redefinition of Englishness—a way, that is, for the pastoral culture of Lucy Swithin to reassert itself against the imperial and patriar-chal politics of Bart Oliver.

The project of separating a humane English tradition from the accreted discourse of imperial nationalism took on a new plausibility for intellectu-als in Woolf's circle during the late 1930s. Woolf herself clearly knew a good deal about the changing status of the British Empire during the in-terwar years, in part through her intellectual and domestic partnership with Leonard Woolf, who was one of the most acute observers of colonial resistance and imperial decline.[75] From his early tour of duty in Ceylon as a colonial officer (1904–11) through his years as a foreign policy advi-sor to the Labour Party, Leonard Woolf had firsthand knowledge of the colonial system. For him, the end of the British Empire was apparent long before formal decolonization.[76] In *Imperialism and Civilization* (1928), Leonard Woolf presciently identified the significance of Asian and African independence movements: "the subject peoples everywhere are at-tempting to throw off the domination of Western States and the tyranny and exploitation of Western civilization. The outcome of this movement of revolt will probably be of supreme importance in the history of the next hundred years."[77] Throughout the 1930s, Woolf was urging politicians in London to come to terms with their "contracting civilization."[78] In his view, Britain's own untenable institutions, especially the overseas empire, would destroy its civilization, even without Hitler's help.

Virginia Woolf knew Leonard's views about the corrupting effects of empire on English society and about growing political resistance to overseas British rule. It is therefore not surprising that *Between the Acts* registers the incipient end of the British empire, nor that Woolf could write in 1936 that "Things—empires, hierarchies—moralities—will never be the same again."[79] At a point when empires—and the hierarchies they both supported and were supported by—were being dramatically transformed, Woolf began to imagine the potential for improvement in the social life of English women. In her late-thirties work of social criticism, *Three Guineas*, Woolf offers a clear exposition of the links between imperial and patriarchal politics, noting that they both contributed to Europe's (and Britain's) headlong descent into war. What is less often noticed about *Three Guineas* is that Woolf's analysis, despite its grim perspicacity about patriarchal aggression, also makes room for a creative vision of an English society redeemed from imperial and warmongering politics.

In Woolf's analysis of English power, patriarchal and imperial institutions are deeply entrenched and mutually reinforcing. Woolf frequently returned to the idea that an unbalanced sexual-aggressive drive, central to the ways and means of patriarchal power, both fueled and was fueled by the imperial enterprise. For Woolf, empire was the mark of tyranny within English domestic life and, on the macropolitical stage, the direct cause of dangerous European rivalries. At the moment of the fascist challenge, *Three Guineas* exposes the everyday roots of both gender and national politics in late imperial Britain. Woolf observes, of a hypothetical woman, that when "consciously she desired 'our splendid Empire' . . . unconsciously she desired our splendid war" (*TG* 39). The book addresses the pitfalls of feminist empowerment: women as well as men can fall prey to a masculine, conquering ethos. Women who gain power in English institutions may be agents of progress and transformation, or they may be recruited into the jingo camp: "if you succeed in the professions, the words 'For God and the Empire' will very likely be written, like the address on a dog-collar, round your neck" (*TG* 70). Woolf urges any woman entering the professions in Britain to "absent herself from military displays, tournaments, tattoos, prize-givings, and all such ceremonies as encourage the desire to impose 'our' civilization or 'our' dominion upon other people" (*TG* 109). The quotation marks around "our" underscore Woolf's point that the imperial mission belongs neither to women nor to their version of Englishness.

But if *Three Guineas* marks a fine awareness of imperialism's effects on English institutions, it also proceeds from the possibility that the moment was ripe for the reform of those institutions, that the waning power of empire was, even then, beginning to remove crucial sources of inspiration and justification for patriarchy. When Woolf discusses the possibili-

ties of a free women's university stripped of masculine pomp and ceremony, she imagines an institution directed toward the cultivation of
knowledge and art rather than toward the production of martial young
men for empire (TG 30–34). In this way, Woolf wonders whether to seize
an historical opportunity to remake English society without the macho
underpinnings provided by a now fragile imperialism. Woolf does not
blindly celebrate nationalism, nor is she sanguine about the prospects for
women in English society, but she recognizes the importance of national
attachments at a moment when England's boundaries are stiffening
against European aggression and contracting with imperial decline. Under
the circumstances, *Three Guineas* suggests that women should neither
ignore nor reject nationalism but should redefine it for themselves; the
outsider must "analyse the meaning of patriotism in her own case" (*TG*
107). Such an act of analysis and of creative redefinition informs Woolf's
fiction in the late 1930s.[80]

For Woolf, then, the political crises of the time compelled intellectuals
to think nationally but also shifted the ground of national identity, so
that it might now possibly be redeemed by a humane and peaceable Englishness. The pastoral traditions represented in *Between the Acts*—remember that La Trobe has purged English history of its martial dimensions—are a bulwark against the twin barbarisms of continental fascism
and British imperialism. But while the image of a rehumanized and innocent England runs below the surface of the novel, so too do the images
of a writhing Darwinian swamp. These two versions of the national unconscious—the pastoral and the savage—are both fantasies of historical
reversion. The pageant's ritual reenactment of island history is a controlled experiment in devolution and collective memory designed to mitigate the uncontrolled experiment in barbarism and blood politics unfolding in Europe.

It is impossible to ignore the thematic impact of these historical factors
on *Between the Acts*. The broad dialectic that leads to violent conflict
between genders, races, and nations seems to operate for Woolf, finally,
as a kind of frightening master narrative, saturating other stories and
histories with its governing tropes of creation and destruction. It satu-
rates narrative itself, in other words. Thus, in *Between the Acts*, the interpolated nonnarratives—visual symbols, lyric moments, snatches of song,
outlines of history, and finally the pageant-play—are the textual locations of an alternative and nondialectical version of history associated
with peaceful and insular continuities. In formal terms, the pageant's
recursiveness and repetitiveness forestall narrative progress. Where *The
Years* labored to show history unfolding in narrative terms, *Between the
Acts* uses the pageant to recast history as heritage—as the rehearsal of
familiar gestures, songs, and scenes.[81] Woolf (like Forster) struggles to

break narrative momentum by posing insular culture against European civilization, the long slow drip of tradition against the rapid transformations of capitalist modernity, enduring pastoral folkways against perpetual Hegelian struggle.

In the end, however, the narrative frame seems to contain and outflank the ritual scene. Still wary about the putative consolations of English identity, Woolf wraps the summer pageant in an ironic and time-haunted narrative that cannot forget modernity; she, unlike Forster, is not fully able to rebaptize the island as innocent.[82] The contest between traditional and dialectical time, which takes the form here of a genre contest between pageantic ritual and modernist narrative, ends with a return to the cycles of sex, violence, struggle, death, and birth that organize the daily lives of characters like Giles and Isa Oliver. Once the pageant has concluded, Giles and Isa return to their private "heart of darkness" to fight, copulate, and possibly reproduce themselves (219).[83] By placing a Conradian echo in the scene, Woolf signals the reemergence of a modernized, barbarized world of civilizational struggle, played out in the smallest domestic arenas as well as in the vast theater of international rivalries.

The novel's conclusion seems to resolve the genre contest between pageant and narrative in favor of the latter: the play is textualized and ironized, its communicative powers subordinated to those of the frame narrative. The insular ritual of the pageant is designed to evoke culture without barbarism, to offer a model of social cohesion without authoritarian control. But Woolf cannot fully endorse it, precisely because even this apparently humane version of group identity—this myth of Englishness—cedes too much ground to conformist, traditionalist, and sexist structures of power.[84] Perhaps, too, the formal structure of the novel seems ragged or unresolved because Woolf is engaged in a transitional experiment with the limits of textual expression and with the powers of ritual performance. The ritual remains flawed and incomplete: its capacity to create or reflect the collective can only, after all, be temporary. For this reason, the novel reaches its highest pitch of stylistic dissonance and self-consciousness during the denouement, when it must confront the breakup of the pageant audience.

The end of the pageant becomes a moment of truth for Miss La Trobe, who suffers dramaturgical agony as she confronts the disintegration of her compound audience into individual atoms. Woolf lingers over the moment of dispersal, recalling the scene in Powys's *A Glastonbury Romance* when "everyone seemed to become a separate individual again" (Powys 605). As in earlier novels, Woolf concentrates on moments when public and private gears mesh and unmesh, when, for example, the individual guests at Mrs. Dalloway's party or Mrs. Ramsay's dinner of *boeuf en daube* become, in an almost magical, always ephemeral way, a unit—

and then, in jerky spasms of disengagement, decompose back into separate souls. *Between the Acts* expands such moments of unity/dispersal into a more overtly political story about the problem of national identity. Here a gramophone delivers an unpleasant harangue to the audience members, forcing them to recognize the death of the collective. Both the gramophone's message and the scene more generally oscillate jerkily from announcements of dispersal to exhortations of togetherness: "O let us, the audience echoed (stooping, peering, fumbling), keep together. For there is joy, sweet joy, in company. *Dispersed are we*, the gramophone repeated" (196). As the civic ritual comes to an end, the narration gives way to a long medley of conversational snippets—what Patricia Laurence sees as a kind of "communal voice" or fugue.[85] Jumping from voice to voice in this Babel of separate souls, Woolf produces the liberal novel's version of a crowd scene: a group caught in that delicate and brief instant of disengagement from collective consciousness, when the community dissolves into the "orts, scraps, and fragments" of a modern society.

And yet Woolf presses beyond the familiarly modernist condition of atomization to confront a central paradox of the liberal imagination. Through ingenious attention to the streaky powers of ritual, the novel represents a group's wish to avoid collective identity as a positive feature *of* its collective identity. In the novel, Woolf frequently returns to this classically liberal (and English) notion of social cohesion based on the promotion of individual freedom. It is expressed as a fond but anxious wish by an anonymous member of the pageant audience: "if we don't jump to conclusions, if you think, and I think, perhaps one day, thinking differently, we shall think the same?" (200). This paradox underlies all the communitarian yearning condensed into Forster's motto "only connect." As the audience members prepare to return to their own private lives, they are united by a common wish for community and vexed by their equal commitment to dispersal. "Dispersed are we" becomes a group chant, its unanimous repetition belying its content. Or, as the gramophone burbles, "*Unity—Dispersity. . . . Un . . . Dis . . .*" (201). This imploding verbal sign of political inconclusion signifies Woolf's unwillingness (or inability) to think beyond the paradox of negative liberty or to endorse rituals of belonging without exposing their authoritarian undercurrents.[86]

Between the Acts is a tragic document of the liberal imagination under pressure, forced to confront the political limitations of the "English way." But it is also a text that looks forward toward a more coherent yet less hierarchical form of national culture and toward new forms of literary expression appropriate to such a culture. The interpolated national pageant exposes the historical limitations of—without fully departing from—a worldview dedicated to liberal individualism expressed in the language of modernist irony. In making a community ritual such a central feature of the plot, Woolf experiments with the aesthetic and social implications of a potentially organic (but also potentially authoritarian) form of national culture. The novel's interpolation of ritual continually reminds us that novels themselves are "socially symbolic acts," that is, mediated and elaborated forms of what were once storytelling rituals.[87] La Trobe's wary and self-reflexive show generates a metafictional commentary on the novel's own covert ritual function. This point can be made simply by saying what readers have long sensed, that the pageant plot gives Woolf a chance to meditate openly about her own purposes and effects as a writer and to come to terms with the social limitations of high-modernist literary institutions. Since the ritual breaks down whenever La Trobe tries too hard to assert her artistic vision, the text yields a parallel and autocritical insight about the ineffectiveness of elite experimental literature in a fragmented, liberal-pluralist society. Woolf thus performs an "anthropological turn" on her own literary practice, gaining critical and historical distance on the modernist aesthetic by juxtaposing it to the immediacy and collectivity of group ritual.

As an artistic surrogate for Virginia Woolf, Miss La Trobe looks for devices and techniques that will create harmony between her own eccentric voice and the demands of a sometimes philistine and truculent audience. La Trobe's experiments with music, for example, seem designed to reduce the distinction between two models of the artist's vocation, one in which the artist imposes unity on a fragmented audience and one in which the artist ritualistically evokes or channels unity from an audience that already possesses it in the form of group identity. That oscillation structures an ambiguous moment at the end of *Between the Acts*. As the pageant draws to a close, there is confusion at the gramophone—and at this moment the experiment is no longer really La Trobe's but Woolf's: "The records had been mixed. Fox-trot, Sweet Lavender, Home Sweet Home, Rule Britannia—sweating profusely, Jimmy, who had charge of the music, threw them aside and fitted the right one—was it Bach, Handel, Beethoven, Mozart or nobody famous, but merely a traditional tune?" This question goes unanswered, but the music begins:

> Like quicksilver sliding, filings magnetized, the distracted united. The tune began; the first note meant a second; the second a third. Then down beneath a force was born in opposition; then another. On different levels they diverged. On different levels ourselves went forward; flower gathering some on the surface; others descending to wrestle with the meaning; but all comprehending; all enlisted. The whole population of the mind's immeasurable profundity came flocking (188–89)

The passage describes the one-making effect of music on the distracted spectators, though of course the grammar of Woolf's writing creates a pitch-perfect equivocation between a unity of the "whole population" and a unity of the single mind's "immense profundity." Moreover, Woolf stages the mix-up at the gramophone in order to advance this question: is the unity effect achieved because of *formal* perfection created by an Artist, or is it achieved because of a preexisting *cultural* cohesion preserved by the people's anonymous creativity? The confusion—never resolved—between individual composer and traditional tune allows the text to make clear its own ambivalent division between a modernist ideal of the artist's individual sensibility and an emergent investment in the creative consciousness of the folk.

Woolf's representation of a collective artistic agency is emergent in two senses: first, it marks a relative but nonetheless identifiable shift in emphasis for Woolf's own writing; second, it marks Woolf's place in a wider late modernist shift away from the prevailing assumption of social fragmentation (palliated by an individual vision of aesthetic or mythical order) and toward an exploration of the sources of collective, often national, identity. As I will suggest in chapter 3, for example, Woolf's use of music to split the difference between aesthetic wholeness and social unity resonates in a number of ways with Eliot's contemporaneous work in *Four Quartets*. And of course the recirculation of pageantry among other English writers of Woolf's generation suggests that her experiment can be understood as part of the anthropological turn in which domesticated rituals seem to inflect perspectival narration and textual irony.

In narrativizing ritual, Woolf struggled not only to represent the present to itself but to invent a ritual that could register an uneasy and partial investment in national community. In the pageant's final scene, La Trobe makes a gesture that, against all odds, seems to answer both to modernist political irony and to Woolf's growing investment in the possibilities (and limitations) of collective self-representation. La Trobe instructs the actors to turn a series of cracked and homemade mirrors on the audience. Her last ruse—the trick of mirrors—shifts attention away from symbolic content and lays bare the aesthetic transaction itself. It converts the neotraditional pageant into an avant-garde gesture embedded within a modernist novel. In a bravura revision of the "mirror of fiction" trope, Woolf defamiliarizes modernist narrative style. At that point, the gramophone proposes: "let's talk in words of one syllable, without larding, stuffing or cant. Let's break the rhythm and forget the rhyme. And calmly consider ourselves" (187). The machine's dream is the substitution of elaborated literary style with a spare aesthetic of self-contemplation on the collective level.

Songs My Uncle Taught Me

Woolf uses the figure of Miss La Trobe to examine the effects of artistic "one-making," but the problems that Woolf wishes to explore only repeat themselves at the level of the surrogate who, like Woolf, is profoundly attuned to both the value and the danger of communal art. Thus, in a Chinese box of displaced artistic agency, Miss La Trobe herself employs a surrogate: the hidden gramophone that issues disembodied voice-overs during the pageant. These distancing mechanisms complicate the transaction between actors and spectators in the pageant (and between text and readers in the novel). At a certain point, Woolf turns the experiment in displaced expression into an exploration of collective reception. At the moment of dispersal, Woolf initiates a stylistic experiment, representing the voice of the audience as a collective in free indirect discourse. In earlier Woolfian ventures into fugue-style renderings of group voice, each snippet of conversation could, theoretically, be assigned to an individual speaker. In certain passages in *Between the Acts*, though, Woolf gives one voice to a group consciousness:

> Feet crunched the gravel. Voices chattered. The inner voice, the other voice was saying: How can we deny that this brave music, wafted from the bushes, is expressive of some inner harmony? "When we wake" (some were thinking) "the day breaks us with its hard mallet blows." (119)

The combination of gramophone speeches and collective discourse modifies Woolf's narration of consciousness and represents the two great challenges to the liberal/modernist subject in 1930s culture: the machine and the masses. By registering the growing and global importance of collectivist national culture, Woolf objectifies her own celebrated techniques for narrating consciousness, providing a lucid case study in the precise interplay between political and aesthetic change in late modernism.

Of course, a familiar narration of consciousness operates at various points in *Between the Acts*, but Woolf organizes the story to emphasize the collective sources of thought rather than its eccentric individual play. Where the earlier Woolf tended to make mental records of fleeting visual and emotional impressions, here she makes mental transcriptions out of the words, songs, phrases, and tropes of a preexisting and durable cultural archive.[88] This marks only a relative shift in Woolf's style; her high modernist representations of mental life were always iterative and citational and therefore, in an important sense, always social. However, in this novel, the pageant's stock of English literary conventions (drawn from Shakespeare, Shelley, Tennyson) begins truly to saturate the inner language of the novel's protagonists, turning stream of consciousness into a game of unfree association. "The play keeps running in my head," says Isa. She and William Dodge acknowledge that their verbal repertoires are made up of overlapping cultural stuff: "They were conspirators; each murmuring some song my uncle taught me" (105). The position of the pageant in the text places rhetorical emphasis on the power of inherited culture to both inform and restrict the mind's verbal and mnemonic pathways. Instead of being used to individuate characters, this version of Woolfian consciousness tends to underscore their shared debt to national tradition. The inflection of Woolf's most distinctive technique, the narration of consciousness, by the gravitational force of national tradition makes sense when we recall that she was at work on a synoptic history of English literature during the composition of *Between the Acts*. The two extant essays from that unfinished critical project, "Anon" and "The Reader," suggest that Woolf intended to emphasize the continuities of English literature from its very beginnings to the present day.[89] Like Mrs. Swithin's *Outline of History*, "Anon" begins with England's geographical separation from the continent, so that insularity once again frames the birth of culture. From there, Woolf's fantasy of origins reaches all the way back to the prehistoric moment when nature begat culture in the form of human imitations of birdsong.[90] As in *Between the Acts*, Woolf seems taken by a vision of English literature's primitive bases, describing forms of culture so rooted in the local ecology that they ring in echoes with the singing birds and the lowing cows. Both the novel and the late essays generate images of a kind of cultural unconscious figured as a pool or "reservoir of common belief": "Behind the English lay ages of toil and love. That is the world beneath our consciousness; the anonymous world to which we can still return."[91] If Woolf seems to indulge in what we are now quick to expose as a bad-faith quest for national essence, she also (characteristically) refrains from fixing a prelapsarian point of origin. In the passage just cited, she also warns against the ideal of a golden, unself-conscious culture: "[t]here never was a time when men and women were without memory" ("Anon" 385). Every history, she suggests, has a prehistory; every story of origins gives way to another. Woolf's point is not to establish a fixed and Edenic cradle of the English genius but to gather into one sustaining narrative the expressive capacities that she associates with her island home.

The anthropological quality of Woolf's project leads her to emphasize dramatic and ritual forms (including pageantry) as the primal art of England. In "Anon," Woolf does not idealize the premodern artist, but rather an entire kind of symbolic transaction shared by artist and audience. The object of Woolf's historical imagination is a cultural situation where the separation into expressive subject and receptive audience does not even make sense: "the audience was itself the singer" ("Anon" 382). Anon, which stands for a pre-aesthetic ideal of authorship submerged into pastoral community, is, for Woolf, "the common voice singing out of doors."

Like most stories that begin with a pastoral ideal, Woolf's "Anon" tells of a fall from grace. From the aesthetic Eden of common culture to early modern patronage to late modern privatization of artistic production and consumption, Woolf recounts the social and institutional separations that gradually but unmistakably produce the alienated modern(ist) writer. Moving indoors and into specialized spaces, Anon "acted more and more his own art," gaining creative freedom but growing more divided from the values of the community. With the rise of the book, literature becomes a storable cultural treasure, but it loses its direct and live connection with the audience: "It was the printing press that finally was to kill Anon." At this point, "the individual emerges"; the modern artist develops a signature and a name; the anonymity of premodern cultural expression gives way to personal style ("Anon" 383–85).

When we read "Anon" alongside *Between the Acts*, the effect of splicing a group ritual into the modernist narration of consciousness comes into sharper focus. In "Anon," Woolf describes the slow transformation of a bardic culture whose themes were "great names, great deeds, simple outlines" to a modern society whose writers learned to focus on the "single subtlety of one soul" (394). The proper theater of an older common culture was slowly and inevitably replaced by the "theater of the brain," a centuries-long process that reaches its peak in the modernist novel of consciousness (398). Woolf's late essays thus describe the modernization and autonomization of Art—the very problem that preoccupied not only the continental avant-garde of the 1930s but also the Auden circle of politically committed poets in Britain. If "Anon" provides a history of art's segregation from broad social power and meaning, *Between the Acts* imaginatively reverses that history. The pageant-novel redirects attention from the "theater of the brain" to a more public and communal theater, thematizing at every turn the political and aesthetic tension between the two arenas. In presenting the encounter between the drama of private souls and the drama of group identity, Woolf draws on pageantry as a traditional form that is still viable in modern England. Her wary nativism bears interesting points of contact with that of T. S. Eliot. During the thirties, Eliot, like Woolf, not only took explicit account of the problem of modernist alienation in its full historical and institutional form but also turned to Anglocentric traditionalism when contemplating remedies for art's autonomy from culture. Despite his growing investment in an elitist, masculinist, and Christian notion of the public sphere, Eliot would certainly have seconded Woolf's call to revive modernist art with "something drawn from the crowd in the penny seats and not yet dead in ourselves" ("Anon" 398). For Woolf and Eliot were not just demystifying island stories but also reinventing them, turning fears of historical regression into a vision of restored contact between artist and audience in a postmetropolitan English culture.[92]

Theatres of the Brain

Although Woolf's interest in national ritual was both partial and belated, the pageant-novel's version of anonymous and participatory expression nevertheless seems to fulfill an old modernist ideal. Its hybrid form frees Woolf to some extent from the critical irony that so many modernist experiments in fiction and poetry, though designed to achieve impersonal voice, have been received and canonized as examples of virtuoso personal style. Under the political pressures of the late thirties, modernists found new approaches to the problem of literary objectivity or anonymity. Woolf's turn to the anthropological scene of ritual, for example, broadens the sociohistorical basis of perspectival narration beyond the historical fantasy of *Orlando*, beyond the serialized viewpoints of family saga in *The Years*, and beyond even the dazzling experiments in fugue consciousness in *The Waves*. In an early musing about the novel, Woolf wrote:

> why not Poyntzet Hall: a centre. all lit. discussed in connection with real little incongruous living humour; & anything that comes into my head; but "I" rejected: "We" substituted . . . "We" . . . composed of many different things . . . all life, all art, all waifs & strays—a rambling capricious but somehow unified whole.[93]

It is no accident that in her attempt to compose a "We," Woolf turns to the kinds of culturally sanctioned meaning associated with country rituals. This particular method for reaching a first-person-plural perspective moves Woolf beyond the simulation of idiosyncratic (yet putatively universal) mind-effects so central to her success as novelist of the psyche. No longer content to oscillate between the personal/impersonal poles of high modernism, she composes a form designed to evoke and express the collective values of a knowable community and to be, in that sense, *trans*personal.

If Woolf's invocation of national ritual tempers her rendering of consciousness, it does not reflect a sudden turn from "individualist" to "collectivist," but it does reflect the emergence of new forms developed in response to the crisis/opportunity of national retrenchment. Woolf's semi-ironic shift toward English tradition encourages a relatively more socially inflected understanding of consciousness and reduces (again, in relative terms) the centrality of the autonomous psyche as an object of modernist representation. To date, the general critical consensus on *Between the Acts* has, I think, overemphasized Woolf's (liberal-feminist) fear of the collective and underemphasized the appeal of a ritualized nativism that reintegrates artist and audience into a common culture.[94] But I do not want to argue, from some stringently Lukacsian perspective, that Woolf had, at long last, learned to transcend "modernist subjectivism." Instead, it might be more profitable to ask what can be learned from this case about the relation between the modernist language of consciousness and "metropolitan perception." What, in other words, does it mean to claim that Woolf's attempt to substitute a "We" for the modernist "I" depends on the recrudescence of national feeling? What does that substitution—or shift in emphasis—reveal about the larger process of demetropolitanization in England and its effect on modernist style?

In recent years, critics have begun to understand metropolitan conditions as a crucial factor in the formation of modernism's theater of the mind. In one recent version of the argument, Franco Moretti has offered, via Georg Simmel, a theoretical account of the stream of consciousness technique as a device for managing the overstimulation of the modern urban subject.[95] Raymond Williams takes the co-presence of diverse languages and cultures in the metropole as crucial for the development of modernist subjectivity.[96] Similarly, for Kumkum Sangari, the multicultural welter of imperial capital cities is inseparable from the "freewheeling appropriations" of an "assimilative bourgeois consciousness."[97] To put the argument schematically, we might say that a high modernist aesthetic dedicated to idiosyncratic mental processes tends to assume that human consciousness is a universal currency or that its language is at least transcultural.[98] In other words, the canonical works of high modernism represent subjectivity by shuttling between individualizing and universalizing discursive modes, between *psyche* and *myth*—a cosmopolitan short circuit that often bypasses determinate social configurations such as classes, genders, and nations.[99]

The case of *Between the Acts* as a document of late modernism extends and retrospectively (as it were) clarifies these claims about the relation between metropolitan settings and the classic high modernist project of writing "consciousness." In *Between the Acts*, Woolf demystifies that literary project just as her thematic focus shifts in the direction of national culture. With a sometimes burdensome degree of self-consciousness, the novel explores the growing historical tension between the universal subject of modernism (psyche/myth) and the demands of a *particularized* collective, defined, in this case, by nationhood. In moving from languages of the psyche that are archetypal and mobile toward those that are more culture-bound, Woolf manages to register the broader transition in English literature from metropolitan modernism to minor culture. Woolf's cultural turn proceeds under the sign of the nation because it seemed both possible and necessary to resignify England as a meaningful (but geopolitically minor) social collective. As I noted earlier, Jameson's thesis on modernism and imperialism holds that modernist style was predicated on the unknowability or lost totality of daily life in the European metropolis, a condition of "meaning loss" perpetuated and exacerbated by the fracturing of the nation into core and colonies. By implication, then, the reconsolidation of culture through a genre that composes the nation's fragments into unified local time and space would both signal the end of imperialism and destabilize modernist style. And this, I think, is precisely the relation between national history and literary form in *Between the Acts*.[100]

In moving from the 1920s artist Lily Briscoe in *To The Lighthouse* to the 1930s dramaturge La Trobe of *Between the Acts*, Woolf has shifted emphasis from private production ("I have had my vision") to collective reception ("I have made them see"). And Woolf's last meditation as a common reader, *Reading at Random*, makes plain her stake in the total circuit of expressive culture, as opposed to the elite institutions and segregated spheres of modern art. In the story of "Anon," what gets lost to modernity is the "impersonality" and "generality" of song, the unselfconsciousness of an art that borrows, repeats, and "can say what every one feels" (397). "Anon" imagines (but cannot execute) the forfeit of artistic privilege in the interest of a more communal form of expression.[101] It defines the long historical emergence of autonomous *art* and its eclipse of a recognizably insular ideal of expressive *culture*—an ideal associated with the broad human Englishness of Shakespeare's time, when the folk and the genius were one. To the extent that modernism had assimilated the concept of the individual genius as the seat of aesthetic value, Woolf's cultural history tries to think beyond modernism. Thus, when La Trobe's actors urge us to "break the rhythm and forget the rhyme" and "calmly consider ourselves," when they turn the shattered mirror of the national pageant onto the audience, they are laying bare the logic of Woolf's cultural turn. Their gesture evokes her vision of a spontaneous community which *is in itself* meaning and which therefore renders obsolete the modernist artist's gift of form.

This domestication of ritual (whose cracked looking glasses echo Joyce's definition of postcolonial Irish art) represents an uncannily apt choice in a culture that is just beginning to accede to its own logic of cultural nationalism, that is, in a culture beginning to recognize itself as one nation among many, eccentric and postimperial. But it would be reductive to read late Woolf for some ultimate statement about the aesthetic or political value of either a common culture based on national belonging or of a high modernist Art based on rational cosmopolitanism. What her late writing offers is a sharp but balanced historical reflection on the advantages and disadvantages attached both to modernist practices and to their potential obsolescence. In "Anon," for example, Woolf frames the emergence of the modern artist not only as a fall from grace but as a successful aesthetic adaptation to modernity. Modern(ist) writing came to achieve an astonishing degree of skill and beauty, but it was often, for Woolf, "a suspended derelict irrelevant beauty" ("Anon" 398). Woolf balances her account of art's irrelevance in "Anon" by reckoning with both the dangers and the comforts of a more communal aesthetic in *Between the Acts*. As the novel vividly suggests, national tradition could easily sponsor stultifying ideologies and mob aesthetics—effects that threaten to curb liberal freedom and bring to ground the "suspended beauty" of modernist art. On the other hand, the ritual invocation of national tradition seems to pose a meaningful shared history against the social fragmentation of the metropolis and against the social marginalization of modernism.

Thus two models of the "location of culture"—the fading world of elite cosmopolitanism and a revived core of insular nativism—are relativized in late Woolf: each is shown to have its own liberating perspectives, aesthetic potentialities, and social blind spots. But the two models are not simply held together through irony as the opposing poles of a stable and structural dichotomy. Indeed, my reading of Woolf in the context of national retrenchment is designed to show that her texts register a historical process. Such a reading kicks the cosmopolitan/nativist dichotomy into dialectical motion and reveals to us some of the ways in which modernists conceived the transition from metropolitan literature to national culture in England. Like Eliot's *Four Quartets*, to which we will shortly turn, *Between the Acts* situates itself at the switchpoint between two cultural epochs—a fact that accounts for its jerky, balky, and elliptical qualities. Rather than read those qualities as aesthetic flaws or content ourselves with repeating truisms about Woolf's ambivalence in the face of nationalism, we can perhaps understand those formal properties of the novel as signs of a necessarily incomplete historical project. *Between the Acts* thematizes but does not fully realize the end of an era.[102] It remains poised between a residual model of the cosmopolitan genius ironically distanced from social collectives and an emergent model of the anonymous artist absorbed back into shared national traditions. This is what English modernism looks like as it transforms itself into something new.

THREE

INSULAR TIME: T. S. ELIOT AND
MODERNISM'S ENGLISH END

.

The Antidiasporic Imagination

ON THE WHOLE, it would appear to be for the best that the great majority of human beings should go on living in the place in which they were born."[1] This celebration of roots was written by one of the twentieth century's most famous literary migrants. A few years before distilling his antidiasporic impulses into the typically sweeping, deceptively modest dictum cited above, T. S. Eliot made his point even more directly by following the trail of his family's colonial migration back to their native English village, East Coker. In the poem "East Coker," Eliot imaginatively reverses his forebears' journey—tacitly expressing his disapproval of their failure to "go on living in the place in which they were born." I see this reversal as a crucial factor in understanding Eliot's later career. And I take Eliot's work during the 1930s and 1940s as exemplary of a wider set of intellectual homecomings and modernist valedictions. His writing reflects the stylistic, generic, and cultural transformations that I have described as the demetropolitanization of English literature; moreover, by virtue of Eliot's central position in London literary circles, his writing also helped produce those transformations.

As my discussion of *The Rock* in chapter 2 suggests, Eliot spent the 1930s adjusting his literary practice to his sense of a broad European crisis and a particular English solution. His vision of national culture promised ambiguous results for high modernism; after all, in Eliot's view, modernism's styles and institutional structures were developed to fit an era of futility and anarchy. If the privations of war, depression, and imperial decline could inspire the English to rediscover their Burkean roots as an organic community, the modernist aesthetic might itself become obsolete. In the discussion that follows, I will explore the ways in which Eliot's cultural ideals condition the self-canceling dimensions of his late literary practice.

We begin this reading of Eliot where the analysis of Virginia Woolf left off: with the rediscovery of culture as a specifically national object. At this crucial turning point in the late 1930s, Eliot echoes Woolf insofar as he connects the reemergence of English culture not only with the eclipse of metropolitan modernism in general but with the displacement of privatized exchanges by ritual and dramatic occasions. Eliot's ideal of communally produced meaning—in which drama becomes once again the most vital literary genre—is deeply intertwined with his Anglocentrism. It draws together Eliot's longstanding suspicion of romantic individualism (as a bad basis for art or interpretation) with an increasing investment in local and bounded definitions of culture. In other words, Eliot's late cultural turn manages to synthesize and, in a sense, activate some of his earliest ideas. In his antihermeneutic essay "The Interpretation of Primitive Ritual" (1913), for example, Eliot notes that a ritual collapses the moment of performance into the moment of interpretation.[2] But self-determining rituals (unlike modernist texts) can operate only in an organic community such as the one Eliot associates with pre-Revolutionary England or the one he envisions for postimperial England. Closed, hierarchical societies and conventional forms are the lynchpins of Eliot's classicism; they represent a set of values that remains fairly constant for him. What is less fully understood, however, is the shift in Eliot's career from articulating those ideals as impossibilities (and therefore the source of modernist irony) to addressing the historical circumstances under which they become possibilities.

One way to chart this change in emphasis—and to grasp its significance for English culture in the phase of imperial contraction—is to note the shifting valence of the term "tradition" in his writing. In *After Strange Gods* (1933), Eliot begins by declaring the need to broaden the narrowly literary definition of the term that he advanced in "Tradition and the Individual Talent" (1919). The earlier essay defines tradition as an undying European canon, putting aesthetics beyond the reach of history. By contrast, the later Eliot seeks to conjure a geographically narrower but socially broader notion of the timeless: it belongs properly to a single (national or racial) people, but it inheres in their total way of life rather than in the aesthetic realm alone. In *After Strange Gods*, he notoriously takes tradition to mean the "blood kinship of 'the same people living in the same place.' "[3] Continuity or "permanence" (the word Eliot would have preferred) depends not on the cosmopolitan aesthetics of European literature but on the ethnic cohesion of English culture.

It has become conventional to think of Eliot's later work as the product of either a simple minded Tory retreat into traditionalism or an exhausted personal retreat into Christianity, both taken as inevitable expressions of Eliot's latent and rigid conservatism. But Eliot's cultural turn was neither inevitable nor simple. The usual biographical explanation obscures Eliot's place—which is at once idiosyncratic and exemplary—in a wider culture of national retrenchment. Moreover, Eliot's conservatism and especially his anti-Semitism have tended to obscure the fact that antidiasporic thinking ran across the political spectrum in 1930s England.[4] Indeed, I take the

emergence of a wider discourse of insularity on both the left and the right
to indicate not just the political stripes of one or another segment of the
educated classes but rather a broader structural shift associated with the
contraction of empire and the collapse of interwar cosmopolitanism. For
example, although Eliot's politics clashed more or less openly with the
prevailing liberal opinions of the Bloomsbury circle, his views on imperialism in fact converge to a surprising degree with those of Leonard Woolf,
who was not only Bloomsbury's main political writer but also the framer
of the Labour position on empire.

Woolf's writings do not condemn Europeans for arrogating to themselves the right to occupy and govern foreign lands. In fact, Woolf (like
Eliot) takes pains to point out that imperial institutions have been enlight-
ening as well as exploitative. Nonetheless, he criticizes imperialism for
creating a "conflict of civilizations" that usually ends in disaster.[5] In *Imperialism and Civilization*, Woolf suggests that people do better to stay with
their own kind and in their native land. When Asian and African popula-
tions live in countries dominated by white Europeans, the inevitable result
is exploitation, hierarchy, and violence. Likewise, according to Woolf
(who, as a Jewish Englishman, experienced both assimilation and ethnic
alienation), colonialism and migration have created intractable racial
problems for whites in East Africa and the Japanese in California, that is,
for "alien, unassimilated bodies" within (putatively) homogenous nations.[6] The principle works in both directions: keep "Africa for the Africans," but also keep "Europe for the Europeans." Woolf's Ceylon fiction
addresses the epistemological limitations of the imperialist enterprise: Englishmen and women who set out to "know India" always discover the
futility of such a project. Woolf pits real experiences against "false ideas"
of empire, whether the latter are inspired by liberal idealism about human-
itarian aid, religious idealism about conversion, or jingoist idealism about
Britain's greater glory. The colonies simply cannot be made sense of—the
logical corollary being, of course, that only one place can really be known
or represented, encompassed or plumbed, by an English writer: England.

In Woolf's thinking, then, the best hope for peace comes when each
nation develops within its own borders, leaving interactions for the private citizen, the occasional trader, and the trained diplomats of the League
of Nations. But what makes Woolf's work in the thirties apposite to a
reading of late Eliot is not just the mutual reinforcement of antidiasporic
beliefs and anti-imperial positions; it is his mooting of the politics of empire by the larger historical and tectonic shift whereby European imperialism—whatever one had thought of it—was coming to an end.[7] Comparing his perspective to that of St. Augustine during the collapse of the
Roman Empire, Woolf seeks to look beyond merely local and political

conflicts in order to grasp the massive historical transformations happening around him, to make rational and recuperative preparations for the end of Pax Britannica.[8]

Like Woolf, Eliot often cast himself in the role of Augustine during the 1930s and '40s, though for Eliot the dying fortunes of an imperial civilization become the occasion to formulate newly vital notions of the City of God. Even more to the point, Eliot's identification with Augustine becomes the basis for a complex autobiographical and allegorical poem that is deeply invested in reimagining national time and space: *Four Quartets*. By the time Eliot wrote *Four Quartets* he had already entered the Anglican Church and assumed English citizenship. Such formal acts of affiliation are indicative of Eliot's lust for roots: they make it tempting to think of the poet in these years as an ancient, grim, and determined salmon, swimming upstream against the currents of modernity and diaspora in order to find his beginnings, and of course, his ends. In this chapter, I am going to expand this received biographical reading by arguing that the poem exemplifies a wider turn from cosmopolitan aesthetics to national culture.

Four Quartets was Eliot's last great poem and the only major poetry he wrote during the last few decades of his life, when he was the very definition of a literary institution. It is both a modernist monument and a poem that addresses and enacts the historical obsolescence of modernism. In other words, it positions itself on the dialectical threshold between a modernist world in which art compensates for social and psychic fragmentation and a newly emergent community in which art integrates itself into the inherited wisdom of an entire culture. The poem's account of civilizational crisis becomes the occasion not only to imagine national renewal, but also to dissolve a romantic notion of poetry as a self-authorizing discourse into a newly emergent and classical concept of national culture. In *Four Quartets* and in Eliot's cultural criticism of the period, England, once a center of expanding temporal power, becomes the heartland of an antimodern reversion. The events of the 1930s signal a new phase of insularity and stasis for English culture, making London a privileged vantage point from which to apprehend the intersection of history and eternity.

Because Eliot occupied and defined an institutional and intellectual center of English letters during the 1930s and 1940s, his writing both reckons with history and helps to make it. The consequences of Eliot's own insular reorientation are visible not only in *Four Quartets* but in his major works of cultural criticism, *The Idea of a Christian Society* and *Notes towards the Definition of Culture*. In the chapters that follow, I will reread those documents to try to understand Eliot's shifting theories of culture and their correlation with changing generic and stylistic commitments. And because I take Eliot as both central to and exemplary of the culture of retrenchment in the English midcentury, I will also refer outward from Eliot to other writers and developments of the 1930s and 1940s.

Metropolitan Standard Time

In chapter 2, I discussed Virginia Woolf's unfinished project *Reading at Random* as an account of English literary history featuring a lost "common voice singing out of doors" and the consequent development of a socially alienated literature whose beauty was "suspended" and "derelict." Eliot's version of that story is well known; it features a devolution from the common genius of seventeenth-century culture into the undisciplined personality-mongering of romantic poetry. Like Woolf, Eliot fashioned his idiosyncratic history of English letters in part to explain the predicament of the alienated bourgeois artist in his own time. Eliot, though, had a more radical investment, not just in charting, but in righting, the course of English literature. For him, the political and economic crises of the 1930s betokened an opportunity to recapture the lost organic culture, to activate historically what had previously been the unfulfillable social and literary ideals of a young crank.

Eliot's 1921 review on the metaphysical poets contains the (in)famous critical observation that, sometime in the seventeenth century, "a dissociation of sensibility set in, from which we have never recovered."[9] Eliot, never a timid critic, goes on to dismiss two centuries and more of English poetry by pointing out that "while the language became more refined, the feeling became more crude." From Milton and Dryden to the late Victorians, English poets "thought and felt by fits, unbalanced"; worse still, they "reflected" and "ruminated" (*SP* 65). In Eliot's view, the work of these poets relies on an aesthetic of indulgent expressiveness. Quite apart from its sentimental and unbalanced nature, the problem with this poetry is its partiality, its lyric fitfulness, its inability to address the fullness of a complex modern civilization.[10]

The fracture in English culture that Eliot locates in the late seventeenth century, and his valuation of a mythic prior state of cultural and psychic harmony, can be understood in historical terms as a response to the English Civil War and the subsequent destruction of traditional communities by industrialization. After these long revolutions, Eliot's England has a split identity. On one side lies an embattled conservative culture staked out by the three terms with which Eliot famously identified himself: royalist, classicist and Anglo-Catholic. On the other side lies the triumphant modernizing strain in English culture based on Protestant, reformist, and ultimately secular forces—forces that bring with them a host of undesirable developments, including, most pertinently here, imperialism and romanticism.

Imperialism and romanticism bear an important but largely submerged relation to each other in Eliot's thinking. The link is hinted at in a 1919 *Athenaeum* review, where Eliot describes George Wyndham's essays as "the expression of this peculiar English type, the aristocrat, the Imperialist, the Romantic, riding to hounds across his prose, looking with wonder upon the world as upon a fairyland."[11] Eliot returns to the same theme a few pages later: "It would be of interest to divagate from literature to politics and inquire to what extent Romanticism is incorporate in Imperialism; to inquire to what extent Romanticism has possessed the imagination of Imperialists, and to what extent it was made use of by Disraeli. But this is quite another matter."[12] Eliot's explicit speculation about the romantic formation of imperial discourse remains a tantalizing suggestion, but the implicit linkage between romantic individualism and imperial expansion has much wider historical and conceptual significance in his subsequent thinking about English culture.

For Eliot, imperialism supplied the cultural meaning around which modern Britain organized and justified itself: empire building was not just one feature of the post-Revolutionary nation; it was the nation's central mission. And though imperialism borrowed institutional energy and inspirational rhetoric from Christianity, its baleful achievement was the worldwide export of secular and individualist values. Eliot was no critic of empire per se, but he denounced the British colonial enterprise in practice for stripping other peoples of their religious beliefs and leaving behind an anemic and alien spiritual life (*NDC* 138–39). England, too, was undone by the expansion of the modern state; the entire imperial era of Britain's history from the Renaissance to the twentieth century represents for Eliot a falling away from a golden age of premodern English culture.[13] The great divide that marks the beginning of the dissociated sensibility thus corresponds historically to a fracture in national identity that was exacerbated and perpetuated by overseas expansion.

As a self-consciously postlapsarian modernist, Eliot readily identifies the social rifts (and, let us not forget, the compensatory aesthetic privileges) of metropolitan perception. In this sense, Eliot himself has an account of the relationship between imperialism and modernism, one that accords at key junctures with theories developed in the name of cultural materialism. Eliot's near contemporary Georg Lukács, for example, tended to emphasize the problem of partial and dissociated societies as the fatal flaw of modernist literature. Like Eliot, he linked the incapacity of modern literature to address social wholes with its overcapacity to give expression to the "inner voice" of romantic subjectivity. Eliot recognized the parallels between Marxist or dialectical thought and his own sense of the vital interconnectedness between art and other levels of historical experience; moreover, as Michael North has suggested, he recognized a parallel or compatible critique of liberalism in the West.[14] Although Lukács's sense of the fragmentary and subjective nature of modern literature was not particularly attuned to imperialism (except as an element or stage of capitalism), it is the case that his presentation of the problem of lost totality shares with Eliot's a classicist investment in small, bounded places as against expansive civilizations. His idea of a harmonic or "integrated" culture rests very strongly on the (notional) boundedness of the Greek world; totality was there available within a small circle, whereas "[o]ur world has become infinitely large . . . such wealth cancels out the positive meaning—the totality—upon which their life was based."[15]

Lukács's general reading of modern literature reemerges in Fredric Jameson's more detailed explanation of the stylistic mediations that mark British modernism as the literature of the high-imperial phase of capitalism. For Jameson, as we have noted, the crucial representational problems of modernism (to which the modernists developed ingenious formal and figurative responses) stem from the absent totality of a modern colonial system in which production occurs offsite. Translated back into Eliot's terms, then, poetry under metropolitan circumstances cannot be "comprehensive"; it is always partial or "fitful," always based on particularized views, momentary impressions, bursts of lyric expression. In the absence of the organic English culture evidently enjoyed by the metaphysical poets—in the absence, that is, of a unified sensibility or a knowable community—poetry can only offer compensatory gestures to a secularized, fragmented urban readership. If the models of Williams, Lukács, and Jameson seem at times to imply an improbable and deterministic relationship between historical conditions and literary style, then perhaps we can recover Eliot's own language to recognize the aptness and subtlety of their insights. As Eliot would have it, the poetry of dissociated sensibility thrives in a culture that is dividing, expanding, and becoming more heterogeneous; in short, it thrives in metropolitan or imperial contexts.

Eliot's 1930 essay "Religion without Humanism" makes the link between fragmented souls and fragmented societies clear in this way: "I believe that at the present time the problem of the unification of the world and the problem of the unification of the individual, are in the end one and the same problem; and that the solution of one is the solution of the other. Analytical psychology . . . can do little except produce monsters; for it is attempting to produce unified individuals in a world without unity. . . . The problem of nationalism and the problem of dissociated personalities may turn out to be the same." For Eliot, souls can only be reunited when societies are reunited; until that point, the individual, and the individual's artistic or discursive products, will be mere "bundles of

incoherent impulses and beliefs."[16] The problem of "dissociated personalities" is thus also the aesthetic problem of Woolf's "derelict beauty"; until
a core (national) culture is restored, poetry may have emotional and sensuous power, but it will remain fatally incomplete. In the form of self-
conscious interiority, fragmentary perspective, or the atomized subject's
lyric plaint, such poetry always bears the signs of its merely partial vision
and its segregation from the wider culture.

Imperialism, then, animates and drives the centrifugal culture of post-
Revolutionary England, extending and prolonging the social fragmentation of modernity, while poetry (in what Eliot would identify as a broadly
romantic mode) provides it with representations of—and aesthetic compensations for—its fallen state. Of course, this description of a fallen aesthetic for the imperial age captures nothing so much as Eliot's own master-
work, *The Waste Land*. Eliot himself seemed to recognize his predicament;
in an essay on Baudelaire, he writes: "It must not be forgotten that a poet
in a romantic age cannot be a 'classical' poet except in tendency. If he is
sincere, he must express with individual differences the general state of
mind—not as a *duty*, but simply because he cannot help participating in
it" (*SP* 233). Plagued by the contradictions of a modern bourgeois existence he could neither escape nor embrace, Eliot the critical historian could
only imagine what Eliot the poet could not have: the sense of belonging to
an integrated, premodern community. Even as early as 1917, Eliot was
aware that perfect form would require not so much stylistic achievement
as social transformation. In "Reflections on *Vers Libre*," he writes: "Only
in a closely-knit and homogeneous society, where many men are at work
on the same problems, such a society as those which produced the Greek
chorus, the Elizabethan lyric, and the Troubadour canzone, will the development of such forms ever be carried to perfection" (*SP* 36). The future
tense of this sentence's main clause (in which "closely-knit and homogeneous" societies are projected into *future* possibility) contains the seed of
Eliot's mature work of the thirties and forties. In *The Waste Land*, however, Eliot still expresses the "general state of mind" using an experimental
form that admits the unfortunate circumstances of modern secular culture
and confronts the degraded milieu of the metropolis.

The Waste Land seeks to overcome the partial, lyric mode of romanticism by interpolating many styles into a long poem structured by thematic
and allusive systems rather than by the poet's own tender miseries or inner
voice. But the poem's aesthetic coherence can only substitute for a missing
organic culture; from the perspective of the classicist Eliot, it must be
understood as a second-best alternative based on culturally deracinated
"myths and symbols." A classic example of metropolitan perception, *The
Waste Land* mixes urban vignettes with source materials from alien cultures in the service of its own self-authorizing aesthetic. The anthologizing

and anthropologizing dimensions of the poem enable a formal synthesis based in large part on imperial knowledge—including, for example, the worldwide mythic correspondences of Frazer's *Golden Bough*. Its combination of urban ennui and deep anthropological play reflects Eliot's best effort at unsettling the lyric conventions of the nineteenth century, but the poem still registers its author's dissatisfaction with the broken culture and broken sensibilities that it is constrained to feature.

This reading of Eliot's metropolitan (or high modernist) phase turns largely on the poet's assimilation of a certain political geography, that is, on the lost totality of the British imperial state (à la Jameson) and on the related dilutions and divisions of English culture charted by Eliot in his own writings. But if the fissures of imperial *space* posed a challenge to modernist representation, then so too did the hollow *time* of secular history. Broadly speaking, we might say that the modernists took themselves to be waging an aesthetic and philosophical battle against a regime of dehumanizing, mechanical time. When the high modernists came of age, history seemed to be moving forward in pure, linear time as bourgeois triumphalism and European expansion reinforced the basic narrative of progress. D. H. Lawrence laments the situation: "Our idea of time as a continuity in an eternal straight line has crippled our consciousness cruelly."[17] For dissenting modernists like Lawrence, modernity's temporal regime did not represent rational progress so much as the painful succession of one valueless moment by another—what Frank Kermode calls *chronos*, the blank unfolding of time or "mere successiveness."[18] As an artistic counterdiscourse, high modernism seeks to give narrative form, aesthetic meaning, or spiritual value to time—to endow it with what Kermode calls *kairos*. *Kairos* refers to meaningful or shaped or end-directed time, time that integrates past, present, and future. Some of British modernism's most ambitious projects were motivated by the ideal of kairos and its opposition to linear history. Think, for example, of the alternative temporalities implied by Joyce's Viconian cycles, Yeats's occult repetitions, or Lawrence's apocalyptic endings. These counternarratives to secular, linear time were self-consciously marginal positions taken against the mainstream bourgeois view of history.[19]

The time of "mere successiveness" plagued Eliot, too, in his high modernist phase. *The Waste Land*'s historical horizon requires that it acknowledge the conditions of "metropolitan standard time": time drained of its meaning and space spattered into the fractured (albeit stimulating) life of the European capitals. However, Eliot's later work moves away from this high modernist formation precisely insofar as it assumes, not the continued dominance, but the potential and imminent failure, of the linear time guaranteed by modern progress and expansion. In other words, Eliot begins in the 1930s to think of his own nonlinear temporal models (based on Christian eternity) as something more than a vexed wish expressed in art. Modernism's fierce investment in the principle of kairos—its cultural Bergsonism—seemed suddenly to be confirmed and reinforced by the external machinations of history. With imperial decline and fascist rebarbarization working to discredit the progressive narratives of secular modernity, kairos migrates from its confinement within the aesthetic sphere to become the principle of what Eliot will imagine as a potential cultural revival. Under this new dispensation, his writing no longer needs to rage at shapeless time, nor to retail aesthetic wholeness to an unwhole and untimely metropolis. Instead, it begins to posit and elaborate a distinctive (and eschatological) shape for English culture.

This process, I will suggest, determines the central time-space thematics of *Four Quartets*, where chronos and kairos seek reconciliation in the ancestral village of East Coker and in the frail monuments of Little Gidding. Before turning to *Four Quartets*, however, it is worth situating Eliot in a (relatively underexplored) prewar culture of imperial contraction and reviewing his avowed positions on Englishness, modernism, and national culture. Eliot's two major works of social criticism, *The Idea of a Christian Society* and *Notes towards the Definition of Culture*, help establish Eliot's exemplary place within the network of discursive shifts that I have described as demetropolitanization. Both offer insight into Eliot's mediation between modernism's obsolescent and "derelict" beauty and the imminent possibility of a more socially integrated but less aesthetically heroic national culture.

Anglocentric Revivals

If there is one literary device that defines Eliot's place in the wider movement of retrenchment and revival in the 1930s, it is the domestication of the quest romance. As suggested in chapter 2, *The Rock* (1934) represents Eliot's first attempt to rewrite the metropolis of *The Waste Land* into a distinctly English *paysage moralisé*. *The Waste Land* organizes its shards of language and myth via the conceit of a moving observer in space. Its multicultural voyage gives an ironic and urban spin to two of the classic genres of imperial literature: the travel narrative and the adventure tale.[20] By contrast, *The Rock* reformulates the quest as a journey across time framed within one central and monocultural story: the persistence of English Christianity. Without positing an actually existing organic culture, it asserts the continued desirability of—and sudden new potential for—such a culture in postimperial England. Its version of the quest story is correspondingly more literal and urgent, less ironic and aestheticized, seeking to restore religious meaning to a genre that had come to index the impossibility rather than the presence of spiritual fulfillment. In a sense, *The Rock* reappropriates the quest tale for Christian purposes and, in the process, implicitly rejects nineteenth-century secular and imperial quest tales as mere adventurism, the pap of a corrupt culture.

The theme of a reenchanted or resacralized England defines a cluster of thirties and forties writers and distinguishes them from the more familiar "minor-chord" chroniclers of late imperial Britain, such as W. H. Auden and Graham Greene. The revivalist writers (including Eliot) tended to take national retrenchment not as the occasion for bleak cosmopolitan irony but for the recovery of literary themes and genres generally out of favor during the high modernist period. In the domestic romances of the time, England figures not as the tepid, grey civilization devoid of supernatural mysteries but as the potentially sacred ground underneath the layers of modernization.

Mary Butts's *Armed with Madness*, to take one salient example from the late 1920s, narrates the possible recovery of the Sanc-Grail on English ground. Indeed, when it appears at one point that the cup has been imported from India rather than unearthed locally, it immediately loses its value; in this scene, Butts self-consciously underscores the importance of insular rather than imperial sources of spiritual power.[21] Like *A Glastonbury Romance*, *Armed with Madness* schools English aesthetes (lately returned from the zone of continental modernism) in the fierce, uncanny power of their own terrain, which brews and bubbles with undercurrents of an animist, not Freudian, kind. Indeed, also like Powys, Butts uses the plot of rural vitalism, the "deep Pan" of the English country, to write against the novel of consciousness and its emphasis on psychological realism, which she associated with Bloomsbury modernism. Butts's interest in the domesticated quest romance as an Anglocentric and countermodernist genre intersects not only with the devolving high modernism of Eliot but with an array of other rural-religious fictions of the 1930s.

The so-called Oxford Christians, or Inklings, for example, emerged in the 1930s as well, to play popular variations on the domesticated quest romance and to reenchant the English landscape. The Inklings—whose members included C. S. Lewis, J.R.R. Tolkien, and Charles Williams—provide explicit and thematic versions of the nativist romance that appears in an abstract, mediated form in late Eliot. They shared with Eliot a certain conservative and religious formation and social ties in English literary circles. As I noted in chapter 2, Charles Williams, now relegated to the margins of literary history, was an actively publishing novelist, poet, dramatist, and critic during the 1930s; as editor of the Oxford Press, he engaged in a relationship of reciprocal sponsorship with Eliot.[22] Like Tolkien and Lewis, Williams grafted Christian theology onto popular fictional forms. But where Tolkien and Lewis gained fame in the world of children's fantasy literature, Williams borrowed his plot structures from such subgenres as the imperial adventure, the detective thriller, and the invasion-scenario novel.

Williams's "spiritual shockers" *War in Heaven* (1930) and *Shadows of Ecstasy* (1933) use pulp fiction devices to organize weighty religious themes for English readers. Williams dispenses with the comforts of middle-class morality, leaving in its place a strict Christian ethic. Eliot championed his works, declaring that a Williams novel could be read as entertainment on the train *and* as a profound narrative of the "struggle between Good and Evil as carried on, more or less blindly, by men and women who are often only the instruments of higher or lower powers."[23] Williams's work thematizes the romance of retrenchment as a recurrent, self-conscious, and self-consciously postimperial quest for local sources of magic. In *War in Heaven*, for example, Williams narrates the exploits of Sir Giles Tumulty, a globe-trotting anthropologist (à la Indiana Jones) who makes his greatest discovery not in the remote tropics but in rural England. Tumulty believes he has found the Holy Grail in an ordinary village churchyard. Profiteers quickly descend on the village to exploit Tumulty's discovery, setting into motion a nasty competition. Despite the predictable satire of local greed and vanity, Williams's transposition of the Grail quest to 1930s England is intended to draw attention to the real Christian roots of English life.

With the central figure of Giles Tumulty, erstwhile imperial adventurer, Williams makes his first attempt to rewrite colonial romance in Anglo-Christian terms. In *Shadows of Ecstasy*, however, Williams links the domesticated quest plot even more conspicuously to the moment of imperial decline. The plot turns on a massive anti-European revolt by the colonized nations of Africa (who are led by Nigel Considine, a renegade English adventurer). Here Williams updates the invasion thriller, yoking it to a positively Eliotic fantasy of desecularization on the home front. Rather than expose military unpreparedness or racial decline (the stuff of turn-of-the-century invasion fiction), Williams is out to suggest the *spiritual* vulnerability of England. He packs a stunning variety of occult sensations into the book, including sorcerer's apprentices, witch doctors, zombies, hypnosis, spirit possession, and sexual magnetism. He conspicuously rewrites Haggard's imperial romances, bringing Zulu kings to London. But despite the glut of "thriller" elements, the story unfolds as a somewhat clunky novel of ideas. At times, it reads almost like an exposition of Eliotic doctrine, with the story lines converging on the central conceit that post-Christian Europe has lost its spiritual identity and has foundered on various inadequate secular substitutes.

Those inadequate substitutes more or less define the cast of characters: Sir Bernard, a belly doctor, bases his worldview on science; Philip, his son, is committed to erotic fulfillment; Roger Ingram, a literary scholar, holds to the separate authority of art; and Ian Caithness, an Anglican priest, represents a somewhat defanged and complacent bourgeois church. Reason, Love, Poetry, Religion: these guiding values are reduced to mere hobbyhorses in the novel's satiric machinery. Having established the essential hollowness of intellectual and professional life in modern London, Williams introduces Nigel Considine, the renowned explorer who divides the world into two camps: a senescent Europe and its vigorous tropical "children." Considine propounds a radical theory of "ritual transmutations of energy" that transform men into immortals, ecstatically free from ordinary desires and from mere rationality.

Traveling to Africa to perfect his occult powers beyond the sway of European scientific orthodoxy, Considine soon accumulates worldly power by fomenting anticolonial revolt among various tribal leaders. His African "High Executive" chooses to invade England because London is "the center of the white race."[24] The immediate military goal of the invaders is African freedom, but Considine's real mission is to awaken the irrational and magical forces that are brewing just beneath the surface of modern Britain. The African High Executive thus exhorts the English people to break the chains of bourgeois rationalism: "It [the Executive] urges the English to consider carefully what they are fighting, and if any among them believe that in love and art and death rather than in logic and science the kingdom of man lies, it entreats them [to submit]" (169). Faced with that choice, Roger Ingram, the literary intellectual, becomes a Considine follower, imagining the African revolt as an irresistible force, "a huge Africa in the shape he knew from maps sliding over the water—only of course *not* sliding, but marching, millions on millions of black manikins" (217). The novel's Africans are generic and massive: a stereotyped body of "children of mankind" in whom magic and ecstasy still reside. Williams thus borrows some of the most hackneyed and reductive Manichean themes from the imperial archive, but reverses their valuations in order to mount a critique of Enlightenment rationalism.

But of course Williams, a dedicated Christian, does not wish to replace secular science with pagan idolatry. Although the revolution begins with a seductive antirationalism, it moves spectacularly past the point licensed by Williams's Christian humility. In the end, Considine's revolt fails, and Considine himself is exposed as a corrupt version of Conrad's Kurtz: the charismatic, polymathic European who, rejecting the hypocrisy of modern bourgeois life, goes too far into the heart of darkness. Considine is a perfect composite bogeyman for a conservative thirties intellectual: his revolt combines the irrational forces of mass culture, global finance, and occult vitalism. In its failure, though, Considine's ecstatic movement reflects the vulnerability of a spiritually bankrupt culture.

The point of Williams's plot is that secular Europe makes easy prey for the *wrong* form of irrationalism—a point that anticipates Eliot's later observations on fascism. For Williams, as for Eliot, the principles of pluralist England are not principles at all; they are a moral vacuum that leaves the country open to class revolution, imperial bloat, economic collapse, and cultural inanition. In *Shadows of Ecstasy*, the protagonists learn too late what modern England has lost: a proper, measured respect for nature and God, appreciation of social hierarchies, and the binding value of Christian traditions. Indeed, the one consistent value that emerges in the novel is respect for the "mighty forms" of the English seventeenth century. Williams uses an inverted imperial romance—the conquest of the center by the colonies—in order to imagine or propose the revival of a traditional spiritual and communal life in England. The novel's motivating fantasy is that the sudden end of imperialism becomes an occasion to repair the damage done to England by modernity. And it is this fantasy that defines the conservative (Eliotic) response to British decline as an occasion to stop projecting grand mystery onto the periphery and to recapture it within a respiritualized core.

The anti-Enlightenment, counter-Revolutionary values that motivated Williams at the crucial moment of civilizational contraction also animate the work of J.R.R. Tolkien, perhaps the most enduringly popular Inkling. Like Williams, Tolkien uses narrative fantasy to engage and emplot the kinds of Christian quests that emerge as shrouded allegory in Eliot's poetry. Despite Tolkien's assiduous avoidance of contemporary political reference, his works can be understood as part of a distinctive romanticization of Englishness that flourished in the 1930s. Fred Inglis has, for example, situated Tolkien's "anti-modernist" nostalgia in the context of an entire wave of thirties culture that includes Vaughan Williams and Benjamin Britten, the artists John and Paul Nash, and politicians like Winston Churchill and Lord Reith—all figures invested in the "myth of an atavistic transhistorical Englishness."[25] Of course, a romance of Englishness had sustained both imperial and anti-imperial forms of thinking in Britain long before the 1930s; we have to distinguish among various strands of that romance in order to isolate the new and significant features of this imminently *post*imperial moment in English literature. In the case of Tolkien and the other Oxford Christians, it is more than simply the coincidence of imperial contraction and a burgeoning school of Anglocentric fantasy. This group of writers understood their literary function to be quasi-shamanistic; as "sub-creators" of the divine pattern, they mediated the universe's mysteries for the workaday minds of modern readers.[26] Their shared concept of authorship also reconceived the metropolitan marketplace as an organic culture. The Oxford Christians wanted to restore a kind of mythic truth-value to literature, rather than the specialized value that accrued to the popular realism of the Victorians or the alienated virtuosity of the modernists. In other words, their anthropological vision of the writer's role was determined neither by market relations nor by freestanding aesthetic ideologies but by the production of a complete allegorical system of truth that would resonate with an English audience's latent Christianity—a literary self-conception that corresponds in obvious ways to the later Eliot's.

It is, of course, the completeness of Tolkien's fictional universe that accounts for his sustained popularity; few fantasy worlds come with the full genealogical and etymological density of The Hobbit and The Lord of the Rings. These works reflect—indeed, are organized by—a deep connection to archaic elements of English language and landscape. A scholar of Old English, Tolkien explicitly conceived of his work as the discovery of "a mythology for England," as a "body of more or less connected legend . . . which I could dedicate simply: to England, to my country."[27] Like Kipling and Eliot and many others who mined the old island for its magical resources, Tolkien came to England as a colonial outsider. Born in South Africa, he spent his first few years in Bloemfontein before his family resettled near Birmingham, so that his home country was in some sense also a foreign place: "the place where I belonged . . . was totally novel and strange."[28] These biographical facts, combined with the contemporaneity of The Hobbit and "Burnt Norton," make it interesting to read Tolkien alongside Eliot. As outsiders-cum-insiders, both writers manage to glimpse an innocent ideal of Englishness underneath the metropolitan crust of fading industry and empire. Tolkien's fiction evokes timeless, rural England: a country shire, plenty of food, artisanal production, stable social relations, a commonly felt sense of tribal belonging, the warm comforts of ale, roasts, and tobacco after dinner. But as this list suggests, we are talking about a deliberately modest and homey brand of myth making. These cozy atmospherics offer nice dramatic contrast to the heroic quests that structure Tolkien's plots. In this sense, Tolkien's hobbits offer a distilled and historically apt version of little England's self-image on the eve of the Second World War: as Gareth Knight observes, they are a small "race" that is "parochial, conventional, . . . but capable of immense loyalty, devotion and—when pushed to it—heroism."[29]

In Tolkien as in Eliot, realistic and romantic elements converge in a discourse that manages to both reenchant England and recover its ordinariness. These writers have an Anglocentric vision of the "mythic everyday" as a set of vital yet plain traditions that defines, not just a polity, but a community. It is to such a vision that Eliot dedicates his essay on The Idea of a Christian Society (1939). However, Eliot disavows both candied images of Merrie Englande and triumphalist stories of national progress.

As he wrote to Bonamy Dobrée in 1939, Eliot feared "galvanisation into artificial revival" as much as he feared further spiritual decay.[30] The unflexible anti-utopian foundation of *The Rock* remains firmly in place: a state of grace—whether individual or national—can only be pursued with humble fidelity and no hope of actual reward. Despite his dedication to rebuilding the root stock of a cherished national culture, Eliot is by no means sanguine about England's redemption from modernity.

Eliot begins *The Idea of a Christian Society* by deprecating liberal England's lack of purpose or identity: "By destroying traditional social habits of the people, by dissolving their natural collective consciousness into individual constituents . . . Liberalism can prepare the way for that which is its own negation: the artificial, mechanised, or brutalised control which is a desperate remedy for its chaos."[31] Liberalism breeds social atomization, whose aesthetic result is the alienated high art of European modernism; that same atomization also triggers the political reaction of European fascism. So far, this would be a familiar parsing of Eliot's thought in terms of class division at home and totalitarian politics on the continent, with Eliot's own position staked to an embattled and insular minority culture of Christian traditionalism. What has been less noted is Eliot's implicit argument that the contracting British state had already begun to make liberal pluralism untenable. He argues that a pallid philosophy like liberalism could only serve as a functional social consensus during the era of "free exploitation" and of industrial/imperial growth (*ICS* 14). In the absence of that growth, the emptiness of "worm-eaten" liberal thought becomes glaringly apparent, destabilizing the pluralist democracies. Without a colonial mission, Eliot suggests, England's lack of communal purpose is crippling: liberalism gives way to ever more nebulous versions of itself, creating the vacuum to be filled by the shrill and dangerous politics of the 1930s.

The Idea of a Christian Society seizes on the potentially fruitful cultural possibilities of a homogeneous and unencumbered England. The *idea* of a Christian society is the idea of restoring positive values to a nation long held together by the negative freedoms of liberalism and by the faltering ideology of empire. The essay invokes a rule of inverse proportion, as it were, between the obvious exhaustion of the imperial mission and the potential energy of a domestic cultural revival.[32] The centuries-long dilution of what was, for Eliot, a poignantly finite entity, English culture, has now reached a crisis point: "At a period when each nation has less and less 'culture' for its own consumption, all are making furious efforts to export their culture, to impress upon each other their achievements in arts which they are ceasing to cultivate or understand" (*ICS* 32). But crisis points are also turning points: Eliot calls for the domestic rebuilding of

English culture to replace its global export, arguing that a "Christian organization of society" is "perhaps now more than at any previous time possible."[33]

Rather than produce more and more refined comparisons of world cultures on the model of Frazerian anthropology, Eliot calls for the English to attend to their own languishing traditions. The artistic ideals implied by this rhetoric are impossibly prelapsarian: artists cannot simply cultivate authenticity once they and their traditions have been integrated into the international traffic in ideas. But what makes this essay interesting is not so much its conservative goals as its anthropological methods. He proposes that England learn to emulate primitive societies "upon a higher plane," without "sentimentalising the life of the savage" (*ICS* 49). His effort to lay bare the primitive roots of English community becomes clear in this condescending commentary on D. H. Lawrence:

> The struggle to recover the sense of relation to nature and to God, the recognition that even the most primitive feelings should be part of our heritage, seems to me to be the explanation and justification of the life of D. H. Lawrence, and the excuse for his aberrations. But we need not only to learn how to look at the world with the eyes of a Mexican Indian. . . . We need to know how to see the world as the Christian Fathers saw it; and the purpose of reascending to origins is that we should be able to return, with greater spiritual knowledge, to our own situation. (*ICS* 49)

Clearly Eliot has no wish to persist in artificial or mimetic forms of primitivism that try to borrow back tribal virtues from the colonies. Instead, he proposes a revival based on pre-Revolutionary England, which he idealizes as a permanently exemplary organization of church and state, of art and faith, of town and country.

The Idea of a Christian Society takes up the possibility of reestablishing a proper (premodern) relationship to God and nature in surprisingly pragmatic terms. For example, in a fascinating literalized version of the "waste land" conceit, Eliot laments the problem of soil erosion that has forced English agriculture overseas. Like all true organicists, he takes seriously the origins of the term "culture" in agriculture, venerating the life of the soil as the basis for good and proper social relations. Without the engagement of English workers in producing the total food supply for the island, Eliot fears continued cultural and spiritual decay (*ICS* 49). In a 1938 *Criterion* commentary, he makes his point plain:

> To understand thoroughly what is wrong with agriculture is to understand what is wrong with nearly everything else. . . . What is fundamentally wrong is the urbanization of mind . . . which is increasingly prevalent as those who rule, those who speak, those who write, are developed in increasing numbers

from an urban background. To have the right frame of mind it is not enough that we should read Wordsworth, tramp the countryside with a book of British Birds and a cake of chocolate in a ruck-sack, or even own a country estate: it is necessary that the greater part of the population, of all classes (so long as we have classes) should be settled in the country and dependent upon it.[34]

If England, facing isolation from continent and colonies, were to become a more complete and self-sustaining domestic economy, then the ground for cultural revival would be prepared. In this sense, the political crises of the 1930s inspired Eliot to contemplate the possibility of restoring precisely the kind of economic relations that Jameson sees as missing from metropolitan life.

Eliot's preoccupation with the lost balance between town and country and his interest in reintegrating a fractured economy point up the comprehensiveness of his interest in the process of demetropolitanization. This is no mere literary movement or stylistic revolution but a chance to herald full-scale changes in economy and culture. Eliot's Tory theorization of the relationship between culture and economy begins to look back on the era of modernism and imperialism from the vantage point of some future, more complete national culture and economy. His phrase "urbanization of mind" diagnoses the problem of the modern in terms that comport with the Weberian concept of rationalization, with Simmel's account of the metropolitan mentality, and with Lukács's rhetoric of lost totality.[35] Eliot's most forceful case for a "Christian society" turns on the *integration* of otherwise fragmented classes and ideas into a more complete social vision, a "pattern into which all problems of life can have their place" (*ICS* 50).

Eliot's radical-conservative sense of the possibilities for social and aesthetic change in the 1930s thus connect his thinking to a broad materialist critique of capitalist anomie and reification. But his articulation of organic-conservative *values* is probably better understood within a British lineage of anti-industrial nostalgia that includes Burke and Coleridge. Eliot's general debt to these latter figures has been well and amply studied, though it is worth recalling them here in order to emphasize how important the rhetoric of insularity was to their views of national culture. Burke's image of a compact and fruitful plot is (as noted in chapter 1) the national beau ideal that attracted Eliot (and Forster) to an Anglocentric romance of retrenchment. After all, Burke's valuation of homogeneous, closed societies translated into skepticism about the dangerous infinities not only of the French Revolution but also of the British Empire—another modern form of European politics spilling out of an old nation's borders. As for Coleridge, the ideal of an equipoise between "Permanence" and "Progress," as articulated in On the Constitution of Church and State, is distinctively English and insular.[36] What may sound at times like political theory is in fact national history: "It is the chief of many blessings derived from the insular character and circumstances of our country, that our social institutions have formed themselves out of our proper needs and interests."[37] Coleridge's myth of insularity—a myth according to which England's political innocence depends on its status as a kind of cultural Galapagos cut off from dangerous continental influences—resurfaces in Eliot's antidiasporic imagination during the 1930s.[38] In the organic-conservative tradition of thought, bounded insularity had once provided England with the conditions for good politics and good art; it is not surprising, then, that Eliot could greet the retrenchment of the British Empire as an occasion to reconsolidate the lost wholeness of national culture.

Through the shared rhetoric of cultural revival, Eliot and other thirties intellectuals (not all of them conservatives) laid claim to national heritage in the name of a resurgent myth of organic community. But as Louis Menand notes, Eliot's increasing commitment to a religious version of orthodoxy and tradition carries him beyond the bounds of the Burke-Coleridge organicist lineage, to a point where supernatural stability eclipses natural growth.[39] It is precisely Eliot's central notion of Christian eternity that marks his Englishness as a nativism rather than a nationalism. Redeemed or nonmechanical temporalities do not correspond to the life of a modern, pluralist nation, which, as Benedict Anderson and Homi Bhabha have argued, requires the empty homogenous time of secular modernity. Eliot's late writing on temporality provides a crystalline example of the rhetorical process that Bhabha describes as "the teleology of progress tipping over into the 'timeless' discourse of irrationality."[40] Eliot's England, then, is not a nation but a community of belief that displaces nationhood while claiming its name and its territory.

Eliot's conservative vision of the English past requires no further commentary in itself, but it becomes more interesting when reconstructed as part of a larger response to imperial twilight on the part of English intellectuals who presided over the modulation from a cosmopolitan-elite model of Literature to a national-popular model of Culture. That broad project engaged not only the Anglican conservative Eliot and the Bloomsbury liberal Woolf but also, as I will suggest in chapter 4, the leftists of the early days of Cultural Studies. In their phase of the process, modernists like Eliot and Woolf called upon traditional and classbound notions of Englishness, but they called upon them in the interest of a more capacious, participatory and "ordinary" idea of culture. For the Eliot of *The Idea of a Christian Society*, the aesthetic culture of the metropolis was beginning to yield its place in history. Modernist formations and institutions begin to seem like a provincialism of the mobile cosmopolitan elite, who crossed national borders freely but remained alienated within their own societies:

"We write for our friends—most of whom are also writers—or for our pupils—most of whom are going to be writers; or we aim at a hypothetical popular audience which we do not know and which perhaps does not exist. The result, in any case, is apt to be a refined provincial crudity" (*ICS* 31). Art's alienated status—its sequestration in the circles of cosmopolitan modernism—would, Eliot implies, be mitigated by the establishment of a Christian society. The potential reintegration of art and community in England, then, would be a happy by-product of the end of metropolitan perception. Eliot clarifies his position in a 1937 *Criterion* commentary: "Perhaps modern art is international, and if so, that may help account for its weakness. I cannot think of art as either national or international—these, after all, are modern terms—but as racial and local; and an art which is not representative of a particular people, but "international," or an art which does not represent a particular civilization, but only an abstract civilization-in-general, may lose its sources of vitality."[41] If art is to retain its source of vitality, then, it must do so in the framework of a locally and racially defined culture. Naturally, then, for Eliot, England must come to name not the administrative capital of a multinational empire, nor a modern multicultural nation, but an organic and traditional culture. The redefinition of tradition from an amoebic international canon to an ethnically exclusive culture is a gesture that marks Eliot's reaction to the heavy weather of 1930s politics and economics. But Eliot's thinking was neither merely reactionary nor merely nativist. He did not rest content with the idea of a Christian society developed in the course of the 1930s but complicated and extended his thinking on national culture in his major critical work of the 1940s, *Notes towards the Definition of Culture.*

Notes from a Shrinking Island

The concept of "Christian society" gave Eliot a way to broker an English peace between universal truth and local history, but it also forced him to place perhaps too much emphasis on the coherence and importance of a single national culture. Like Forster and Woolf, Eliot valued an organic English way of life but harbored serious doubts about nationalism in most of its available forms. In *Notes towards the Definition of Culture* (1948), he complicates the myth of insularity with reference to European connections outside England and regional diversity within England. In a series of canny double maneuvers, he builds difference back into his model of a self-identical, self-possessed England. Although few commentators have considered the essay in this context, *Notes towards the Definition of Culture* is a document of postwar *and* postempire reconstruction: in it, Eliot considers the problem of preserving cultural dynamism in an England already reverting to minor or insular status.[42] The essay aims to register the historical necessity of nationalized culture without capitulating to mere nativism or losing sight of what Eliot takes to be the transnational truth of Christian incarnation.

Tempering the programmatic idealism of *Idea*, *Notes* strikes a more analytical pose, stating over and again that culture evolves in an unconscious, undirected process. Eliot's insistence on that point reflects his horror at fascism's attempt to administer cultural order from the top down. In this treatise, Eliot confronts a very basic problem: as an organicist, he cannot advocate for a particular culture-building program but must concentrate on "preparing the ground" for a revitalization that can only proceed on its own. Authentic culture, in his view, bubbles up from the soil and takes slow shape in a defined space. Chthonic Burkean metaphors dominate the essay's language and give continual emphasis to the idea of a natural web or ecology of cultures. Thus, in Eliot's model, England has emerged slowly as a distinctive national entity, but it occupies only one level within a system of cultural diversity that includes both sub- and supranational entities. This layered model allows Eliot to acknowledge that England is neither fully autochthonous nor exceptional while isolating and celebrating a dense and coherent body of national traditions. Amidst the frayed and tattered networks of the global web, England can be seen as a solid object or a core culture: in Eliot's view, this is not "invention" but rediscovery.

The essay warns against the fantasy of resurrecting some putatively original culture: "I am quite aware that any local 'cultural revival' which left the political and economic framework unaffected, would hardly be more than an artificially sustained antiquarianism: what is wanted is not to restore a vanished, or to revive a vanishing culture under modern conditions which make it impossible, but to grow a contemporary culture from the old roots" (*NDC* 127). Straining toward transitivity, the verb "to grow" signifies the trouble with Eliot's noninterventionist intervention: who or what "grows" a culture? (the same question has afflicted post-Keynesian politicians who wish to claim credit for "growing" an economy that also grows itself). Clearly, for Eliot, cultural revival must be unaware of itself as such; it can be neither sentimental nor governmental. Eliot's account of English life describes a sad devolution from *having a culture* to "knowing culture." Of course, Eliot cannot simply wish away the self-conscious multiculturalism that emerged on the way to international and imperial modernity, but he does make that form of self-consciousness the true object of analysis in *Notes*.

In fact, *Notes* reads at times like a survey of the inevitable and malign cultural effects of migration and colonialism. Modern imperialism has created mongrel and self-conscious cultures on *both* sides of the colonizer/ colonized divide, from England to India to the settler colonies of Australia, New Zealand, Canada, and the United States. In the latter cases, the settlers could only bring "a part of the total culture" of their homelands (*NDC* 138), producing a bastardized partial culture of the kind Eliot himself abandoned when he made his way back to the putative totality of the Anglo-Christian homeland.

Notes idealizes closed and homogenous societies whose cultural identity is based on spontaneous self-possession rather than on a weary, worldly knowledge of the other. But it is precisely that worldly knowledge of the other (in the form of the ethnographic archive) that gives Eliot the material to frame and exemplify his idea of unself-conscious cultural being. The Bornean Dyaks, for instance, are cited as a tribe that has a culture without knowing it in the decadent European way (*NDC* 96). And, speaking more generally, Eliot writes:

> The researches and the theories of anthropologists have played their part, and have led us to study the relations of imperial powers and subject peoples with a new attention. Governments are more aware of the necessity of taking account of cultural differences; and to the degree to which colonial administration is controlled from the imperial centre, these differences become of increasing importance. One people in isolation is not aware of having a "culture" at all. (*NDC* 165)

Here Eliot is not concerned to critique ethnocentrism, just *self-consciousness* about cultural difference. The imperial center or metropole had become a factory for national comparisons and a marketplace for the consumption of difference. The half-buried subtext of the essay turns on the question of whether, with the props of empire removed, such a center could remove itself from the play of differences and "reascend to origins." Although framed as a general analysis of the culture problem, the essay often implicitly takes England as the paradigmatic metropolitan space— the leading edge of modernity and therefore of modernity's end.

After England, the most significant national example in *Notes* is India, a country crippled in Eliot's view by its incongruous mix of traditions— a patchwork culture made still less coherent by the half-secular, half-Christian British Raj. Eliot particularly regrets the more recent phases of British rule, in which the colonizers exceeded their economic mission in order to impose alien cultural practices on India. Cultural imperialism had, by the 1940s, left India in a lamentable state of "partial westernisation," its people discontented with native values and doomed to invidious knowledge of cultural differences (*NDC* 166).[43] The failures of empire, then, are not political:

To point to the damage that has been done to native cultures in the process of imperial expansion is by no means an indictment of empire itself, as the advocates of imperial dissolution are only too apt to infer. Indeed, it is often these same anti-imperialists who, being liberals, are the most complacent believers in the superiority of western civilisation, and at one and the same time blind to the benefits conferred by imperial government and to the injury done by the destruction of native culture. According to such enthusiasts, we do well to intrude ourselves upon another civilisation, equip the members of it with our mechanical contrivances, our systems of government, education, law, medicine and finance, inspire them with a contempt for their own customs and with an enlightened attitude towards religious superstition—and then leave them to stew in the broth which we have brewed for them. (NDC 167)

With typical antiliberal conviction, Eliot makes clear that the most dangerous legacy of colonialism is the spread of Enlightenment rationalism and the consequent erosion of local customs and beliefs.

If colonialism erodes traditional life, national culture kept inside its "natural" or conventional boundaries, can guarantee, by contrast, a certain degree of authenticity and continuity. Indeed, although *Notes* gives due recognition to various strata of culture, what finally goes unchallenged here is the preeminence of the nation as the proper seat of *a* culture. As an unmarked singular noun, "a culture" in these essays almost always corresponds with political nationhood, that is, with the state. By contrast, subnational units (such as Scotland or Wales) are understood as components *within* a culture and supranational units (such as Europe) are understood as systems *to which* a culture or cultures may belong. Even at this semantic level, the essay assumes that anthropological totality is proper to the nation-state. The national bond supersedes internal antagonisms and affiliations; it is always more significant than the "community which each class has with its counterpart in another society" (NDC 124). This formulation not only opposes (in predictable Tory fashion) the idea of working-class internationalism but also casts doubt upon the solidarity of the cosmopolitan elites whose internationalism was so central to the development of interwar modernism.

While celebrating the roots of a viable national culture, though, Eliot does not shrink from pointing out the historical artificiality, political danger, and aesthetic stultification implied by crude nationalism. In the appendix to *Notes*, entitled "The Unity of European Culture," he argues for England's place within Christian Europe as a useful counterweight to the narrow horizons of insularity.[44] As Frank Kermode (among others) has noted, Eliot's church represents a continuous and properly European cultural unit—a holy empire—that extends from Virgil through Dante to the present.[45] With the imminent loss of such non-Christian annexes as India,

Eliot now can imagine England's reintegration into that original and legitimate *imperium*, the "universal church" of Christian Europe, which fostered the "highest culture that the world has ever known" (*NDC* 106). Consistent with the organic logic developed in *Idea*, England (since its colonization by Rome) *represents* Christendom gnomonically; it is an independent and complete Christian society. In this way, Eliot trades the old internationalism of the empire with its secular model of expansion, assimilation, and hybridization, for a more static model of representativeness. The nation does not transmit its values by imperial dynamism but incarnates them.

Seen in retrospect, then, Eliot's work seems to manage England's transition from empire to nation by insisting on the value of bounded particularity. This aspect of the essay is nowhere more clear than in Eliot's brief, prescient treatment of Anglo-American cultural relations. The essay describes a new phase of Western imperialism, casting the United States as the border-spilling colossus dealing fatal blows to local culture: "America has tended to impose its way of life chiefly in the course of doing business, and creating a taste for its commodities . . . I mention that influential and inflammable article the celluloid film. American economic expansion can be also, in its way, the cause of disintegration of cultures which it touches" (*NDC* 168). Where British imperialism once threatened the integrity of traditional cultures in places like South Asia, now the traditional core culture of England itself was becoming vulnerable to the colonizing forces of Hollywood.[46]

Eliot's insight into this reverse colonization points up not just England's eclipse by American power but also the relative advantages of English citizenship. An island nation makes a much more suitable home for a conservative soul than does an expanding multicultural empire. Such a soul naturally viewed the provincialization of English culture not as a loss of global prestige so much as a gain in cultural vitality and coherence. Robert Crawford has characterized Eliot's career as energized throughout by a provincial identity defined against an English center, but I think that Eliot maintains his provinciality in the wartime period precisely by coming to occupy the English center.[47] Eliot was in fact quite explicit about the desirability of English intellectuals learning to see themselves as regional: "The problem [of cultural diversity] can only be properly seen when Englishmen become regionalists too."[48] Following a path already blazed by the merciless course of history, Eliot proposes that England now become a self-contained regional culture rather than an unmarked center of comparative knowledge.

Where *Idea* lays claim to national culture from a particular (and somewhat farfetched) antimodern vantage point, *Notes* has a less tendentious rhetoric that aligns it with a different branch of thirties writing: the documentary geared to the description of culture as a quotidian, ordinary, and popular way of life. Culture, Eliot writes, comprehends such things as, "Derby Day, Henley Regatta, Cowes, the twelfth of August, a cup final, the dog races, the pin table, the dart board, Wensleydale cheese, boiled cabbage cut into sections, beetroot in vinegar, nineteenth-century Gothic churches and the music of Elgar" (*NDC* 104). George Orwell's almost contemporaneous essay "England Your England" offers a similar catalogue: "[t]here is something distinctive and recognizable in English civilization. . . . It is somehow bound up with solid breakfasts and gloomy Sundays, smoky towns and winding roads, green fields and red pillar-boxes."[49] These evocations of a shared national culture work by appealing to details that are homey yet stirring, apparently realistic yet also highly conventionalized. It is precisely here, where Eliot tries to cloak the theoretical bones of a culture concept in the real flesh of everyday English life, that the true import of his cultural criticism comes to light.[50] His treatises couch a conservative romance of Englishness in the rhetoric of anthropological realism. The ordinariness—even the populism—of the dart board and the beetroot are fused to the concept of a "total way of life" in a move that sanctifies and unifies ways of life that are neither sacred nor homogenous. But the point is not so much to call out the ruse in Eliot's rhetoric as to recognize its historical importance in midcentury England: after all, the fusion of romantic and realistic elements in Eliot's concept of national culture are what make him so central a figure in the period and what carry his influence beyond the narrow confines of his sectarian interests all the way to the origins of Cultural Studies in the 1950s.

If Eliot urges England to come to terms with its own particularity or provinciality, he also recognizes in *Notes* that England retains its central status in the older cultural system of the British Isles, which includes the Celtic "regions" or, as he calls them, England's cultural satellites. To understand the role of the so-called Celtic fringe in Eliot's vision of postimperial English culture, we need to review three related problems that have surfaced in the analysis of Eliot so far. First, having suggested the value (indeed, the necessity) of a consolidated Anglo-Christian culture, Eliot must come to terms with the potentially stultifying effects of homogeneity. Second, having projected a return to organic community as one consequence of demetropolitanization, Eliot has to consider that the subordination of the specialized arts to a living "total culture" would obviate the need for romantic, lyric expression. As a successful poet of the modern era, Eliot naturally retains a latent attachment to those specialized aesthetic forms that provided sustenance during the long, dark era of secular modernity. Third, having attempted to take stock of both sameness and difference within a single national culture, Eliot must confront the central problem of perspective—the problem that has since taken root as the disciplinary crisis of anthropology. Eliot's acute analysis of this last problem reads like an excerpt from the playbook of anthropological theory: one cannot know one's own culture without knowing other cultures, yet one cannot really know other cultures so long as one truly belongs to one's own (*NDC* 113–14). To summarize: Eliot needs a source of cultural difference, one that can be counted on to provide a certain kind of lyric poetry (as a pleasing compensation for the continual disintegration of art and religion), and one calculated to provide a manageable quantum of cultural difference. Enter the Celt as proximate "other."[51]

Notes towards the Definition of Culture describes Scotland, Wales, and Ireland as "satellite cultures" because of their dependence on the English language, but emphasizes their vital and distinct contributions to English poetry. The Irish, for example, with the vestigial lilt of their native language, add an enriching rhythm to English (*NDC* 127). In a similar access of Anglocentric condescension, Eliot asks whether "the Welsh *qua* Welsh are of any use" (*NDC* 130). The answer is yes, but not as an autonomous culture so much as colorful providers of the "cultural friction" that catalyzes the English literary tradition. Indeed, Eliot concludes, "the disappearance of the peripheral cultures of England . . . might be a calamity." Eliot's conception of an archipelagic "ecology of cultures" thus combines a Darwinian head with an Arnoldian heart: it acknowledges that imperial powers absorb smaller and weaker cultures but maintains an interest in preserving rare cultural game to enrich the life of the otherwise philistine modernity of the major power.[52] At the same time, however, Eliot is eager to reattune the ear of his readers to "the more humble local peculiarities of England itself" (*NDC* 131–32). The essay establishes a mixed and dialectical position on the Celtic fringe: it assumes English dominance, but it also relativizes England as one national culture among others. Because it relies on England's linguistic hegemony, the essay is able to try to reclaim for England the status of a whole and wholly particular national culture. In other words, Eliot finally wishes to try to seize an opportunity to undo the imperial/Arnoldian legacy, that legacy which held that England was the spiritually defunct modern center for a set of satellites that possessed vital folk cultures.

Eliot's blueprint for spiritual revival in England depended on the relativization of England, on remaking it as a national culture that no longer consumed the rich traditions of subordinate nations while letting its own attenuate and ossify. This commitment no doubt motivated Eliot's sponsorship of a figure like Hugh MacDiarmid, the Scottish poet and nationalist who offered an explicit and prescient case for the relativization of English culture. Eliot's *Criterion* published MacDiarmid's seminal essay "English Ascendancy in British Literature," which offers an early formulation of literary and cultural questions that we would now recognize as postcolonial. MacDiarmid not only addresses the lost traditions of Irish and Scots writing due to England's "sorry imperialism" but takes account of the emergence of "genuine independent literatures" in the rest of the English-speaking colonies and dominions. Here MacDiarmid alludes matter-of-factly to contemporary "changes in the Imperial organization which will deprive England of the hegemony it has maintained too long."[53] MacDiarmid's essay thus marks a moment in the 1930s when an English intellectual like Eliot could start to come to terms with the literary-historical effects of national retrenchment.

Like Eliot, MacDiarmid sees a convergence of two broad and potentially salutary processes at work in 1930s Britain: the relative diminution of English imperial power and the relative eclipse of literary institutions by national-popular culture. He argues that the work of cultural revival in all the "British" nations will restore a folk vitality that had been lost in the era of the lonely modern genius. Echoing Eliot's essay on Marie Lloyd and affirming Eliot's efforts to revive the verse drama as a neotraditional popular from, MacDiarmid writes: "The only literature which is at the same time vital and popular, is the literature of the music-hall. . . . But it is just a possibility—and no more than a possibility—that the music-hall song and its allied forms—music-hall patter and revue libretto—contain the germ of a new popular poetry. It is significant that the only poems which suggest such an art are some of Mr. T. S. Eliot's recent poems."[54] MacDiarmid's motto here might also be Eliot's: "get back behind the Renaissance," meaning return literary practice to that cherished point where it was possible to have what he calls a "self-contained national culture." He expands his critique of Renaissance internationalism:

> The antithesis of Renaissance art in this regard is national art. To some it may seem as if the Renaissance has justified itself in thus introducing a common strain into the art-consciousness of all European countries. That common strain was certainly brilliant, shapely, worldly-wise, strong, if not indeed gigantic, over-abounding in energy, in life. Yet all the time there was a latent weakness in it, a strain, a sham strength, an uneasy energy, a death in life. . . . It therefore dazzles us rather than moves us.[55]

This passage anticipates Virginia Woolf's diagnosis of modern art's fall into "derelict irrelevant beauty" and captures the dissatisfaction registered by Eliot with both Renaissance internationalism and romantic individualism. Much as he valued the European tradition, Eliot (unlike Pound) came increasingly to subordinate an intercultural pantheon of genius to a more insular and self-contained notion of national culture.

The MacDiarmid connection suggests how significant Eliot's awareness of England's dwindling hegemony was to his ideas of cultural revival in the 1930s and '40s, even if that awareness was sometimes only tacitly expressed. The complicated and highly mediated brand of nativism that emerges out of *Idea* and *Notes* bears comparison to an array of anti- or postimperial nationalisms for which MacDiarmid was an early spokesman. Like so many postcolonial intellectuals in the era of the early Cold War (and despite the obvious historical differences involved in writing, as it were, from the center), Eliot interprets the end of empire as an opportunity to grow a new national culture from old roots—roots long obscured by the impositions of imperial modernity. That the modernizing forces of imperialism emanated from the ruling class of Eliot's own adopted nation does not make it any less plausible that Eliot would celebrate their diminishment.

If we read *Idea* and *Notes* as a double response to the moment of national retrenchment, we can see a dialectic of local and supralocal culture, a two-stage attempt to manage the obsolescence of metropolitan aesthetics and the emergence of a newly cohesive and significant national culture. Even so, these essays in cultural criticism do not quite arrive at a conceptual formation that is able to do justice to the claims of English culture as a particular totality while avoiding the pitfalls of cultural relativism—the pitfalls of merely belonging to Forster's "drab sisterhood" of nations. In order to synthesize the local and the universal in a manner befitting the imperial crisis and national opportunity, Eliot required the complex and allegorical form of *Four Quartets*. Its poetic language and structure recast and fuse the dilemmas that remained imperfectly inscribed into the serial and discursive logic of Eliot's critical writings. In the pages that follow, I reread *Four Quartets*—with its infamous paradoxes and dizzying repetitions, its spinning images and tight structures—with an eye toward relating its form to a particular set of historical developments. As I read it, *Four Quartets* both reflects and projects a new, postimperial horizon for English culture and a new, classical aesthetic dispensation. That aesthetic depends on the capacity of national tradition to give shape to temporal history and, moreover, to play host to absolute truths that outstrip the limitations of temporal history. In a sense, then, the rereading of Eliot's late criticism and poetry through the lens of colonial and postcolonial history allows us to come to terms with their relationship to a now (in)famous category of analysis: national allegory.

Four Quartets and the Chronotope of Englishness

To reread *Four Quartets* in the context of imperial contraction is to bring new critical tools to the longstanding debate about the poem's relationship to nationalism. The debate divides those who see the poem as ultimately Anglocentric, territorialized, provincial, or patriotic from those who see the poems as ultimately abstract, deterritorialized, conceptual, nonnational(ist). Critics on both sides have been stymied by Eliot's labeling of the last three quartets as "patriotic" poems: is this a possumy trick or sincere self-description? In the end, I think most readers of *Four Quartets* discount the possibility that Eliot is imagining a uniquely or even necessarily English redemption of time, pointing out, in the words of one critic, that Eliot's "true *patria* is in the hereafter."[56]

We can perhaps shift and update the terms of this debate if we concentrate on Eliot's role in the midcentury reconceptualization of English culture as a concrete totality. In my view, the poem's overarching investment in Christian renunciation does not exclude its relation to specific events and conditions in England. This is not to argue that the poem advocates for nationalism (implicitly or explicitly) as a *value*, but that a new and historically contingent concept of national culture is among the poem's conditions of possibility. Such a reading does not simply split the difference between the local and the universal; it describes their reciprocal constitution as made possible during a certain phase of national retrenchment in England. If the poem refuses either the "localist" or the "universalist" reading taken separately, it does so because of its place at the diachronic switchpoint of a major historical transition, in which the very meaning of culture in England had to be comprehensively rethought. Our reception of the poem should, therefore, try to account for changes both in material history and in the discursive responses to that material history that changed Eliot's conception of national culture in the period 1935–45. With the broader transition in view, we can be precise about the poem's mediation between metropolitan modernism and the revived regionalism of British poetry in the second, "postimperial" half of the century.

Four Quartets records the full phenomenological density of the here and now even while attempting to transcend the here and now. The poem's beauty and complexity stem from its superimposition of those two processes onto each other, so that its subject remains attached to local dimensions of history ("Now . . .") and geography (". . . and in England"), but cannot meaningfully dwell in those dimensions without aspiring to grasp larger patterns of time (eternity) and space (the universe). The poem recognizes that historical time only has meaning in relation to worldly entities like the nation or the person. At the same time, it sees those entities as screening out a more capacious and eschatological time. Using an extended allegorical form, it coordinates the two types or "levels" of time, conferring the significance of a more stable and infinite pattern on the agonies and vicissitudes of merely personal or merely historical experience. The presence of an allegorical method could itself be said to signal Eliot's turn from a classicist critique of romanticism to a classical practice per se, since allegory is the form capable of registering the completeness of human sensibility and social organization, the form that gradually disappeared in the long Romantic era.[57]

Although it is possible to pursue questions of national history through a thematic reading of *Four Quartets*, such a reading would be of limited value without an accompanying consideration of how shifts in national history are registered and mediated by form. In particular, Eliot sees a new way to use allegory that had perhaps not been possible so long as he was positioned as the deracinated and ironic urban persona trading in symbolist aesthetics. Allegory, as it operates in *Four Quartets*, requires an idea of national culture; it seeks meaning across time but from within the fixed bounds of a given tradition. The commitment to allegory thus marks a distance from *The Waste Land*, which seeks "myths and symbols" that confirm meaning's travel across cultures.[58] If England exerts gravitational pull on *Four Quartets*, it also allows for an unbounded set of temporal reflections. This relation between restricted notions of cultural space and dilated, deepened representations of time defines the "chronotope of Englishness" that organizes *Four Quartets*.[59] Needless to say, I take this most fundamental feature of the poem as reflective of the larger relationship in midcentury England between imperial contraction (compression of space) and historical self-consciousness (which for Eliot means the effort to mesh the gears of secular history and Christian permanence).

With this larger perspective of *space* in mind, let us begin by noting that all four *Quartets* are, more humbly, poems of *place*. The overall pattern of the poem's geography is that of an out-and-back movement, from England to America and back to England. "Burnt Norton" refers to a Gloucestershire country house that Eliot visited in 1934; "East Coker," is the village in Somersetshire where the Eliot family lived, the place from which Eliot's ancestor Andrew Eliot left for the new world; "The Dry Salvages," takes its name from three islands off Cape Ann, in Massachusetts, where Eliot vacationed as a boy; and "Little Gidding" refers to an English village that was home to the seventeenth-century Anglican religious community founded by Nicolas Ferrar. Beyond these mostly rural settings, Eliot's original title for the sequence was "South Kensington Quartets"—a reminder of the central role that London continues to play in Eliot's work. The last three are wartime poems; in them, as many critics have noted, the speaker views the city from the perspective of a local air-raid warden.

Spirits in Place: "Burnt Norton"

The opening five lines of "Burnt Norton" make an inhospitable threshold for the reader:

> Time present and time past
> Are both perhaps present in time future,
> And time future contained in time past.

If all time is eternally present
All time is unredeemable.[60]

At once diffident and dogmatic, these lines establish the central theme of "Burnt Norton" and of *Four Quartets* in general: the problematic intersection of time and the timeless, of competing temporalities defined by secular history and Christian eternity. The co-presence and mutual inherence of past, present, and future mean a rejection of the idea that historical epochs are fundamentally distinct. But what are the historical conditions that motivate Eliot to make this syllogism and then to extend it into long poetic form? My reading of the poem proposes that Eliot's antihistoricism can itself be historicized, that is, explained by reference to a particular epochal transition.

"Burnt Norton" quickly trades its syllogisms for ghostly evocations of a rose garden, creating an odd tonal mix. Yet both sections of the poem engage the Proustian problem of lost time. The rose garden seems initially to trigger personal recollections, but Eliot makes the garden out of non-memories, out of what might have been (one enters the garden, after all, through a portal that "we never opened"). The scene's motif of invisible laughing children has been linked to Rudyard Kipling's story "They," which features a ghostly country house populated by skittering, tittering childhood spirits.[61] Certainly the comparison clarifies the tone of "Burnt Norton," which is more uncanny than a nostalgic idyll but less spooky than a ghost story. What is still more suggestive about this connection is that the enchanted gardens in "They" form part of Kipling's larger turn away from imperial settings and toward a romance with rural England—a turn that Eliot celebrates in his 1941 introduction to Kipling's verse.[62]

The garden scene in "Burnt Norton" initiates a pattern of ephemeral visions that shapes the opening sections of all four parts: next come the Tudor dancers of "East Coker," then the vanished fisherfolk of "Dry Salvages," followed by the Royalist ghosts at "Little Gidding." "Burnt Norton" also establishes the importance of intricately permuted verb tenses (a technique on display in "Ash-Wednesday" as well) to Eliot's larger discussion of temporality. The poem reckons with a past that can neither be revived nor revisited, yet which haunts the present as an adumbration of the way things ought to be. Eliot needs language that can do justice to the irreversibility of modernity *and* to the permanent value of ideals established in England four centuries ago. To pull off this delicate feat, he filters the past (both personal and national) through a screen of contorted conditionality.

Complicated tenses, elaborate paradoxes, and even simple puns help establish the poem's idea of times and places that are both fleeting and permanent. Hence the modesty topos that precedes our glimpse of the rose-garden:

> My words echo
> Thus, in your mind.
> But to what purpose
> Disturbing the dust on a bowl of rose-leaves
> I do not know.   (14–18)

The frailness of Eliot's afflatus indicates that the poem binds its own meaning up with an inaccessible past and a future that continually recedes into potentiality. Still, the rose garden (favored locale of medieval Christian allegory) evokes a childhood that could have been, a love that almost was, a spiritual state—both individual and collective—that might yet be. As the passage reaches its high pitch of enchantment, a dry concrete pool fills with water: "And the pool was filled with water out of sunlight, / And the lotos rose, quietly, quietly" (37–38). This revivification turns on the verb "rose"; the shift from noun (rose garden) to verb (lotos rose) indicates the poem's own movement from a static description of fallen, abandoned "dry" states (à la *The Waste Land*) to a dynamic allegory organized by the action of revival.

It is fitting, then, that the next section opens with a methodological reflection on allegorical language and procedure, equipping the poem at large with its basic technology of correspondence:

> The dance along the artery
> The circulation of the lymph
> Are figured in the drift of stars   (54–56)

The passage establishes a choral voice in counterpoint to the veiled autobiographical references of section 1 and announce a series of alignments between body and nature, soul and cosmos. The parallel drifts of organismic and universal systems signify the symmetries of a divine plan, but they also provide, in formal terms, a basis for the poem's overall allegorical pattern, in which the story of the poet's struggle to recover a workable sense of his position in time recapitulates the wider community's struggle to recover a workable sense of its position in history. The first fifteen lines of section 2 propose a narrative arc not of redemption but *toward* redemption. They pan back to a cosmic perspective from which all entwined dyads (organic/inorganic, blood/wire, garlic/sapphire, boar/boarhound) are absorbed into an ultramundane order of stars.

The poem shifts its frame of reference to reveal that apparent opposites are not only resolvable but in fact already and always resolved at a higher level. Although the resolution "lifts up" paired opposites, it does not resolve them dialectically. Rather, the poem describes a process of revelation, in which all merely temporal contradictions are reconciled to each other from a transhistorical perspective. The resolution does not transform the clashes of the present into some new and dynamic state (with its own contradictions) but absorbs them into a pattern that is, in a word, timeless. It is as if the poem wishes to suggest that dialectical thinking represents the best human *approximation* of divine thinking, but remains naturally limited by its lack of transcendental concepts. However, even if there is a pattern beyond or above history, we cannot simply overleap time to reach it. Humans must, after all, suffer time as imperfect souls. This principle of original sin, the foundation of Eliot's antiutopian thinking, is thus the foundation of his commitment to history as such. His poetic achievement is to keep framing and reframing the reciprocal relationship between historical experience and celestial order. Allegory works to sublate temporal phenomena into eternal order, but it also prevents the poem from prematurely leaching real time out of human experience. It is in this sense that *Four Quartets*, though it has been received by many readers as a retreat from history into religion, is actually a confrontation between history and religion.[63]

The imagery of "Burnt Norton" sets the mold for that larger confrontation through a series of spatializations of time—not just the particular geography of rural England that seems to imply its own "lost time" in section 1 but also the famous "still point of the turning world" in section 2, which defines a temporal problem in terms of its location. In place of the moving observer of *The Waste Land* (whose motion in space allows, in the Aristotelian fashion, the apprehension of time), "Burnt Norton" centers on the "still point," a poetic representation of immobility designed to reverse the Aristotelian formula and indicate timelessness. The poem thus revises the chronotope of the modernist urban quest. Where urban transport appears in other modernist works as a vehicle for sensory stimulation and social commingling, here the London tube serves as a figure for a blank and static purgatory.

In fact, Eliot revisits and revises several key motifs drawn from his earlier and most successful poetry. For example, the London section of "Burnt Norton" reworks at large the spiritually agonized cityscapes of Eliot's first two volumes. Of course, the "twittering world" of the city is still a blasted and wasted space, but the poem emphasizes passage beyond, not in, it. Where *The Waste Land*'s final section represents a thunderous but distant apocalypse, "Burnt Norton" points to a more immediate but more muted, almost involuted, transcendence of urban squalor. The city here is less a sensuous attractive-repulsive habitat of the kind Eliot learned to represent from Baudelaire than an austere site of self-denial and thus of ascetic withdrawal. When we read the lines "Desiccation of the world of sense, / Evacuation of the world of fancy" against the concluding stanzas of "Preludes," for example, the poet's evacuated imagination contrasts sharply with his earlier luxurious investment in curling, clinging fancies gathered around the city's refuse. The younger Eliot had mixed sensual excitement and moral horror into a distinctively metropolitan irony; the Eliot of *Four Quartets* seems to damp down the sensuous details and the emotional pangs in favor of longer, slower emotional rhythms designed to capture not so much the agony of bourgeois civilization as the process by which such agony is purged and purified. Likewise, the flash of the kingfisher's wing as a twilight augury in section 4 seems almost directly to invert the Fisher King—a sly echo of *The Waste Land* that emphasizes the difference between pervasive multicultural myths and bare allegorical signs.

Backed by the dim dusk of the Underground in section 3 and the flower-wilting twilight of section 4, the poem repeatedly dramatizes its own withdrawal from the merely sensuous to the allegorically significant, from elaborately self-justifying imagery to precise, partially glimpsed omens. Thus in *Four Quartets* Eliot displays an austerity or purity that departs from the verbal richness of his earlier work.[64] For readers devoted to Eliot's earlier work, the stylistic asceticism of *Four Quartets* can seem forbidding. But it is only when he removes the sensory clutter and kaleidoscopic urban detail that the poem can approach what he now represents as the purifying darkness of redemption.

The tension between verbal detail and patterned meaning becomes explicit in the final section of "Burnt Norton":

> Words move, music moves
> Only in time; but that which is only living
> Can only die. Words, after speech, reach
> Into the silence. Only by the form, the pattern,
> Can words or music reach
> The stillness, as a Chinese jar still
> Moves perpetually in its stillness.   (143–49)

The time-ridden aspect of language itself can be purged in pure form, in a classical pattern that removes all traces of partiality, temporality, mortality—all the trivial signs of a merely personal style, all the accidental phenomena of a merely historical moment. The poem announces a classicist attempt to effect pure form while acknowledging that its attainment may be beyond the artistic power or the historical horizon of its maker. Classical perfection, as embodied in the Chinese jar, is a hallmark of closed, traditional societies, where aesthetic production is based on rule-based design rather than on personal expression. In other words, such forms emerge and hold value within a community of utterly and unconsciously shared values. Eliot seems bent on a new type of classicism, for which the conditions of possibility—so palpably absent in the modernist metropolis—now seem to be realized in a society coalescing around its traditional, insular core.

For Eliot, classicism defines both ethical and aesthetic ideals, linking an ascetic Christianity back to Hulmean formalism. Moreover, the process required to achieve such ideals applies both to the individual (the poet) and to the culture (the nation). Consider a typical temporal conundrum in "Burnt Norton":

> To be conscious is not to be in time
> But only in time can the moment in the rose-garden,
> The moment in the arbour where the rain beat,
> The moment in the draughty church at smokefall
> Be remembered; involved with past and future.
> Only through time time is conquered. (90–95)

The riddle of these lines has been unraveled before: consciousness (of values, of essences beyond the merely temporal) requires a suspension of time, but experience and memory (which are made of time) are necessary preconditions and preparations for that consciousness. In personal terms, the passage seems to suggest that an achievement of a spiritually meritorious kind of consciousness, an awareness of permanence, depends on living through moments defined by an ordinary and painful knowledge of loss. What has been less often considered is the poem's allegorical extension of this same principle to the collective or cultural level. From that perspective, we might think of history (experience) as the necessary precondition for collective spiritual readiness. A collective ability to conceive of timelessness requires having suffered and lived through a certain accumulation of (national) experience. To put it another way: there is a necessary quantity of moments, of accumulated cultural tradition, that lays the groundwork for a culture's ability to project itself beyond history. English Christianity, with its historical depth and stability (as idealized by Eliot), has accreted a sufficient amount of continuous experience for it to get beyond mere historical time. Thus Eliot's provisional "conquest of time" depends on a cultural formation whose specific history allows it to store—and to symbolize—transhistorical values.[65]

Significant Soil: "East Coker"

If this reading of "Burnt Norton" seems to stake abstract temporal conceits too closely to the ground, then perhaps the genealogical romance of "East Coker" can be said to confirm the importance of native soil. Eliot's search for his own aboriginal English identity is one of the many meanings embedded in the sphinxlike opening line: "In my beginning is my end." The homecoming of "East Coker" does not simply reverse the diaspora of the English Eliots, it also shifts the enchanted meditations of "Burnt Norton" into a more direct presentation of England as a kind of historical preserve. It evokes the rural past in order to isolate values that have, so to speak, survived modernity, but it does not propose a nostalgic return to vanished folkways. In fact, the opening lines reject easy recuperations of time, suffusing their images with the pathos of historical loss:

> In my beginning is my end. In succession
> Houses rise and fall, crumble, are extended
> Are removed, destroyed, restored, or in their place
> Is an open field, or a factory, or a by-pass.   (1–4)

Like the garden of "Burnt Norton," the abandoned fields and lanes of East Coker will become the setting for a brief glimpse of a happier time and a brief surge of hope. As before, the poem's language emphasizes not the memory itself so much as its fragility.

With this in mind, we can follow Eliot's pathway through a Somerset-shire lane to the Tudor period. Moving cautiously forward, the poem discovers a rustic scene, presented in words cited from *The Boke of the Governour* by Tom Eliot's forebear and namesake Sir Thomas Elyot:[66]

> In that open field
> If you do not come too close, if you do not come too close,
> On a Summer midnight, you can hear the music
> Of the weak pipe and the little drum
> And see them dancing around the bonfire
> The association of man and woman
> In daunsinge, signifying matrimonie—
> A dignified and commodious sacrament.
> Two and two, necessarye coniunction,
> Holding eche other by the hand or the arm
> Which betokeneth concorde. Round and round the fire
> Leaping through the flames, or joined in circles,
> Rustically solemn or in rustic laughter
> Lifting heavy feet in clumsy shoes,
> Earth feet, loam feet, lifted in country mirth
> Mirth of those long since under the earth
> Nourishing the corn. Keeping time,
> Keeping the rhythm in their dancing
> As in their living in the living seasons   (24–42)

I quote at length because the most noticeable feature of this passage about rhythm is its own stately rhythm: Eliot holds both the dance and the lines to a slow, measured time with flatly accented syllables. The words themselves bespeak a series of "necessary conjunctions"—images of joining, of pairs, of completed circles, of the rhyming and jibing of nature and culture in the romanticized agrarian space. Eliot's words *keep time*: in both form and content, they capture the ways in which moving bodies and verbal expressions can give shape to time. The poem's own rhythms, in this sense, provide a formal proxy for the redemptive time of the ritual circle.

Using Tudor orthography and ancestral citation, the scene evokes a specific place and time, but treats it as a zone of anthropological time-lessness where the rhythms of music and the seasons replace the time-worn "ruined houses" motif of the opening section. The conjugal dance takes place in the kind of organic community that Eliot idealizes in his cultural criticism: a place where time and the timeless do not need to be labored back into conjunction by dint of virtuoso poetic effort but consort innocently in the realm of the everyday.[67] Yet if the gaze of the reader tarries too closely, too lingeringly on the rustic dance, the scene threatens to become a mere touristic sop to sore metropolitan eyes. The fragility of this *tableau vivant* captures the predicament of Eliot's revivalist writing: any call for a "revival" functions perforce as a sign of loss and belat-edness, as an index of the long hard fall from gemeinschaft to gesellschaft.

The strains apparent in Eliot's vision of the English past announce more than a complication of atavistic theme; they also point to a self-conscious crisis of poetic means. Thus section 2 of "East Coker" opens in a tight metrical form bound together by close rhymes and hieratic symbols, but quickly gives way to a deflationary, prosaic self-commentary. The initial, highly patterned movement echoes the cosmic correspondences of "Burnt Norton," playing a refrain on the stars/wars rhyme to indicate the return of the poem's bass note, a deep allegory of elemental and universal strug-gle. The plight of the poem's speaker carries over, too, so that the language of lost time meets the language of cosmic allegory and mixes with it. At this point, the theme of temporal disturbance extends to several levels of the poem: the poet's awareness that his life's autumn brings not accumu-lated wisdom but a renewed sense of inadequacy mirrors a larger collapse of linear time in the natural world (the "disturbance of spring" haunts a late November).

As these fairly conventional lyrical images turn to prose, autobiographi-cal elements rise to the fore, providing a tally of the poet's dissatisfaction with writing that does not come any closer to truth than it ever did:

> That was a way of putting it—not very satisfactory:
> A periphrastic study in a worn-out poetical fashion,
> Leaving one still with the intolerable wrestle
> With words and meanings. The poetry does not matter.   (69–72)

This passage, read in the context of the entire sequence, signals a determi-nation to generate poetic forms adequate to the moment. Eliot declares the inadequacy of older types of symbolic condensation or periphrasis;

the passage's images of fire and ice—conventional signs of apocalypse—are "worn-out." Aesthetic recapitulations of apocalyptic time (a hallmark of modernist writing) are losing their power and interest. The oscillation between periphrastic and discursive language in Four Quartets bespeaks a newly skeptical attitude toward poetry itself. Just as "East Coker" begins to gather symbolic momentum, signifying aspects of eternal time that cannot be addressed in prose, Eliot switches over to prosaic lines that deflate the incantatory power of the more formal passages. It is as if the poem seeks to dissipate its own energy, the prose supervening to announce its own referentiality and transparency. Unlike poetic language, prose tends not to arrogate independent or absolute value to itself. It may not be hyperbolic to say that for Eliot at this point, the self-authorizing formal power of high modernist poetry would verge on a kind of secular idolatry—displacing or distracting from belief rather than encouraging or expressing it.

In a sense, then, the text works antipoetically, exposing the limits of poetry even as it extends them. Alternating between tight hieratic verse and slack essayistic prose, Eliot avoids the middle ground of modernist vers libre and pastiche. Throwing the value of periphrasis into question, the poem announces its own intention to find a transparent (yet visionary) form. Of course, few contemporary readers find Four Quartets especially accessible, perhaps because its content becomes more profound and paradoxical even as its form becomes more discursive and direct. The difficulty stems from complex extrapoetic concepts, not from the a priori symbolist principle that poetry cannot name its object. The poem challenges its own authority by questioning the potency of language-in-itself and by establishing a conspicuous commitment to the vitality of collective practices. Ambivalence about the value of poetic language is not new for Eliot, but his striving after objective style—the old struggle to make Inner Voice yield to Outer Authority—finds a new toehold in the projected image of an English national culture. Within that culture, a classical brand of artistic impersonality could come out from the shadows of Eliot's critique of romanticism. In Four Quartets, the impersonal ideals that motivated the younger Eliot's experimentation now reach fulfillment not as a function of style per se but as a function of extratextual assumptions about cultural solidarity or national tradition.[68]

The old romantic-classical contest between artistic expression of self and artistic submission to collective values returns in "East Coker" and recalls a set of images from "Burnt Norton," wherein the darkness of spiritual redemption competes with the light of aesthetic pleasure. In "East Coker," the purifying darkness surfaces in the trope of "death the mighty leveler":

> The captains, merchant bankers, eminent men of letters.
> The generous patrons of art, the statesmen and the rulers,
> Distinguished civil servants, chairmen of many committees,
> Industrial lords and petty contractors, all go into the dark,　(104–7)

This vision of darkness rising leaves the self-important elite of a secular civilization without a "motive of action." But material decay prefigures spiritual redemption. This passage records Eliot's unsentimental response to the historical crises of the 1930s in the form of a national allegory, offering a vision of remote salvation to a nation in immediate decline. Faced with war—and with the wider failures of cosmopolitanism—these poems propose a kind of national ascesis. Ascetic themes also cinch the poem's basic allegory: for both an old master poet and an old European nation, the same dark night of the soul becomes a station on the long stony path to redemption. In this time and place, for both poet and nation, the way down becomes the way up.[69]

The poem's delicate investment in ascetic rebirth should not, of course, be taken as a patriotic pep talk; it does, however, urge patience on both the suffering soul and the faltering nation. In a series of similes, Eliot qualifies the process of self-negation whereby a "dark night" (modeled on that of St. John the Divine) becomes a lingering prelude to salvation:

> I said to my soul, be still, and let the dark come upon you
> Which shall be the darkness of God. As, in a theatre,
> The lights are extinguished , for the scene to be changed
> With a hollow rumble of wings, with a movement of darkness on darkness,
> And we know that the hills and the trees, the distant panorama
> And the bold imposing facade are all being rolled away　(113–19)

Grover Smith identifies the "rumble of wings" as a neat sonic device for referring to the air war, but a larger historical process may inform the entire theatrical metaphor.[70] The removal of the "distant panorama" and the "bold imposing facade" do not just evoke a momentary suspension *between the acts* of a play but also provide an oblique commentary on England's narrowing horizons and hollow facades.[71]

The next attempt to figure the purifying darkness elaborates the idea of consciousness suspended in time:

> Or as, when an underground train, in the tube, stops too long between stations
> And the conversation rises and slowly fades into silence
> And you see behind every face the mental emptiness deepen
> Leaving only the growing terror of nothing to think about;
> Or when, under ether, the mind is conscious but conscious of nothing　(120–26)

The terror of everyday "mental emptiness" captures in psychological terms the exacting state of readiness demanded by Eliot's idea of a purgatorial threshold. Such readiness replicates the equipoise of the still point in "Burnt Norton": the image of a train caught between stations revises the kinetic organization of such metropolitan modernist classics as *Ulysses* or *The Waste Land*, where cognitive and aesthetic faculties are catalyzed by movement. In this poem, the suspension of the journey, the negation of movement, and the absence of distracting "panoramas" all contribute to the receptiveness of both soul and community. The master trope of immobility runs across the quartets, reworking Eliot's richly agonized "metropolitan perception" into a kind of sensory negation. In fact, Eliot seems deliberately to revise his own image stock as a way to mark out new territory. Hence Prufrock's etherized evening sky (a projection of the suffering bourgeois ego) becomes an etherized mind whose ascetic receptiveness extends outward from the subject to an entire community.

If *The Waste Land* represented a degraded city, void of meaning except for that derived from the self-authorizing form of the poem itself, *Four Quartets* points to a wider culture teetering on the threshold of redemption. But salvation is by no means guaranteed even for the fit soul or the fit society. Lest the poem's vision of self-possession (individual or national) produce a sanguine attitude about human perfectibility, section 4 of "East Coker" reminds us of the essential ill-health of a sinful humanity. Where the younger Eliot imagined that Art could give order to a disordered society, the Eliot of *Four Quartets* tends to subordinate artistic to cultural order, individual expression to collective tradition. Hence section 5 returns Eliot to the limits of his own poetic achievement:

> So here I am, in the middle way, having had twenty years—
> Twenty years largely wasted, the years of *l'entre deux guerres*—
> Trying to learn to use words, and every attempt
> Is a wholly new start, and a different kind of failure
> Because one has only learnt to get the better of words
> For the thing one no longer has to say, or the way in which
> One is no longer disposed to say it. And so each venture
> Is a new beginning, a raid on the inarticulate
> With shabby equipment always deteriorating
> In the general mess of imprecision of feeling,
> Undisciplined squads of emotion. And what there is to conquer
> By strength and submission, has already been discovered   (177–88)

Eliot's admission that the old techniques of writing are now "shabby equipment" and that the old themes are "the thing one no longer has to say" convey his valedictory stance toward the literature of the interwar years. High modernist practice must be reconceived and reinvented, as part of a continual coming-to-terms with history and with the truths that, for Eliot, lie beyond history.

The poem not only announces its own passage beyond the cult of aesthetic originality but also begins to recalibrate and reorient the language of conquest with its "no worlds left to conquer" motif. The passage goes on to contravene the modern or romantic doctrine of originality ("there is no competition") whereby the artist is a contending genius determined to produce what has never been seen before. Modernism, in this sense, could be seen already in retrospect as the last phase of a misguided secular culture of innovation and expansion. As noted above, Eliot had always sensed a link between the romantic drive to originality and the imperial drive to new territory. In response to these twin and quintessentially modern drives, the poem simultaneously classicizes its own aesthetic and domesticates the rhetoric of expansion. "East Coker" ends by reworking two key narratives of empire, the discovery and the mission, so that they describe the recovery and conversion of England itself.[72]

In the final section of this dazzlingly centripetal poem, then, Eliot arrives back at the starting point to find that the recovery of his roots at "East Coker" has aesthetic and philosophical consequences:

> Home is where one starts from. As we grow older
> The world becomes stranger, the pattern more complicated
> Of dead and living. Not the intense moment
> Isolated, with no before and after,
> But a lifetime burning in every moment
> And not the lifetime of one man only
> But of old stones that cannot be deciphered.   (196–202)

Here the poem cuts a fine distinction between the allegorical method of "a lifetime burning in every moment" and the epiphanic (high modernist) investment in the "intense moment isolated."[73] Indeed the entire poetic sequence offers a buried commentary on the limits of modernist poetry as an aesthetic of autonomous fragments (as in The Waste Land). Eliot makes his interest in the programmatic subordination of autonomous fragments to the overall meaning clear in his late essay on Yeats (written at almost the same time as "East Coker"): "The course of improvement is towards a greater and greater starkness. The beautiful line for its own sake is a luxury. . . . What is necessary is a beauty which shall not be in the line or isolable passage, but woven into the dramatic texture itself" (SP 255).[74] In the allegorical organization of Four Quartets, images and lines have meaning only in relation to a spiritual narrative that preexists and provides cultural ground for the text. Whereas The Waste Land borrowed Frazer's mythological positivism, laying bare the common threads of quest narratives from many cultures, *Four Quartets* returns to the runic roots of allegory, finding scripts and stones that cannot be fully collated, interpreted, or known.

If the figure of indecipherable stones neatly captures Eliot's gnostic classicism, it also gives concrete form to Eliot's confrontation with history as the unfolding of a partially glimpsed allegory in which personal and communal crises are simply blips in a cosmic pattern of recurring struggle and deferred redemption. Authentic national and personal self-conceptions, therefore, depend on partial recoveries of the past combined with disciplined rejections of nostalgia. The past can no more guarantee redemption of time or from time than can the future. The assimilation of eternal to historical time can only be approached asymptotically; it cannot be achieved on the secular plane of history or mortality. What must remain elusive—and yet continually sought—in *Four Quartets* is precisely that awareness of the co-presence of time and the timeless that would give shape and meaning to biological and historical entities, to souls and to nations.

Wild Time Unseen: "The Dry Salvages"

"The Dry Salvages" moves the sequence from England to America and to the waters of Eliot's youth: the Mississippi River and the ocean off Cape Ann in Massachusetts. As the master tropes of section 1, the river and the sea seem to both reinforce and to oppose each other; it is difficult to parse the prepositional distinction between the river "within" us and the sea "all about" us. In one sense, the two bodies of water metaphorize anew the relationship between individual and collective experience. The river recalls a personal past (the "nursery bedroom"), whereas the sea expands into layers and depths that include all of biological and geological creation ("the whale's backbone"). True to the theme-and-variations structure of *Four Quartets*, Eliot here produces a new set of temporal and spatial figures that are not simply adjacent to, but embedded in, one another, as allegorical sets and subsets to each other.

Elaborating the marine motif, the first section establishes a cultural site in which the apprehension of nonlinear time is possible. The "time not our time" in this poem (like that of the enchanted garden in "Burnt Norton" or the rustic dance of "East Coker") emerges from a reverie that fuses memories of childhood to evocations of primitive culture. In this case, the poem envisions fisherfolk whose rhythms chime with both time and the timeless. The clanging bell at the end of the section first sustains, then terminates, the keynote of that wild time, "older than the time of chronometers"—the time that cannot subsist in history-haunted societies that have forsaken their gods.

Section 2 inveighs against the complacent historicism of the modern temper, posing the poetry of "natural" and cyclical human labor against a prosaic meditation that rejects popular "notions of evolution." The organic life of the fisherfolk stands as a distant exemplary image of an unchanging life where harsh, ongoing struggle brings scant reward, but where humans maintain the proper humility before fathomless nature. Eliot wishes to expose the superficial meliorist cant by which modern individuals and modern societies congratulate themselves on their victories over time. Humanism's fatuous notion of progress has convinced us that we can assign our own meaning to the irreducible mysteries of time. Writing against the secularized or psychological (i.e., modernist) notion of epiphany, Eliot recodes defining moments as lucky extrusions of collective and cosmic experience whose proper emotional correlate should be not self-satisfaction at human insight but "primitive terror" at human ignorance. To assimilate and mute that terror with rationalist psychology or with the "assurance of recorded history" blinds the modern mind to deeper layers of struggle. But the ambition of the poem is not simply to dismiss the surface buzz of modern knowledge in favor of ancient portents and struggles; it is to try to discover the mutual inherence of the two registers of experience, the two layers of temporality, so that readers can see them not just as "mere appearance" and "true reality" but as two versions of the same thing, two reciprocally constituted elements of time.

Section 3 of "The Dry Salvages" returns to a syllogistic mode, dissecting modernity's fallacious habit of misassigning origins and ends. Dissection then gives way to exhortation, as readers are urged to reconceive their place in time, to recognize that "time is no healer" and that the self does not exist in the luxury of time's improvement, but dies as an evanescent ripple in a vast temporal ocean. The poem wishes to dislodge the habit of linear thinking, to find a way to pry back the layers of secular time-consciousness and restore a kind of time-innocence, a new dispensation under which time would mean a natural persistence and a divine insistence, not the human(ist) clock that ticks forward in an endless trivial spillage of time.

Given that this is the so-called "American" quartet, it might be tempting to argue that the poem associates the apprehension of "wild time" or time-innocence with the American frontier. Indeed, the title "Dry Salvages" signals primitivism insofar as Eliot tags it as derived from the phrase "les trois sauvages" (though his derivation may be incorrect, it is still relevant interpretively). And the poem describes a brawny brown river god of the Mississippi as a kind of animist divinity. However, the poem's full view of life on the Mississippi ends up focusing more on the enterprising energies of the new republic than on the atavistic spirits of its frontier. America, in fact, exemplifies, not the persistence of older communities of belief, but the rapid modernization that separates its citizens from the "daemonic, chthonic" time of the river god. By implication and by its position relative to the other three quartets, the poem tends to point the reader back to England, which is not only Eliot's ancestral homeland but also a nation that has exhausted itself on the secular, mechanical, imperial enterprises of modernity.

Section 5 of "The Dry Salvages" contains the poem's most overt broadside against the preening fallacies of humanist, historicist, and technological triumphalism. As always, the poem insists on the limitations of human foresight. In this passage, we can grasp with utter clarity the difference between *The Waste Land* and *Four Quartets*. The Frazerian undercurrents of the former tended to emphasize myth making as a cross-cultural effort to make meaning out of a bewildering collective fate; by contrast, the gnostic undercurrents of *Four Quartets* suggest that culture should not interpret the unknowns of human experience so much as forestall excessive curiosity about them.

Thus, "Dry Salvages" catalogs a range of vain human methods of divination (from astrology and graphology to cow guts and tarot cards), observing a consistent inability to conceive eternity. Over the course of the poem, Eliot rejects secular interpretation as incomplete. Attempts to grasp the meaning of historical time founder on the rock of eternal time; they fail to make sense of authentic human destiny:

> For most of us, there is only the unattended
> Moment, the moment in and out of time,
> The distraction fit, lost in a shaft of sunlight,
> The wild thyme unseen, or the winter lightning (211–14)

We only have "hints and guesses" about the past and the future, a meager understanding of our place in the universe. Such hints and guesses fill the poetry of secular modernity: they are the symbolic and epiphanic moments of romantic expression, but they offer no comprehensive or abiding insight into the deeper narrative of redemption adumbrated by *Four Quartets*.

The ascetic and gnostic ideals embodied in "The Dry Salvages" mean that religious striving should continue without immediate promise of reward; they implicitly reject the existential heroism of the modern individual who struggles against meaninglessness, even that specialized modernist hero, the artist, who seeks to overlay historical chaos with formal order. Instead, the poem proposes a humble acceptance of the moment when life (whether individual or collective) reverts back to patterns whose significance is suprahuman and suprahistorical:

We, content at the last
If our temporal reversion nourish
(Not too far from the yew-tree)
The life of significant soil.   (235–38)

The conceit of "temporal reversion" speaks to the idea of death made tolerable not so much by expectations of a hereafter but by the reversion of life to "significant soil," to an eternal pattern whose closest proxy on earth is long-lived national tradition. And if we remain in doubt about whether the enchanted nexus of tradition and territory has, for Eliot, a particularly national dimension, then his elaboration of the figure of "significant soil" in "Little Gidding" lays such doubt to rest.

World's End: "Little Gidding"

The first three quartets begin by measuring the passage of time (figured as lost youth, crumbled houses, the modernized river), then give way to scenes of suspended time. But "Little Gidding" announces the motif of frozen time from the very first:

Midwinter spring is its own season
Sempiternal though sodden towards sundown,
Suspended in time, between pole and tropic.   (1–3)

Like those earlier images of an eternal present (the enchanted garden, the rustic dance, the *ostinato* of the sonorous buoy bell), this interseason generates beautiful lines but makes tough conceptual demands upon Eliot's presumably secularized readership. As metaphor and metaphysical conceit, "midwinter spring" defines a frozen moment of recognition, but it also figures an eternity that spills beyond the horizons of both the past and the future as conceived by humanists and historicists. When the snow blossoming on the hedgerows of "Little Gidding" threatens to billow outward and claim the poem for eternity's sake, Eliot's stern negations quickly intercede to remind us that this is not a romantic affirmation of limitless life but a scrupulously turned image of death-in-life.

In other words, "Little Gidding" reestablishes the keynote of *Four Quartets*: not the denial of historical time, but the coordination of that time with a more profound but less apparent eternal order. The opening lyric, dedicated to an anomalous springtime outside the "scheme of generation," captures the poem's effort to subdue the bad infinities of mere sequence with the permanence of pattern and rhyme. This delicate process—which requires that the poem neither surrender to the demands of clock time nor renounce them altogether in a premature grab for eternity—moves gingerly. "Little Gidding" approaches Little Gidding the way "East Coker" approaches East Coker, with a set of reverential conditional phrases: "If you came this way, /. . . If you came at night like a broken king / If you came by day not knowing what you came for" (21–28). These eggshell-thin exigencies (impossible to fulfill) are designed to reprove a touristic dalliance with national innocence. In this village, Nicholas Ferrar founded a religious colony that Eliot takes to be the sacred center of royalist Anglican culture. The poem commemorates the martyred King Charles's visit to the colony, which was later "desecrated by the Roundheads."[75] For Eliot, Little Gidding is a specific site that incarnates the values of pre-Revolutionary England, a permanent set of truths made valid by devotion. But:

> There are other places
> Which also are the world's end, some at the sea jaws,
> Or over a dark lake, in a desert or a city—
> But this is the nearest, in place and time,
> Now and in England. (36–40)

Little Gidding has no exceptional status; it is simply the handiest example of a place where prayer and faith have elevated a human community beyond mere worldliness. Still, we should not miss the significance of nearness and exemplarity; the poem stakes itself to the idea that culture and belief proceed from the ground beneath your feet.

The double logic of place-and-placelessness mirrors the more familiar formula of time-and-timelessness in the poem. The first section of "Little Gidding" closes by converting time into space while emphasizing the reciprocal necessity of the local and the transcendent:

> Here, the intersection of the timeless moment
> Is England and nowhere. Never and always. (54–55)

In a visual pun befitting the metaphysical protocols of the poem, "nowhere" can read as "now/here": now and here or, as in "Burnt Norton," "quick now, here now, always." Thus, even as the line wants to explode outward toward abstract indeterminacy, the word manages to split on itself and return us to the immediate site. This tight superimposition of the transcendent and the local is what perpetuates the critical debate about the poem's Englishness—a debate complicated by the poem's further conflation of the national and the local. Does "nowhere" take England or Little Gidding as its opposite? Is it *in* Little Gidding that "England" becomes a name for the intersection of time and the timeless? How does England go from being a *setting* for this intersection to being the very incarnation of it?

Lifting the poem's perspective from these questions back up to the level of vast, celestial correspondences, the second section of "Little Gidding" shifts from jagged discursive lines to well-rounded lyrical ones. The lyric recapitulates the first three quartets, declaring the respective deaths of their signature elements: air, earth, water. The final fiery lines diminish all merely human toils and achievements in favor of a supratemporal perspective; they anticipate section 4, where the tightness of the rhyme scheme (pyre, fire, suspire, fire) creates a fierce centripetal and apocalyptic energy.

Having put into view the cosmic machinery above all human action, the poem turns to a last extended meditation on the meaning and limits of the poetic vocation, the celebrated vignette in which Eliot casts himself as Dante to Virgil (and as Hamlet to a "familiar compound ghost"). The ghost's bitter lessons bring home to the thinly veiled Eliot figure the fact that he must constantly reequip himself for confrontation with the purgatorial unknown. The passage stages a retrospect of Eliot's career and makes an oblique valedictory comment on the poetic epoch (modernism) that is passing as Eliot approaches his mortal end. Poetic power, like other forms of human achievement, is subject to this text's strictly anti-Promethean and antiprogressive values: a lifetime of verse making does not afford the mature poet any ready-made solutions to the problems of the present. Under the circumstances, the best he can do is avoid various forms of secular bad faith. Since the poem begins by vesting its interest in a particular historical arrangement of human community at Little Gidding, then steers the poet into a blankly purgatorial and antiutopian position, it must find a way to reconcile its local cultural ideals with its commitment to the hereafter. This problem takes shape in section 3 with an explicit address to the provisional value of national sentiment:

> Thus, love of a country
> Begins as an attachment to our own field of action
> And comes to find that action of little importance
> Though never indifferent.   (163–66)

In Eliot's idealized dialectic of native attachment, the subject transmutes mere patriotism, enlarging that sentiment into something less literal, less territorial. But the phases of this process cannot simply be ignored, as in a rational cosmopolitanism that negates local roots by the mere will of a free-floating individual subject. "Little Gidding" thus offers an oblique rebuke to modernist-era cosmopolitanism. National sentiment (like attachment to the self and its desires) serves as a stage to be transcended on the way to "another pattern," to a "love beyond desire." Since attachment to the native "field of action" remains crucial (if preliminary) to the poem's dialectical *via negativa*, it is possible for us to say that the local and the transcendent are not so much two poles at opposite ends of a structure as two interlocked phases in an unfolding process that embraces them both. The process describes a way to relativize the value of secular nationhood (a worldly attachment among others) without abandoning the recognition that certain national ideals have been the most viable form for proper collective attitudes toward nature and God. If Eliot enshrines a particular version of English history, he tries to avoid a historicist idolatry by enshrining it dialectically as the necessary first step on the way to transcendence.

The historical present cannot be o'erleapt by radical visions of the future, nor of the past:

> We cannot revive old factions
> We cannot restore old policies
> Or follow an antique drum.   (189–91)

It is part of this poem's discipline that scenes of the past (such as the king's visit to Little Gidding) remain half-glimpsed, crowded with conditionals and negatives. The poem does not call for England to fight its Civil War all over again for the soul of the nation but instead proposes a "purification of the motive / In the ground of our beseeching" (202–3). Factions and policies of the seventeenth century are long gone; what remains, what can be "taken from the defeated," is a "symbol perfected in death."[76] We can read this as Eliot's idiosyncratic brief for national life in 1941. For its historical flesh and blood, it depends on a particular conservative myth of Englishness, but for its values it claims an apolitical commitment to endure, submit, withstand, and beseech—a Churchillian rhetoric purified of mere patriotism by the appeal to eternity.

As we draw toward the end of this long sequence of rhetorical checks and formal balances, Eliot's meditation on Little Gidding's national significance gives way, once more, to a tight incantatory lyric whose salvational ambitions are conspicuously sub- and supranational. Section 4 aims at the allegorical levels of the suffering soul and corrupted humanity rather than at the mediating levels of the nation with its merely "historical" fate. In a method perfected with the quatrain poems of the late 1920s, Eliot saves his lightest verse cadences for his heaviest metaphysical cargo. Two oddly lilting seven-line stanzas return us to the cosmic and Manichean patterns that always underlie—but can also be dimly felt in—the course of human events. *Four Quartets* seems to have moved conspicuously away from the "mythic method" Eliot outlined in his famous essay on *Ulysses* and applied in *The Waste Land*. In that method, so closely associated with canonical high modernism, order and meaning are imposed by the artwork onto the meaninglessness of contemporary history. Here, by contrast, a profound commitment to Christian eschatology means that order predates and outflanks the poem.

The final section of "Little Gidding" echoes the first by invoking a sacred space that is both national and supranational:

> A people without history
> Is not redeemed from time, for history is a pattern
> Of timeless moments. So, while the light fails
> On a winter's afternoon, in a secluded chapel
> History is now and England.   (237–41)

History—seen redemptively now as "a pattern of timeless moments"—*is* England. This final move from "in" to "is" (from location to essence) cuts against the logic of mere exemplarity by which Eliot and many of his readers have tended to deflect or deemphasize the poem's Anglocentrism. Even with the temporal qualifications (on this afternoon, in this chapel, at the moment of dusk), the poem suggests that history can be transfigured from a mere sequence of events happening in England into a permanent pattern that can be called England. In that case England occupies the dialectical space of reconciliation between time and the timeless; it names both history as experienced by mortals and an organic set of values that transcends the laws of historicism. In a deeply Burkean appeal to the nation, Eliot predicates the possibility of historical meaning itself (i.e., history as a pattern) on "England." A genuine awareness of both history and eternity demands shared values and practices. Proper attitudes toward nature and God cannot simply be a matter of the individual conscience, as in radical Protestant and romantic thinking; they depend on collective daily life. For all practical purposes, they depend on a knowable and bounded notion of national tradition, on the "blood kinship of the same people living in the same place."

But the twin or dialectical meaning of nationhood has to be kept in view: "England" does not stand for coherent patterns as against the mere unfolding of history, rather, it names the capacity of a people to comprehend both sequence and pattern, both time and the timeless. History, even with its meaningless shape, remains the necessary plane of existence for both the soul and the collective—and a necessary precondition for any apprehension of the time that is beyond history. In a sense, the historical quandary of the poem involves a gnostic limitation: the human mind must acknowledge its scant knowledge of eternity; the relative comforts of a national tradition are only mitigations of that fundamental and terrifying ignorance. "Little Gidding" thus ends by affirming a permanently Sisyphean situation:

> We shall not cease from exploration
> And the end of all our exploring
> Will be to arrive where we started
> And know the place for the first time.   (243–46)

Although exploration here clearly carries more metaphorical than literal value, it is perhaps no coincidence—indeed, this is the substance of my interpretation of the poem's place in English history—that the language used to frame Eliot's ethos of continual self-discovery manages to evoke the new inwardness of a contracting nation-state. This quest—centripetal, recursive, recuperative—reformulates the national idiom of expansion even as it refers us back to Eliot's own personal recovery of origins.

In the quest to recover original identity, the basic allegory of "Little Gidding" continues to operate: the recovery is of a culture made exotic to itself and of a soul made other to itself. In collective terms, this means the cultivation of an estranged view of England, so that native intellectuals can reinvent the nation as the object of its own anthropological knowledge. In autobiographical terms, that means the estrangement of the master poet's career, his humble willingness to relearn his craft under new circumstances. The formerly alienated modernist Eliot thus comes to project his own integration into the community, not only as shamanistic voice, but as fateful embodiment and representative of a larger, historically inevitable process. A particular version of national history allows Eliot to cast himself as a representative man, providing at last a successful poetic means to objectify the self. It is the combined force of the allegory's pervasiveness and its austerity that frees Eliot to speak as and about himself without the savage-comic masks of his Laforguean youth. *Four Quartets* is in this sense both his most and least autobiographical poem.

The Anglocentric Muse

If *Four Quartets* aligns the fate of suffering soul and contracting nation, it also—by dint of that allegorical logic—revises the symbolist aesthetic so crucial to Eliot's early experiments (up to and including *The Waste Land*). Where symbolism lends itself to the authority of aesthetic forms (and of distant Platonic ideals), allegory aims for completion through and reference to collective tradition. To invoke the symbol/allegory divide in this general way is to propose that *Four Quartets* operates with an assumption of a shared cultural situation—a cultural circuit between text, artist, and audience.[77] As a historically embedded form, allegory tends to both assume and project cultural order. By the time of *Four Quartets*, Eliot had replaced his high modernist sense of the "futility and anarchy of contemporary history" with the idea that reality already contains a pattern.[78] Such a shift depends on the restoration of a meaningful, manageable English (i.e., classical) culture, one that vitiates the bad effects of historical time in ways not previously available to poets working in what Eliot considered the long romantic era (i.e., from Milton to modernism). Marking the transition to a new era, *Four Quartets* binds together and

authorizes its elements (lines, images, vignettes) according to their relation to a culture, not, as in The Waste Land, in relation to cosmopolitan
aesthetics. When, at the end of "Little Gidding," Eliot refers to the "complete consort dancing together," he is not engaged in self-referential self-
congratulation but rather in a declaration that the poem's meaning takes
root in some prior and extrinsic set of complete meanings. The poem's
power is a function not of literary genius or autotelic formal perfection
but of projected adequacy to both Christian and national narratives.

   I do not propose a stark divide between a symbolist Waste Land and
an allegorical Four Quartets, nor a model of historical determination by
which Eliot was somehow constrained to work in one mode or another
under certain macropolitical conditions. Rather, I am trying to track a
relative shift in method by which some of the allegorical presuppositions
of Four Quartets can be understood in relation to the historical context
not just of World War II (as has been customary) but also of that larger
process of imperial contraction around which this study is organized. The
poem implies its own location within a historical transition that I have
described as the passing away of metropolitan modernism. But of course
the most compelling sign of Eliot's adaptation to new ideas about culture
and literature is his turn from poetry to various kinds of drama during
the last thirty years of his life. Eliot's movement toward the pageant-play
and verse drama—his search for a public, sacramental language—makes
sense in light of his own belief in the possibility of a new organic culture.

   But if the later phases of Eliot's career are based increasingly on eschewing the private reading practices of high modernism in favor of a völkisch
revival of verse drama, why propose that Four Quartets—a difficult and
often autobiographical text—constitutes Eliot's fullest imaginative response to a new epoch? Why not consider the drama more directly? The
first answer to that question is that the poem, despite its sometimes obscure, hieratic, and self-referential techniques, was meant to be resonant
and accessible for its audience. Indeed, Eliot conceived of the poem dramatically—not as a mere device (e.g., Prufrock's soliloquy) but as words
meant for performance. The first sections of "Burnt Norton," which were
lifted from Eliot's play Murder in the Cathedral, set the tone for the entire
poetic sequence. We know, too, that Eliot had in mind that these poems
would be broadcast on BBC radio rather than consumed in the hothouse
parlors and little magazines of high modernism. But the second, more
important reason for reading Four Quartets as the major text of Eliot's
valediction to the metropolitan era is that the poem is so clearly itself
of the transition. It cannot simply project itself forward into a postwar,
postempire English community, nor can it imagine itself back into the
cosmopolitan days of 1922; the text's dialectical relationship to history
keeps it poised at the fading edge of the high modernist era.

Thus, while Eliot's prose and verse of the time herald the reintegration of art into culture, he retains a modernist skepticism about the premature subordination of aesthetic to social value. Seeking a more direct, dramatic exchange with audiences, he nonetheless remains committed to an Adornean law of form, that is, to the idea that complex modernist forms are required in order to see (and compel readers to see) beyond the world of received ideas and social convention. This predicament explains the power and peculiarity of *Four Quartets*: it is meant to work as an allegory that speaks publicly about collective fate and as a prophecy whose grim eschatology redresses the public's vulgar historicism.

In the attempt to marry pure form to recognizable content, to conjoin his own priestly vision of ascesis to the popular understanding of political crisis circa 1940, Eliot turns not just to the multivalence of allegory but also to the unique properties of music. Music functions as both a figurative and a structural device in the poem, a governing aesthetic (and in the end political) principle that combines formal complexity (the elaborate theme-and-variations of the five-part "sonata" structure) with primitive directness. Of course, music as an idealized "form without content" had been a symbolist/modernist desideratum since Valéry and Pater. Eliot's early poems in fact aspire to follow rhythmic imperatives above all; they also incorporate frequent musical quotations and allusions. But for Eliot, the real fulfillment of musical ideals had to wait until the classical consolidation of *Four Quartets*, for the moment when he could see the converging destinies of poet and nation within a panoramic double-helix model of time. At that moment, the poem can establish a patterned relationship between the deep structures of history and the deep structures of its own form. The impersonality of musical form—its repetitive, layered, classical pattern—sublates the idiosyncrasies of verbal style into a kind of writing degree zero, a writing whose blankness (as Barthes conceived it) overarches all the social differentiations attached to conventional literary style.[79] Eliot, for his part, looked for ways to purify his own somewhat accidental notions of Englishness into a historical vision that would speak to and for the nation at its moment of crisis. Though still a vestigially modernist work, *Four Quartets* thus reworks the modernist problematic, lifting the agonized perpetual oscillation of the personal/impersonal polarity out of the aesthetic arena and into the putatively more capacious arena of culture.[80]

The importance of music to that project will become clear if we recall Virginia Woolf's late writings on English culture. As observed in chapter 2, Woolf's ideas of primitive English art and of contemporary English community converge around musical scenarios in *Between the Acts*. When words fail, music emerges as a socially integrative medium; Miss LaTrobe, the desperate dramaturge, uses music to unite a dispersing crowd. In their later works, both Woolf and Eliot cast music as an impersonal and transpersonal medium. They share a fascination with polyphonic or choral voices in classical drama and with disembodied sources; thus the gramophone in the bushes in *Between The Acts* echoes the "unheard music" in the shrubs of "Burnt Norton." In such scenes, music reflects a primal connection between artist and audience and conjures up atavistic hints of a common culture long since vanished in England. In both texts, artistic production and reception are renaturalized by music, removed from the agonized modernist context of social segregation and returned to an innocent moment of cultural totality. Musical form thus seems not to traduce the demands of high modernist difficulty but to reintegrate artistic and social power.[81] It promises a synthesis of the social realism and avant-gardism whose midcentury tug-of-war had such a defining (and paralyzing) effect on European literature. For Eliot in particular, if the musicality of *Four Quartets* offers a new method to treat the old problem of literary impersonality, it is partly because historical conditions seemed to promise the revival of a native classical culture in England, one where the lonely plaint of the Artist could be eclipsed by the genius of tradition.

It is important to remember that this reading of the poem and its place in literary history, while it depends in part on a historical argument about material changes in the politics and economics of English national life, is predominantly a more modest and local argument about how T. S. Eliot made sense of those changes. Eliot imagines that a common culture might reassociate (as it were) the dissociated sensibility and retotalize a fragmented, unknowable society. His poetry reflects those imagined possibilities in its allegorization of individual and national destiny, in its establishment of a classic kind of allegory. Even if a salvific destiny is perpetually deferred, the sublation of merely personal or local-historical concerns to a higher-order struggle has a moderately redemptive effect. And even if Eliot's late work depends on an artificially homogenized or prematurely circumscribed notion of national culture, it nonetheless tries to engage a collectivity in ways that improve on an elite-cosmopolitan model of modernist art. Eliot's imagined restoration of England's insular totality repairs the social fractures identified by Jameson's model of modernism and imperialism. In *Four Quartets*, as in late Forster and late Woolf, the key spatial referent is indeed no longer dangerous infinity, but bounded place. And in the process of trading the aesthetic order of high modernism for a broader cultural notion of order, Eliot demystifies his own style. This would seem to confirm, by extrapolation, Jameson's model: if high modernism's cultural and economic schisms underwrite a kind of mystification of style, an abstraction of imperial relations into modernist technique, then the collapse of the colonial economy back down to its more "knowable" national shape might conceivably correspond to the demystification of those same modernist techniques. At least so it is in "East Coker": the return to origins exposes "a worn-out poetical fashion."

Read in this way, *Four Quartets* makes it possible to see the convergence between a valedictory revision of an insufficiently classical modernism and the reconsolidation of national culture in the wake of empire. Only with a particularist culture concept in place can Eliot generate the apparently transhistorical meditations on time that drive the poem. As noted above, Eliot's notion of timelessness in 1919's "Tradition and the Individual Talent" had a restricted provenance: canonical art is timeless, but the rest of human endeavor is subject to an unforgiving mechanical time. By contrast, *Four Quartets* seeks to conjure a much wider notion of the timeless, one that inheres not merely in high art but in the values and practices of an entire culture, a total way of life. Within a meaningful and manageable national tradition, Eliot can begin to see beyond the social depredations of mechanical time—chronos—to the redemptive time of kairos. Rather than howl against and ironically dispose a fragmented, reified modernity, he pursues a redemptive brand of Englishness based on the long, shaping forces of insular tradition. In a sense, the late Eliot wants to recover Englishness as a cultural particularity precisely so that it can be transcended, not geographically but temporally and transcendentally. Suspended "between pole and tropic," Eliot's England is an island of bounded space that redeems time. It is in this sense, finally, that England *is* history. Where the high modernist Eliot was locked in a battle with dominant historical notions of linear time, the Eliot of 1940 begins to imagine himself aligned with a newly ascendant instantiation of organic time under the sign of national culture.

Eliot's late writing manages both to relativize England as one culture among many after empire and to re-exceptionalize England as a peculiarly cohesive "traditional" culture. The two processes depend on each other; they constitute the dialectical logic of the local and the universal by which Eliot imagines (and comes to exemplify the design of) postimperial English culture.[82] If England can be returned, via Eliot's ministrations and minor prophecies, to a sense of itself as an anthropological object (as a culture with positive content, not as an Arnoldian-imperial custodian of other cultures), then it can free itself from the modern curse of secular historicism. Eliot's representation of this possibility suggests a new national way to transcend the local: instead of exporting and attenuating cultural values through empire, English culture can now attain extralocal significance by sheer exemplarity. What was once a universaliz*ing* (i.e., self-extending) English culture becomes a universaliz*able* (i.e., exemplary) national culture. Eliot's complex response to the moment of retrenchment thus marks itself as a paradigmatic moment in the history of lost European universalism. National culture here means neither membership in the "drab sisterhood" of nations foretold by Forster nor in the baggy liberal empire he chronicled but status as a concrete unity and totality. The notion of the "anthropological turn" shows that Eliot's nativism proceeded alongside a corresponding recovery of cultural totality. As I will explore in the next chapter, the implications of that recovery extend beyond our understanding of Eliot or even of modernist literature; they help set the stage for ideas that have broadened the class franchise of "culture" while narrowing and territorializing its ethnic and national dimensions.[83]

FOUR

BECOMING MINOR

T. S. ELIOT's renewed commitment in the thirties to the local and racial bases of art stems, as we have seen, from his sense of historical opportunism: as British horizons shrink, Eliot imagines a salutary restoration of English particularity. *The Idea of a Christian Society* puts forward Eliot's most concentrated claim for the distinctiveness of an Anglo-Christian culture whose heart is still beating; *Notes towards the Definition of Culture* offers theoretical modifications of that core culture relative to its component parts and its place in the wider world. In both texts, Eliot drives home the point that English art and literature will continue to deteriorate so long as they float in the empty ether of rational cosmopolitanism and liberal pluralism. Here, for example, is Eliot's brief against Englishness as merely a generic name for the unrooted: "The Englishman . . . does not ordinarily think of England as a 'region' in the way that a Scottish or Welsh national can think of Scotland or Wales; and as it is not made clear to him that his interests also are involved, his sympathies are not enlisted. Thus the Englishman may identify his own interests with a tendency to obliterate local and racial distinctions, *which is as harmful to his own culture* as to those of his neighbours" (NDC 126; emphasis added).

Although framed as a description of national habits, this statement also has the force of an injunction to English intellectuals to redeem their traditions from a diffuse and deterritorialized pseudoculture. For Eliot, the moment is ripe to redirect English sympathy away from imperial dissemination, away from a patronizing custodial relationship to peripheral folk cultures, and back toward a cultivation of Englishness itself. As real political forces conspire to isolate England, Eliot sees his chance to reattach English sympathies to a properly bounded national culture and to expose rational cosmopolitanism as an insidious, culture-killing ideology.

Eliot's localism establishes a keynote that sounds through several different strands of Anglocentric discourse in the midcentury period: the idea that England's imperial past and provincial future can both be mitigated by the recovery of its national culture as a significant totality. Late modernism, represented by Eliot, thus helped give shape to the anthropological turn that increasingly defined literary and cultural institutions in postwar England. As we have seen, the thirties writing of Forster, Woolf, and Eliot initiates two historically linked discursive processes that define the anthropological turn: the relativization of England as one national culture among many and the relativization of elite literature as one form of expressive culture among many.

Eliot's insistence on a local, racial definition of culture counters what I have been calling the Arnoldian legacy, in which England came to represent itself as a spiritually etiolated modern state surrounded by more colorful, more vital satellite cultures. Arnold's England is a thing of patches without essence, caught up in knowing and typifying other (subordinate) cultures. This national lack drew the attention of the Scots nationalist Hugh MacDiarmid, who, some sixty years after Arnold, affirmed that "England . . . is a composite—not a 'thing in itself.' "[1] If Englishness came, in the years between Arnold and MacDiarmid, to constitute a mobile and composite metaculture, it also continued to name a hegemonic nationalism replete with mythic self-representations, ripe and ready for colonial export. In the highest phase of British power, Englishness seemed to perform a short circuit from the local to the imperial, from cozy shire to red-mapped planet. It represented, in other words, a universalist doctrine that displaced its own inner core of nationalist content by projecting cultural essence outward to the colonies or backward into pastoral yore.

The curious contentlessness of imperial English nationalism, trenchantly identified by Arnold, Eliot, and MacDiarmid, has also attracted the attention of contemporary English leftists. Tom Nairn and Perry Anderson have, as we have seen, updated and clarified the problem of England's cultural depletion under British hegemony. In Anderson's analysis, the anthropological visibility and wholeness of tribal societies in the colonial periphery drew attention away from comprehensive sociological observation of English culture and society.[2] The Nairn-Anderson theses of the seventies proposed that the imperial legacy of cultural blankness or missing totality at the center was never really undone, even in the era of decolonization. By contrast, I have been suggesting that certain intellectual movements or literary formations, beginning in the thirties, responded to imperial retrenchment by inverting Nairn and Anderson's inward lack/outward presence formula. Indeed, the late modernist version of the anthropological turn, even in its limited or compromised form, initiates and therefore gives shape to a new confrontation with England as a cultural whole.

It should be clear from the outset that I am analyzing intellectual projections of English unity, not making claims about the social reality of those projections. While the shrinking of the imperial state gave material and symbolic impetus to intellectuals interested in the cohesion of national culture, it is perhaps worth stating the obvious fact that imperial decline, even now, has not aligned the English nation and the British state. Moreover, decolonization has not restored a lost cultural purity to England any more than it has to England's ex-colonies. In England, as many observers have noted, the immediate postwar period saw nostalgic invocations of cultural wholeness challenged by the dawning recognition that the post-imperial nation would be a multicultural and heterogeneous place. If there was an Anglocentric and anthropological turn among intellectuals bent on remaking England into a knowable community, it was a largely discursive event, even a fantasy. But the nature of that Anglocentrism remains important, not only because we need to understand and remember the baleful effects of nativism, but also because the reconsolidation of Englishness seems so intertwined with the broadening definition of culture in the period.

To pursue this point, I am now going to examine three different intellectual formations through which midcentury England can be seen to regain its cultural particularity and visibility. First, the economic and cultural writing of J. M. Keynes, a Bloomsbury intimate, not only provides a salient instance of English intellectual response to British contraction but reveals the formative role of a late modernist literary milieu in the emergent discourse of English particularism. In this sense, Keynesian thought mediates between pre- and post–World War II generations of intellectuals and points up the importance of imperial retrenchment for the development of English Cultural Studies. Secondly, then, I will examine the early work of Cultural Studies intellectuals, who bring the logic of the "anthropological turn" that was initiated in the thirties to its institutional and academic fulfillment. If we reconsider figures like E. P. Thompson, Raymond Williams, and Richard Hoggart in this context, it becomes clear that their groundbreaking and integrative analyses of culture were substantially (if somewhat tacitly) shaped by the assimilation of anthropological holism in and to postimperial England. At the same time, of course, England became a site of reverse colonization, in which both workers and intellectuals from the (ex-)colonies migrated to the center in unprecedented numbers. A wave of colonial writing in and about England emerged in the fifties, and, as we will see, a number of its novelists (including Doris Lessing, Sam Selvon, and George Lamming) converge with the Cultural Studies intellectuals, not just in time and place, but in the project of making England over into a minor culture susceptible to romantic discourses of local color and to realist protocols of ethnography.[3]

Since scholarship on British decline has tended to focus on the bleaker, more ironic aspects of imperial loss and on associated retrograde and xenophobic forms of nativism, it seems important now to reassess the recuperative discourses of Anglocentrism that emerged at the same time and that, in their own way, decolonized England. In order to situate these recuperative Anglocentrisms within a more familiar landscape of decline and a more familiar history of English literature after modernism, I will, in conclusion, briefly address "next generation" writers, such as W. H. Auden, George Orwell, Graham Greene, and Evelyn Waugh. In these cases, the postmetropolitan phase of English life does not offer an opportunity to democratize culture or to shift the terms of literature away from metropolitan anomie. Instead we see variations on the theme of an individual soul (especially the cosmopolitan traveler) caught in a tragic world or in an English nation increasingly bereft of any hope for moral, political, or artistic renewal. I take the canonical writers of the Auden-Orwell generation as a countertradition to the redemptive culturalisms of both left and right.

Because native culturalism became, in my view, the mother tongue of Englishness after empire, it remains relevant not only to contemporary literature and criticism but also to any historical account of late modernism and late imperialism. With that in mind, we can shift from close textual work on literary forms to somewhat broader cultural formations, beginning with the transitional figure of J. M. Keynes, who was both an aging modernist aesthete and the chief architect of the contemporary welfare state. In what follows, I read the work of Keynes as a useful guide for understanding the relation of economics and culture in England during the transitional period between metropolitan modernism and global postmodernism.

The Keynesian National Object:
Late Modernism and *The General Theory*

We are used to hearing about J. M. Keynes as the theoretical architect of international monetary agreements and of a general "deficit economics" that was transplanted and adopted by many governments after World War II. But Keynes was also a Bloomsbury intellectual of the 1930s, and his writings register a particular historical event: the decentering of English capital and the decentering of England as a cultural capital. As an economic statesman, Keynes brokered the agreements under which a fading Pax Britannica gave way to the (short) American Century. His role in what Hugo Radice calls the "economic introversion of the 1930s and 1940s" can only be fully understood in the context of distinctly English social predicaments and cultural resources.[4] Naturally enough, most economic historians and biographers have emphasized Keynes's contributions to postwar monetary policy and theory. But when we reread Keynes alongside his English literary contemporaries, we gain new insights not only about the consequential afterlife of Keynesian thought but about the historical conditions for its emergence. To that end, I will propose a shared context for—and related textual impulses in—Keynesian economics and the modernist writing examined in chapters 2 and 3. Keynes's *General Theory* takes its place among self-conscious attempts by modernist writers in the 1930s to come to terms with the obsolescence of their most successful intellectual habits of the 1920s and to recover a usable core of English national culture from the derelict body of British imperialism.

In September 1938, as the Sudetenland crisis broke in central Europe, Keynes addressed a private gathering of the Memoir Club with an autobiographical paper entitled "My Early Beliefs." His memoir provides a useful glimpse of a Bloomsbury intellectual's commitments as they were tempered by events of the late 1930s. For the circle of friends in attendance, the memoir also told the story of their own intellectual formation, of their familiar debt to G. E. Moore, the philosopher-don of Edwardian Cambridge. Keynes recalls the intellectual milieu of Moore's Cambridge: "Nothing mattered except states of mind, our own and other people's of course, but chiefly our own. These states of mind were not associated with action or achievement or with consequences. They consisted in timeless, passionate states of contemplation and communion, largely unattached to 'before' and 'after' " (*CWK* 10: 436). The "youthful religion" that Keynes and his fellows imbibed at Cambridge was, however, only partially Moorean: "We accepted Moore's religion, so to speak, and discarded his morals. Indeed, in our opinion, one of the greatest advantages of his religion was that it made morals unnecessary—meaning by 'religion' one's attitude towards oneself and the ultimate and by 'morals' one's attitude towards the outside world and the intermediate" (*CWK* 10: 436). Moore's great gift to the embryonic cultural formation of Bloomsbury was the rational removal of the "intermediate"; his philosophy implied a socially *unmediated* relationship between the individual and "the ultimate." Looking back on this aesthetic education thirty years later, Keynes acknowledges the detached and sheltered quality of Moore's connoisseurship of mental states. In fact, he criticizes the philosophical attitude that Lukács famously denounced as modernist subjectivism. Although in "My Early Beliefs"—a text contemporaneous with *Between the Acts* and *Four Quartets* and driven by similar ambivalences—Keynes cannot fully abandon Moorean values, he recognizes the limitations of passionate self-contemplation: "one cannot live today secure in the undisturbed individualism which was the extraordinary achievement of the early Edwardian days" (*CWK* 10: 444). Keynes does not simply diagnose a youthful error, he claims the historical obsolescence of rational individualism, as constituted against inherited culture and "the intermediate." The memoir thus balances fond evocations of Bloomsbury's formative milieu with a distinctively late-thirties suspicion of that milieu.

Keynes's memoir not only marks the end of an era but connects that era's "undisturbed individualism" to the prevailing economic conditions and assumptions of a classically liberal society. In it, Keynes admits that he and his companions adhered to an increasingly frail aesthetic and philosophical individualism that was, even in its heyday, constituted as much *by* as *against* the logic of laissez-faire capitalism. Looking back, Keynes recognizes that Moorean ideas, though they appeared to offer a refined haven from the corrosive effects of utilitarianism, were fully implicated in an entire Victorian socioeconomic structure whose day had passed.

However, when the young Keynes came into his own as an intellectual in the years just after World War I, he still maintained his allegiance to the civilized individual, building a reformist economics out of the refined antimaterialist sentiments of his university days. In his major works of the 1920s, including *A Tract on Monetary Reform* and *A Treatise on Money*, Keynes focused on the problems caused by an increasingly disruptive force in twentieth-century capitalism: money. At that time, British economists generally held to the classical view that the marketplace was a magical mechanism guaranteed to spit out the best results for the most people. Keynes sought to reveal the limitations of the classical model and, in particular, to suggest that laissez-faire thinking was no longer adequate to the situation of the British economy. The *Tract* and the *Treatise* describe the prevailing monetary system as anything but a perfect, self-adjusting machine. They draw particular attention to the problems engendered by the gold standard, which, in Keynes's view, produced unstable transactions and irrational speculation. When tied to gold, money could not act as a balancing and ordering device; it became a commodity subject to unbridled, high-velocity market action. Where the gold standard had once created both order and advantage for free-trading Britain, it was now generating disorder and disadvantage. In Keynes's view, gold also threatened Britain's economic self-determination, subjecting it not only to that ingot-swollen parvenu, the United States, but to the vagaries of imperial war and commercial adventure. As long as the gold standard prevailed, the international quest for mineral reserves would drive European aggression and imperial rivalry. Keynes's proposed monetary reforms, based on currency reserve formulas, promised a more rational—and more national—system.

But Keynes met with little success as a crusading monetary reformer in the 1920s. Instead, his achievement was representational: he developed a supple and powerful language for capturing the quicksilver flows of metropolitan capitalism. He exposed the complex unreality of the economy by pointing out how expectations rather than facts determined outcomes; in fact, third- and fourth-order expectations *of* expectations had come to govern fundamental economic conditions in a speculative roundelay. In describing this unstable economy, Keynes developed an original style that was, as Robert Skidelsky puts it, "full of fancy, sparkle and paradox."[5] The French journalist Marcel Labordère praised Keynes's *Tract*, for example, as "amongst the most purely aesthetic pages . . . which have ever been written about economics" (*JMK 158*). It was the irrational motion of money, its chaos-breeding velocity, that inspired Keynes to develop his own mobile army of metaphors and to employ witty, ironic juxtapositions of absurd economic facts. In short, while Keynes's efforts to represent the irrationality of market behavior in the 1920s may not have knocked Britain off the gold standard, they led to the development of an innovative and idiosyncratic literary style.

Keynes's writing came into its own in the same marketplace that inspired such landmark displays of metropolitan modernist style as T. S. Eliot's *The Waste Land* and Virginia Woolf's *Mrs. Dalloway*. Those works helped make Eliot and Woolf the key canonical representatives of a 1920s London modernism that gained high-cultural power while absorbing some of the shocks of more radical, continentally inflected avant-gardes. If Eliot was the house poet of the interwar English metropolis, and Woolf its novelist, then Keynes was its economist. His experimental style answered to the complex, highly volatile urban economy that inspired Georg Simmel's classic essay "The Metropolis and Mental Life." Simmel places a strong emphasis on the unprecedented and dizzying effects of money; in Simmel's metropolis, money liquidates preexisting forms of cultural affiliation and cultural distinction, suspending individuals in a democratizing social medium. Simmel's analysis of the rapid-fire cognitive tricks and turns—what he identifies as "the dominance of the intellect"—required by life in the urban economy has helped literary critics, in their turn, to see the modernist representation of consciousness as part of a distinctly *metropolitan* language of art.[6] This modernist style developed into its canonical form during the 1920s, the same decade in which Keynes's own technique was maturing, in a city whose arteries coursed with unruly money.

The initial connections between Keynes's economic observations and the development of modernist style have been explored by Jennifer Wicke in an important essay on Keynes and Woolf in the 1920s. Wicke presents both Keynesian and Woolfian style as an attempt to capture in language the unpredictable life of urban markets. What Simmel had implied about the relation between the market and mental life takes on exemplary form in Wicke's discussion. She reads Woolf's language of consciousness—in which the mind's motions are themselves highly mobile ("blooming, buzzing, dispersed and displaced")—in relation to the market economy described most trenchantly by Keynes.[7] Like Woolf, Keynes took stylistic inspiration from irrational, quasi-magical market forces and highly volatile forms of discourse, including fashion and advertising. The dazzling stimuli of the metropole required and inspired beautiful figures of speech and sharp rhetorical turns in Keynes. But if such stimuli were inspiring to Keynes the stylist, they were also troubling to Keynes the theorist.[8]

The incoherent and fragmented economy that inspired Keynes's *Tract* and *Treatise* was shaped not only by unbridled speculation and gold money but by unstable relations between the metropolis and the periphery. Imperialism was, like the other economic conditions described by Keynes, a substantial part of the context for metropolitan perception and indeed for modernist culture at large. Like Simmel's monetary solvent or Woolf's buzzing marketplace, metropolitan perception forms part of the urban environment of high modernism, a place characterized by both epistemological privilege and socioeconomic fragmentation. Moreover, as Fredric Jameson suggests in "Modernism and Imperialism," the colonial economy relocated major elements of the economy overseas, rendering them invisible to British citizens. As we have seen, Jameson argues that modernist texts reflect this state of affairs by gesturing imagistically toward a frightening and unrepresentable spatial infinity, one that is symbolically associated with empire. This suggestive account of the relations between macroeconomic conditions (imperial capitalism) and aesthetic form (modernist style) becomes more concrete when we recover Keynes as a mediating figure for English modernism. Keynes not only theorized the economy, but—like Forster, Woolf, and Eliot—made artful language out of the cognitive maze of the metropole. Like his contemporaries in the modernist canon, Keynes found stylistic success in the representation of social conditions that he explicitly deplored. His major works of the 1920s, the *Tract* and *Treatise*, concentrated on the unruly effects of Adam Smith's machine gone haywire, on economic conditions that he sought to reform out of existence. But it would take the external machinations of 1930s history to give full theoretical coherency and practical force to Keynes's declarations of the "end of laissez-faire."

When the 1930s began with two major financial crashes, Keynes saw not simply the final crisis of Victorian capitalism but an opportunity to restore first conceptual, then actual, order to the economy. Crippling strikes, lingering depression, and stubborn unemployment convinced Keynes that classical economics should be—and perhaps at last could be—comprehensively rethought. At that point, Keynes transformed himself from a dissenting metropolitan into an architect of postmetropolitan economic life. He saw what few wished to confront: that the putatively magical, self-adjusting market could, left to its own devices, reach a static and unsatisfactory condition of low employment. Keynes's central work of the period, *The General Theory of Employment, Interest and Money* (1936), argues that the classical postulates of Smith and Ricardo were accurate only under certain *special* economic conditions and that those conditions had effectively died with Victoria. But *The General Theory* also articulates the position that the British economy could be saved by pursuing a middle way between raw capitalist individualism and the new authoritarian collectivism.

In its bare bones, *The General Theory* holds that the creation of higher aggregate demand via higher rates of consumption will produce higher rates of employment. Keynes attacks the outmoded Victorian virtue of thrift because it unnecessarily depresses the level of consumption. Keynesian economics aims at a healthier domestic consumer market for goods and services. As both a prerequisite and a corollary, wealth inequities would be reduced (but not eliminated—Keynes backs away from radical socialism). Working-class incomes would, after all, need to be higher in order to raise the consumption level. *The General Theory* proposes a return to more stable and fixed relationships between capital and plant, between enterprise and investor. By slowing down the velocity of exchange in modern stock and bond markets, Keynes wants to create an investment system that is based more on communal wealth than on individual profit. At its most ambitious, *The General Theory* offers the hypothetical restoration of a lost condition of full employment. Despite a coolly rational expositional style, Keynes's writings of the 1930s evince a fairly spectacular optimism about solving "the economic problem" altogether and establishing a state-smoothed capitalist equilibrium.

Keynes's brave new world of managed capitalism defined a conceptual and, in the end, a political form whereby collective interests could modify the actions of private individuals and firms. Once Keynes established what the economic slumps had already suggested—that the invisible hand was fallible—he required some alternative mechanism of economic control. What he chose was the state, taken as the benign agent of the national interest. In *The General Theory*, Keynes advances a neomercantilist case for the importance of a nationally organized marketplace. In fact, Keynesian theory assumes not just a marketplace but an economic *community*. No longer would individuals and firms be the atomized units of a free-trading world; they would become citizens in a definable and manageable national economy. The chief political implication of Keynes's paradigm shift was, of course, the replacement of a laissez-faire liberal oligarchy by a more activist economic policy implemented by the state. Such a system is the main legacy of Keynesian economics today.

However, given his classically liberal suspicion of state power and his growing sense of the potential dangers of central planning in Stalinist Russia, Keynes needed to conceive of the state as something other than an authoritarian institution. Seeking to avoid the twin dangers of the old individualism and the new conformism, Keynes found the necessary conceptual and rhetorical resources in the softer half of that political hybrid "the nation-state"; that is, he invoked the nation as defined by English cultural traditions rather than the state as defined by British imperial power. Like many others in the Bloomsbury circle, Keynes distrusted vulgar patriotism, but believed that the English had a particular genius for measured and voluntarist forms of community. Piero Mini argues, in fact, that Keynes's investment in notions of collective interest should be understood as an extension (and therefore a revision) of G. E. Moore's narrowly conceived circle of friends.[9] But if Keynes's liberal notion of community bore the rhetorical blush of friendly, voluntary belonging, it had its roots in a more conservative strain of British political thinking stemming from Burke and Coleridge. The mainstream tradition of civil nationalism disavows but depends on a Burkean logic of cultural identity that was, I think, quite central to *The General Theory*'s innovative turn to the state-managed economy. Whatever Burkean notions about national culture were lodged in Keynes's mind, their full activation had to await the moment when he traded in cosmopolitan individualism for a new kind of reckoning with "the intermediate." Skidelsky describes Keynes's progress in this way: "Eventually Keynes came to understand that the search for truth could take place fruitfully only within a shared cultural framework" (*JMK* xix). During the 1930s, Keynes eschewed his attachment to the pure or universal rationalism of metropolitan souls and developed an intellectual practice framed by cultural givens. *The General Theory* makes a titular claim to broad applicability, but it was written from within the conceptual boundaries of Keynes's own declining nation.

If Keynesian theory depended on a set of premises about English cultural cohesion, those premises were, as we have seen, themselves gaining a new form of visibility and currency during the 1930s. *The General Theory* casts one eye backward to a residual, laissez-faire imperialism and one eye forward to an emergent, postimperial welfare state. Keynes's economic thinking responded directly to the end of an entire—and, for Britain, specially charmed—phase of free-trade international capitalism. He makes this point clear in a 1934 *New Statesman and Nation* editorial, part of a debate with G. B. Shaw: "Queen Victoria died as the monarch of the most capitalistic empire upon which the sun has (or has not) set. If Shaw had kept up with the newspapers since the death of Queen Victoria, he would know that a complex of events [has] destroyed that form of society" (*CWK* 28: 33). Keynes's position does not just rehearse a familiar Bloomsbury dissent from imperialism; it expresses his assurance that the edifice itself, good or bad, was collapsing.[10] In his view, mainstream British economists had not grasped the nature of the epochal changes afoot, nor the possibilities for a new economic order.

Keynes's own grasp of the end of Pax Britannica combined with his appreciation for the traditions of English liberal statehood to produce a coherent concept of the national interest. The imperial British economy had developed "excessive facilities for foreign lending and the purchase of properties abroad . . . [which] frequently stood in the way of . . . full employment at home" (*CWK* 7: 337). *The General Theory* would, if put into practice, remove the need for colonies to absorb surplus capital, and reduce aggressive competition for overseas markets (*CWK* 7: 382).[11] By both acknowledging and accelerating the end of the free trade era, Keynesian economics turned attention to restoring plenitude to England's domestic markets. For Keynes, then, imperial decline implied, not the loss of colonial lucre, but a historical opportunity to improve the nation's health and to rethink its economic shape.

To read *The General Theory* in its 1930s English context means more than just recognizing its Anglocentric liberal predicates and its flirtations with a neo-Malthusian view of the national interest. This context also allows us to see that Keynes's ground-breaking attention to a complete, or "macro," economy emerged from a moment of insular contraction. Imperial decline and diplomatic isolation gave national shape to Keynes's thinking. *The General Theory* revives an older ideal of concrete, bounded communities in order to reinvent the rules for survival in the abstract world of international finance capitalism. In a sense, his economics both pre- and postdates Adam Smith; it uses both ends against the fading middle of classical, laissez-faire, gold-standard economics.

Before Keynes, economists generally analyzed the behavior of individuals and firms within a given market. Classical economics thought of the national income (or debt) in terms more or less dictated by the metaphor of the nation-as-household. Keynes vigorously disputed the terms of this metaphor, pointing out that a simple extension of household virtues (including thrift) to social aggregates led to bad theory and bad policy. He rejected the idea of explaining the larger economy by microeconomic analogy and classical market rules. As political scientist Timothy Mitchell has recently argued: "*The General Theory* replaced this abstraction [the market], which had no geographical or political definition, with the 'economic system as a whole,' a system whose limits correspond to geopolitical boundaries."[12] The Keynesian turn of the midcentury established a tighter discursive and statistical net around national economies, with world-changing results. From that point forward, national economies became dynamic objects susceptible to state intervention. As Richard Adelstein observes, whereas earlier economic models "conceived of the national income as a *descriptive statistic*, a measure of the economy's performance at any moment and a signal that action of some sort might be desirable, Keynes allowed it to become a *dependent variable*, an object of policy that could be scientifically predicted and manipulated by the politically neutral technique of the state's economic engineers."[13] Keynes's ability to remake the nation into this particular kind of "object" was conditioned by the contraction of British borders, which triggered both an actual and a symbolic reorganization of the nation during the 1930s.

In particular, Keynes's reconceptualization of the economy reflects the fraying tether between nation and empire. As Mitchell notes: "Previously it made little sense to talk of, say, the British economy, so long as Britain's economic realm was thought to include India and its other colonies."[14] Beyond this, *The General Theory*'s projection of a complete economy converges with a wider intellectual current in thirties Britain, one that carried the methods and protocols of imperial knowledge homeward, where they became available techniques for national self-representation. Keynesian economics does not explicitly reflect the domestication of anthropology, but it mirrors the holistic logic of viewing society as a layered and knowable totality.[15] Moreover, Keynes's own intellectual progress charts a path from the colonial periphery back to the domestic economy. His economic primer was the Indian economy, which, from the distance of several thousands of miles, could be grasped by the young civil servant in Whitehall as a dynamic and correctable monetary *system*. Then, during the interwar decades, he gradually transformed such early scale-models of a money economy into the bases of British macroeconomics. In a somewhat more mediated way, Keynes used his famous "banana parable" as an initial lesson about the ill effects of thrift in a closed economy (*JMK* 323–25). The parable's version of a primitive, one-celled economy does not have any specific political referent, but the example alludes implicitly to the single-commodity economies of the tropical periphery. One way to understand the Keynesian paradigm shift is as the application of banana-parable lessons to the advanced capitalist economies of the declining imperial center.

Keynesian economics, then, can be seen as both a representative case and a causal agent within a larger intellectual transformation that brought the concept of social totality from the imperial periphery back to the national center. If Keynes had some qualms about Englishness as an ontology based on deep ethnic or territorial essences, he had no reservations about restoring the nation's epistemological boundaries: "The nationalising of knowledge is the one case for nationalisation which is overwhelmingly right" (qtd. in *JMK* 268). When viewed in this light, *The General Theory* makes possible some historical modifications of Perry Anderson's famous thesis about the "absent centre" of British national culture. Writing in the 1960s, Anderson observed that Britain never produced a "classical sociology" of the kind represented by Weber, Durkheim, and Pareto, but did produce a "brilliant and flourishing anthropology" during the modernist era. "British imperial society *exported* its totalizations onto its subject peoples. There, and there only, it could afford scientific study of the social whole. 'Primitive' societies became the surrogate object of the theory proscribed at home. . . . The miniature scale of primitive societies, moreover, made them exceptionally propitious for macro-analysis."[16] For Anderson, the particularly English aversion to thinking of society as a structural totality persisted into the 1960s, with some limited exceptions. Given Anderson's basic thesis about the displacement of social totality into colonial anthropology, it makes sense that the midcentury erosion of the British imperial system coincided with a set of "anthropological returns" whereby the thought of social totality came home to roost.[17] Keynes identified the changing status of British imperial capitalism, recognizing the obsolescence of precisely those conditions that had undergirded Britain's "flourishing anthropology." By the same token, Keynes's foray into "macro-analysis" effected what Anderson himself at one point describes as a "retotalization" of domestic economics.[18] As we reread Keynes in relation to European *and* colonial crises, we can see that Keynesian ideas of the 1930s became exemplary and shaping forces beyond the field of economics. For example, those ideas gave shape to two key transformations in midcentury British culture: (1) the reconception of the imperial state in specifically national terms (a process whose logic has, of course, carried through to the current devolution debates in Scotland and Wales); and (2) the migration of available models of social totality from the colonial periphery to an increasingly compact territory at home.

Keynes's work of the 1930s allows us, moreover, to rethink imperial decline not just as Europe's loss of the metropolitan power to universalize but also as the recovery of cultural particularity. The point can be made by recognizing that *The General Theory* is both more and less "general" than previous economic theories. It is more general in that it conceives of the economy as a *total* and integrated system rather than as a set of individual markets and firms, buyers and sellers. But it is less general in that it is designed for a world organized by *particular* (culturally located and politically defined) economies rather than by potentially universal rules about market behavior. I have suggested that the "macro" dimensions of Keynes's theoretical breakthrough are in fact intimately connected to his national situation. Keynes's new grasp of economic aggregates occurs within an intellectual culture that was rapidly confronting its own particularity. His writing helps bring to an end the era during which the island was the sociologically invisible center of a world empire replete with anthropological knowledge.

Keynesian economics responded to the crises of the 1930s by projecting a recuperative *national* future implied by shrinking *imperial* horizons, by coming to terms with English cultural traditions as resources for improving the British state, and by exploring new forms of social aggregation and new languages for collective experience designed to supersede the forms and languages of the laissez-faire 1920s. These strategies, which also emerge in the contemporaneous work of Forster, Woolf, and Eliot, modified both metropolitan perception and modernist anomie with a more restrictive, but more cohesive, model of national culture. Keynesian economics thus replicates the Anglocentric and anthropological turn taken by modernist writers. For Keynes, the nationalization of economic thinking was no doubt made urgent by the pressure of European events, but it was also made possible by the shaping forces of imperial retrenchment. The death of cosmopolitanism motivated Keynes to strike an uneasy peace with Englishness, not just as a source of pragmatic wartime solidarity but as a newly salient resource for mitigating old problems based in the metropolitan era. In this sense, the transformative vision of Keynes's *General Theory* (1936) can profitably be compared to Woolf's unstinting critique of patriarchy in *Three Guineas* (1938) and Eliot's comprehensive rejection of liberal pluralism in *The Idea of a Christian Society* (1939). Of course, as dissenting intellectuals and cosmopolitans, the feminist Woolf and the classicist Eliot did not simply retreat into the established framework of national culture; instead, they imagined the potential reinvention of that culture at a moment of dire historical necessity. In *Three Guineas*, Woolf outlines with grim perspicacity the mutually reinforcing links joining patriarchy to patriotism to imperialism to capitalism to war. However, as I have suggested, she also makes room for a creative vision of national culture rebuilt without the macho underpinnings provided by a now fragile imperialism—a national culture at last redeemed by the pastoral literary traditions of humane Englishness. In *The Idea of a Christian Society*, Eliot attempts to insulate England by exhuming a set of archaic but mythologically coherent traditions that had been layered over by the liberal, expansionist version of the modern British state. Despite important ideological differences, these projects share an investment in English civil traditionalism as an inalienable core of value.

The project of postimperial domestic salvage was similarly central to Keynes's analysis of the economy. But Keynes's involvement in national affairs also extended to direct sponsorship and advocacy of the arts in ways that make his late career resonate even more closely with those of Woolf, Forster, and Eliot. Keynes was the key founder, planner, and fundraiser for the Cambridge Arts Theatre, which opened one day before *The General Theory* was published in February 1936; the two projects expressed Keynes's overlapping interest in cultural and economic revival (*JMK* 536). In that same year, Keynes published "Art and the State," calling on the modern state to foster the aesthetic well-being of citizens.[19] In particular, Keynes champions the performing arts as a way to satisfy "the human craving for solidarity" (*CWK* 28: 347). With the great success of fascist ceremony in view, Keynes advocates a counterfascist art for liberal England. The Western democracies' failure to develop ceremonial and communal forms was, he thought, "a weakness not to be ignored." His emphasis on public ritual makes sense not only as a response to fascism but also as part of the growing application of anthropology to domestic English life during the 1930s. If events on the continent suggested the need for national art, then anthropological self-consciousness provided one basis for reinventing domestic rituals that could be "expressive of ourselves" (*CWK* 28: 346). Like many writers of his time and milieu, Keynes was beginning to question the value of privately produced and privately consumed literary forms like poetry and fiction, the modernist genres par excellence. In "Art and the State," he develops the following hierarchy: "Architecture is the most public of the arts, the least private in its manifestations and the best suited to give form and body to civic pride and the sense of social unity. Music comes next; then the various arts of the theatre; then the plastic and pictorial crafts." Keynes concludes his list "with poetry and literature," which are "by their nature more private and personal" (*CWK* 28: 345). His proposal for state-sponsored art is designed to supersede both the philistinism of the Victorian bourgeoisie and the rarefied artistic institutions of modernist elites.

It was just at the time that Keynes was offering this brief against the privatization of modern art that Forster, Eliot, and Woolf were partaking in the curious revival of interest in pageantry, which (as I discussed in chapter 2), they used to explore the claims of public ritual as against private textuality and interiority.[20] Keynes's call for "public shows and ceremonies" thus converges with the activities of his closest literary associates, who were themselves trying to adjust the cosmopolitan modernist aesthetic to the imperatives of national revival. In *The General Theory*, Keynes introduced new techniques for representing economic aggregates rather than individual agents. Similarly, Woolf tried in *The Years* and *Between the Acts* to modify the techniques of perspectival narration and to broaden the social and historical dimensions of her fiction without abandoning the claims of the eccentric soul. Keynes and Woolf shared a lifelong Bloomsbury commitment to free-thinking individuals, but their late works register new appreciation for the inevitable, sometimes irrational power of group identity.[21] *The General Theory* embeds the old microeconomics in the nascent language of macroeconomics. In *Between the Acts*, Woolf ventures an analogous revision of the stream of consciousness technique by exploring the individual psyche as it is informed and re-formed by the pressures of inherited, public, and especially national culture.

Eliot's later work, of course, attempts an even more thoroughgoing departure from representations of the atomized bourgeois soul in the city, gravitating toward the broader problems of culture and religion. While Keynes would have evinced some secular liberal suspicion about Eliot's essentially religious definition of culture, he too was seeking to refine his own youthful devotion to the autonomous self with a greater awareness of the "order and pattern of life amongst communities and the emotions which they can inspire" (*CWK* 10: 449).[22] In the larger history of British politics, the overlap between Keynes's liberalism and Eliot's conservatism may come as no surprise. However, this particular intersection clarifies the role of Keynesian economics in the midcentury rhetoric of *cultural revival*. Keynes believed that national disengagement from the vicissitudes of global laissez-faire might reestablish the island nation as a stably populated, fully employed, and self-determining polity, which could in turn support a healthier culture. In the new era, dynamism would be measured not by the expansion of political boundaries but by the evolution and refinement of civilization *within* them. Timothy Mitchell describes the economic half of this Keynesian equation: "Once economic discourse took as its object the fixed space of the nation state . . . it became both possible and necessary to imagine economic growth in new terms, not as material and spatial extension, but as the internal intensification of the totality of relations defining the economy as an object."[23] As we saw in our reading of the choruses from *The Rock*, Eliot too was proposing that English culture switch gears from self-extension to self-discovery, an idea that rested on his sense of an opportunistic correlation between the decline of the bloated British empire and the revival of its vital national core.

The intersections of Keynesian theory and Eliotic criticism shed light on late modernism's close relation to emergent discourses of national collectivity in the West. We are used to thinking about this final phase of Anglo-American modernism in terms either of its horrified retreat from, or its secret affinities with, totalitarianism, but it is also true that modernist writing of the 1930s and '40s participates in the arrival of a more domesticated brand of collective politics. Indeed, the changing styles and doctrines of modernism in this period coincide with an emergent cultural logic of the welfare state, particularly in their absorption of individual atoms into collective forms. Michael Szalay has recently offered a persuasive account of this cultural passage as it pertains to New Deal America. In particular, Szalay argues that Wallace Stevens manages the mediation of lyric experience into public representation just as he imagines the integration of private agony and private risk into the aggregated, impersonal order of social security.[24] Szalay's subtle reading of Stevens's place in our insurance society is useful for reflection on 1930s English culture because it identifies a related case of midcentury modernism responding to the corporate turn, not just by defending the private freedoms of the artist, but by recognizing new resources for the development of literary impersonality. In England, the emerging language of collectivity referred less explicitly to the competence of the managerial state, preferring the rhetorical comforts of cultural cohesion. As I have suggested, the sweet tropes of national tradition were a crucial factor in Keynes's own willingness to accept state control over the free market as the lesser of two evils. My emphasis on English nostalgia (vs. American enterprise) invokes a rather inert national cliché. But it also marks a distinction between midcentury U.S. culture, in which Szalay can see a modernist poetics as homologous to New Deal social insurance, and midcentury English culture, in which modernists were exploring the uneasy absorption of the metropolitan subject back into folk histories and civil traditions.

By grouping Keynesian economics with late-1930s English literature under the rubric of metropolitan twilight and national recovery, I have risked deemphasizing important variations in social, political, and aesthetic commitments. For example, the argument seems to have collapsed the liberal rationalism of Keynes into the arch-traditionalism of Eliot. Keynes's humanism did contradict Eliot's stern Christianity; however, they both criticized the "pathologies" of what Eliot saw as vacuous pluralism and what Keynes called "capitalistic individualism" (*JMK* 538). Despite their manifest differences, they both invoked a native, Burkean genius for the common life in their attempts to ward off mass politics and mass culture. Eliot's Tory dreams echo beneath the surface of Keynes's rational reinvention of the economy. A few years before publishing *The General Theory*, Keynes announced his high regard for the "harmonies and qualities of a sound national economic life" (*CWK* 21: 206). A 1932 radio broadcast on British trade made his position clear:

> the pursuit of agriculture is part of a complete national life. I said above that a prosperous motor industry was a national necessity, if only to give an opening to one kind of typical Englishman. It is true in the same way that another kind needs . . . contact with the changing seasons and the soil. To say that the country cannot afford agriculture is to delude oneself about the meaning of the word "afford." A country which cannot afford art or agriculture, invention or tradition, is a country in which one cannot afford to live. (*CWK* 21: 209–10)

Pointing out the damage that international free trade had done to "the old established traditions of a countryside," Keynes issues the following call to reform: "let goods be homespun . . . and, above all, let finance be primarily national" (*CWK* 21: 207). Here the English genius for mechanical arts and rural crafts trumps the efficiencies of global capitalism. Keynes wished to reorder the economy to preserve not just English prosperity but an entire way of life. His program converges with Eliot's rather unlikely foray into agricultural reform in the late 1930s. As we saw in chapter 3, Eliot literalized the waste-land conceit in his lament about contemporary soil erosion in England (*ICS* 49). He urges his adopted nation to restore its agrarian foundations in order to make more direct links between society and nature, between culture and agriculture. Like Keynes, Eliot saw the renewal of a more complete and self-sufficient insular life as both economically feasible and culturally desirable. For his part, Keynes was more resistant than Eliot to the mesmeric power of gemeinschaft nostalgia, but his economic thinking nonetheless reveals a certain appetite for organic community underneath the liberal statecraft.[25] In 1933, abandoning his faith in free trade, at last Keynes offered this argument for "national self-sufficiency": "I am not persuaded that the economic advantages of the international division of labour today are at all comparable with what they were. . . . I become doubtful whether the economic cost of national self-sufficiency is great enough to outweigh the other advantages of gradually bringing the producer and the consumer within the ambit of the same national, economic, and financial organisation" (*CWK* 21: 238). Here Keynes proposes that the salvage of the national culture may come from the restoration of a *total economic life* on the island.[26]

Keynes's interest in the domestication of the national economy repairs, at least theoretically, the most basic fractures of the colonial system. After all, the Keynes of the 1930s was pointing to the salutary economic *and* cultural effects of bringing production and consumption within a single national ambit, of restoring precisely the kind of economic relations whose absence Fredric Jameson takes as a precondition of modernist style. In fact, Keynes's plans for taming capitalism were designed to manage a process of economic introversion that was already underway and that had already begun to impress itself on English intellectuals in the 1930s. As Jameson's model would predict, the reemergence of a more knowable, more bounded, more complete economic life in the nation seems to have triggered a demystification and destabilization of modernist style itself. It was, as we have seen, at this point in the late 1930s that Woolf and Eliot were modifying some of their most successful literary techniques. In their 1930s writing, Eliot, Woolf, and Keynes actively managed the transition away from the rich phenomenology but reified social relations of the metropolis. They explored a potentially meaningful recovery of national culture, describing a world more structured by the "order and pattern of life amongst communities" (*CWK* 10: 449)

The demystification of idiosyncratic modernist style in late Eliot and late Woolf was matched, in a sense, by stylistic modulations in Keynes's own work of the 1930s. *The General Theory*, with its conceptual *gravitas*, features a relatively ordered and somber use of language. Although the Modern Library recently named it one of the ten best nonfiction works of the century, *The General Theory* has never been seen as the best *written* of Keynes's books. Its increased theoretical and social range seems to have interfered with Keynes's usual stylistic finesse and playful experimentation and muted the "linguistic vivacity" that characterized his 1920s writing (*JMK* 470). As an economic reformer, Keynes aimed to restructure the free marketplace by slowing it down, stabilizing its more mercurial tendencies, and bringing it under the managerial hand of the nation-state. His goal was to make capitalism more humane and less mysterious. The unexplored irony of Keynes's project is that this new version of capitalism became less complex and delightful as an object of representation. Shifting away from virtuoso representations of economic disorder, Keynes traded the pleasures of form for the consolations of reform. Soon after *The General Theory* was published, Keynes himself evinced nostalgia for the time when economic writing could proceed by intuitive dazzle and rhetorical derring-do as against the more ascetic totalities of mathematical and econometric description that would come to dominate the "Keynesian" era (*JMK* 611). His own stylistic inventiveness, like the literary pyrotechnics of the high modernists, was outmoded in part because he began to reconceive his work in relation to a more complete and knowable social object. In *The General Theory*, then, as in *Four Quartets* and *Between the Acts*, we can grasp that elusive, elegiac moment when modernist style begins to identify itself as a relic of prewar metropolitan life.

The shared context of Keynesian theory and late modernism makes evident a certain relationship between historical and formal changes during an initial phase of demetropolitanization in British culture. But of course Britain did not become an economic or cultural island in the wake of Keynesian theory or high modernism. Even if we restrict our observations to Keynes, we have to recognize that his 1930s versions of national community were modified by alternative, supranational ideas in the 1940s, as evidenced by his contributions to the postwar monetary order of Bretton Woods. Still, a rereading of Keynesian economics and modernist writing helps isolate a distinctive, if incomplete, kind of historical transition. The route Keynes traveled from Moore's Cambridge to Bretton Woods exemplifies that larger transition. His "early beliefs" thrived in the relatively unmediated space between a free-floating subject and a rational universe permeated by the ethos of cosmopolitanism. But his later theories registered the sometimes violent reassertion of "the intermediate" and in particular of the nation-state. In the 1930s, Keynes theorized that the state power *could* mediate relations between individuals and the world, between souls and markets, because he had begun to recognize that national culture *already did*. Keynes had once participated in what Jennifer Wicke rightly describes as the modernist project of making imaginative order by dint of a powerful, innovative "cast of mind overlaid on the blooming, buzzing confusion of the market."²⁷ In the next phase of his career, though, Keynes looked for order not in the modernist mind but in a more properly *social* mediation of the disorder of laissez-faire capitalism. For Eliot and Woolf, as for Keynes, intellectual or *artistic* mediation between autonomous subjects and universal conditions was gradually displaced by more determinatively social forms of mediation between the individual and the general, between psyche and myth. When these English modernists began to disengage from the tenets of cosmopolitan individualism in the 1930s, they took national culture not simply as a spectral constraint left over from the *ancien régime* but as a real social form that could impart social coherence and artistic relevance.

Naturally, the Keynesian state (and its affective core of national culture) threatened certain individual freedoms available in the high modernist, laissez-faire metropolis. But it also offered to deliver the alienated modernist subject into a more public, communal arrangement for the production and consumption of art. Keynes's rethinking of the economic situation foreshadowed the end of metropolitan modernism as a culture marvelously free from territorial legacies, but increasingly subject to the unrelenting and lonely logic of the marketplace. By trying to improve on a "decadent international but individualistic capitalism" (CWK 21: 239), Keynes was also looking beyond the horizons of an "international but individualistic" *modernism*.²⁸

In the Keynesian transition of the midcentury, then, English intellectuals confronted their territorial and cultural particularity anew. If, for example, Keynes's youthful atomism was in some sense conditioned by the structure of imperial capitalism, his mature organicism was, in turn, conditioned by the *relative* retrenchment of British capital into a national form. His efforts to counteract the effects of an increasingly homogenized world culture and the international division of labor were in one sense nostalgically antimodern and antimodernist. On the other hand, they formed part of the dialectical emergence of new discursive and economic forces that superseded metropolitan perception and superannuated modernism. Keynes's contributions to the rethinking of national life as an integrated and particular totality thus carried over into many other postwar and postcolonial models of national culture that emerged in the wake of European imperialism.²⁹

Local Color: English Cultural Studies as Home Anthropology

Keynes's response to the conditions of midcentury—his belief in the "nationalisation of knowledge," his implicit recourse to English tradition as the basis for a newly collective rhetoric of state-sponsored art, his emphasis on public and popular culture, and his domestic application of models of social totality derived from more "primitive" economies—all reflect (and participate in) the reshaping of English destiny during the transition from empire to welfare state. In these ways, Keynesian thought not only mediates between economic and cultural history but throws into relief some discursive continuities between the pre- and postwar phases of retrenchment. To be more precise, Keynes's rethinking of the nation as a *system* both registers a residual modernist confrontation with the failure of cosmopolitanism and paves the way for an emergent, Anglocentric Cultural Studies.

The official origin story of English Cultural Studies generally includes backward references to Eliot, so it is not immediately surprising to see the field as emerging out of a dying modernism, despite the obvious variations in politics that separate a conservative like Eliot (or even a liberal like Keynes) from the postwar New Left. Most accounts of this ambiguous genealogy behind Cultural Studies frame the relation as one of intellectual influence; by contrast, I propose to describe a shared context to which Anglocentric intellectuals, from Eliot to F. R. Leavis to Raymond Williams, all respond in turn. The nativist problem frequently crops up as a kind of original sin in many academic histories and intellectual memoirs of Cultural Studies.[30] Rather than rehearse those internecine arguments, which generally seek to expose romantic impurities lurking in the heart of early Cultural Studies, I propose to address the nativist problem within the broader historical context of the anthropological turn. Such an approach moves us beyond the limitations of an influence model or a purely intellectual genealogy—in which Anglocentrism is no more than a humanist error—and allows us to come to terms with the historical and symbolic constraints operating on English intellectuals during the moment of imperial retrenchment. Such an approach, in other words, frames the problem of Cultural Studies nativism within a necessary and dialectical transition from universalist to particularist concepts of culture. With that principle in mind, we can reexamine some of the field's founding texts, largely conceived and composed in the late fifties: Richard Hoggart's *The Uses of Literacy* (1957), Raymond Williams's *Culture and Society* (1956) and *The Long Revolution* (1961), and E. P. Thompson's *The Making of the English Working Class* (1963).

Hoggart, Williams, and Thompson retain the status (and the gendered implications) of founding fathers in Cultural Studies because their work broke the ground for new, comprehensive approaches to English society. Their analyses of national culture as a dynamic system challenged decades of Whig historiography and Tory iconography, promoted working-class agency to the center of literary and historical attention, and inspired a new era of what Tom Nairn has called "bookish populism."[31] In the last decade, most assessments of early Cultural Studies have drawn their conclusions based on the political virtues (attention to the working class) and vices (inattention to race, gender, and sexuality) of the postwar New Left. But when we place Hoggart, Williams, and Thompson in the context of a domesticated anthropology that also draws from late modernist ritualism and thirties documentary realism, we can unfold a richer explanation of the Anglocentric predicates of Cultural Studies.

In the dialectical transformation of England from unknowable modern center into a full-blooded and self-knowing culture, figures as different as Eliot and Leavis and Williams all used the language of national tradition to address the problem of cultural wholeness. It was at this point, writes Francis Mulhern, that "[p]sychology, anthropology and Marxism struggled for rights to synoptic explanation in the domain that had formerly been monopolized by religion, systematic philosophy, liberal economics and sociology."[32] In the struggle for synoptic explanation, Eliot, Leavis, and Williams all saw English tradition as something to be transvalued rather than cast off (or, for that matter, accepted uncritically).

Despite a common orientation to English particularism, Eliot, Leavis, and Williams differed sharply in many ways. For example, the culturalism of both Eliot on the right and Williams on the left challenged the preeminence of literature itself in ways that Leavis could not have countenanced. For Leavis, literature was "the main surviving witness of an existential integrity that had disappeared from the social world."[33] In a world falling ever farther from the ideals of organic community cherished by Leavis, great English writing had a special redemptive vocation. He aimed to democratize, not anthropologize, the old high literary culture. In this sense, Leavisite criticism represents not the romance of retrenchment (as I have been calling it) but a more familiar discourse of national decline associated with figures like Graham Greene or George Orwell.

Leavis and his house journal *Scrutiny* stood for the redemption of a corrupt world by heroic literary individuals. By contrast, Eliot and other modernists turned in the end to national culture as a means to reverse, or at least mitigate, the social autonomization of art. In this way, Eliot, Forster, Woolf, and Keynes anticipated Cultural Studies: they imagined that the end of empire could separate authentic and humane English traditions from the excesses of the modern British state, closing the gap between culture and society.[34]

The points of convergence between these two phases or variations of Anglocentric revivalism should not, of course, obscure the differences between representative figures like Eliot and Williams.[35] Where the populist Williams redefines culture in terms of its makers at every level of society, Eliot insists programmatically on the stewardship of a traditional elite based on Coleridge's clerisy. Moreover, Williams's secular definition of culture contradicts Eliot's essentially religious one. Williams explicitly rejects any premise about "an ultimate, essential condition of man" (including the doctrine of original sin that underwrites Eliot's classical and religious sensibility), preferring to address specific manifestations of the human in society.[36] Finally, Williams implicitly poses his concept of a "knowable community" against Eliot's Burkean concept of an organic community. For Williams, the concept of a cultural system is meant to describe heterogeneity, dynamism, and transformation from below, whereas for Eliot the importance of grasping the many levels within a single culture is to appreciate the equilibrium that keeps all the constituents fixed in their proper place in the hierarchy. With these differences in mind, it is easy to see why Williams dismissed Eliot's ideas of English culture as warped and abstract.

However, while we acknowledge the abstract and even tendentious quality of Eliot's troglodytic ideas about Englishness, it is important to note that Williams's investment in concrete, lived experience requires—like all forms of realism—its own (more subtle) kind of abstraction and condensation. Indeed, as Williams himself notes in *The Long Revolution*, it is quite impossible to come to terms with the full nature of modern culture and society without abstracting from the whole.[37] Moreover, it is in some ways the central insight of *Culture and Society* that the affinity between radical and conservative anticapitalism consists precisely in a shared wish to recover forms of wholeness underlying the rationalized and reified fragments of modern society. Both late modernist aesthetics and early Cultural Studies wanted in some sense to reconcile the heterogeneity of real culture with the abstract unity of the nation. It is therefore worth suspending the left/right binary long enough to consider the historical process that drives the national abstraction on both sides. These two varieties of anticapitalism both turn to a domesticated anthropology of culture in order to reclaim Englishness—and thereby to gauge the deep cultural effects of British contraction.

For Eliot as for Williams, socioeconomic and cultural conditions determine each other. It makes sense, then, that both could see a slowdown in Britain's imperial and industrial expansion as a potential slowdown in the pace of social atomization and therefore as an opportunity to reconceive the island nation in terms of its once and future territorial and cultural integrity.[38] In *Culture and Society*, Williams writes that the very idea of cultural integrity—of culture conceived as a "whole way of life"—comes to modern literary intellectuals through Victorian anthropology and sociology, although those nascent social sciences owed much to a romantic literary tradition that had already (in aversive response to industrialism) broken culture off from society in the first place (CS 233). This historical give-and-take between literature's implied critique of industrial society and anthropology's formalization of that critique reaches what appears to be a new phase in Williams's own time:

In common thinking, the mediaeval town and the eighteenth-century village have been replaced, as examples [of life free from modern industrialism], by various kinds of recent simple societies. These can reassure us that the version of life which industrialism has forced on us is neither universal nor permanent, but can also become a kind of weakening luxury, if they lead us to suppose that we have the "whole arc" of human possibilities to choose from, in life as in the documents. The alternatives and variations which matter are those which can become practical in our own culture; the discipline, rightly emphasized, drives us back to look at these within our own complex, rather than outwards to other places and other times. (CS 233)

The passage charts the movement from romantic ideals of cultural authenticity based in the past to more recent (i.e., modernist-era) anthropological projections of "simple societies" based on those in the colonial periphery. But it also sets out a new imperative to forego the fantasy of evolutionary anthropology and to reformulate the tribal romance of the "simple society" into a practical and comprehensive criticism of England itself.

Culture and Society, like Eliot's Notes towards the Definition of Culture, imagines a radical reconfiguration of the splintered laws of culture in postwar England. Williams rejects the idea of the artist as "abnormal" and alienated, writing that "[t]he renewed emphasis on communication [among contemporary artists] is a valuable sign of our gradual recovery of community" (CS 250). He situates himself on the cusp of a historic opportunity to relocate wholeness in English culture, to repair conceptually an entire tradition of thought that, beginning in the Renaissance, had split off "individual" and "society" as reified categories increasingly divorced from the real web of social relationships (LR 76). Like Eliot, Woolf, and Keynes, Williams renarrates the gradual divorce of high art from the common culture as one symptom of a profound atomization that peaked in the modernist era, but that might admit of remediation during the radical reorganization of British capitalism after 1930.[39]

To this account of Anglocentric and holistic convergence between intellectual projects from different decades and different political traditions, one might well object that Williams has, after all, only an epistemology of Englishess while Eliot has something like an ontology. In this view, Eliot's nativism depends upon a rooted essence of culture, whereas the work of the postwar New Left was predicated on the minimal, even procedural, gesture of limiting their work to a national (not nationalist) sphere. In this view, furthermore, even if the early work of Cultural Studies bears the traces of nativism, such nativism was not historically or theoretically necessary to their project; it is a romantic leftover easily purged by subsequent generations. However, in their shared attempts to transform British universalism into English particularism, the writers in question were shaped not just by the promptings of the creative individual mind but by the available stock of rhetorical resources and indeed by historical forces associated with a massive geopolitical *transition*. It makes sense, then, that Cultural Studies intellectuals reinvented English exceptionalism despite their radical politics. Likewise it makes sense that Eliot, despite his apparent arch-nativism, in fact demystifies English essence in *Four Quartets*. And Eliot was not the only modernist who did so: both Woolf's insular yet antifoundational history of culture and Keynes's unmistakably English yet demonstrably "general" theory of employment exemplify the complex shading between ontologies and epistemologies of Englishness endemic to this era of transition. That same subtle mixture has been exposed as part of the appeal of English Cultural Studies by Paul Gilroy, who points out that Raymond Williams's valuation of long experience does not invoke simply a neutral empiricism but constitutes, in the end, a logic of "ethnic absolutism."[40]

Once we take Gilroy's critique on board, the active question becomes whether or not Cultural Studies *needed* its restrictive model of Englishness in order to generate its ground-breaking insights into class and culture. Could Cultural Studies have absorbed the ethos of anthropological holism for the purposes of inventing a systematic *approach* to culture without at the same time installing that holistic ethos in the culture itself, thereby reifying Englishness? In my view, the answer is no. And this despite the fact that intellectuals like Williams are impressive precisely because they scrupled over the difference between a utopian *method* that projects totality into the future as a socialist goal and a conservative *fantasy* that asserts totality as the organic, indestructible birthright of Englishness. In short, early Cultural Studies bears within it the limitations of its own complex historical moment. During the thirty-year interregnum between empire and welfare state, the rhetoric of home anthropology allowed English intellectuals to equivocate between a culturalist ethos based on immanent wholeness and a materialist model based on social antagonisms. As those intellectuals transferred anthropological thought from the periphery to the center, they revealed its own conceptual doubleness in the split between a primitivist romance (in which Englishness could be reauthenticated as an almost tribal identity) and a functionalist method (in which England had to be grasped heuristically as a bounded unit for the purpose of representing its social heterogeneity). Early Cultural Studies embodies rather than resolves this split, which is why the specter of nativism has haunted the field ever since.

The domestication of anthropology seems to account theoretically for the innovative methodology of Cultural Studies *and* for its latent organicism, but we should test this explanation against textual facts by analyzing anthropological effects in the work of Williams, Hoggart, and Thompson. Williams's early work, dedicated in large part to literary-critical treatment of "great men" drawn from a traditional elite, might seem at first to stand as counterevidence. But *Culture and Society* and, even more, *The Long Revolution* do try, in a sense, to anthropologize the literary canon. In his essay on the "creative mind," for example, Williams integrates artistic production into a more general and participatory model of "communication"; not incidentally, the essay echoes both Woolf and Eliot by invoking a primal scene of English art in which the distinction between artist and audience is yet to be invented (*LR* 25–39). Here Williams does not simply preside over a "slippage" between culture as art and culture as a "whole way of life" (as many casual critics would suggest) but in fact attempts a theoretical reconciliation of the two. By insisting that individual creative acts—in any social domain—articulate shared values, Williams lays the foundation for an anthropology of art. In the process, Williams broadens the definition of culture to include not just artifacts but practices; and practices require ethnographic, not literary, interpretation. More to the point, Williams's anthropological turn in *Culture and Society* and *The Long Revolution* coincides not accidentally but integrally with his axiomatic (though often tacit) assumption that culture is national.[41]

And not just national but *English*: as Williams himself would later reflect, *Culture and Society* was "informed by a very specific national consciousness" that was neither Welsh nor British.[42] As a Welsh native studying English culture in a British state, Williams could be said to follow in the steps of Eliot and Orwell—two colonial outsiders who fascinated Williams, in part because they produced such resonant accounts of *English* life. Williams's own anthropology of the English led him to confront the classic problem of ethnographic fieldwork: how does the "participant-observer" find a position that is sufficiently external to the specimen culture to allow for an objective grasp of patterns yet sufficiently internal to allow for a nuanced and subjective understanding of experience? The tension between abstraction and experience (the philosophical problem bridged by Eliot with the critical apparatus of the "objective correlative") repeats itself in an anthropological key for Williams, who finds a provisional solution in the celebrated idea of the "structure of feeling" (*LR* 48).

Williams's ingenious attempts to modulate his own ethnographic distance from English culture defines what is perhaps the most significant point of intersection between his early work and the (otherwise quite dissimilar) early work of Richard Hoggart. Hoggart (who went on to head the Centre for Contemporary Cultural Studies at Birmingham) made his breakthrough with *The Uses of Literacy* (1957), itself a creative experiment in domestic ethnography. The book describes the habits of the English working class in an effort to protect those habits from erosion by an inauthentic mass culture and from stereotypical misrepresentation by the metropolitan elite. Wishing to avoid both florid romanticization and arid abstraction, Hoggart blends ethnography with memoir. To achieve subjective depth and authenticity, he bases half the book on memories from his own working-class boyhood in Leeds; to achieve objective credibility, he conducts field work in contemporary urban neighborhoods.

Although Hoggart's experimental form of autoethnography-cum-autobiography is designed to finesse the gap between participant and observer, it often runs aground on the same shoals that sank the Mass-Observers of the thirties. Like them (but with less scientific confidence and therefore more rhetorical appeal), Hoggart aims to represent the working class from within, not from above. Like them, he falls into a longer history of autoethnographic writing about the working class in England (a history that extends back into nineteenth-century discourses of folklore, local history, and ethnology), while also seeking to break with that history by removing the bourgeois filters from descriptions of working-class life. But Hoggart's split form and self-conscious methodology cannot fully remove those filters, especially since he rewrites the gap between his own rude youth and later educated sensibility as the gap between an authentic working-class past and an increasingly inauthentic working-class present. His ethnographic idiom thus seems to echo the work of Mass-Observation (which in turn echoes the faintly condescending, obsessively detailed functionalism of Malinowski). We learn that "canary-breeding is not increasing, but there is a growing interest in some other forms of cage-bird breeding, notably of budgerigars."[43] In working-class neighborhoods ("each as homogeneous and well-defined as a village"), "the oral tradition is still strong," and "[d]reams are not to be ignored . . . because they foretell" (UL 59, 31, 30). Hoggart sounds a bit like a puritanical and masculine Margaret Mead when he describes the sexual lives of young working-class women and their "brief flowering period" (UL 51). In short, despite Hoggart's ingenuity and his sensitivity to the problems of working-class representation, exoticism shapes his ethnography.

The real achievement of The Uses of Literacy stems not, then, from its positivist view of working-class authenticity but from its attempt to describe a cultural system. And that systemic, economic, and relational model of culture depends in Hoggart's case, as in Williams's, on patterns within bounded nationhood. Although Hoggart draws evidence from particular urban neighborhoods, he proposes more general conclusions about "English life" (UL 246). My point here is not to cavil over methodology in an important book now a half-century old but simply to note that the national framework is a necessary part of both the substance and the rhetoric of the new culturalism. Hoggart and Williams generate their most interesting models for the relation of class and culture by working empirically and ethnographically within a field defined by them as English (not British, not regional). As Stanley Aronowitz has suggested, it is as an ethnographer of national culture that Williams develops the innovative "vocabulary of immanence" through which he can treat "works of art as constitutive material signs."[44] Aronowitz pays tribute to Williams's empirical achievements, but points to a theoretical vacuum resulting from Williams's assumptions of wholeness in the national culture.

Aronowitz's skepticism about the coherence of Williams's cultural object joins a large body of commentary, which has included a second generation of theoretically driven cultural leftists such as Terry Eagleton and Perry Anderson. E. P. Thompson crystallized the main point of contention as early as 1961, with his rejoinder to Williams that a "whole way of life" should rather be conceptualized as a "whole way of struggle."[45] Since then, this central divide—between empiricism and theory, or romanticism and structuralism, or humanism and Marxism—has divided Cultural Studies into what Stuart Hall has usefully summarized as "two paradigms." The fundamentals of the debate are well known and not fully germane to the present discussion, so I will confine myself to two observations about it.

First, the debate seems to divide the adherents of English particularism from those who wish to purge their theory and their politics of any hint of nativist or even national exceptionalism. But in some sense the entire field of conflict, not just one of its poles, seems governed by the historical peculiarities of England's absorption of both Marxist and anthropological concepts of culture. The emergence of Cultural Studies as a domesticated anthropology for the postimperial period has, as I have suggested above, generated a legacy of built-in contradictions about English cultural wholeness and peculiarity. These contradictions are best understood not as political error or humanist heresy but as effects of the difficult transition between imperial universalism and national particularity. The original class-and-culture formulations of Cultural Studies bear their residual Anglocentrism as a kind of necessary mark of history.

And this leads to my second observation, which is that English Cultural Studies unfolded dialectically within a changing national context, so that Thompson's rejoinder to Raymond Williams rather neatly anticipates Perry Anderson's later response to Thompson himself. Anderson challenged the empiricism and holism of Thompson's early work on William Morris and of Thompson's monumental *The Making of the English Working Class*, two books whose recovery of popular national traditions played a key part in the rise of left culturalism. For Anderson, Thompson indulges in "proletarian positivity" as opposed to a more austere and theoretical view of the proletariat as a negativity that will transform history.[46]

The consolidation of national identity by Cultural Studies acted, of course, to contain social differences (gender, class, religion, race, sexuality), but it also focused attention on those differences within the framework of an "entire way of life." This double effect stems from the equivocation between two forms of wholeness, one "cultural" and oriented to integration, one "social" and oriented to differentiation. Or, as Anderson reframes the problem, the tension is between Marxist and sociological versions of totality: the Marxist concept denotes "a 'complex' totality of different levels, not to be reduced to each other, but 'loaded' by the greater weight of one level within it, such that dynamic contradictions are generated by discrepancies between them." By contrast, the social wholes of Weber or Durkheim—and of what I have been calling the anthropological ethos—are "tacitly circular" and "reciprocal." They explain the reproduction, not the transformation, of a society.[47] The versions of a complete national economy/culture at work in Keynesian and late modernist writing are clearly of the second variety. But they were also dialectical precursors to the cultural materialism of the postwar English leftists, including Anderson himself.

Rather than pass the nativist problem back and forth as a political football, it is perhaps more useful now to think of Cultural Studies nativism as the conceptual language available to intellectuals who faced the task of rewriting universalism during the first sustained phase of decolonization. This task no doubt confronted other Europeans, but my hypothesis (which ironically but necessarily reproduces the logic of exceptionalism) is that English intellectuals worked in a special historical context. In that context, it was possible to absorb the lost privileges of imperial centrality by restoring to England its historical privileges as the archetype of modern industry and empire, and therefore the archetype of a new age of postindustrial, postimperial national life. The archetypal turn of thought—in which England is somehow the "most typical" modern society because it is the *oldest* modern society—retains a second-order universalism for a national culture in the process of losing its first-order universalism (the classic form of European humanism based on geopolitical centrality). This second-order universalism, based not on the unmediated human *subject* as a universal type but on the national *culture* as a universal type, is precisely the inner form that links Woolf, Eliot, and Keynes to Hoggart, Williams, and Thompson. All of these intellectuals ascribed to England a particular kind of cultural depth, integrity, and recuperative commonality expressed as the postimperial core of a shrinking island. Without the claim to archetypal status, England would have to subordinate itself fully to the logic of particularity, taking its place in Forster's drab sisterhood of nations, alongside Guatemala and Belgium. But the recuperative model of historical depth and cultural integrity confers on England a "first among equals" status in the world after empire. In their reformulations of English destiny, Eliot, Keynes, Williams, and Thompson replace the imperial and Arnoldian claim to metacultural modernity with an opposite claim to historical priority in the organic formation of a national tradition, a claim of privileged capacity to produce, as it were, the very stuff of culture (and, by extension, to produce Cultural Studies itself).[48]

The discourse of particularism in midcentury England contains, then, a buried cargo of universalism. The key texts of early Cultural Studies feature redemptive claims about England's first-in, first-out relationship to both modernity and its discontents—claims that make England at once the most atomized society and the most integrated culture.[49] In *Culture and Society*, for example, Raymond Williams identifies a slow-cooked critical tradition of writing about culture as an English endowment based on the fact that industrialism hit first and hardest in England (*CS* xi). The idea of England's archetypal modernity takes on more explicit form in *The Country and The City*: "Since much of the dominant subsequent development, indeed the very idea of 'development' in the world generally, has been in these decisive directions, the English experience remains exceptionally important: not only symptomatic but in some ways diagnostic; in its intensity still memorable, whatever may succeed."[50] This passage follows from a description of British industry and empire (as the "decisive directions of modernity"), then makes a telling shift from British to "English" as it turns from the material facts of modernity to the intellectual countertradition cherished by Williams as part of the national "experience."

For E. P. Thompson, as for Williams, the English experience refers to a cultural landscape in which the expression of dissent from modern capitalism has an especially rich lineage, both high and popular. Thompson's *The Making of the English Working Class* works from the premise that English priority in modernization makes the formation of its working class both typical and atypical. In the introduction, Thompson notes that some forms of dissent that are sadly but safely obsolete in England are still current in the colonial world, so that "[c]auses which were lost in England might, in Asia or Africa, yet be won."[51] From a synchronic and political point of view, it is possible to read Thompson's work as reflective of an entrenched contradiction *between* universalism and particularism.[52] But from a historical point of view, Thompson's work reflects the experience of intellectuals whose task it was to make the transition *from* British universalism *to* English particularism.

In this sense, *The Making of the English Working Class* tends to substantiate the basic insight that the postimperial wave of domesticated anthropology was—if restrictive with regard to race, gender, and other forms of social differentiation—productive in reconceptualizing class and culture within a systematic or "retotalized" national frame. Like Williams and Hoggart, Thompson uses the national frame to describe a complete circuit of class relations rather than an isolated and autonomous working class. The restructuring of English destiny in the fifties certainly informed Thompson's own cultural turn, since it was a crucial part of the recovery of England's native integrity and democratic vitality. My claim is not that imperial decline necessitated or determined Thompson's method for representing English history but that, in a broad sense, the newly contracted national horizons seem to have translated into a more intensive and comprehensive set of projects concerned with the internal mechanisms of English culture and society.

Moreover, as the case of Thompson makes especially clear, the recovery of England's cultural depth and working-class cohesion in the fifties was often framed as a form of resistance to U.S. cultural hegemony. Keynes and Eliot had already registered the threat of Hollywood to the cultural integrity of smaller nations, among whom England was ever more likely to be numbered. For Hoggart, too, the protection of working-class authenticity against mass-cultural incursions was a specifically national mission. In *The Uses of Literacy*, he associates derivative and shallow cultural forms with the power of American media, as evidenced by his discussion of "juke-box boys" and their callow imitation of American style (*UL* 246–50). Similarly, Raymond Williams's early work tends to associate a "poorer kind" of mass culture with U.S. power and a retrievable, authentic popular culture with Englishness. Looking back on his early work, Williams reflects that the goal of postwar leftwing-culturalism was to find ways to allow England "to persist in its own terms."[53]

But Thompson was the most vocal champion of English integrity; his brand of Cultural Studies was overtly dedicated to reviving distinctive national traditions against the homogenizing violence of U.S. capitalism. His prodigious and energetic rearticulation of humane, radical-democratic traditions as a hallmark of Englishness was galvanized by his antipathy to the "Natopolitan" world of the Cold War, in which the British state acted as a faithful lackey to U.S. power. A 1951 essay on William Morris offers rich evidence of the ways in which Thompson and the English New Left were dedicated to protecting England against "American penetrations." This was, above all, a cultural(ist) mission. Thompson issues a battle cry to intellectuals on the shrinking island to pay "even more attention to our own history and cultural achievements."[54] Although it would be unfair to pin a case for Cultural Studies nationalism on this single early document, it nonetheless illuminates the relationship between fading British hegemony and the rising discourse of English cultural integrity.

Thompson's work offers in fact the best example of what we might call the pleasures of postimperialism among the founders of the New Left. There is something profoundly recuperative about the particularism of

The Making of the English Working Class; it taps into a resurgent idea of the English national genius for culture itself. Thompson's book appreciates and exhumes local and insular sources of worker solidarity, unalienated labor, communal cohesion, public joy, peasant vitality—all of the things presumed lost to England in the long rationalizing process of modernity, then projected outward into the colonies by metropolitan intellectuals like Arnold. Part of the crackle of Thompson's work and much of its lingering appeal come precisely from his efforts to restore to English history a sense of its own folk culture, its own broad popular energies.

Although Thompson's work on English class and culture seems to leave imperialism out *of* the story, the changing nature of British power forms an important context *for* the story. Rob Gregg and Madhavi Kale have argued that Thompson's influential account of the making of the working class has tended to obscure the significance of race, empire, and gender in English history. Even more to the point, Gregg and Kale show that Thompson's manifest blind spot about the effects of empire corresponds ironically to his own latent formation by imperial concerns (chiefly via the figure of his father, E. J. Thompson). Their discussion of the "imperial residue" in E. P. Thompson's work establishes him as a figure quite similar to Keynes or Woolf as I have presented them in this study: influenced a good deal more than is generally recognized by the experience of British imperialism (as mediated by friends and close family connections), but influenced in such a way as to concentrate attention on the potential vitality and unity of English culture (posed implicitly against and *after* imperial adventurism). Furthermore, just as the late modernists under examination above registered the end of empire as an occasion to recuperate or transform insular traditions, Thompson's work in the fifties and sixties betrays a wish to "rise above the politics of the inter-war years to something transcending the imperial context."[55] Even if Gregg and Kale are right that Thompson never fundamentally challenges his father's imperial values, it is perhaps even more important to note that—avowed values aside—Thompson's entire project seems at a deeper level to assimilate the fading hegemony of British universalism to the emergent significance of English particularism.

Similarly, Raymond Williams's failure to fully theorize race and empire was, in a sense, the blind spot that structured an entire anthropological set of insights into English culture. In that sense, Williams's work was deeply (if not always explicitly) responsive to the contraction of the British empire. Gauri Viswanathan makes the case that Williams's model of English culture "left a nebulous space that at one level seemed to allow for the potential broadening of that analysis of [the] English to include colonizer-colonized relations but at another implicitly resisted such further refinements."[56] Even when, near the end of *The Country and the City*,

Williams does consider imperial relations, Viswanathan points out that a model of modernization whose contours are determined by a national (indeed insular) view is not well suited for extension to the imperial sphere.[57] Since the late fifties, Cultural Studies intellectuals, including Stuart Hall and Paul Gilroy (and the collective that published *The Empire Strikes Back* in 1982), have, of course, expanded and changed the field to address, not just empire, but questions of race and immigration in Britain. Gilroy, for example, has criticized the national and ethnographic specificity of English Cultural Studies while extending cultural analysis in diasporic directions.[58]

With differing emphases, Gregg, Kale, Viswanathan, and Gilroy (among others) have rightly revealed, and begun to transcend, the limitations of an original Cultural Studies model of class and culture based on English national history. As their work suggests, a history of English class formation that leaves out race and empire is not only artificially insular and incomplete as national history but an insufficient basis for reconceiving the history of colonial relations and of transnational movements. Their critiques refer back to Raymond Williams and E. P. Thompson appropriately enough, since Williams and Thompson (with Hoggart) continue to exercise a powerful influence on cultural criticism and social history, whether or not those practices go by the name of Cultural Studies. However, when we analyze the formative stages of English Cultural Studies, we need to situate both its blindnesses and its insights within the historical horizon of a postimperial moment now fifty years old.

When we do so, three significant conclusions emerge. First, if English intellectuals of the modernist period tended toward cosmopolitan formations and primitivist forms, and if, moreover, those forms conduced to a kind of obscurity about the dynamics of class and culture at home, then binding the new class-culture analysis to national experience through radical Anglocentric thought had a certain revisionist logic about it, and was perhaps even a historical necessity. This does not mean, of course, that Cultural Studies had to exclude race or gender in order to see class clearly, nor that the cultural dynamics of class could only be grasped in an artificially circumscribed national laboratory. But it does mean that it was, at a certain point, analytically productive to concentrate on class and culture within the national sphere.[59]

Moreover, the circumscription of national culture endemic to this mid-century period and to the formative moment of Cultural Studies was not simply a superstructural event; that is, we are assessing not simply the decision of intellectuals to "ignore" empire or race but also the structural conditions of imperial decline in England. And this is the second conclusion to be drawn about Cultural Studies nativism: that it was part of a distinct phase in a larger dialectic of decolonization. As I have suggested,

I view the anthropological holism—and the corresponding analytical limitations—of those early Cultural Studies methods to be substantially informed (but not determined) by the transition from laissez-faire empire to welfare nation-state. This situates an English time and place—a history in short—for what Paul Gilroy in a more theoretical vein calls the "fatal junction of the concept of nationality with the concept of culture."[60]

When I suggest, then, that Williams's project "includes" empire not at the level of content but as an enabling condition for its address to the "peculiarity of the English," this is more than a theoretical twist on Gilroy and Viswanathan. Although it is significant that the national limitations of early Cultural Studies were both analytically productive as a form of home anthropology and historically symptomatic of imperial decline, there is a further point about decolonization to be made here. To draw this third conclusion, we have to begin by recognizing that cultural decolonization requires two historically complementary (but logically opposed) revisions of the myth of Englishness. Just as British colonial discourse managed to frame its peripheral objects as at once radically exotic and politically assimilable, it projected its own nationalism in the form of a contradiction. In colonial modernity, Englishness represented both an insular wellspring of distinctive values and an almost blank Arnoldian metacultural capacity to absorb and govern the cultures of its periphery. The English difference was, then, both a cultural essence and an essential culturelessness.

As a result, to decolonize the English means not only to demystify the myths of English cohesion and insularity (the approach more or less taken by critics like Said, Viswanathan, and Gilroy when they seek to give proper historical due to racial and imperial histories *within* the modern nation) but also to demystify English universalism. There is, then, a critical decolonizing force to ethnographies of the English that make its national culture the object of particularist and local-color discourses. Such ethnographic work redresses the universalist assumptions that, as Tom Nairn puts it, made the hegemonic English proof against stereotype. Stuart Hall's career exemplifies the double and complementary project of de-essentializing Englishness while also insisting on its cultural particularity. On the one hand, his analyses of an urban, multiethnic Britain in the seventies implicitly challenged monocultural and pastoral myths of the English experience. On the other hand, in more recent work on ethnicity, Hall has recognized the importance of direct address to a "conception of 'Englishness' which . . . because it is hegemonic, does not really represent itself as an ethnicity at all."[61] The complementary work of decolonization, then, is both to insist on a multicultural reality against a monocultural myth and to reduce the myth of Englishness to its own inner particularist form by means of ethnographic essentialism. At a certain point, Cultural

Studies nativists demystified the rhetoric of Englishness as an invisible, normative incarnation of the human; later critics like Gilroy began to demystify the ethnically absolutist rhetoric of "this island race." In fact, these efforts are, not simply complementary and sequential, but integrated in the same process, since they constitute a coordinated critique of the universalist excesses of imperialism and the particularist excesses of postimperial nationalism.[62]

If this study emphasizes one side of the problem by insisting on the critical force of English particularism in the period after empire, it is no doubt because I have framed my account of Cultural Studies against the legacies of high modernism. From the *literary*-historical perspective, the most striking development in the midcentury is the displacement of metropolitan perception by emergent realist, ethnographic, and systemic forms for representing national culture in England. As I have suggested throughout, Williams's original concept of metropolitan perception captures the historical ground out of which emerged a series of interlocking modernist features: (1) a cosmopolitan humanist language supported by English cultural hegemony; (2) a European artistic elite increasingly bound to itself and split from its constituent societies; (3) growing anthropological knowledge of (and aesthetic interest in) "total" primitive societies in the tropics; (4) a related mystification of the cultural system at home as hopelessly fragmented and therefore unreal; (5) the tendentious polarization of high and low culture in the absence of any systematic grasp of cultural production and consumption; (6) charged and antinomial relations between aesthetic form and social relevance, between lonely artists and their philistine public, between the language of subjectivity and objectivity— all of which resulted in (7) fierce experimental efforts in literary style that simultaneously reconcile (at the level of form) and recapitulate (in an ironic aesthetics of failure) the besetting schism between art and society. This litany draws together two historically related forms of modernist alienation that have not always been articulated to each other, one associated with imperialism and one with aestheticism. In brief, metropolitan perception reveals the historical link between a culturally disembodied modern center, defined against the embodied folk cultures of its global periphery, and an alienated aesthetic elite, defined against the mass cultural energies of its social periphery.

With that model in mind, we can see that Cultural Studies nativism, or the anthropologization of English culture, plots the joint end of imperialism and modernism. It simultaneously relativizes England as one particular culture among many in a global system and relativizes the high aesthetic as one specialized element among many in a national culture. In England, the idea of a national culture—conceived not just as a static alternative to, but as historical supersession of, the modernist Great

Divide—allowed figures as different as T. S. Eliot and Raymond Williams to rethink the disintegrative problem of minority culture in terms of an integrative minor culture. In a sense, anthropological functionalism migrated back from periphery to center, bringing with it a challenge to the supreme nonfunctionality of the art object that prevailed in certain quarters of modernist aestheticism (and in its critical offshoot, the New Criticism). If this postimperial and relativist turn destabilized some of the epistemic privileges of aestheticism and cosmopolitanism, it also promised to restore some hope for a reconnection between high art and a socially deeper, but politically narrower, culture. The discourse of culturalism in England, running from right to left, from thirties to fifties, from Eliot to Williams, was in this sense a dialectical antithesis to metropolitan modernism: not simply its political antagonist but a historical event that superseded it.

The various generations and iterations of the nativist problem in Cultural Studies, then, take on a new meaning when contextualized within a decolonizing "anthropological turn" embracing both late modernism and the New Left. These two Anglocentrisms represent an arc of thought that not only registered the end of empire but also "shifted the whole ground of debate from a literary-moral to an anthropological one."[63] As the prominence of names like Stuart Hall and Raymond Williams (not to mention T. S. Eliot) in this conversation reminds us, the anthropological view of England, as a place at once alien and knowable, has often been produced by resident outsiders (and here we might, from the point of view of gender, include Woolf in that category too). Williams and Hall, two key figures in early Cultural Studies, were not just outsiders but migrants from the colonial semiperipheries of Wales and Jamaica.[64] The defamiliarization of English traditions by colonial intellectuals in the fifties reached a fascinating convergence, in fact, not just in the new Cultural Studies but in literary writing as well.

Ethnography in Reverse: (Post)colonial Writers in Fifties England

The blind spots of early Cultural Studies with regard to race and empire seem ironic in retrospect since that field's emergence coincided with the arrival of newly visible postwar colonial immigrants in Britain and with the burgeoning presence of black writers in English literature. A few commentators have noted the connection; in *The Black Atlantic*, for example, Paul Gilroy proposes that "the entry of blacks into national life was itself a powerful factor contributing to . . . the formation of both cultural studies and New Left politics."[65] Gilroy cites the contributions of intellectuals like C.L.R. James and Stuart Hall to those intellectual fields but mostly poses the *fact* of colonial immigration against a *discourse* of English culture and society. More remains to be said about how imaginative writers from the (ex-) colonial periphery generated a literature that, like the critical discourses of Cultural Studies, aimed to particularize Englishness. In this section, then, I turn to representative figures from the wave of Asian, African, and Caribbean writers coming to England during the fifties: Sam Selvon, George Lamming, Doris Lessing, and Nirad Chaudhuri. The point is not so much to look for direct exchange or influence between colonial intellectuals and the members of the New Left (although Doris Lessing and Stuart Hall provide salient instances of such an exchange) but rather to juxtapose common responses to and redefinitions of Englishness during this phase of decolonization. Ioan Davies characterizes the larger process in this way: "The shift in British culture was from a confident imperial centre to one which was ultimately confronted by its own conquests. Not surprisingly, therefore, thinking about that culture involved a new form of theorizing—the inside making sense of its new naked self and the outside grasping what might be salvageable of what had made it marginal."[66] In this section, then, we are shifting attention from the "inside making sense of its new naked self" (that is, the reconception of late English modernism and of early Cultural Studies in a shared postimperial frame) to some examples of the "outside" performing its own kind of cultural and ethnographic salvage work on the shrinking island.

The texts I examine here remind us that the fifties were marked by a vivid and resurgent (though by no means monolithic) myth of English social cohesion and by an equally vivid set of material changes (including immigration) that challenged that myth. Far from engendering the monocultural England imagined by insular atavists such as Enoch Powell, the end of empire in fact only intensified the cultural mixing and migratory traffic that had long characterized life under the British crown. Nonetheless, Powell's rhetoric of Anglocentric continuity, in which imperialism features as an accidental and temporary aberration, does capture a powerful, semiburied ideology of shared insular experience. As we have seen, the recovery of a vital English core from a crumbling British exoskeleton has been a compelling trope in a variety of midcentury Anglocentrisms. In those Anglocentrisms, the logic of ethnic and territorial belonging displaces the principle of civic or universal subjecthood upon which, at least theoretically, the British imperial project relied.[67] Kobena Mercer points out that Powellism itself was not some brute bioracial essentialism but rather a powerful "*cultural* construction of Little England" whose assumptions and effects were racially exclusive.[68] Paul Gilroy, too, has been concerned to identify the ethnic absolutism, the Burkean ideological spine, that subtends contemporary concepts of English national culture:

the idea that England is a "culturally homogeneous" nation based on long, settled, shared experience.[69]

Naturally, then, the new postcolonial immigrants often faced an exclusionary logic of belonging and provoked a crisis in the definition of British subjecthood.[70] This crisis forms both the social context and thematic content for much colonial writing in the fifties. It is only fitting, then, that colonial writers participate in stripping away the ideological veils that had made British imperial nationalism a universal, unmarked, and transferable category of identity. Like their Anglocentric contemporaries in the New Left, migrant writers of the fifties represent English culture in terms of a particular and situated body of traditions rather than a mobile and extensible set of principles.

The story of the material and discursive shift from an empire based on universal Britishness to a nation based on exclusive Englishness—the story whose complex aesthetic manifestations have occupied the center of this book—has a fairly straightforward legal and political dimension. In her work on postwar immigration law, for example, Kathleen Paul shows that Labour leaders initially attempted to preserve imperial connections by affirming the British subject status of citizens from the dominions and colonies. However, that "inclusive formal nationality policy" was increasingly at odds with an "exclusive constructed national identity." In the decades following World War II, British political history testifies to the growing power of the latter.[71] From the Nationality Acts of the 1940s to the restrictive immigration acts of the 1960s, policy shifted from accepting the logic of imperial universalism to circling the wagons around an ethnocultural idea of Englishness. The transitional and ad hoc quality of Labour policy from 1940 to 1960 mirrors what I see in the cultural arena as an uneasy blend between a dying universalism and a rising particularism.

Within this broad transition of the postwar period, colonial workers and their families were transforming the condition of England, just as an increasingly visible group of colonial writers were transforming the condition-of-England novel.[72] Of course, writers from the colonies and ex-colonies had been a formative part of the London literary scene for decades, from Henry James and T. S. Eliot, to Oscar Wilde and W. B. Yeats, to Katharine Mansfield and Jean Rhys. Still, though, the colonial writers of the 1950s represent a distinct phase in the remaking of English culture insofar as their work participates in the transformation of center-periphery relations at the end of empire. West Indian writers like Selvon and Lamming represent a new cultural formation, both because they (unlike Eliot or Mansfield, say) were seen as artistic voices from within a non-elite migrant community and because they gained cultural authority by depicting England from the point of view of racially marked estrangement.

Like the Cultural Studies ethnographers, these immigrant writers look on inherited conventions of English culture through the lens of an alien knowability, generating a similar tension between a recuperative romance of Englishness and a disillusioned critique of Englishness. In Samuel Selvon's 1956 novel *Lonely Londoners*, for example, the central character, Moses, has thoroughly demystified immigrant life in the metropolis, yet continues to imagine England as the source of his future and his fate. Through Moses, Selvon maintains a broad sympathetic perspective on the urban disillusionment of the West Indians in postwar London, including the recent arrivals who, like the ambitious provincials of so many Victorian novels, come to the city with great expectations. Although the novel captures communal spirit within certain Caribbean enclaves in London, its main trajectory is toward a kind of ironic urban detachment, even atomization: "It have people living in London who don't know what happening in the room next to them, far more the street, or how other people living. London is a place like that. It divide up in little worlds, and you stay in the world you belong to and you don't know anything about what happening in the other ones except what you read in the papers."[73] Selvon's evocation of the yellow-fogged, beehive city as host to a million lonely souls often seems to echo T. S. Eliot's urban anomie. However, if we consider the central figure of Moses, we can also see that the disillusionment plot does not, in the end, cancel out the romance of arrival so much as fuse with it to create the ironic equipoise embodied in Moses, whose irony is the basis, in fact, for Selvon's own aesthetic.

As Kenneth Ramchand suggests, Selvon structures the novel so that Moses, a grim veteran of life in Lonely London when the story begins, has a kind of partial or vicarious resurgence of hope through his contact with newer arrivals like Galahad. For islanders like Galahad, London is still in many ways the center of the world: "that circus [Piccadilly] have a magnet for him, that circus represent life, that circus is the beginning and the ending of the world. . . . people sitting and standing and walking and talking and laughing and buses and cars and Galahad Esquire, in all this, standing there in the big city, in London" (*LL* 90). Galahad's awe— a newcomer's exoticizing naiveté—meets Moses's dry familiarity. From there, the novel blends and fuses those modes of experience. It trips episodically and achronologically from one to another of Moses's acquaintances, never straying far from Moses's own stabilizing perspective. The narrative structure presents emigration, expectation, disappointment, and acculturation in jerky juxtaposition rather than in smooth sequence. By moving rapidly among several characters and by alternating between the raw thrills of first contact and the mature reflections of long dwelling, the novel generates a kind of collage of arrival that reconciles these two modes and culminates in Moses's jovial irony. Moses is the Tiresias device of this novel, having foresuffered all; as the lonely Londoners tell stories in his basement flat, what Moses hears is the substance of the story: "Sometimes listening to them, he look in each face, and he feel a great compassion for every one of them, as if he live each of their lives, one by one, and all the stress and strain come to rest on his own shoulders" (LL 139).

Having reversed the innocence/experience plot by narrating Galahad's gradual rejuvenating influence on the worldweary Moses, the novel culminates in Moses's final bemused detachment from England. In the end, Moses's London is neither Eden nor Babylon—not a mythic location at all, but a particular cultural setting that, like Jamaica or Barbados or Trinidad, comes with its own ways and means, its own hazards and opportunities. Moses's final equidistance from Galahad's wide-eyed pleasure and his own cynical pain has two related implications. First, this plot establishes a way for the migrant intellectual to represent England beyond the Manichean logic of colonial and postcolonial history, beyond its symbolic status as either mythic homeland or mythic antagonist and into the realm of a quotidian, deromanticized contemporaneity. From the realistic and even neutrally anthropological vantage point of Moses/Selvon, English culture is ordinary. Second, the plot blends protagonist (Moses) into author (Selvon): the almost inevitable result of Moses's mature equanimity is his musing on the possibility of writing a book from the point of view of the sympathetic, ironic, and lonely Londoner. These two processes, taken together, provide a quick insight into the development of cultural authority for the West Indian writer in fifties England. It is, after all, Moses's ironic vantage point on London that has allowed Selvon to relativize English culture and to make his way on equal terms into English literature.

Of course, this reading has the danger of resolving too neatly some of the sexual and racial themes of the novel into the universal solvent of the protagonists's aesthetic equipoise. What remains to be examined are the consequences of the cultural relativism on which Moses's irony is predicated. After all, even if the novel rewrites Englishness as a particular identity suspended in attraction/repulsion with equally particularized non-English identities, there are still substantial economic and social disadvantages for the non-English, nonwhite Londoner. Like others of his generation, Selvon represents the disconnection between black London and white London as an obvious fracture in the idea of shared imperial subjecthood. Moreover, he rewrites the old romance plot of colonial allegory by describing a series of exploitative (even when comic) and exoticized sexual adventures across the racial divide. Reflecting on the unfamiliar sexual tastes and mores of London, Moses (in a streaming interior monologue) describes the common run of English girls who "want you to live up to the films and stories they hear about black people living primitive in the jungles of the world that is why you will see so many of them African fellars in the city with their hair high up on the head like they ain't had a trim for years" (*LL* 108). In this way, Selvon observes both the willingness of black immigrants to trade on sexual exoticism and the depressingly predictable forms of desire among English characters unable to break from primitivism. The repetitiveness of this sexual economy—in which reciprocal exoticisms only confirm the incommensurability of the two cultures/races even (or especially) when black and white bodies come together—is, more than anything else, what makes London lonely for Moses. His only recourse seems to be to withdraw from the sexual roundelay altogether.

In a sense, Moses's progress towards jovial sympathy and consolidated individuality depends precisely on achieving distance from both English and West Indian exoticisms and their corresponding racialized structures of attraction/repulsion. The novel's sophistication depends, as I have suggested (following Ramchand) on the sophistication of Moses's ethical and existential vision, a process which in turn depends on his ability to relativize England and the English, to push beyond both an inherited colonial awe and a subsequent (but equally overdetermined) anticolonial antipathy. Moses's ability to distance himself from this discursive double bind represents an interesting variant, I think, on what James Clifford has called "ethnographic self-fashioning."[74] That is, Moses achieves a kind of rhetorical authority and existential flexibility by positioning himself as a mobile, detached, ironic, and sympathetic self in an alien community, a participant-observer suddenly able to see with x-ray vision through the ideological assumptions and cognitive habits of both his host culture and his home culture. We might, though, call this *reverse* ethnographic self-fashioning, since Moses's field work—and there is much incidental and ethnographic commentary on the peculiarities of the English along the way—takes place in a not-fully-decentered metropole. Moses's selfhood—or Selvon's representation of Moses *as* a self—is thrown into high relief by the background of a racially and culturally totalized England. This version of black postcolonial subjectivity confirms by implication the peculiarity and cohesion of postwar Englishness. When, on the last page of the novel, Moses reaches an existentially triumphant (though politically anxious) moment of interiority, he imagines his own stability among "the black faces bobbing up and down in the millions of white, strained faces" (*LL* 142).

As the black faces in that sentence attest, Selvon's formula is not simply a single black subjectivity forged in the ethnographic crucible of white London. Indeed, Selvon takes pains to situate Moses's interiority within a collective West Indian identity formed against white Englishness. The critical consensus on *Lonely Londoners* would tend, in fact, to emphasize the novel's rendering of a group identity for West Indian immigrants. In that reading, the most important feature of the book is its flexible Creole idiom (in first and third person narration) that "draws expertly upon the whole linguistic range available to the literate West Indian," creating "a modified dialect which contains and expresses the sensibility of a whole society."[75] Stuart Hall established this interpretive focus in an early essay that credits Selvon (and George Lamming) with developing a literary technique that outstripped modernist subjectivism by rendering a "stream-of-social-consciousness."[76] This view is seconded by Lamming himself, who claims that one of the most significant contributions of the West Indian novel is that it represents the life of the masses. Lamming sees this as a dramatic departure from the tradition of the upper-middle-class English novel.[77] He praises Selvon's work as the closest thing there is to an authentic fictional representation of "the people" in contemporary English fiction, going on to note that, for the native Anglo-novelists, "there are really no people" (*PE* 45). This reading of Selvon's fiction remains important because, as noted above, Moses comes to consciousness through and in, not against, the nascent West Indian collectivity in London. Selvon's portrait of ethnographic self-fashioning in the encounter with a native English culture is inseparable from his achievement of literary authority as the representative of a new minority culture in Britain. However, it is equally important, I think, to recognize that Moses's ironic sensibility, conveyed by interior monologue, contains the key decolonizing force in the novel insofar as it inverts a trite colonial model of white subjectivity honed against the backdrop of a racially subordinated collective.

Stuart Hall's reading of "social consciousness" extends from *Lonely Londoners* to Lamming's *The Emigrants* (1954), though in this case too the narrative of arrival and acculturation unfolds largely in terms of the problem of black subject formation. Much more than Selvon, in fact, Lamming concentrates on the subjective consequences of the reciprocal exoticism that structures the relationship between English and West Indian characters. Indeed, as the essays in *The Pleasures of Exile* (1960) indicate, Lamming's writing manages to capture many of the same psychosexual nuances of the colonial encounter that Fanon captured in his Hegelian and psychoanalytic idiom. *The Pleasures of Exile* opens famously by exploring the critical possibilities of the Prospero-Caliban motif, particularly as it applies to the condition of West Indian intellectuals in the era of decolonization. In the drama of reverse colonization, Lamming casts the West Indian as a Caliban who travels back to Prospero's island and into the literary depths of English, forcing Prospero to relearn his role (*PE* 13). Having been the most thoroughly "colonial" type in the world—split completely from cultural roots in Africa or Asia

and forced to occupy a subordinate role with regard to distant Europe—
this Caribbean Caliban seeks to rewrite the master narratives of European
culture. And, now that Caliban lives on Prospero's island, "it is Prospero's
turn to submit to the remorseless logic of his own past. . . . Colonised by
his own ambition, Prospero's role is now completely reversed" (PE 85).
Lamming's elaboration of this logic of reversal is notable because it addresses both sides of the colonial divide, focusing on shared histories and
reciprocal effects.

From one perspective, Lamming's fairly sympathetic interest in the effects of decolonization on "Prospero" and *his* island (England) might
seem to be an unfortunate, even neocolonial recourse to the center just at
the point when Caliban's efforts should be turned to the reclamation of
his own history. And yet Lamming's double focus on Caliban and Prospero—and on Caliban in the land of Prospero—had, I think, a crucial
decolonizing vocation in the 1950s. By framing the problem of colonialism as a problematic legacy for both ex-colonizer and ex-colonized, rather
than repeating the belated or derivative politics that so many have found
lodged in that terminological back-formation, the "postcolonial," Lamming's essays began to clear the way for a new era. Moreover, by addressing England's metamorphosis into its own colonial contact zone
with its own limited and particularist culture, Lamming begins quite directly to rewrite the legacy of Englishness ("our once absolute Prospero")
as an unmarked, unmediated, and self-determining metaculture of the
center. While acknowledging the obvious (and often violent) differences
between the historical roles played by England/Prospero and the Carib-
bean/Caliban, Lamming nonetheless seeks to balance accounts by describing the ironic symmetries involved in the colonial encounter: "Papa was
a colonial; so am I; so is our once absolute Prospero. For it is that mutual
experience of separation from their original ground which makes both
master and slave colonial. To be colonial is to be in a state of exile" (PE
229). The common state of exile posited by these essays challenges inherited imperialist assumptions about the radical difference between colonizer and colonized. Faced with the typical imperialist double-bind rhetoric that both assimilates and exoticizes the colonized, Lamming relativizes
the colonizer's own perspective. In his writing, the English and the West
Indian are distinct and mutually exclusive cultures (not assimilable to
each other under the old universalist rubrics of British subjecthood); they
are symmetrical and reciprocal in their difference from each other (not
divided into an unmarked Arnoldian center and a "colorful" exotic mar-
gin). Rather than reify and mystify the historical roles of conqueror and
conquered, then, Lamming seeks to unfold a relational, and at times even
a recuperative, model of exile.

The "pleasures of exile" that Lamming extends to both Prospero and Caliban in his essays do, however, clash in tone with the rather more somber agonies of his fiction. For example, although *The Emigrants* is, I think, committed in principle to the relativization of English social and cultural power, the novel describes educated and working-class West Indians for whom London remains—at least initially—the "Headquarters" of the anglophone world (*PE* 24). Moreover, the novel describes a brutal round of dashed hopes, baffled intimacies, racist encounters, and sexual exploitation among the West Indians in England. Its plots and themes resonate closely with Selvon's *Lonely Londoners*: the high hopes of new arrivals, the growing ambivalence about England, and the almost instant formation of a West Indian community out of the regional and class diversity of exiled islanders. It opens by registering the oddness of transatlantic travel, the historical ironies of Afro-Caribbean traffic that have brought an unnamed emigrant voluntarily to leave his warm island for gray, war-broken England: "Unemployment, the housing shortage. He stood on the deck considering the newspaper report. It did not matter. No. It did not; for there beyond the water too large for his view was England rising from beneath her anonymous surface of grey to meet a sample of the men who are called her subjects and whose only certain knowledge said that to be in England was all that mattered."[78] As in Selvon's fiction, the emigrants soon discover the limitations of merely official belonging. But where Selvon uses the figure of Moses to capture the dramatic progress from hope through disillusionment to ironic detachment, Lamming's version of that storyline unfolds more or less extra-diegetically, in the knowing, politically sophisticated voice of the third-person narrator.

For the characters themselves, the plots of economic struggle and racial disadvantage do not resolve neatly, but for the narrator, England becomes—just as it does for Moses in *Lonely Londoners*—an existentially neutral zone, a *paysage demoralisé*. Stripped of its Manichean politics and recoded as neither a colonial promised land nor an anticolonial enemy camp, England becomes, in other words, a more genuinely postcolonial landscape. This does not imply that Lamming's England is culturally or historically blank. Quite the opposite; it features a fully integrated and richly realized society but one that, by the end of the novel, must be understood in relative terms, not as the spellbinding homeland of an "absolute Prospero":

> it would be a lie to deny that on the ship and even in the hostel, there was a feeling, more conscious in some than others, that England was not only a place, but a heritage. Some of us might have expressed a certain hostility to that heritage, but it remained, nevertheless, a hostility to something that was already a part of us.

But all that was now coming to an end. England was simply a world which we had moved about at random, and on occasions encountered by chance. (E 237)

This passage captures the critical insight harvested, as it were, from all the suffering of the emigrants in the course of the novel; its speaker has glimpsed a demystified England, denuded of its mythic accretions and moribund imperial discourses.

In *The Emigrants*, as in *Lonely Londoners*, the demystification of Englishness lays the foundation for a particular narrative of black subject formation. Here, instead of Selvon's generalized Creole dialect, though, we find a rather philosophical idiom that is strikingly redolent of Sartrean existentialism. On board the ship bound for England, for example, the narrator bathes the emigrants and their frail hopes in an atmosphere of merciless, reasonless fatality, generating a rather austere perspective from which the men appear merely as "heavy black flesh" (E 82). This objectifying view in a sense preempts the racial objectification that will occur in England and almost seems to deflect its political implications. But of course the detachment and self-alienation behind this existential idiom is itself already a racial and colonial matter. The cultural dislocation of the emigrants predates their journey to England and gives shape to their private experiences of disorientation, so that the crisis of meaninglessness can only be articulated in terms of England's role as ontological anchor: "Did it really matter? If each had been turned into a mere object it would not have mattered whether there was a place called England" (E 83). The painful condensation of souls into heavy flesh, of subjects into objects, becomes the master trope of Lamming's novel, because it captures the rerouting of the emigrants's desires through the metropole.

In England, objectification unfolds almost immediately as an exchange of reciprocal exoticisms, so that the white natives and the black arrivants continually reveal their separate but equal estrangement from the idea of a shared "British" subjecthood. Here, for example, Lamming describes the reaction of the Plymouth port officials to the West Indians who have obviously taken great pains to come to England:

They were bewildered by this exhibition of adventure, or ignorance, or plain suicide. For a while the movies seemed truer than they had vouched for, the story of men taking ship with their last resources and sailing into unknown lands in search of adventure and fortune and mystery. England had none of these things as far as they knew. . . . For a moment the officials thought of the islands the passengers had come from, and the whole spectacle seemed more fantastic. These islands off the gulf of Mexico that made an archipelago of unutterable beauty had bred lunatics. . . . They could not understand what England meant to these men. (E 108)

The bureaucrats in this passage are baffled by the emigrants' vision of England as a land of adventure, even enchantment—and only further baffled when they consider that, in their own packaged imagery, the West Indies were the *real* enchanted isles. The scene thus codes the English as natives of an exotic land while exposing them as exoticizers in their own right.

The fact that this scene takes place in a customs house, in the space of state authority over human traffic, underscores the failure of the official policy of shared or universal subjecthood. It sets in motion, in other words, a narrative based on the logic of unbreachable (and multiple) cultural particularisms as the end-stage of imperialism; what Fanon called the spatial principle of "reciprocal exclusivity" in the colonial zone comes back to reorganize the metropolis itself.[79] Like Selvon, Lamming emplots that logic in terms of recurrent and dispirited scenes of cross-racial sex. The sexual episodes provide a crystalline and rather Fanonian narrative instance of the psychosexual damage inflicted by colonialism on both sides of the divide.[80] Thus, the impotent Englishman Frederick has been unmanned, it seems, by losing his administrative post in Nigeria; he plans to return to Africa to "get back [his] strength" (*E* 253). Meanwhile, the schoolteacher Dickson feels his life and identity "drained away" by the "eyes of others" when he is put on display as a sexual object by Englishwomen captivated by his black body (*E* 268).

What seems reminiscent of Fanon in these encounters is not simply the racialized desire (as in *Black Skin, White Masks*) but the Hegelian and Sartrean resonances in Lamming's evocation of a furious lack structuring the encounter between black and white characters. Lamming's dual-sided sympathy allows him to present the problem of exile and lack in both English and West Indian characters—and, moreover, to narrate the formation of black consciousness in London via the hard-earned appreciation of Prospero's own forms of postcolonial emptiness. This face-off of dualing brands of existential crisis, then, tables the vexed politics of colonial/postcolonial.

Of course, such balance only emerges in the long course of the narration. Indeed, Lamming's use of sporadic first-person narration testifies to the agonized production in the novel of a private and interior self, threatened materially and politically by racism, but stabilized existentially by the encounter with Englishness. The first-person voice (never anchored to a name or a clear identity) seems to speak as a type of the educated West Indian man developing a refined and resolute sense of his selfhood against the backdrop of postcolonial migration: "I felt my freedom fresh and precious. It was a child's freedom, the freedom too of some lately emancipated colonials. . . . It was a private and personal acquisition, and I used it as a man uses what is private and personal, like his penis" (*E* 8). Because private freedom is conspicuously sexualized early in the novel, readers are prepared to interpret later sexual episodes as subplots within the larger trajectory toward existential freedom. Such freedom, it turns out, is at best a mixed Sartrean blessing, with no political guarantees (and little to offer West Indian women), but it is a compensatory "pleasure of exile" in England.

If Lamming's novel explores the formation of black subjectivity against an objectified white English culture, it also—like Selvon's—situates that individuating process within a *social* process defined by the formation of a new West Indian community. Dwelling on the informal meetingplaces of the new immigrants, Lamming insists on the collective basis for the emergence of black interiority: "It was here in the room of garlic, onions, and mist that each became aware, gradually, anxiously of the level and scope of his private existence. Each tried to think, for that too was a kind of action" (*E* 192). The last line captures Lamming's own gradual and anxious development of a case for the relevance of the West Indian artist or intellectual in a time of postcolonial struggle.[81]

Indeed, the insistence that thought, too, is action reminds us that the novel wishes, not just to narrate the plight of West Indian labor in England, but to justify the possibilities of West Indian literature in England. To do this, Lamming embeds the story of black subjectivity within the history of West Indian community and kicks both stories—the individual and the collective—into action by posing them against the obdurate integrity of postimperial English culture. The rhetorical authority of the West Indian or black British writer emerges out of the relativization of Englishness, a discursive technique that clears the space for an emigrant to represent, not sub-British identity, but a self fashioned in the traffic between two (at least formally and ontologically) equal and opposite cultures. And that self-fashioning is ethnographic to the extent that England can be represented in its new historical guise as a knowable national culture.

It should come as no surprise, then, that Lamming frequently makes the reverse colonization plot over into a plot of reverse ethnography, putting England squarely into a framework of postempire particularism. This pattern emerges early in the novel, aboard the ship bound from Guadeloupe to Plymouth, when the narrator meditates on the accent of one of the emigrants in this way: "It was as though you had taken a willing London Cockney and put him in some cultural laboratory" (*E* 57). The evocation of a Cockney in the culture lab prefigures an entire "peculiarity of the English" motif that recurs through the text, subjecting white natives to the kinds of typifying and stereotyping statements that, as Nairn suggests, were so often missing from the discourse of imperial, Arnoldian Englishness. Like Eliot, Orwell, and the Mass-Observers before him, Lamming ends up writing about the quotidian habits of the natives—their rabid love of football pools and the daily paper, for example (*E* 113). Such moments might well be put down to the obvious thematic material of a novel about immigration to England were Lamming not so intent on drawing our attention to the larger historical significance of an Anglocentric (but not English) anthropology. At one point, for example, the impotent Frederick observes that colonial students in Britain seem drawn to social anthropology, giving rise to the following exchange:

> "But if a colonial student does social anthropology," the other man said, "whose customs will they investigate?"
>
> "The West Indians can go to Africa," the man said, "and the Africans to the West Indies."
>
> "Or they can both come to England," Frederick said, "where the customs are indeed very queer."
>
> "Do you really think there would be much to find in our society?" the warden asked.
>
> "I don't know how much they'll find," Frederick said, "but there must be a damned lot to look for." (*E* 157)

Driving home his point with a not very subtle irony, Lamming immediately introduces into the scene an Englishwoman who gushes to a West Indian (whom she has mistaken for African) about the splendors of African costume and dance. With this, Lamming exposes the fatuousness of the old colonial exoticism, juxtaposing it to the new and counterdiscursive potential of Caliban's field work conducted on Prospero's island. Later, we learn that Azi, a talented African emigrant, has kept Western culture in his ethnographic sights for years: "he had a very queer interest in Christianity. Nothing to do with conversion. Just the kind of interest a visiting European might have in tribal customs" (*E* 251). The middle sentence points up the fact that Lamming's emigrants have less interest in "going native" than in extracting knowledge from England. Over the course of the novel, indeed, it becomes clear that the remaking of England into an object of local-color discourse does not so much perpetuate an older Anglocentrism, in which imperial power took the form of English invisibility, as describe a new Anglocentrism, in which the loss of imperial power results in a reverse-ethnographic visibility.

Reverse ethnography gives *The Emigrants* its central technique for rendering the mutual estrangement between English and West Indian cultures as a symmetrical face-off rather than a belated colonial romance. Although the novel chronicles the lingering effects of that romance—showing the emigrants as susceptible both to a golden image of an English promised land and a countervailing demonization of England—it *ends* by converting that colonial and Manichean structure into a more existentially neutral form of postimperial anthropology. When interpreting novels, one must attend to the entire narrative process, which in this case means that we attend to the relativization of Englishness over the course of the book. Like *Lonely Londoners*, the novel generates a new perspective on England itself and encodes the nascent literary and intellectual authority of non-English anglophone writing.

As I have suggested, the objectification and anthropologization of English national culture was a historical task proper not only to these migrant writers but to native intellectuals of the New Left; it was, in other words, a historical task proper to the moment of postimperial reconstruction of Englishness in the fifties. With Britain's imperialist self-image still clinging to life in the decade of the Suez crisis, migrant writers—like Cultural Studies intellectuals—objectify English culture, not to reify its traditions in an access of Anglocentric nostalgia (though as we have seen, some of this effect necessarily filters through), but in order to puncture the universalist assumptions once propped up by British power. This particularizing task does not offer any real solutions to the increasingly urgent problems of justice in the multiethnic nation-state, but it nonetheless represents a crucial first phase of decolonization *in* England. For this reason, it is worth arguing that the tropes and methods of reverse-colonial ethnography have a special significance in the midcentury, even though they can be seen in colonial and postcolonial writing from earlier (and later) eras.[82] As I suggested in chapter 1, the documentary and "home anthropology" movements of the thirties in England initiated the cultural turn and confirmed its tight correlation with the contraction of the empire. By the fifties, the project of domesticated anthropology and the resurgent discourse of English culturalism were not only affirmed by migrant intellectuals like Selvon and Lamming but gaining institutional credibility through the efforts of the New Left.

As we have seen throughout this study, to approach postempire England anthropologically is both to demystify an old high culture (with its universalist aspirations) and to remystify a new national culture as either prototypically even exotically, integral. It is for this reason that the rhetoric of the "peculiarity of the English" can remain a central concern for such ideologically diverse figures as T. S. Eliot, E. P. Thompson, Enoch Powell, and George Lamming. For a West Indian like Lamming, the pleasures of reverse ethnography no doubt flow in part from the ironic construction of the English as quaint natives; whereas for the Cultural Studies intellectuals, a broadly functionalist model of art and entertainment within the national arena helped generate new analytical insights about the class dynamics of both elite and popular culture.

These Anglotropic projects converge in the work of Doris Lessing, a colonial writer and left intellectual whose 1960 autobiographical novel

In Pursuit of the English both anthropologizes England and seeks to lay bare the workings of class society. What's particularly apposite about Lessing's story of a single mother making the postwar migration from the colonies (here Rhodesia) is that she identifies England as the most typical example, indeed the ur-example, of class society. The narrator (like Lessing, a young leftist) frames her own journey to London as a kind of mock-ethnological quest for the real England: she goes out to encounter class society in its authentic historical habitat. The novel begins, in fact, with the narrator's reflection on her own analogy between English and working-class culture: "I have been thinking for some time of writing a piece called: In Pursuit of the Working Class . . . I have chased, off and on, and with much greater deviousness of approach, the working-class and the English."[83] *In Pursuit of the English* provides a salient example of the rewriting of the old Arnoldian metaculture into a newly inclusive picture of English society, that is, into an object of ethnographic curiosity and an unusually crystalline model of modern class society.[84]

Lessing self-consciously situates her narrative within the postwar tide of "reverse immigration," describing her protagonist as one of those new "horizon conquerors" from the colonies who "now set sail or take wing for England, which in this sense means London, determined to conquer it, but on their own terms" (15). Once in England, Lessing's narrator sketches a satirical portrait of lower-middle-class domestic life, thematizing her own ironic distance from the extended family of major characters as a colonial anthropologist's methodological pose. Initially, the narrator gently ironizes her own high expectations of English authenticity, finding that what she considers the "true English" are as elusive as the vanishing tribes of the South African desert: "like Bushmen in the Kalahari, that doomed race, they vanish into camouflage at the first sign of a stranger" (9). She emphasizes English peculiarity by associating it with her own English father's eccentricity, supposing that his "splendidly pathological character"—so problematic in the colonies—"would merge with the local scene without so much as a surprised snarl from anyone." This framing commentary kicks the novel into gear by establishing Lessing's own assumption that Englishness is that odd, elusive cultural essence from which "one is an exile" (8). As in the other emigrant fictions we have considered, her representation of London local color replaces the received notions of English centrality with a new awareness of English ex-centricity.[85]

In this broader fifties discourse of reverse colonialism, the work of the Indian belletrist Nirad Chaudhuri represents a self-consciously apolitical and Anglophilic pose that clashes not only with the mood of anticolonial struggle then prevalent in so much of the periphery but also with the political commitments of most of the writers examined in this chapter. Chaudhuri's 1959 travelogue *A Passage to England* departs sharply in tone (and genre) from the fiction of Selvon, Lamming, and Lessing, but it was well known in its day (as Dipesh Chakrabarty suggests, its author's "legendary name now stands for the cultural history of Indo-British encounter") and is worth revisiting for its specific and striking investment in postimperial and Anglocentric culturalism.[86] Chaudhuri sets out to reflect in writing what he discovered in person on his relatively brief stay in England: that England and India are two incommensurate cultures (now officially separated) whose bizarre historical pairing under the British crown never made very much sense. This puts *A Passage to England* in the line of *A Passage to India* and the Forsterian tradition of genteel anticolonial writing, tinged with ironic melancholy. But Chaudhuri seems more committed to a postcolonial logic of cultural particularism, dismissing internationalism in art as "shallow, insincere, and sterile."[87] In Chaudhuri's work, English national culture—no longer the invisible center around which deep, sincere, and fertile cultures orbit—has itself become authentically provincial.

Not surprisingly, then, Chaudhuri fixes his gaze on what he takes to be representative scenes associated with "Timeless England" (3). Expecting to find a drab and defeated welfare state, Chaudhuri seems surprised to discover that "timeless England" is in fact everywhere present and that he need not exert himself much in order to succumb to its exotic allure. If Chaudhuri presents what we would now call an essentialized version of England, he fully matches it to his own romanticized version of "timeless India"; in this sense, the text's juxtaposition of two separate cultural ecologies establishes, as John Thieme suggests, a "relativistic ambience" (63). In the hands of a colonial intellectual, even a conservative and Anglophilic one, the mysteries of deep England can be seen, not as the reproduction of colonial ideologies of Englishness, but as the reversal of the old colonial romance that projected inner mystery, folk vitality, and cultural integrity to distant nations.

Cultural integrity or "wholeness" defines one of Chaudhuri's recurrent themes; he frequently notes that his outsider's eyes allow him to see English culture as a whole in a way that insiders may not, particularly not those commonplace, dispirited liberals who have "Old England in the blood and the Welfare State on the brain" (4). The national prophets of loss and decline, fretting over England's modernity, cannot in fact see the nation in its entirety, as can Chaudhuri. Whereas the irrepressibly empiricist English typically reduce "the idea of England to one concrete particular," Chaudhuri instead fuses "the details into a general idea" (55). Chaudhuri defines his own recuperative, even enchanted, experience of England in terms of a totality that cannot quite be grasped by the beleaguered and presbyopic natives, who are having suddenly to retrain their metropolitan eyes on a nation that has itself become an embodiment of the local and the provincial. Chaudhuri's evocation of a hopelessly complex and divided society in India forms a sharp contrast with England's relatively uniform whole (73). This observation chimes with the fifties rhetoric of a classless society, the idea that rising prosperity was blurring the signifiers of class (and regional) difference in England. Moreover, it captures Chaudhuri's sense that England's relatively circumscribed and integrated cultural system allows for a more holistic and populist brand of culture.

Indeed Chaudhuri envisions post-empire England as the very homeland of cultural populism, finding himself charmed by the historical recovery, cultural diffusionism, and adult education that were so central to the emergence of Cultural Studies as an academic enterprise. More to the point, he observes the popularization of English arts and letters as a replacement mission for imperialism: "Those who were devoting themselves to the work of conversion to civilization, the new missionaries of our times, were a very attractive set of men" (168). For Chaudhuri the new mission implies not just a fussy antiquarian stewardship of national heritage but a robust democratization of the cultural endowment—an intensive development of Englishness for the era when its export was no longer possible or desirable. After all, Chaudhuri notes in his conclusion, the end of European imperialism "leaves to all Western nations, and Englishmen among them, only one thing to fall back on: their historic civilization" (222). The culminating insight about cultural integrity and revival buoys Chaudhuri's mood to the point of an almost giddy sense of restored "national destiny" for a people that one might otherwise expect to lapse into morbid fascination with the imperial past. As Chaudhuri sees it, England in the fifties is intact and surprisingly harmonious: "So far as I could see, there was not only no rancour on account of the loss of India, there was not even any hangover of the psychological tension to which I have already referred, and which life in India generated in Englishmen. Their proper environment seemed to have reclaimed them, and restored their natural self. I might use a musical term and say that it had effaced the accidentals and re-established the normal key" (125). Chaudhuri's Anglophilia naturalizes an insular national identity, a little Englandism that, as we have seen, crops up on both the left (E. P. Thompson) and the right (Enoch Powell) during this era. His manifest pleasure at England's restoration of its insular self manages—despite its flirtation with the fatuous—to cement the point that England has become precisely the kind of vital, authentic, even popular national culture that was once the object of the invidious, imperial Arnoldian vision. Chaudhuri's appreciation, Anglophilic though it may be, exoticizes and particularizes the English, absorbing the once-absolute center into a discourse of local color. Moreover, Chaudhuri's recurrent interest in the democratization of England's "historic civilization" diverts him from the objectifying discourse of English quaintness long enough to appreciate its native twin: the recuperative and populist language of culturalism associated with the New Left.

However, the full array of recuperative Anglocentric discourses in fifties writing itself represents only one strain within a broader postimperial literary culture. It is important to frame our view of native culturalism in England against the prevailing modes of high literature in the period from 1930 to 1960, especially since so many canonical writers of that period (Auden, Orwell, Waugh, Greene, Lowry) are associated with a literature of British decline that is neither culturalist nor redemptive, even when it is Anglophilic. As I will suggest in the conclusion that follows, these other writers maintain the modernist problematic of alienated art in a way that the historical modernists themselves did not. In a sense, they narrate the loss of metropolitan perception *without* the corresponding compensations of a new cultural integrity. Their melancholic tales of decline throw into relief the more radical or recuperative culturalisms of right and left. Both sides mine the imagery of Englishness, but while the culturalists seek to transform its contemporary meaning, the writers of the next generation mourn its dwindling significance.

Conclusion: Minority Culture and Minor Culture

The writers and intellectuals featured in this study generally take *imperial* decline to imply some form of *national* revival. By contrast, most of the writers typically associated with the ebb of British power—Graham Greene, Malcolm Lowry, Evelyn Waugh, George Orwell, Philip Larkin, even, to some extent, W. H. Auden and the critic F. R. Leavis—take imperial decline to imply national decline. Where intellectuals invested in redeeming Little England tend to use an anthropological language of culturalism, most of the writers listed above, forming a familiar postwar minicanon, remain at least implicitly committed to Literature's special status. Where the Anglocentrists of late modernism and early Cultural Studies tend to rearticulate value in terms of an integral national culture, the "next generation" writers remain committed to the existential integrity of the individual subject in a fallen world.

It is generally understood that both the context of imperial contraction and the question of elite literature's social relevance are important shaping factors in the development of English literature after World War II. Too often, though, readers and critics connect these two factors through the logic either of raw coincidence or of overcooked causality (as discussed at the outset of the book, it is impossible to maintain that geopolitical power correlates to, let alone causes, great literature). Instead, I want to propose that, in the absence of a transformative anthropological model of cultural integrity in which literature could be seen as a meaningful social act, traditional writers and critics resorted to a seductive, but merely metaphorical, linkage between the decline of English society and the marginalization of literature. But metaphors have power too. Just as the adherents of the "anthropological turn" helped to create a discourse of Anglocentric revival that has had real effects on English society, those who resisted the nationally restrictive and culturally populist logic of the anthropological turn created a powerful discourse of national decline by fusing literary nostalgia to political regret.

It is telling, for example, that Graham Greene, one of the most noted chroniclers of empire's burnt-out ends is also famous for having separated his works of fiction into literary "novels" and popular "entertainments." This is precisely the kind of resigned distinction between the literary and the popular that was rejected by the native culturalists (including Eliot, who championed Charles Williams because his novels promised to reintegrate literature's didactic, spiritual, aesthetic, and crowd-pleasing functions). Even in its artistic successes—the spare clockwork fatalism of Greene, the fierce prosaic rectitude of Orwell, the easy cosmopolitan brilliance of Auden—the canonical literature of the "next generation" attests to the dwindling possibilities of an authentic common culture. It tends, instead, to be fixed to the plight of the conscientious soul in a corrupt, groupthinking world. Such, in fact, was the charge made by E. P. Thompson in his 1960 essay "Outside the Whale," where he takes Orwell and Auden as exemplary of English literature's political disillusionment.

To divide a culturalist discourse of national transformation from a broader individualist discourse of national decline might appear to be a crude gesture, even if we restrict our observations to the tight group of male authors that are often taken by U.S. readers to represent English writing between 1930 and 1960. Nonetheless, the next-generation writers do by and large think elegiacally rather than transformatively about English traditions. In the case of Auden, for example, Englishness finally stands for the cloying and claustrophobic legacy to be left behind on the way to lyric cosmopolitanism. Auden's career offers what is perhaps the clearest instance of the problem of national culture for English writers after modernism. Partly because of the famous symmetry between Auden's removal to America and Eliot's self-styled repatriation to England, Auden seems to epitomize the internationalist tide pulling against the Anglocentrism described in this book. Auden leaves an early career rooted in national tradition to become a roving poet-without-borders, while Eliot leaves the cosmopolitan and cross-cultural orientation of his early career in order to root himself in a national tradition. The transatlantic chiasmus of Auden and Eliot is not a question merely of location or theme but also of form, and all that form implies about literature's relation to its audience. If Auden and Eliot each had a more "national" and a more "cosmopolitan" phase, it is instructive to note that Auden's early, and Eliot's late, dramatic experiments both correspond to the more national phase. Auden's political engagement in the thirties is inseparable from a thematic interest in the condition of England and from an aesthetic stake in the social, collaborative elements of drama.

In this sense, the Auden of the 1930s would seem to confirm much of what I argued in chapter 2, insofar as he participated in a late modernist turn geared simultaneously to the problems of national tradition and to the potentialities of nonnaturalist dramatic genres. Auden's early forays into Group Theatre reflect, I think, his timely interest in developing new forms for an England at the end-cusp of its high modernity, for a decaying industrial and imperial society ready to redeem its socially fractured artistic institutions through shared ritual. Like Eliot and Woolf, Auden offers his own miniature history of the schism between art and society: "As long as society was united in its religious faith and its view of the universe, as long as the way in which people lived changed slowly, audience and artists alike tended to have much the same interests and to see much the same things. It is not until the great social and ideological upheavals of the sixteenth and seventeenth centuries that difficult poetry appears. . . . The more homogeneous a society, the closer the artist is to the everyday life of his time."[88] The familiar chronology of this passage (harking back to the seventeenth century) identifies it as a specifically English story; its tone marks it as a prehistory of the modern artist's segregation from everyday life. Auden's diagnosis of the artist as an increasingly lonely clairvoyant in a context of social instability (taken from his 1938 essay "Light Verse") thus resonates closely with Woolf's contemporaneous story of Anon's displacement by the derelict and beautiful forms of modernity. However, where Woolf and Eliot end their careers by coming to new terms with national culture, Auden begins there and moves away. My readings of Eliot and Woolf have not been motivated by a desire to celebrate nativism as the only arena for engaged writing (still less by the desire to castigate cosmopolitan writers like Auden for "abandoning politics"), but rather by curiosity about how late modernism's cultural/nativist turn can be understood in terms *other* than that of an entwined geopolitical and aesthetic process of decline. Since modernism's experimental vitality is so often assumed to be coextensive with its internationalism, it has become too easy, I think, to forget that literary creativity can flow from the social challenges of national engagement as much as from the existential challenges of exilic wandering.

Auden's work is apposite to these larger questions, because even as it breaks from England's new national cohesion after empire, it still represents English insularity in the wake of British retrenchment. In "Letter to Lord Byron" (1936), for example, the speaker marks his own distance from Byronic exploits by suggesting that contemporary poets have a less grand, more domestic set of concerns to address. Living in the era of "Britannia's lost prestige and cash and power," the contemporary poet can see on the home front what Byron, in the heroic age of British adventurism, could not: "Injustice just outside your lordship's door: / Nearer than Greece were cotton and poor." Moreover, the poem links cosmopolitan distraction to the postromantic shift whereby poetry went from being "attendant" to social problems to being increasingly "independent" of them.[89] These aspects of Auden's lighthearted address to Byron seem to imply, in a sense, that the social conscience is domestic, or at least that imperial distraction and artistic rarefaction had been mutually reinforcing factors in the production of a detached, exoticizing, and metropolitan art.

It is not surprising then that Auden's more overtly political period corresponds to the decade of his greatest interest in the condition of England. And yet, though the work represented in *The English Auden* (covering 1927–39) does indicate Auden's debts to a native poetic tradition, it also reminds us that Auden was already, long before going into exile, distancing himself from that tradition. In several poems, the lyric speaker is suspended in a timeless pastoral scene, but Auden extends Housmanesque repose into the territory of gentle parody. Moreover, his speakers roam beyond the English greensward, looking back and down at it from an almost jovial perspective. Auden's aerial views on England, identified by Valentine Cunningham as a hallmark of the thirties, intensify the estrangement of his poems from the English landscape, literalizing his flight from the nets of national tradition.[90]

On the one hand, then, Auden blows the clean air of contemporary reality into an England already beginning to enshrine (and entomb) itself in the Anglocentric and insular imagery of pap nativism. His distanced views replace pastoral myth with the detritus of decaying industry and disrupt the concept of a unified island by cross-hatching the landscape with the marks of mobility, of social difference, of regional variety. On the other hand, however, there is a perhaps unintended or ironic secondary layer of literary effects in these poems of estrangement: after all, as the cosmopolitan ego moves off, it leaves behind a *reconsolidated* concept of England as the abandoned thing, the prisonhouse of culture. A nascent citizen of the world, Auden tends to overviews that confer on England precisely the unified (and claustrophobic) quality that the poet wishes to escape. The overview makes England—qua island—both a knowable and a provincial unit, the antithetical ground to cosmopolitan possibility. In "Dover" (1937), for example, the "immense improbable atlas" beyond the white cliffs bespeaks a global commercial infinity, making England into the cozily knowable unit against which a poetic vision can expand.[91] Similarly, in the utterly composed lyric "Look, stranger, at this island now" (1935), Auden emphasizes the attainment of a viewpoint—a place ("here") and a time ("now")—that allows a "full view" of the island to enter the speaker's mind and memory. The full view—the glimpse of an island now seen as a totality—is, however, finessed by the poem's final lilting simile:

> And the full view
> Indeed may enter
> And move in memory as now these clouds do,
> That pass the harbour mirror
> And all the summer through the water saunter.[92]

In the end, the poem is not about the England seen in full view but about the seeing itself, so that the completeness of the view is inseparable from its attenuation: by the logic of the simile, it is not just a reflection but the memory of a reflection. This figurative turn defines Auden's mixed but exemplary legacy to a culture that is becoming minor: his clear-eyed estrangement from the hallowed marks of Englishness tends to relativize national myth, but his cosmopolitan flights from the island have the subtle, scale-shifting effect of confirming, from a distance, that England has become its own province, and that the culture of the whole nation has become a consolidated *Ding-an-sich*.

Auden's "full view" of the island requires the development of a literary perspective estranged from England and its national myths—an effort that does not so much transform or transvalue Albion's myths as abandon the territory. In Graham Greene's midcentury fiction, too, those insular myths tend to remain intact despite obvious threats from economic and political crises on a global scale. Greene opens *A Confidential Agent* (1939) on a ship approaching Dover under white fog and gull cry, striking an Audenesque pose not only in imagery but by framing England as an almost exotically snug society removed from the violence of the continent. The novel's perspective unfolds through the eyes of "D," a foreign agent for whom England has become a fond memory, a half-remembered dialect, a "rather literary" land.[93]

This agent's cultivated distance from England is mirrored thematically by Mr. Muckerji, a Mass-Observer who views England (like the colonial immigrants discussed in the previous section) ethnographically. Indeed, Greene seems quite self-consciously to echo Kipling's *Kim* by intertwining anthropology and espionage, though here both endeavors have been transplanted back to the heart of English culture—a fact which is itself symptomatic of the collapse of British power.[94] Both Muckerji and "D" (especially in his formal capacity as the focalizing consciousness of the narrative) make English life into an object of intense scrutiny, an object that is, in that distinctively anthropological fashion, both alien and knowable. Muckerji's methods combine attention to working-class minds (tracking rumors "all untrue, of course, but it shows the working of their minds") and attention to the total circuit of behavior, manners, and practices that make up daily life in his urban arena. More to the point, Muckerji frames his observations of the book's plot (a spy vs. spy game that includes a fake suicide and stolen documents) in terms of a direct comparison between local mores and those of "tribes in West Africa." Muckerji's scientific observation of English life proceeds from the Mass-Observation tenet that scientific reportage will replace traditional literature's narrow interest in the lives of the few. Muckerji pins his hopes to a broader form of representation (more anthropological than literary) by whose logic his work will one day appear in a "big book—without my name."[95] Greene's novel thus links the relativization of England—its new status as an ethnographic object—to the increasingly fragile status of traditional novels, with their individuated authors and morally exemplary protagonists.

Of course, no writer better exemplifies the movement from imperial disillusionment to domestic (and working-class) documentary than George Orwell. Born in the Asian empire, Orwell was a colonial outsider who, like Kipling (and, in a crucial sense, Eliot) had the "eyes of the observer, of the man coming back to England . . . eyes full of [the] experience of imperialism."[96] Unlike Kipling and Eliot, though, Orwell was a political radical; his documentary fictions of the 1930s seemed vigorously to resist the pastoral blandishments of official Englishness. And yet Orwell too ended up manifesting a latent pastoral romanticism—a tendency heightened and rigidified by World War II and the disillusionment that followed from the Spanish Civil War. Orwell's evocation of English life in his wartime writing echoes Eliot's catalog in *The Idea of a Christian Society*: "The clatter of clogs in Lancashire mill towns, the to-and-fro of the lorries on the Great North Road, the queues outside the Labor Exchanges, the rattle of pin-tables in Soho pubs, the old maids biking to Holy Communion through the mists of the autumn mornings."[97] Orwell's attempt to do documentary justice to the bitter social divides of the class system in the thirties gives way to emphasis on the "emotional unity" of the country that he figures as "an everlasting animal stretching into the future and into the past."[98] Like Eliot (and, from the opposite direction, like Raymond Williams), Orwell expressed dissent from ruling ideologies not by eschewing national tradition but by attempting to extract a good nationalism based on ordinary, quotidian, shared English habits.

So far, then, Orwell's investment in Englishness—in both its documentarian commitment and its conservative pastoralism—would seem to align itself with the figures whom I have described as converting imperial crisis into national revival. However, Orwell's evocations of Englishness project not cultural revival so much as political despair. What he calls the "deep, deep sleep of England" offers an idyllic memory, but one that can only fuel a doomed nostalgia.[99] Orwell's Anglocentrism finally defines itself as doomed liberalism, in that it seems to give up on the possibility of group politics altogether. His career moves from anthropological salvage operations in working-class England to deep pessimism. By the late forties, when he was writing *1984*, Orwell's recoil from mass politics had hardened into the lonely and bleak antiheroism of Winston Smith. For Winston, as for Orwell, there are no redemptive resources to be mined from the shared traditions of a national culture. Far from participating in an Anglocentric revival, Orwell exemplifies the foreclosure of the existential novel. His only recourse is to unspool the hopeless tale of a feeble Winston Smith going down in the face of a drunken, broken proletariat and a remote, unbreakable State.

The ideological aridity of *1984* gives it a certain desperate period resonance but also makes it a claustrophobic novel, in which the provincialism of post-1945 England translates into a mean Cold War existence as Airstrip One. England's reduced estate and the dead ends of literary humanism become, likewise, the thematic core of Evelyn Waugh's satires of the 1930s and 1940s. Waugh depicts a depressing and decaying England unredeemed by any prospect of cultural consolidation. Indeed, in *A Handful of Dust* (1934), reduced estates and dwindling imperial opportunities combine to form the plot and predicament of Tony Last, the cuckolded and belated protagonist. Waugh takes his title from Eliot's *The Waste Land*: the "handful of dust" expresses his dispirited view of a civilization that Eliot was by this time seeking to redeem. *A Handful of Dust* opens with a vignette of destruction: a burned house whose only hope of renovation is that it will be Beaverized, that is, made over by the hopelessly tacky parvenu, Mrs. Beaver. Waugh's misanthropic, misogynistic tone extends to almost all the characters in the novel, with the exception of the residually noble, if hapless, Tony Last.

Last's fate corresponds to that of his unsightly ancestral home, Hetton, a device Waugh uses for some not very delicate satire of Anglocentric heritage and country-house tourism. Hetton, "formerly one of the notable houses of the county," has already been rebuilt and is now, like everything else in Waugh's disenchanted England, "devoid of interest."[100] Slow to recognize its death, Last finally reaches a moment of clarity: "His mind had suddenly become clearer on many points that had puzzled him. A whole Gothic world had come to grief . . . there was now no armour, glittering in the forest glades, no embroidered feet on the greensward; the cream and dappled unicorns had fled."[101] In the end, Last throws himself into tropical adventure. His journey to the South American jungle in search of a mythical pre-Columbian city becomes an undignified mock-heroic quest, replete with biting flies, itchy rashes, clinging mud, and frequent vomiting. Abandoned by Indian guides, a feverish Last is rescued, but then held prisoner, by a daft English hermit, Mr. Todd. Last's captor is a farcical version of Conrad's Kurtz; the child of missionaries, he lives utterly apart from England but is inordinately fond of Charles Dickens. In the closing pages, we see Tony Last condemned to a lifetime of reading and rereading Dickens novels to his mad warden deep in the Amazonian jungle. Waugh cuts right to the absurdity of a culture that is frozen into repetitions of a nineteenth-century identity disseminated to every corner of the planet. Last's fate as a zombified reader captures one aspect of the British empire's legacy to English culture: a forced diet of the fetishized markers of a vanishing Englishness. Having clung to his Victorian ideas—first as a manor house gentleman in the era of suburbanization, then as a would-be jungle hero in the era of imperial decline—Tony Last himself comes to grief. Neither imperial romance nor domestic revivalism can save him.

A Handful of Dust offers a satirical acknowledgement of its own self-enclosure in the elite traditions of English country-house and imperial-romance fiction, all the more so because it is only able to invert and parody those genres rather than write its way out of their shadow. Waugh reveals how tightly the sad tale of decline is linked to a fetishization of the Literary (a linkage whose logic directly counters the discourse of Anglocentric revival based on reintegrating literature into culture). In this sense, Waugh's Dickensian jungle torture provides a grotesque and satiric reflection of the tight relationship between imperial decline and a fetishized Great Tradition of the kind associated with F. R. Leavis and Scrutiny. It is hard to overestimate Leavis's importance to the literary culture of midcentury England, especially since he was both a champion of native English writing and a liberal defender of what he called "minority culture": an antagonist, then, of both cosmopolitan modernism and a degraded "mass civilization." Leavis's defense of great literature takes place in the context of a belief in England's more or less irreversible (and more or less generically modern) decline. The loss of cultural wholeness, for him, continues apace through the phase of imperial retrenchment.[102] Moreover, that loss can only be individually palliated, not collectively transformed, by the cultivation of a great native literature in which images of wholeness remain encased, like flies in amber.

Where culturalists of both the right and the left wanted, in a sense, to depersonalize literature by subsuming it into a functionalist model of culture, Leavis continued to champion the free individual as the locus of value, in books, as in society. In this, he retains the first-order universalism, the unreconstructed humanism, of the Arnoldian legacy even as he inflects it with a more self-consciously parochial and populist idiom. As Francis Mulhern notes, for the typical act of Leavisian criticism, "the medium of the essentially human, it turns out, is English."[103] The values of the *Scrutiny* group thus throw into relief the basic divide that I have proposed between (1) a residually humanist literary defense of Englishness, tied to the belief that England was going downhill all the way and (2) an emergent cultural defense of Englishness tied to the belief that England could be revived as an authentic, integrated culture in the postimperial world.[104]

The *Scrutiny* critics shared with the "next generation" writers (Auden, Orwell, Greene, Waugh, Larkin) a basic belief in the ethical and existential value of literary humanism as against the dangerous edicts of mass politics. They continue to represent a conscientious aesthetic in an age of groupthink even as the first generation of English modernists were trying to strike a separate (if uneasy) peace with the corporate and collectivist future. As I have argued at large, aging modernists like Eliot, Woolf, and Forster inflected their thirties writing with an organic Anglocentrism that had, during the twenties, been buried under—or fused to—the language of cosmopolitan subjectivity. By rewriting private textuality into public ritual, by formulating a concept of national culture designed to address the rift between audience and artist, by registering the end of an "international but individualistic" modernism, that generation I think attempted to *manage* rather than to resist (or simply accede to) the anthropological turn. They took the signs of British decline as an occasion not simply to revive English universalism but to reinvent it as a form of cultural authenticity for the era of decolonization. In this sense, and despite the political ironies, the modernists have staked a claim for contemporary relevance.

If the Leavis/*Scrutiny* position saw great literature redeeming a corrupt culture, the late modernists and early Cultural Studies intellectuals saw national culture redeeming rarefied Art. Leavis's literary humanism attached itself to the values of a fragile "minority culture" *within* England, whereas the culturalist position attached itself to England's emergent status as "minor culture."[105] This model of a contest between residual humanism and emergent culturalism clarifies by historical retrospect what I attempted to articulate through literary-critical readings in chapters 2 and 3, which is that the stylistic shifts of late modernism catch a major culture in the act of becoming minor. In both late modernism and early Cultural Studies, English intellectuals seem to register the loss of British hegemony by (1) adapting the language of the universal human subject to the language of an archetypal cultural subject and (2) projecting the integration of autonomous literary values into a more socially complete but nationally restrictive (i.e., anthropological) model of culture.

All of this confirms, I think, David Lloyd's powerful claim that there is
a deep and understudied connection between "the erosion of the aesthetic
domain and the demise of colonialism itself, a connection which implies,
it may be stressed, not the end of hegemony but possibly its migration to
another necessarily less discrete sphere."[106] As I noted in the introduction,
Lloyd suggests that the material bases of European (particularly British)
imperialism are inseparable from the development of an aesthetic culture
understood as the domain of archetypal ethical subjects. Metropolitan
modernism, we might hypothesize, represents both the peak and the dialectical switchpoint of that aesthetic culture, in which the ethical subject
seems at once to float free of determining discourses and to be entirely
constructed by them; in which aesthetic discourse seemed, in Woolf's
words, at once beautiful and derelict; and in which European humanism,
described by Sartre as the obverse of imperial power, seemed to reach both
its apotheosis and its twilight. To return to the scene of late modernism in
England, where those antinomies unraveled into dichotomies, is to grasp
with new clarity the interconnection between postcolonial critiques of
Western imperialism, philosophical critiques of the sovereign subject, and
cultural critiques of literary humanism—to see that these are not static
and academic points of debate but a series of dynamic, consequential
historical events, whose legacy of anthropological relativism continues to
shape ethnic and national identity, not to mention literary and historical
knowledge, today.

This is an English story, and more. The discourse of midcentury Anglocentrism typifies, as it were, the return of anthropology from the periphery
to the center after empire. It also represents an episodic cross-section of
the dialectical process whereby European nations, once the preeminent
consumers of cultural authenticity (in the Arnoldian vein), have now become preeminent producers of it.[107] And it exemplifies the ways in which
native culturalism, on the rebound from empire, can inspire both the fetishization (as in the Heritage movement) and the modernization (as in
Cultural Studies) of tradition. In this sense, England's demetropolitanization reveals another historical and dialectical irony: the fact that native
intellectuals in England confront problems of cultural revivalism that are
comparable with, if not parallel to, the problems confronting writers in
former colonies, from Ireland to Nigeria to Jamaica to Pakistan, who
must negotiate between the liberating and stultifying effects of celebrating
national essence.

As Sean Golden describes the process, "English writers are faced with
developing a post-traditional English literature, no longer metropolitan
and tolerant of provincial, i.e. colonial, upstart crows, but itself provincial, measuring and defining itself in light of American and other literatures."[108] Seamus Heaney makes a similar point in "Englands of the

Mind" by suggesting that English poets like Ted Hughes, Geoffrey Hill, and Philip Larkin "are afflicted with a sense of history that was once the peculiar affliction of the poets of other nations who were not themselves natives of England but who spoke the English language." Thus English poets are "now possessed of that defensive love of their territory which was once shared only by those poets whom we might call colonial—Yeats, MacDiarmid, Carlos Williams." Heaney's reading of Hughes, Hill, and Larkin describes a process whose initial phases I see in late modernism's nativist turn: "Their very terrain is becoming consciously precious. A desire to preserve indigenous traditions, to keep open the imagination's supply lines to the past, to receive from the stations of Anglo-Saxon confirmations of ancestry, to perceive in the rituals of show Saturdays and race-meetings and seaside outings, of church-going and marriages at Whitsun . . . a continuity of communal ways."[109]

For English intellectuals invested in the reconstruction of a cohesive national culture after empire, the return to native rituals, to historical supply lines, to the everyday habits of a genuine people have an almost irresistible allure. Like any of the other cultures taking new post-British shapes after empire, England has been susceptible to the loving but narcissistic clench of nativism.

In tracing the historical shift from a cosmopolitan to a provincial literary culture, a literary critic is best qualified to analyze the rhetorical and aesthetic forms associated with certain imaginary projections of national (or nonnational) identity. Moreover, it seems to me that citizens of the world are as likely to ignore determinate forms of social difference as are parochial nationalists: neither thinking "within" nor "beyond" the nation is any guarantee of good politics or good art. For these reasons, I have aimed not to moralize about different languages of nationalism but to historicize their literary and cultural implications. For example, my point in this conclusion has not so much been to champion the cultural revivalists over the bleaker prophets of decline—nor to hypostasize the basic difference between them—but to take stock of the problematic that defines the relation between them. To wit: certain forms of thinking about literature's *relative* position within culture tend to operate most powerfully within a national space; likewise, and as a corollary, most intellectuals who are committed to literature's *special* potential to encode universal values tend to operate in a humanist arena defined as cosmopolitan.

If there is a larger theoretical implication beyond the literary history of this project, it is perhaps simply to affirm the difficulty of steering language and culture between the Scylla of rote nativism and the Charybdis of liberal elitism, of keeping nationalism apart from populist xenophobia, transnationalism apart from solipsistic anomie. What the complex transitions of late modernism in England reveal is, not the theoretical impossibility of reconciling those binaries, but the historical necessity of resolving them dialectically, in stages. Reading from late modernism to early Cultural Studies, we can see more clearly a dialectical motion of colonial and postcolonial modernity in its literary manifestations, and we can see the way that literary language itself helped shape the phases of transition from the residually universalist principles of the metropolitan era into the emergent particularism of postwar England. If metropolitan conditions created rich experimental art as well as cross-cultural knowledge, they also tended to mystify the problem of high art and mass culture into an entrenched agon of artistic heroism/failure. On the other hand, if insular discourse reopened the possibility of treating culture in holistic or systematic terms, it also tended to restrict the development of cross-cultural knowledge and even to devolve into identitarian excess. The essentialist pitfalls, aesthetic dead ends, and political dangers of the one are balanced in the other. Beyond these general points, the story of English demetropolitanization insists that we cannot reflexively associate the fate or perceived quality of English literature after 1945 with the fate of the British empire after 1945. With an elaborated historical model of the connections between a fading British hegemony and the changing modes, styles, and values of English literature, we can perhaps come to terms with the loss of metropolitan perception, not as a fable about the death of literature, but as a story about the birth of culture.

NOTES

INTRODUCTION

1. Deleuze and Guattari develop the concept of a "minor literature," exemplified by Kafka and Beckett as radical figures who "deterritorialize" writing from the margins of major (European) languages. Gilles Deleuze and Félix Guattari, *Kafka: Toward a Minor Literature*, trans. Dana Polan (Minneapolis: U of Minnesota P, 1986).

2. Anthony Burgess, "Letter from England," *Hudson Review* 19 (Autumn 1966): 460. Michael Gorra cites from this section of Burgess's essay in his authoritative account of Paul Scott's struggle with the apparently minor status of postimperial British writing (*After Empire: Scott, Naipaul, Rushdie* [Chicago: U of Chicago P, 1997], 34).

3. Colin MacCabe, "Broken English," in *Futures for English*, ed. Colin MacCabe (Manchester: Manchester UP, 1988), 3.

4. The concept of an Anglocentric cultural turn not only accounts for an underappreciated aspect of English modernism, it also looks beyond the antagonism model of modernism and mass culture. Critics working on this question since Andreas Huyssen's *Great Divide* have offered convincing analyses of modernists' appropriation of and fascination with mass culture, which was part of Huyssen's point all along, despite frequent invocations of his modernism as hermetic and elitist (*After the Great Divide* [Bloomington: Indiana UP, 1986]). Recently critics have begun to reconceptualize the high/low divide rather than simply point out the popular-culture affinities of this or that modernist. See, for example, *High and Low Moderns: Literature and Culture 1889–1939*, ed. Maria DiBattista and Lucy McDiarmid (New York: Oxford UP, 1996).

5. Historical and critical work on early and high modernism still continues to dominate in quantity and quality over critical accounts of late modernism, particularly since literary histories of the thirties tend to focus attention on the Auden Generation rather than on the last phase of modernism. Within British modernist studies, the eventful episodes of the avant-garde eruption around 1914 or the *annus mirabilis* of 1922 continue to be the focus of the best contextualizing work. See, for example, Paul Peppis, *Literature, Politics, and the English Avant-garde: Nation and Empire, 1901–1918* (New York: Cambridge UP, 2000); and Michael North, *Reading 1922: A Return to the Scene of the Modern* (New York: Oxford UP, 1999). Tyrus Miller's *Late Modernism: Politics, Fiction, and the Arts between the World Wars* (Berkeley: U of California P, 1999) is a recent and welcome exception to this rule, though it operates largely within the context of European political and economic crisis, not British retrenchment.

6. For recent work on the conditions of modernist production and consumption, see Lawrence Rainey, *Institutions of Modernism: Literary Elites and Public Culture* (New Haven: Yale UP, 1998); and Mark S. Morrisson, *The Public Face*

of Modernism: Little Magazines, Audiences, and Reception, 1905–1920 (Madison: U of Wisconsin P, 2001).

7. Raymond Williams, *The Politics of Modernism* (London: Verso, 1989), 44.

8. In the case of English writing it seems to make more sense to develop the concept of late modernism than to herald the arrival of a proper postmodernism. After all, the concept of postmodernism as a period/style applies better to the visual arts than to literature and better to other cultures than to England. With the exception of some obliging metafictions (e.g., by John Fowles, Jeanette Winterson, or Julian Barnes), it remains difficult to generate a strong account of English literary postmodernism.

9. Terry Eagleton, *Exiles and Émigrés* (New York: Schocken, 1970).

10. Ezra Pound, *How to Read* (New York: Haskell House, 1971), 42–43; qtd. in Michael North, *The Dialect of Modernism: Race, Language, and Twentieth-Century Literature* (New York: Oxford UP, 1994), 92.

11. My reading of Eliot as an English poet stems less from a critical judgment about his true identity than from the fact that, during the period in question (after 1930), he evinces a sustained and recuperative interest in the nature and future of English culture.

12. Thus Irish modernism, where colonialism forms an unavoidable part of both the context and content of major canonical works, has been fairly comprehensively rethought in postcolonial terms, whereas English modernism has not. This state of affairs is exacerbated by the split between popular and modernist literature. Within this lowbrow/highbrow equation, the popular genres of adventure tale, frontier romance, or "barracks-room ballad" dominate the literature of imperialism, while the texts of English modernism (with a few exceptions) have traditionally been read within the bounds of domestic settings and concerns (Fredric Jameson, "Modernism and Imperialism," in *Nationalism, Colonialism and Literature* [Minneapolis: U of Minnesota P, 1990], 44–45).

13. Ian Baucom, *Out of Place: Englishness, Empire and the Locations of Identity* (Princeton: Princeton UP, 1999); Simon Gikandi, *Maps of Englishness* (New York: Columbia UP, 1996); Gauri Viswanathan, *Masks of Conquest: Literary Study and British Rule in India* (New York: Columbia UP, 1989).

14. Jameson, "Modernism and Imperialism," 54–58.

15. Tom Nairn, *The Break-up of Britain* (London: New Left Books, 1977), 297. Nairn elaborates: "A peculiar repression and truncation of Englishness was inseparable from the structure of British imperialism" (79).

16. To the extent that critics have examined Forster, Woolf, and Eliot within the context of colonial history or imperial power, they have tended to focus, naturally, on texts featuring imperial themes or metropolitan appropriations of non-Western cultures. There is, for example, a large body of critical/colonial work on Forster's *Passage to India*, a somewhat smaller one on Woolf's *Voyage Out*, and growing attention to *The Waste Land* in relation to the context of empire. For the last, see Purnima Bose, "'End-Anxiety' in T. S. Eliot's *The Waste Land*: Narrative Closure and the End of Empire," *Yeats Eliot Review* 9 (1988): 157–60; Gareth Reeves, "*The Waste Land* and the *Aeneid*," *Modern Language Review* 82 (1987): 555–72; and particularly David Trotter, "Modernism and Empire: Reading *The Waste Land*," in *Futures for English*, ed. MacCabe, 143–53.

17. *The Collected Writings of John Maynard Keynes*, ed. Donald Moggridge (London: Macmillan and the Royal Economic Society, 1971), 21: 239. Further references to Keynes are from the *Collected Writings* (*CWK*) and are indicated by volume and page number in the text.

18. Hugh Kenner, *A Sinking Island: The Modern English Writers* (New York: Knopf, 1988), 5–6.

19. Since this study examines an Anglocentric vision of cultural integrity figured in the image of a shrinking island, it is perhaps worth noting here that the island of my title is an ideological and metaphorical one, not the actual geographical entity that includes Scotland and Wales. This obvious distinction has only become more relevant as the logic of restrictive cultural nationalism after empire continues to drive the devolution debates in the contemporary United Kingdom.

20. James Buzard, "Ethnography as Interruption: *News from Nowhere*, Narrative, and the Modern Romance of Authority," *Victorian Studies* 40.3 (1997): 450.

21. David Lloyd, "Arnold, Ferguson, Schiller: Aesthetic Culture and the Politics of Aesthetics," *Cultural Critique* 2 (Winter 1985–86): 168.

22. David Lloyd, *Anomalous States: Irish Writing and the Post-Colonial Moment* (Durham: Duke UP, 1993), 42–46.

23. Similarly, Robert Sullivan suggests that the repatriation of anthropology tended not only to defamiliarize social formations in the home country but also to destabilize the concept or form of autonomous individuality ("Marxism and the 'Subject' of Anthropology," in *Modernist Anthropology: From Fieldwork to Text*, ed. Marc Manganaro [Princeton: Princeton UP, 1990], 261).

24. In this sense I am inclined to agree, broadly, with Pericles Lewis's view (*Modernism, Nationalism, and the Novel* [Cambridge: Cambridge UP, 2000]) that modernist representations of the subject tended to expose the sociocultural determinants of character and consciousness even more assiduously than did the great liberal/realist Victorian novels (in keeping with the etiolation of liberal forms of nationalism in England and elsewhere after 1900). In a similar vein, Michael Tratner argues that modernism took definitive shape precisely insofar as it became responsive to the new collectivist political movements and possibilities of the early twentieth century (*Modernism and Mass Politics: Joyce, Woolf, Eliot, Yeats* [Stanford: Stanford UP, 1995], 3–4).

25. The holism of a repatriated or postimperial anthropology of Englishness seemed, at least at a theoretical level, to resolve and supersede the liberal/antiliberal political agon of the modernist period. By addressing its importance to late modernism, we can also ring some changes on the politics of modernism, which is perennially dominated by the question of modernism's resistance to, or secret collaboration with, totalitarianism. Often the result has been to divide the radical avant-gardes from a reactionary Anglo-American modernism, leaving a large gulf between two static categories. Recently, critics have begun to offer a more nuanced approach to corporate politics, in part by addressing the liberal welfare states, which were, after all, more immediately relevant to Anglo-American literature. For a good recent example, see Michael Szalay, "Wallace Stevens and the Invention of Social Security," *Modernism/Modernity* 5 (January 1998): 49–74.

26. In *Aesthetic Theory*, Adorno argues that "art is possible only in that it passed through the subject . . . [t]he objectivation of art through its immanent execution requires the historical subject" (Theodor W. Adorno, *Aesthetic Theory*, trans. Robert Hullot-Kentor [Minneapolis: U of Minnesota P, 1997], 169).

27. *Selected Prose of T. S. Eliot*, ed. Frank Kermode (New York: Harcourt, 1975), 252.

28. As Amanda Anderson notes, the basic opposition between the claims of authentic and affective localism on the one hand and the claims of rational or relativist cosmopolitanism on the other remains unresolved theoretically within the new cosmopolitan studies ("Cosmopolitanism, Universalism, and the Divided Legacies of Modernity," in *Cosmopolitics: Thinking and Feeling beyond the Nation*, ed. Pheng Cheah and Bruce Robbins [Minneapolis: U of Minnesota P, 1998], 265–89).

29. Homi K. Bhabha, *The Location of Culture* (London: Routledge, 1994), 149.

30. Both Eliot and Woolf use national tradition as a nontranscendental category that mediates between the apparent randomness and possible patterning of historical time. Moreover, Woolf's pageant creates a kind of pause, a pastoral suspension of motion, in the ticking clock of European history—an effect that seems to resonate very closely with Eliot's master trope of the "still point." For a persuasive and systematic reading of these writers in relation to purgatorial time on the eve of World War II, see Sebastian D.G. Knowles, *A Purgatorial Flame: Seven British Writers in the Second World War* (Philadelphia: U of Pennsylvania P, 1990).

31. My usage of England/English and Britain/British throughout follows the logic of this basic culture/state distinction.

32. Although this study presents a broadly materialist approach to literary history, it takes Cultural Studies more as an *object* of analysis than as a *method* of analysis. In a sense, my narrative of demetropolitanization and of high modernism's self-obsolescence is something of a disciplinary allegory. It traces and anticipates the broader shift in Anglo-American literary studies from New Critical modernism to the anthropological, even functionalist, assumptions of so much cultural theory today.

33. Stuart Hall, "When Was 'the Post-Colonial'? Thinking at the Limit," in *The Post-Colonial Question*, ed. Iain Chambers and Linda Curti (London: Routledge, 1996), 246.

34. I do not use the word "postcolonial" to describe twentieth-century English culture, because it usually refers to ex-colonies rather than to ex-colonial centers. On the other hand, to apply postcolonial analysis to England need not imply the erasure of history if the term really refers, as Stuart Hall suggests, to "a general process of decolonisation which, like the colonisation itself, has marked the colonising societies as powerfully as it has the colonised" ("When Was 'the Post-Colonial'?" 246). There are certain analytical occasions that call for the term postcolonial to indicate shared post-British predicaments and experiences across the colonizer/colonized divide; attention to these does not imply equivalence across the divide. For example, as Michael Gorra suggests, Britain is a postimperial nation, but also "in a special sense, a postcolonial one, a country whose recent

history of immigration ensures that conflicts of postcolonial identity are now enacted on the site of the imperial power itself" (*After Empire*, 8). In what follows, I use the term "late imperial" to describe the period from 1930 to 1960 and to distinguish it from both the "high imperial" or metropolitan phase (1880–1930) and from the "postimperial" phase (1960 to the present). My usage reflects a purposefully Anglocentric approach, separating rough phases of English history in terms of what I take to be the prevailing relationship between culture and empire. Of course, British *politics* did not suddenly become "postimperial" in 1960 (as evidenced by the Falklands War, the Northern Irish conflict, and devolution).

35. Sean Golden, "Post-Traditional English Literature," in *The Crane Bag Book of Irish Studies* (Dublin: Blackwater, 1982), 427; Seamus Heaney, "The Regional Forecast," in *The Literature of Region and Nation*, ed. R. P. Draper (Hampshire, U.K.: Macmillan, 1989), 20.

CHAPTER ONE

1. *The Collected Tales of E. M. Forster* (New York: Knopf, 1971), 43.

2. Ibid., 48.

3. The combination of a concentric geography of rings (at whose core lies an archetypally English landscape) and a recovered brother/male companion had lasting resonance for Forster. In *The Longest Journey*, for example, the definitive pastoral scene features an encounter between long-lost, then suddenly found, half-brothers Rickie Elliot and Stephen Wonham. In Forster's fiction, the divisions of metropolitan geography operate, at a number of levels, in correspondence with the thwarted desires of homosexual love. As Joseph Bristow observes, Forster wishes for an idealized but often narratively unsustainable synthesis of imperial masculinity with feminized Englishness (*Effeminate England: Homoerotic Writing after 1885* [Buckingham: Open UP, 1995], 55–57). Indeed, the fraternal reunion in the greensward, as a recurrent motif in Forster's early fiction, is almost always ironized or temporized; it represents a wish-fulfilling dimension within a story that also seems constructed to counter or limit that wish with the pressures of a divisive, disciplinary modernity. Whether the authentic or traditional culture featured in a Forster story is markedly English or not, it generally stands in symbolic and geographic counterpoint to imperial modernity.

4. The linkage between the Road and imperial expansion seems even more apparent when we consider that the Gates to the road are named for the gates traversed by Aeneas in Virgil's epic of colonial expansion and settlement (see Judith Scherer Herz, *The Short Narratives of E. M. Forster* [Hampshire, U.K.: Macmillan, 1988], 15).

5. In his 1920 essay "English Character," Forster revives the Arnoldian idea that "the Englishman is an incomplete" or "undeveloped" person requiring an alien supplement, spark, or catalyst (*Abinger Harvest* [New York: Harcourt, 1964], 11).

6. J. A. Hobson, *Imperialism: A Study* (Ann Arbor: U of Michigan P, 1965), 91.

7. Ibid., 11.

8. Ibid., 181.

9. The British intellectual lineage for Hobson's "compact body" rhetoric extends back to Burke and Coleridge (working in the line of German romantics like Herder), both of whom distinguished bounded communities from the universalizable and centrifugal ideologies of national and rational political expansion issuing, like an Enlightenment plague, from revolutionary France. In *Letters on a Regicide Peace*, for example, Burke worries about the fading of "that narrow scheme of relations called our country, with all its pride, its prejudices, and its partial affections. All the quiet little rivulets, that watered an humble, a contracted, but not an unfruitful field, are to be lost in the waste expanses and boundless, barren ocean of the homicide philanthropy of France" (qtd. in Seamus Deane, *A Short History of Irish Literature*[Notre Dame: U of Notre Dame P, 1986], 127). Burke's contracted field (like Coleridge's privileging of culture over civilization, to which we will return in chapter 3) defines a relationship between cultural integrity and nation-state formation that I will refer to throughout as the Burkean or organicist position. A more contemporary instance of modernist-era anthropological thinking, Edward Sapir's "Culture, Genuine and Spurious," also declares the importance of compact and bounded territory for cultural authenticity. Sapir's landmark essay, which appeared in a key modernist organ, *The Dial*, in 1919, bespeaks the widespread anxiety among metropolitan intellectuals that civilizational expansion had come at the cost of cultural intensity. Genuine culture, writes Sapir, "reaches its greatest heights in comparatively small autonomous groups," for it "rarely remains healthy and subtle when spread thin over an interminable area" ("Culture, Genuine and Spurious," in *Selected Writings of Edward Sapir*, ed. David G. Mandelbaum [Berkeley: U of California P, 1985], 328–29). Much in the manner of Eliot and Woolf, Sapir cites Elizabethan England as an exemplary culture (with an organic interrelation of functions) as against a specialized, expanding, sophisticated civilization (315–17). Sapir also establishes the integrative aspirations of the culture concept by arguing that "genuine culture" is neither "high" nor "low" but "merely inherently harmonious, balanced, self-satisfactory" and that it can be found in the "occidental" industrial nations as well as in tribal societies (314). It is from this perspective that the contraction of the British state seemed to entail the restoration of some lost cultural integrity to England.

10. Perry Anderson, *English Questions* (London: Verso, 1992), 24.

11. As Raymond Williams explains, the English countryside took on a special valence as an imaginary homeland during the imperial period; it was the empire man's dreamscape and retirement community (*The Country and the City* [New York: Oxford UP, 1973], 282). The rural, aristocratic, and indeed anachronistic values inherent in such a concept of the English home were often disseminated and reproduced by middle-class workers abroad in the empire. As Patrick Wright (among others) has demonstrated, the ideology of Englishness, including its pastoral mythology, was largely developed *in* and *for* the "massive school house of Empire" (*On Living in an Old Country: The National Past in Contemporary Britain* [London: Verso, 1985, 86]).

12. Michael North describes a particular kind of imperialist nostalgia afflicting intellectuals in 1920s Britain, in which anthropological knowledge both symbolizes and exacerbates the lost "cohesion and solidarity" of a national culture (*Read-*

ing 1922: A Return to the Scene of the Modern [New York: Oxford UP, 1999], 54–58).

13. Gertrude Stein, "What Is English Literature," in *Lectures in America* (New York: Random, 1935), 24. Jameson cites Stein's influence on his essay "Modernism and Imperialism," 66.

14. "What Is English Literature," 42–43.

15. As Jennifer Ashton has noted, Stein's lecture centers on the problem of totality or wholeness, so that the expansion of English culture into the unbounded, unknowable realm of empire has the corollary effect of undoing the completeness, the satisfying insular total style of English literature ("Gertrude Stein for Anyone," *ELH* 64.1 [1997]: 290).

16. "What Is English Literature," 46.

17. "Modernism and Imperialism," 57.

18. In an earlier version of this basic point, Jameson argues that experimental modernist forms "inscribe a new sense of the absent global colonial system on the very syntax of poetic language itself" (Fredric Jameson, "Cognitive Mapping," in *Marxism and the Interpretation of Culture*, ed. Cary Nelson and Lawrence Grossberg [Urbana: U of Illinois P, 1988], 349). Laura Chrisman offers a thoughtful assessment of Jameson's argument, in which she appreciates his formulation of an English modernism that is "rationally and rhetorically opposed to empire yet aesthetically affirmative of it," but also criticizes his depoliticized and existential emphasis on cognitive and perceptual experiences ascribed across the board to metropolitan subjects ("Imperial Space, Imperial Place: Theories of Empire and Culture in Fredric Jameson, Edward Said, and Gayatri Spivak," *New Formations* 34 [Summer 1998]: 68).

19. The problem of England's "meaning loss" or self-alienation in the course of British expansion is crystallized famously in Salman Rushdie's quip, stuttered by S. S. Sisodia in *The Satanic Verses* (New York: Viking, 1988): "The trouble with the Engenglish is that their hiss hiss history happened overseas, so they dodo don't know what it means" (343). Ian Baucom cites this line to open his study *Out of Place*, which proceeds to offer an elegant account of the ways in which British imperial experience has unsettled the tenets of English identity at home and overseas, in both the nineteenth and twentieth centuries. Similarly, Simon Gikandi's *Maps of Englishness* offers rich exemplification of the hollowing-out of Englishness as a cultural entity in the vast field of the colonial encounter.

20. From Forster's July 1920 *Athenaeum* review of H. G. Wells's *Outline of History* (qtd. in Iain Wright, "F. R. Leavis, the *Scrutiny* Movement and the Crisis," in *Culture and Crisis in Britain in the Thirties*, ed. Jon Clark, Margot Heinemann, David Margolies, and Carole Snee [London: Lawrence and Wishart, 1979], 41).

21. Most historians now agree that the commitment to empire became increasingly problematic and draining precisely when Britain entered its most vigorous and notorious empire-building era, in the so-called New Imperialism of 1870–1900. The rapid consolidation and expansion of Britain's formal empire in the period was not a manifestation of Britain's unrestrained vitality but already "a symptom and an effect of her decline in the world" (Bernard Porter, *The Lion's Share: A Short History of British Imperialism 1850–1983* [London: Longman, 1975], xi).

22. V. I. Lenin, *Imperialism: The Highest Stage of Capitalism*, in *Lenin: Selected Works* (New York: International Publishers, 1971), 223.

23. Edward Said, *Culture and Imperialism* (New York: Vintage, 1994), 188.

24. Kumkum Sangari, "The Politics of the Possible," *Cultural Critique* 7 (Fall 1987): 182.

25. As Simon Gikandi puts it: "English modernism is thus the product of a fascinating paradox in the culture of colonialism: it emerges at a time when imperialism seems to have institutionalized a rationalized global community, but it mediates a situation in which the central categories in this institutionalization—temporality, reason, subjectivity—have lost their traditional authority" (*Maps of Englishness*, 165).

26. Benita Parry, "Problems in Current Theories of Colonial Discourse," *Oxford Literary Review* 9 (1987): 55.

27. *Culture and Imperialism*, 188.

28. Stephen Slemon, "Modernism's Last Post," *Ariel* 20 (1989): 3.

29. "The Politics of the Possible," 182.

30. For detailed work on modernism, primitivism, and anthropology, see *Prehistories of the Future: The Primitivist Project and the Culture of Modernism*, ed. Elazar Barkan and Ronald Bush (Stanford: Stanford UP, 1995); *Modernist Anthropology: From Fieldwork to Text*, ed. Marc Manganaro (Princeton: Princeton UP, 1990); and Marianna Torgovnick, *Gone Primitive* (Chicago: U of Chicago P, 1990).

31. *Culture and Imperialism*, 189.

32. In 1914, for example, London's status as a prototypical metropolis and center of brawny imperialism attracted the appreciation of the avant-garde. The original 1914 *BLAST* manifesto announced that the "Modern World is due almost entirely to Anglo-Saxon genius" (*BLAST* 1, ed. Wyndham Lewis [Santa Barbara: Black Sparrow, 1981], 39). Similarly, in 1910 F. T. Marinetti praised British industrial, naval, and imperial power as the product of a "great muscularly courageous race" and hailed the "Futurist genius of England" (*Let's Murder the Moonshine*, ed. R. W. Flint, trans. Flint and Arthur A. Coppotelli [Los Angeles: Sun and Moon Press, 1991], 67, 65). It might be possible, in fact, to separate canonical modernism's general skepticism about British power and progress from avant-garde (vorticist and futurist) enthusiasm; on the latter, see Peppis, *Literature, Politics, and the English Avant-Garde*, 5–6.

33. Jean-Paul Sartre, preface to Frantz Fanon, *The Wretched of the Earth*, trans. Constance Farrington (New York: Grove, 1963), 26.

34. *Culture and Imperialism*, 50.

35. Reflecting on sociology's institutionalization in the period from 1880 to 1914, R. W. Connell writes that the raison d'être of the discipline was to generate "an empirical base for the concept of progress" derived not only from studies of urbanized, industrialized Europe (as subsequent histories of the field suggest) but also from the "ethnographical dividend of empire" which gave crucial confirmation to the model of a modernized Europe surrounded by premodern peripheries ("Why Is Classical Theory Classical?" *American Journal of Sociology* 102.6 [1997]: 1520).

36. *The Break-up of Britain*, 78.

37. Matthew Arnold, *On the Study of Celtic Literature and On Translating Homer* (New York: Macmillan, 1883), 64.

38. Ibid., 102.

39. Ibid., 87. As David Lloyd points out in his acute reading, for Arnold, "the English race, when fully realized as the reconciliation of . . . disparate strains, is itself the synthetic approximation to the Indo-European root" ("Arnold, Ferguson, Schiller" [Introduction, n. 21], 150).

40. Renato Resaldo, *Culture and Truth* (Boston: Beacon, 1989), 68–74.

41. *The Break-up of Britain*, 292.

42. Ibid., 293. G. K. Chesterton, who was, along with Hilaire Belloc, perhaps the most celebrated Little Englander of the Edwardian period, opined: "The English are not Nationalist enough. They love their nation; but they love it almost without knowing that it is a nation" (*As I Was Saying* [London: Methuen, 1936], 118).

43. Georg Simmel, "The Metropolis and Mental Life," in *On Individuality and Social Forms*, ed. Donald N. Levine, trans. Edward A. Shils (Chicago: U of Chicago P, 1971), 333–35.

44. Not coincidentally, Matthew Arnold makes humorous detachment central to the eccentricity of the English (*On the Study of Celtic Literature*, 102). In other words, metropolitan English modernity, or detachment from the tethers of a particular cultural tradition, enables the cultivated perspective required to enjoy and produce irony. This is partly what allows Arnold to imagine that declaring himself a "typical Englishman" is tantamount to a declaration of intellectual neutrality, which is, in a sense, another definition for wit (ibid., 65).

45. *Culture and Imperialism*, 108.

46. *The Break-up of Britain*, 264.

47. Robert Crawford, *Devolving English Literature* (Oxford: Clarendon, 1992), 270.

48. Sean Golden, "Post-Traditional English Literature" (Introduction, n. 35), 427.

49. Keith Tuma has written a thoughtful study suggesting that the centralized nature of British literary culture—the influential presence of a determined amateur or "common reader" resistant to arcane literary professionalization and the autonomization of the high aesthetic—accounts for the apparent underdevelopment or marginalization of modernism in Britain ("Is There a British Modernism?" in *Forked Tongues? Comparing Twentieth-Century British and American Literature*, ed. Ann Massa and Alistair Stead [London: Longman, 1994], 243–48). The force of Tuma's argument would only increase were we to isolate the English case from the British. Margery Sabin has proposed, along similar lines, that modern literature in England tends to hold more closely to traditional and idiomatic language, so that radical avant-gardist repudiations of "common speech" are less endemic to England than, say, to France (*The Dialect of the Tribe: Speech and Community in Modern Fiction* [New York: Oxford UP, 1987], 10–25). This common reader/common language argument helps explain both the semimodernized quality of English modernism and the relative capacity of English intellectuals (including modernists themselves) to decommission high modernist aesthetics in favor of a common culture concept in the thirties and forties.

50. In another influential account of the tepidness of English modernism, Perry Anderson claims that England "produced no virtually significant native movement of a modernist type in the first decades of this century" ("Modernity and Revolution," in *Marxism and the Interpretation of Culture*, ed. Cary Nelson and Lawrence Grossberg [Urbana: U of Illinois P, 1988], 323). For Anderson, England was in a sense already too developed and too bourgeoisified to support the modernist movements that, he claims, "arose at the intersection between a semi-aristocratic ruling order, a semi-industrialized capitalist economy, and a semi-emergent, or semi-insurgent, labor movement" (326).

51. The tension between local and universal claims, between tradition and modernity—so volatile in the more radical modernisms of Europe's semiperiphery—was more muted in an England already given to the universal language of civic rationality. Perhaps this is what Keynes had in mind when he said in 1927, "It is not necessary in England to lead a bold life in order to have bold ideas" (qtd. in Robert Skidelsky, *John Maynard Keynes: The Economist as Savior 1920–1937* [New York: Penguin, 1992], 417). Jean-Michel Rabaté understands London as a *host*, not a *wellspring*, for European modernism, precisely because of its relative surplus of capitalist power combined with its relatively underdeveloped traditions of revolutionary ideology and embedded monumentalism (*The Ghosts of Modernity* [Gainesville: U of Florida P], 192–93).

52. Francis Mulhern, *The Moment of "Scrutiny"* (London: New Left Books, 1979), 181.

53. Indeed it is only by adducing the context of continental pall on cosmopolitanism and the multisited, multidetermined collapse of British power that we can begin to understand the culture of the shrinking island and modernism's fate within it. This requires a certain Anglocentrism in outlining the signs of imperial contraction, but political agency in the colonies was, of course, crucial in this history. Both metropolitan perception and demetropolitanization should be understood here as "*viewed* from the center but not necessarily *determined* at the center" (Frederick Cooper and Ann L. Stoler, "Tensions of Empire: Colonial Control and Visions of Rule," *American Ethnologist* 16.4 [1989]: 617).

54. John Darwin, *The End of the British Empire* (Oxford: Basil Blackwell, 1991), 1.

55. Ibid., xiii.

56. Paul Kennedy, *The Rise and Fall of the Great Powers: Economic Change and Military Conflict from 1500 to 2000* (New York: Random, 1987), 287.

57. B. R. Tomlinson, "The Contraction of England," *Journal of Imperial and Commonwealth History* 11 (1982): 64.

58. E. J. Hobsbawm, *Industry and Empire* (London: Penguin, 1968), 273.

59. Correlli Barnett, *The Collapse of British Power* (New York: Humanities P International, 1986), 207.

60. Barnett, *Collapse of British Power*, 162–64. Like Barnett, Bernard Porter sees the 1930s as the time when important segments of the English public first acknowledged that India might be lost (*The Lion's Share*, 296).

61. Paul Kennedy summarizes the matter in this way: "From Kipling onwards, the most acute imperialists had sensed on what a thin crust of Afro-Asian deference their colonial rule rested. By 1942 at the latest, that superficial layer had

been torn asunder" (*The Realities behind Diplomacy: Background Influences on British External Policy, 1865–1980* [London: Fontana, 1981], 330). Elsewhere Kennedy points out that the dominions "had evolved into virtually independent states" by 1940 (*Rise and Fall*, 315). Likewise Henri Grimal dates the fateful moment for European colonialism to the late 1930s (*Decolonization: The British, French, Dutch and Belgian Empires 1919–1963*, trans. Stephen De Vos [London: Routledge and Kegan Paul, 1978], 113). And John Strachey suggests that although imperial divestment reaches back well into the previous century, the crucial phase of British "disimperialism" takes place in the 1930s, '40s and '50s (*The End of Empire* [New York: Random, 1960], 140).

62. See, for example, T. S. Eliot, "Last Words," *Criterion* 18 (January 1939).

63. *The Diary of Virginia Woolf*, ed. Anne Olivier Bell and Andrew McNeillie (San Diego: Harcourt, 1984), 5: 237.

64. Leonard Woolf, *Barbarians Within and Without* (New York: Harcourt, 1939), 177.

65. E. M. Forster, *Two Cheers for Democracy* (New York: Harcourt, 1951), 48.

66. In a 1949 essay, Forster muses about the potentially regenerative effects of "universal exhaustion"—meaning a respite from scientific, capitalist, and imperial activities, an exhaustion that might lead to renewed spiritual energy in England (*Two Cheers*, 91).

67. This is especially true since imperial contraction inspired a variety of responses in the thirties and forties, many of which do not correspond to the culture of retrenchment described in this chapter. At a political level, for example, both major parties continued to think in terms of imperial continuity as they laid plans for the Commonwealth.

68. For the classic statement that the "welfare ideal" should be England's "national purpose" after empire, see Strachey, *End of Empire*, 229. Strachey's book exemplifies a redemptive, late-fifties call to Keynesian fullness, Burkean boundedness, and creative democracy on the domestic front.

69. As Paul Rich observes: "If the romance had been removed from the posturing on an external imperial plane, it was to some extent being rediscovered within the English cultural and political landscape" ("British Imperial Decline and the Forging of English Patriotic Memory, c. 1918–1968," *History of European Ideas* 9 [1988]: 665).

70. For an excellent recent study on the imperialist codes and tropes used to describe late-Victorian and early-twentieth-century London, see Joseph McLaughlin, *Writing the Urban Jungle/Reading Imperial London* (Charlottesville: UP of Virginia, 2000).

71. John McClure, *Late Imperial Romance* (London: Verso, 1994), 8–12.

72. Terence Ranger, "The Invention of Tradition in Colonial Africa," in *The Invention of Tradition*, ed. E. J. Hobsbawm and Terence Ranger (Cambridge: Cambridge UP, 1983), 215.

73. Raphael Samuel points out that the genealogy of contemporary interest in Stonehenge, druids, and local mysticism leads back to "artists and writers of the 1930s and 1940s—for whom the primitive and the prehistoric was the real classical antiquity" (*Theatres of Memory* [London: Verso, 1994], 229).

74. Richard Dorson, *The British Folklorists: A History* (London: Routledge and Kegan Paul, 1968), 440.

75. Ibid., 392.

76. Ibid., 440.

77. There were, of course, earlier waves of tourism directed at rediscovery of quaint England and earlier literary figures whose work participated in that rhetoric of domestic tourism (Wordsworth's Lake District, Hardy's Wessex). But most commentators agree that the "thirst for the rural" intensified markedly through the 1930s and 1940s. See, for example, John Lowerson, "Battles for the Countryside," in *Class, Culture and Social Change: A New View of the 1930's*, ed. Frank Gloversmith (Sussex, U.K.: Harvester, 1980), 262–63.

78. On this phase of English ruralism, see the influential account of Martin J. Wiener, *English Culture and the Decline of the Industrial Spirit. 1850–1980* (Cambridge: Cambridge UP, 1981), 73–75. Raphael Samuel points out that both heritage preservation and nature conservancy hit a peak in the years just before World War II (*Theatres of Memory*, 229). By 1940 rural England was imagined as a threatened space sheltering and fostering vital cultural values during wartime. For more on the "pastoral as propaganda," see Simon Featherstone, "The Nation as Pastoral in British Literature of the Second World War," *Journal of European Studies* 16 (1986): 159–61.

79. Valentine Cunningham offers a good overview of this ruralist trend, citing titles such as the following: Edmund Blunden's *The Face of England* (1932), A. G. Macdonnell's *England Their England* (1933), Batsford's *The Legacy of England* (1935), G. Wilson Knight's *This Sceptred Isle* (1940), and Morton's *I Saw Two Englands* (1942). See Cunningham, *British Writers of the Thirties* (Oxford: Oxford UP, 1988), 228–30. An inordinate number of the new travel books focused on the (re)discovery of the ideal English Village at the symbolic center of the modern nation: Henry Williamson's *The Village Book* (1930), Edmund Blunden's *English Villages* (1931), Frances Brett Young's *Portrait of a Village* (1937), and, perhaps most revealingly named, C. Henry Warren's *England Is a Village* (1941).

80. As Valentine Cunningham suggests, there was also a deep pastoral streak in much of the "left" poetry of the period (*British Writers of the Thirties*, 234–36).

81. In the visual arts, too, the 1930s marked what David Mellor calls "modernism in recession" and the resultant wish on the part of British painters to "seek consolation in the homely, familiar British pastoral" ("British Art in the 1930's: Some Economic, Political and Cultural Structures," in *Class, Culture and Social Change*, ed. Gloversmith [1980], 185). With growing interest in the "national landscape," painters participated directly in the domestic tourism boom, providing images for travel posters and Shell guidebooks. Bloomsbury's Duncan Grant, for example, provided pastoral images for the so-called "lorry bills" or truck posters. Steve Ellis has offered a useful analysis of competing pastoral styles in the 1930s and '40s, posing the neoromanticism studied by Mellor against a more classical and austere landscape that resonates with Eliot's late poetry (*The English Eliot: Design, Language and Landscape in* Four Quartets [London: Routledge, 1991], 136–40).

82. Malcolm Cowley, "England under Glass," in *The New Republic*, 6 October 1941, reprinted in *Virginia Woolf: Critical Assessments*, ed. Eleanor McNees, (East Sussex, U.K.: Helm Information, 1994), 4: 175.

83. *Theatres of Memory*, 139.

84. Indeed, the anthropologists Marcus and Fischer locate Orwell within the broader framework of the repatriation of anthropology as culture critique, noting that there was "a widespread and self-conscious interwar trend of cultural criticism in England. In many ways, it paralleled the documentary and social-realist concerns of the Americans. The best-remembered essayist and literary figure among English critics of that era remains, of course, George Orwell" (George E. Marcus and Michael M. J. Fischer, *Anthropology as Cultural Critique: An Experimental Moment in the Human Sciences* [Chicago: U of Chicago P, 1986], 186–87).

85. For more on the "salvage imperative," see George W. Stocking, "The Ethnographic Sensibility of the 1920s and the Dualism of the Anthropological Tradition," in *Romantic Motives: Essays on Anthropological Sensibility*, ed. Stocking (Madison: U of Wisconsin P, 1989), 210–12.

86. Mary Louise Pratt, *Imperial Eyes: Travel Writing and Transculturation* (London: Routledge, 1992), 7. James Buzard has offered a persuasive argument for extending the term autoethnography from the anticolonialist settings where Pratt finds it to metropolitan self-representation. See "On Autoethnographic Authority," *Yale Journal of Criticism* (forthcoming).

87. Nineteenth-century autoethnography had often featured a mutual allegorization between the "folk" at home (rural peasants or urban working class) and the "folk" abroad (tribal, primitive, or colonized working class). In the thirties, autoethnographic writing tended not so much to trade between these two "others" of metropolitan intellectuals as to *replace* the primitivist with the domesticated version of the folk. Terry Eagleton describes the shift from primitivism to popular Anglocentrism (though in a somewhat foreshortened historical scheme that jumps from the modernist era to the present): "The exoticism will resurface in the twentieth century in the primitivist features of modernism. . . . [and] . . . crop up rather later, this time in postmodern guise, in a romanticizing of popular culture, which now plays the expressive, spontaneous, quasi-utopian role which 'primitive' cultures had played previously" (*The Idea of Culture* [Oxford: Blackwell, 2000], 12). On the repatriation of anthropology, see also Robert Sullivan, who notes that "[t]here has been a move within ethnographic discourse toward a semiotic demystification of late Western capitalist society as opposed to the earlier concentration on exotic formations" ("Marxism and the 'Subject' of Anthropology" [Introduction, n. 23], 260). Similarly, Marc Manganaro suggests that autoethnography has opened up a critical awareness of "alterity and power" in Western societies (*Modernist Anthropology: From Fieldwork to Text* [Princeton: Princeton UP, 1990], 29).

88. The reversal of fortunes for universalist European culture, described memorably by Sartre as the "strip tease of our humanism" (preface to Fanon, *The Wretched of the Earth*, 24), was particularly striking in the imperial centers of England and France, where, as Sartre notes, humanism had made its most stubborn claims to universality. Suddenly, with the rising and articulate resistance of non-

Western peoples, "France seems exotic in our own eyes" ("Black Orpheus," trans. John MacCombie, in *What Is Literature? and Other Essays* [Cambridge: Harvard UP, 1988], 292).

89. Paul Rich, *Race and Empire in British Politics* (Cambridge: Cambridge UP, 1986), 93.

90. The practice of metropolitan writers performing documentary on the real people of rural and urban England has nineteenth-century origins and, as James Buzard points out, a kind of revival in the 1930s ("Mass-Observation, Modernism, and Auto-ethnography," *Modernism/Modernity* 4.3 [1997]: 105). When Valentine Cunningham describes the autoethnography of Mass Observation as a "brilliant innovation," he does not mean that the tropes and techniques of anthropology had never been applied to English settings before, but that the thirties version was more self-consciously systematic and democratic (*British Writers of the Thirties*, 333).

91. Qtd. in Buzard, "Mass-Observation, Modernism, and Auto-ethnography," 99.

92. Ibid., 102.

93. Buzard, "Ethnography as Interruption," 446.

94. "Mass-Observation, Modernism, and Auto-ethnography," 98.

95. Clifford writes: "For all its supposed relativism, though, the concept's model of totality, basically organic in structure, was not different from the nineteenth-century concepts it replaced" (*The Predicament of Culture: Twentieth-Century Ethnography, Literature, and Art* [Cambridge: Harvard UP, 1988], 273).

96. See *Englishness: Politics and Culture 1880–1920*, ed. Robert Colls and Philip Dodd (London: Croom Helm, 1986).

97. The apprehension of national culture no longer refers to one or another class segment of the culture but to a more integrated and systemic model of class relations. James Buzard, following on (and citing) the historian of Mass-Observation Tom Jeffery, makes a similar point, claiming that the "social crisis in Britain between 1936 and 1939 differed from those earlier spasms of 1918 to 1924 and 1929 to 1933 in that it was felt as 'affecting all classes with equal intensity' " ("Mass-Observation, Modernism, and Auto-ethnography," 106).

98. Of course, even at a time when it was in the interest of British power to distance Englishness from the restrictive logic of localism or of cultural nationalism, English culture was already to some extent relativized and anthropologized. Indeed, as Michael North has recently suggested, it was an irony of imperial culture in the modernist 1920s that "the British perspective" was exposed by empire as "partial and local even in the very act of asserting its universality" (*Reading 1922*, 14). The domestication of anthropology in the midcentury was, then, not a sudden departure, but an intensified and intensifying episode within a longer cultural process. What North sees as a pungently *high* modernist paradox about the localism yielded by—indeed structurally inherent in—imperial projections of universality takes on a new shape in *late* modernism, which makes the latent paradox increasingly manifest, bringing mystified and ironic forms of English parochialism increasingly and directly to the surface.

99. The aging high modernists may have been the last generation to imbue Englishness itself with cultural authenticity, that is, to venture a reconciliation

between the dream of social wholeness and the unruly differences of national life. More contemporary English poets, having assimilated the postimperial or devolutionary logic of cultural particularism, tend to imagine the reenchantment of parts, provinces, and pockets. Along these lines, David Gervais argues that poetic regionalism, which before World War II often signified an identification with England itself, became merely local for postwar figures like Donald Davie, Ted Hughes, Basil Bunting, or Geoffrey Hill ("Ted Hughes: An England beneath England," *English* 42.172 [1993]: 46).

100. C. D. Blanton has noted with useful subtlety that while rationalization may be understood as a process issuing from, and most thoroughly transformative of, England (vis à vis the other nations or colonies in the greater British ambit), it was more a symbolic abstraction than an actual historical transformation that cast England as the prototype of the modern secularized society ("Nominal Devolutions: Poetic Substance and the Critique of Political Economy," *Yale Journal of Criticism* 13.1 [2000]: 134).

101. Marianna Torgovnick points out that Lawrence can do in the Mexico of *The Plumed Serpent* what he cannot in the English novels: imagine a resolution of basic antithetical principles (male/female, active/passive, civilized/primitive) (*Gone Primitive*, 168).

102. *Culture and Society 1780–1950* (New York: Columbia UP, 1983.), 213.

103. Ian Baucom argues that, after centuries of a fundamentally localist ideology that defined the nature of English belonging, *race* rather precipitously usurped *place* as the primary or official signifier of Englishness during the postimperial era (*Out of Place*, 7–14). We might take the spatial and insular forms of Anglocentrism of the midcentury as a crucial but partially obscured step in this larger process, since the invocation of "culture" from late modernism into early Cultural Studies was inseparable from its territorial and ultimately ethnic entailments. This is the thrust of Paul Gilroy's critique of Raymond Williams, whose emphasis on long and settled experience implies (despite its intent) a kind of national belonging that is ultimately ethnic or racial (*There Ain't No Black in the Union Jack: The Cultural Politics of Race and Nation* [Chicago: U of Chicago P, 1991], 49–51). By returning to the scene of modernism's uneasy assimilation of cultural nationalism, we can see with new clarity the historical emergence (rather than just the political bad faith) of certain compromise forms of national identity shaped by the transition from empire to welfare state, that is, from potentially universal definitions of belonging to culturally and ethnically restrictive ones.

104. Gillian Beer, *Virginia Woolf: The Common Ground* (Edinburgh: Edinburgh UP, 1996), 25–26.

105. Franco Moretti, *Modern Epic: The World System from Goethe to García-Márquez*, trans. Quintin Hoare (London: Verso, 1996), 107.

106. In a sense, I am describing a transitional late modernism that tries to preserve the residual hermeneutic depth of the modernist text while capturing the oral spontaneity of ritual and public performance. We can, for example, read *Four Quartets* as both the end of a formally difficult textual practice *and* as the beginning of that practice's transformation into a more public, oral, anti-interpretive perfor-

mance. The narrative structure of Woolf's *Between the Acts* confirms this compromise between textuality and performance as a feature of late-thirties modernism.

107. The prevailing metropolitan view was that tribal cultures did not suffer from the divorce between art and its daily, functional, collective purposes—a view that was manifest in most modernist primitivisms. Seeking a non-western escape route from the legacy of rationalized, autonomous Art, spinning in its own Kantian world of purposeless purposiveness, modernists raided the new ethnographic archive and museum trove of the metropolis. In the thirties, the culture of retrenchment, combined with the imperative to make Western art more conspicuously political, brought the logic of functionalism back home from the periphery. In this sense, the anthropological turn of late modernism allowed English writers to find a new literary language for addressing the social embeddedness and function—not just the social alienation—of their art.

108. By comparison with the linkage of ethnography and surrealism described, for example, by James Clifford, the anthropological turn in English culture is less epistemologically and aesthetically radical. It is not so much an attempted negation of the culture concept as an elaboration of it in Anglocentric and empiricist terms. Jeremy MacClancy has traced the overlapping intellectual milieux of British surrealism and Mass-Observation in the late thirties, noting that the English surrealism/ethnography nexus (embodied, for example, in Humphrey Jennings) was less radical than its anarchic French counterpart precisely in the sense that it was "deeply imbued with a sense of the spirit of England" ("Brief Encounter: The Meeting, in Mass-Observation, of British Surrealism and Popular Anthropology," *Journal of the Royal Anthropological Institute* 1.3 (1995):497).

109. Susan Hegeman, *Patterns for America: Modernism and the Concept of Culture* (Princeton: Princeton UP, 1999), 16.

110. At this point, modernists were beginning to refer the problem of totality not to literary forms but to the culture concept itself, increasingly conscious that, as Adorno puts it, "[a]ntagonisms that are unsolved in reality cannot be solved imaginatively either" (*Aesthetic Theory*, 169). This point is obliquely affirmed by Franco Moretti in his reading of *The Waste Land* as the end of European literature's high phase, in that it "attempted to solve in the literary domain problems that instead required the institution of new aesthetic and cultural systems" (*Signs Taken for Wonders* [London: Verso, 1988], 210). My claim would be a modified version of this rather abrupt periodization, since I think *Four Quartets*, for example, marks a renewed and historically significant attempt to solve some of the same problems in the literary domain. Nonetheless, in the rough spirit of Moretti's argument, I read *Four Quartets* and its contemporaries as transitional attempts to reconcile a primarily textual-private and cosmopolitan-symbolist aesthetic with more public, more national forms like ritual and allegory—that is, with forms that reflexively register the rising importance of "cultural systems" for literary expression.

111. The standard literary histories of the period narrate the destructive intrusion of mass politics (Samuel Hynes, *The Auden Generation* [London: Bodley Head, 1976]), mass culture (Kenner, *A Sinking Island*), or mass technology (Bernard Bergonzi, *Reading the Thirties* [London: Macmillan, 1978]) into modernist aesthetics.

CHAPTER TWO

1. Modernist pageant experimentation in the thirties plays out against a background of new dramatic movements: mass theater, workers' theater, political theater, avant-garde and neoclassical theater. As Valentine Cunningham notes, theater's resurgence was driven by a diffuse sense among British intellectuals that it was a more collaborative and collective form than either poetry or fiction, genres that seemed to be the preserve of the lonely bourgeois mind (*British Writers of the Thirties* [chap. 1, n. 79], 322). The influence of Brecht's openly ideological and "epic" drama, along with the obvious vitality of mass theater and political spectacle on the continent, inspired English intellectuals, especially on the left, to working-class and "agitprop" dramatic efforts. On this background, see Patricia Klindienst Joplin, "The Authority of Illusion: Feminism and Fascism in Virginia Woolf's *Between the Acts*," *South Central Review* 6 [Summer 1989]: 93).

2. L. N. Parker, *Several of My Lives* (London: Chapman and Hall, 1928), 279.

3. Robert Withington, *English Pageantry: An Historical Outline* (New York: Benjamin Blom, 1963), 193.

4. The new, secular local drama was less allegorical than a traditional pageant (most of the actors here tend to represent individual historical figures, not ideas, conditions, or professions). It was also more episodic and larger in scale than the court masque. Parker himself set out a generic definition that insists on distinguishing the historical pageant play from these older genres as well as from the street procession, the gala, the fête, and the *tableau vivant* (Parker, *Several of My Lives*, 278).

5. The town was often embodied by a single actor who would begin the action by striding to center stage and announcing, for example, "Know all men, I am Chester" (*The Chester Historical Pageant Book of Words, July 18–23, 1910* [Chester: Phillipson and Golder, 1910], 14). The municipal figure then remained on stage during succeeding episodes and eras, embodying not just the town but the organic logic of pageantry, whereby the town's continuity reinforces the idea of national permanence. My discussion in this chapter is based on some twenty "books of words" from English pageants produced between 1905 and 1912 (six of these were Parker's own pageants; the rest were produced by such pageant-masters as George Hawtrey, Frank Lascelles, and Nugent Monck).

6. Especially during the years 1900–20, pageantry spread rapidly over both countries. While the municipal pageant remained the most popular kind, several new pageant subjects emerged as well, including institutional history (pageants of a given school or university), literary history (pageants of letters), biblical history (church pageants grown into mass spectacles), scientific and technological history ("pageants of tomorrow"), and even pageants of the African diaspora (W.E.B. DuBois's *Star of Ethiop*). For a good recent account of historical pageantry in the United States, see David Glassberg, *American Historical Pageantry: The Uses of Tradition in the Early Twentieth Century* (Chapel Hill: U of North Carolina P, 1990).

7. The playbill for the 1910 Chester pageant, for example, advertises three thousand performers and seating for four thousand spectators (*Chester Book of Words*). The influx of summer visitors, along with the demand for costumes and

sets, meant that a pageant town would often experience a quite substantial economic revival in addition to the desired folkloric one.

8. L. N. Parker, *Souvenir and Book of Words of the Colchester Pageant, June 21–26, 1909* (Norwich and London: Jarrold and Sons, 1909), xix.

9. Ibid., xvii.

10. Despite pageantry's pretensions to social inclusion, the genre's founder, L. N. Parker, insisted on the need for dictatorial control at the top. In his 1928 autobiography, he writes: "If I were asked to indicate the ideal Master of the Pageant, I should unhesitatingly point to Signor Benito Mussolini" (*Several of My Lives*, 284). Parker's own pageant-mastering took place in a crow's nest over the grandstand roof, where he could "signal to performers, and even tell them exactly what I thought of them through a megaphone, unsuspected and unheard by the audience" (ibid., 280). The figure of the unseen pageant-master becomes, for Woolf, a fascinating fictional device for meditating on the problem of artistic authority. In *Between The Acts*, her Miss La Trobe hisses and groans from behind a screen of trees and bushes as she desperately seeks to maintain control over the dramatic process.

11. *Several of My Lives*, 284.

12. The earl of Darnley, *Frank Lascelles: "Our Modern Orpheus"* (Oxford: Oxford UP, 1932), 34.

13. Qtd. in Darnley, *Frank Lascelles*, 171.

14. *Several of My Lives*, 280. The same ideals inspired a series of Edwardian open-air revivals of Hardy's *The Dynasts* which, like the pageant-plays, focuses on archetypal rural England. In "An Explanation of the Rural Scenes" (1916), Hardy describes the importance of staging *The Dynasts* "in spots that are not more than a mile" from the sites of the events depicted, thus giving "a curious sense of closeness to the action of each scene in point of place, although separated from it in time by more than 100 years" (qtd. in Keith Wilson, *Thomas Hardy on Stage* [New York: St. Martin's, 1995], 99).

15. Qtd. in Withington, *English Pageantry*, 195.

16. The pageants exhibit the kind of ahistoricism that Wright ascribes to national heritage movements in general: "Where there was active historicity there is now decoration and display; in the place of memory, amnesia swaggers out in historical fancy dress" (*On Living in an Old Country: The National Past in Contemporary Britain* [London: Verso, 1985], 78). The ahistorical qualities of the Edwardian pageant movement were not lost on dramatic critics of the day, who disparaged its simpleminded pedagogy and its nostalgic nationalism. Richard Withington cites, for example, the critic John Palmer on pageantry: "At worst they were conspicuous instances of precisely the deliberate cult of innocence and simplicity which is the last possible quarter whither we should look for a revival of the arts. They correspond with the activities of a large class of people who imagine they can recapture the sixteenth century by writing 'Merrie Englande' upon invitations to a contest of brass bands—people . . . who imagine they are putting back the clocks of history by measuring time with a sundial" (qtd. in *English Pageantry*, 209).

17. In his foreword to the York Pageant, Parker makes his own national ambitions clear: "Dilettantes and quidnuncs prate about the National Drama. Here it

is. Drama covering all English history from 800 B.C. to the Great Rebellion; written by Englishmen, set to music by Englishmen, costumed and acted by English men and women—acted by thirteen thousand of them—and listened to by over half a million spectators in twelve weeks . . . is that not National Drama?" (qtd. in Withington, *English Pageantry*, 196).

18. Darnley, *Frank Lascelles*, 124.

19. L. N. Parker, *Book of the Words of the Dover Pageant, July 27–August 1, 1908* (Dover: Grigg and Son, 1908), 69.

20. The pageant boom forms one part of a larger set of historical recuperations and found rituals, of jubilees and festivals, exhibitions and carnivals in the industrialized and imperial nations of Europe during the period 1880–1920 (Paul Connerton, *How Societies Remember* [Cambridge: Cambridge UP, 1989], 63). To get a quick, concrete sense of the contradictions at play in these inventions of tradition, consider the double verb in this remark by Reginald Blunt on the revival of historical pageantry: "England is reawakening to the remembrance that the dramatic sense must be, and has ever been, an integral part of the life of all great nations" (introduction to *The Chelsea Historical Pageant Book of Words, Jun 25– Jul 1, 1908* [Chelsea: Chelsea Pageant Committee, 1908], 11–12). The imperative "must be" combined with the indicative "has always been" underscores the paradox: abiding cultural practices must nonetheless be revived.

21. Although he saw no particular significance in the fact, historian Richard Withington observed in 1918 that, "Scotch and Welsh National Pageants there have been . . . but the English is yet to come" (*English Pageantry*, 203).

22. David Glassberg notes that, although the historical pageant was mostly on the wane after World War I in both England and the United States, the 1930s saw a brief resurgence in England, where civic rituals flourished and where "antimodern folk symbolism and massive public demonstrations remained linked" (*American Historical Pageantry*, 289).

23. Henry Miller and George Steiner praise the novel extravagantly on the cover of the new edition; Steiner calls it "the only novel produced by an English writer that can fairly be compared with the fictions of Tolstoy and Dostoyevsky."

24. It is probably not coincidental that Powys attended the Sherbourne school during the time when Louis Napoleon Parker himself was a master there; it was at Sherbourne that Parker staged the first modern pageant-play.

25. John Cowper Powys, *A Glastonbury Romance* (Woodstock: Overlook, 1967), 21; hereafter cited in the text.

26. Glen Cavaliero instructively contrasts Powys's "anthropology" with Lawrence's "prophecy" (*John Cowper Powys: Novelist* [Oxford: Clarendon, 1973], 181).

27. Even before arriving in Glastonbury, Crow confronts the power of his native landscape at that most classic site of primordial Englishness, Stonehenge. Reeling among the monoliths, Crow experiences a typically Powysian moment: "Stonehenge! He had never expected anything like this. He had expected the imposing, but this was overpowering. 'This is England,' he thought in his heart. 'This is my England. This is still alive' " (97).

28. In an effort to find an antirationalist vocabulary, Powys (like Eliot and Yeats) drew on a diverse cultural endowment, including William James's theories

of consciousness and Taoist religion (as filtered through British anthropology). Powys offered a full elaboration of his beliefs in *The Complex Vision* (1920), a book that resembles Yeats's *A Vision* in title, purpose, and modernist-era mysticism.

29. Qtd. in Dante Thomas, *A Bibliography of the Writings of John Cowper Powys: 1872–1963* (Mamaroneck, N.Y.: Paul Appel, 1975), 139.

30. Powys to W. N. Guthrie, 25 November 1931; qtd. in Charles Lock, "Polyphonic Powys: Dostoevsky, Bakhtin, and *A Glastonbury Romance*," *University of Toronto Quarterly* 55.3 (1986): 271.

31. E. Martin Browne, "From *The Rock* to *The Confidential Clerk*," in *T. S. Eliot: A Symposium for His Seventieth Birthday*, ed. Neville Braybrooke (New York: Farrar Straus and Cudahy, 1958), 57.

32. Eliot's interest in the music hall as a site of popular performing arts reflects a barely submerged fantasy of a primitive/organic cultural life not beset by social divisions; as David Chinitz aptly observes, for Eliot "the music hall thus becomes the English tribal ritual" ("T. S. Eliot and the Cultural Divide," *PMLA* 110.2 [March 1995]: 239).

33. For an overview of the critical dismissals and a detailed reading of the play in the context of its performance, see Randy Malamud, *Where the Words Are Valid: T. S. Eliot's Communities of Drama* (Westport, Conn.: Greenwood, 1994), 31–62. Most critics, including Malamud, do see the ten choruses as valuable sections of the text and agree with their inclusion in Eliot's collected poems. Eliot himself wrote ruefully to Bonamy Dobrée in July 1934: "I don't think my poetry is any good: not *The Rock* anyway, it isn't; nothing but a brilliant future behind me" (qtd. in Dobrée, "T. S. Eliot: A Personal Reminiscence," in *T. S. Eliot: The Man and His Work*, ed. Allen Tate [New York: Delacorte, 1966], 79). Among the disappointed friends who read or saw *The Rock* was Virginia Woolf, who feared that "poor old Tom" was "petrifying into a priest." Woolf writes to Stephen Spender: "The rock [*sic*] disappointed me. I couldn't go and see it, having caught the influenza in Ireland; and in reading, without seeing, perhaps one got the horror of that cheap farce and Cockney dialogue and dogmatism too full in the face. Roger Fry, though, went and came out in a rage. But I thought even the choruses tainted; and rather like an old ship swaying in the same track as the Waste Land—a repetition I mean. But I cant be sure that I wasn't unfairly influenced by my antireligious bias" (Woolf to Spender, 10 July 1934, in *The Letters of Virginia Woolf*, ed. Nigel Nicolson and Joanne Trautmann [New York: Harcourt, 1980], 5:315).

34. Dramatic expression was always a feature of Eliot's poetry, of course, from the overheard monologue of "Prufrock" to the dialogue of the "Game of Chess" section in *The Waste Land*. Eliot began moving toward drama proper with "Sweeney Agonistes" (written in the late 1920s and, though unfinished, staged in London by Group Theatre in the mid-1930s).

35. T. S. Eliot, *The Rock* (London: Faber, 1934), 30; hereafter cited in the text.

36. Charles Williams, *Descent into Hell* (Grand Rapids: William B. Eerdmans, 1972), 76; hereafter cited in the text.

37. Speaking of *The Rock* in a June 1934 letter to the editor of the *Spectator*, Eliot wrote, "[m]y only seriously dramatic aim was to show that there is a possible role for the Chorus" (qtd. in Roger Kojecky, *T. S. Eliot's Social Criticism* [New York: Farrar Straus and Giroux, 1972], 103).

38. T. S. Eliot, "Dramatis Personae," *Criterion* 1.3 (1923): 305–6.

39. The pageant was performed in July 1934 as a benefit for the Abinger Church Preservation Fund. In 1938, Forster wrote his second pageant-play, *England's Pleasant Land*, for the Dorking and Leith Hill District Preservation Society.

40. For a new and sophisticated account of Forster's refusal not just of the marriage plot but of the conventional (i.e., unrealistic) structure of love stories altogether, see Jesse Matz, " 'You Must Join My Dead': E. M. Forster and the Death of the Novel," *Modernism/Modernity* 9.2 (2002): 303–17.

41. "Modernism and Imperialism," 54–58. In Jameson's reading, the negative "infinity" of the imperial-metropolitan economy (as manned, for example, by Henry Wilcox) stands in opposition to the "utopian landscape" of *Howards End* and to the stable values of personal relations embodied in Mrs. Wilcox.

42. *Passage* describes the East as a place that retains mystery and refuses to be known, despite what Sara Suleri calls the narrator's deflationary or "antiexotic" rhetoric (*The Rhetoric of English India* [Chicago: U of Chicago P, 1992], 144). The Marabar Caves, like the rest of India, pose an epistemological and perceptual challenge to the English; they strike both Mrs. Moore and Adela Quested as unbounded and unknowable. At some points, the Indian landscape appears to offer access to the English imagination, but it always retains an element of challenge. And as Penelope Pether points out, the Indian muddle is generally defined against the ordered clarity of Forster's pastoral idealism ("E. M. Forster's *A Passage to India*: A Passage to the Patria?" *Sydney Studies in English* 17 [1991–92]: 115).

43. Suleri, *Rhetoric of English India*, 133.

44. Forster's grasp of imperial decline was quickened not only by his direct experiences of Anglo-India but also by his awareness of anti-imperial resistance movements. A friend of many Egyptian and Indian intellectuals, Forster knew that resistance was a growing force in the colonial world as early as 1919 when he warned fellow Britons about the importance of Egyptian nationalism (P. N. Furbank, *E. M. Forster: A Life, vol. 2, Polycrates' Ring (1914–1970)* [London: Secker and Warburg, 1978], 57–62).

45. When Forster did try to write a new novel in 1943, he could only produce family biography and local history, including a pastoral meditation on his long-time home called "West Hackhurst: A Country Ramble" (Furbank, *E. M. Forster*, 253–54). Although Forster considered his inability to write a new novel a personal failure, it is perhaps more interesting from a critical point of view to note the connection between the rooted English subject matter (the displacement of history by tradition) and the specifically *narrative* failure of inspiration.

46. E. M. Forster, *Abinger Harvest* (New York: Harcourt, 1964), 24: hereafter cited in the text as *AH*.

47. E. M. Forster, *Howards End* (New York: Vintage, 1921), 204.

48. Wright, *On Living in an Old Country*, 85.

49. E. M. Forster, *Two Cheers for Democracy* (New York: Harcourt, 1951), 23.

50. Ibid., 19.

51. Ibid., 31.

52. William Empson, *Some Versions of Pastoral* (London: Hogarth, 1986), 11.

53. E. M. Forster, *England's Pleasant Land* (London: Hogarth, 1940); hereafter cited in the text as *EPL*.

54. Powys frequently intones a similar litany of place names in *A Glastonbury Romance*: "They skirted through the wall of Long Leat Park. They passed Upper Whitbourne; they passed Corsley Heath; they passed Lane End and Gradon Farm. . . ." (106). As Patrick Wright notes, the names of "villages, plants, landmarks, birds, stones and the accoutrements of rural life" become vitally important in the discourse of Englishness during the interwar period: "It is as if the answer to urban modernity was for everyone to learn the names of the plants and places again" (*On Living in an Old Country*, 109–10).

55. "The Nation as Pastoral" (chap. 1, n. 80), 165.

56. The stewards of England's pastoral resources are clearly, in Forster's view, the enlightened gentry or upper-middle class. As Patrick Wright notes, the upper-middle-class pastoral imagination proceeds from the notion that the land has been underappreciated or misused by the lower-middle class (cheap picnickers likely to ignore or disrupt the land's noble essences). One consequence of the thirties boom in domestic tourism was the presence of the "masses" in the countryside, so that elites had to confront the fact that rural England was increasingly an "urban playspace" (Lowerson, "Battles for the Countryside" [chap. 1, n. 79], 258).

57. Of course pageants are intended for spectacular and spontaneous performance, not for close reading. For this reason, Forster himself expressed concern about committing *England's Pleasant Land* to print (*EPL* 9).

58. For a useful discussion of the popular and "mass" forms of post-Wagner German nationalism, and especially of the revival of classical, choral, and outdoor theatrical conventions designed to "bridge the gap between actor and audience," see George L. Mosse, "Mass Politics and the Political Liturgy of Nationalism," in *Nationalism: The Nature and Evolution of an Idea*, ed. Eugene Kamenka (Canberra: Australian National UP, 1973), 42–45.

59. Some left theater groups in the 1930s did, however, use the pageant-play form to represent urban or working-class experience in England. In 1936, the Communist Party staged a "March of History" in a pageantic attempt to suggest that communism was a "vernacular, indigenous force" stemming back to radical progenitors like Cromwell and Milton (*Theatres of Memory* [chap. 1, n. 73]. 207). The "mass theater" movement, like the pageant play, used amateur actors, often in casts of thousands. In the program for the Group Theatre on 1 October 1935, Auden describes some of the communal idealism associated with vernacular performance genres in the period: "Drama began as an act of a whole community. Ideally there would be no spectators. In practice every member of the audience should feel like an understudy . . . the music hall, the Christmas pantomime, and the country house charade are the most living drama of to-day" (*The English Auden*, ed. Edward Mendelson [London: Faber, 1977], 273).

60. Woolf to Stephen Spender, 7 April 1937, in *The Letters of Virginia Woolf*, 6: 116. One problem, she thought, was the dilution of psychological realism: "I expect I muted down the characters too much, in order to shorten and keep their faces towards society."

61. Woolf to Stephen Spender, 30 April 1937, in *Letters of Virginia Woolf*, 6: 123. Woolf's critical intuitions about the need for different levels and hybrid genres grew during the last decade of her career. In 1936, she wrote to her nephew Julian Bell to dissuade him from standard novel writing: "What I wish is that

you'd invent some medium that's half poetry half play half novel. (Three halves, I see; well, you must correct my arithmetic.) I think there ought to be a scrambling together of mediums now" (qtd. in Hermione Lee, *Virginia Woolf* [New York: Knopf, 1997], 603).

62. In "On Not Knowing Greek," Woolf describes the Greek tragic chorus approvingly as "the undifferentiated voices who sing like birds in the pauses of the wind" (*The Common Reader,* first and second series [New York: Harcourt, 1925], 46). This choral ideal will come back a bit mangled, but recognizable, in *Between the Acts.* In the same essay Woolf remarks that there are still some villages "in the wilder parts of England" that possess the kind of "perfect" customary life necessary for classical completeness (40).

63. Virginia Woolf, *Between the Acts* (San Diego: Harcourt, 1969), 6; hereafter cited in the text.

64. As biographer Hermione Lee notes and most contemporary Woolf critics seem to emphasize, Woolf remains ever suspicious of the appeal to national heritage (*Virginia Woolf,* 422). On the other hand, Woolf was certainly capable of a touristic thrill at making contact with the historical depth of England, as when she encountered: "peasants, wandering along the bank, and talking to us, like something in the time of Elizabeth so that I felt I was actually in Shakespeare, one of the northern ones" (Woolf to Ethel Smyth, 26 June 1938, in *Letters of Virginia Woolf,* 6: 246). Gillian Beer has provided a valuable analysis of the ways in which, for Woolf, elements of the past and of "prehistory" remain visible and even unchanged in the present—a logic of conservation that takes on literary form in the pageant-play (*Virginia Woolf: The Common Ground* [Edinburgh: Edinburgh UP, 1996], 8–9).

65. There appear to be two sources for Swithin's outline: H. G. Wells's 1920 *Outline of History* (a text that, as we have seen, also attracted Forster's interest) and G. M. Trevelyan's 1926 *History of England* (Beer, *Common Ground,* 21 and 144). In her diary, Woolf describes Trevelyan's *History* as a product of "the complete Insider." Such Insiders, Woolf notes, "are the glory of the 19th century. They do a great service like Roman roads. But they avoid the forests & the will o the wisps" (*The Diary of Virginia Woolf,* ed. Anne Olivier Bell and Andrew McNeillie [San Diego: Harcourt, 1984], 5: 333). Woolf's version of English history, for its part, sides with "the will o the wisps" of local memory as against the imperial directness of the Roman road.

66. This history establishes the idea that civilization begins with separation from the continent. Naturally events of the late 1930s made this a resonant myth for English citizens who felt civilization threatened by potential contact with the new barbarisms of the continent.

67. From the virile Richard Dalloway in *Voyage Out* to the graying Peter Walsh to the retired Colonel Pargiter of *The Years* to the ancient Bart Oliver, Woolf's career measures the gradual superannuation of the empire man. Old Oliver's vision of the bullock is also a dilapidated echo of Percival's "pair of bullocks" episode in *The Waves* ([San Diego: Harcourt, 1931], 136).

68. Maria DiBattista, *Virginia Woolf's Major Novels: The Fables of Anon* (New Haven: Yale UP, 1980, 196–204).

69. Following the logic of domestic identification, we might say that Isa's fate corresponds to England's and unfolds in relation to the resident power of patriarchal Britain embodied by Giles. Isa's place in an allegory of competing national destinies seems confirmed when we consider that she is exactly thirty-nine, "the age of the century" and that, as Judith L. Johnston points out, her name echoes the Greek word *aisa*, or fate ("The Remediable Flaw: Revisioning Cultural History in *Between the Acts*," in *Virginia Woolf and Bloomsbury*, ed. Jane Marcus [Hampshire, U.K.: Macmillan, 1987], 270).

70. The conflict of values between pastoral Englishness and imperial Britishness appears frequently in Woolf's writing. In novels ranging from *The Voyage Out* to *Mrs. Dalloway* to *The Years*, Woolf pits imperial men against cultured women. In a recent study of Woolf and empire, Kathy J. Phillips illustrates and discusses this pattern, suggesting that Woolf sees imperial and patriarchal enterprises as twin manifestations of an aggressive, misdirected, masculine drive toward conquest (*Virginia Woolf against Empire* [Knoxville: U of Tennessee P, 1994], 224–40).

71. DiBattista, *Fables of Anon*, 193.

72. The pageant-play serves as a useful device for Woolf's project of reclaiming unofficial Englishness because, as Woolf herself points out in *Three Guineas* (1938), pageantry is one of the most "dictated, regimented" versions of public discourse (*Three Guineas* [San Diego: Harcourt, 1966], 114; hereafter cited in the text as *TG*).

73. A few pages later, when the audience begins to lose interest in the pageant, the lowing of the cows draws them back into the dramatic circle. When art falters, the cows "annihilated the gap; bridged the distance; filled the emptiness and continued the emotion" (141). Despite the absurdity of the cows, the scene cannot be read as fully ironic. Woolf is not simply mocking a degraded form of community drama but exploring its cohesive power.

74. If we take *Between the Acts* as a sort of case study of group ritual in an advanced industrial society, we see that its plot corresponds to the three-part model of social drama developed by Victor Turner: (1) an initial separation from daily life in preparation for the ritual; (2) the performance of the ritual itself, which is a time of symbolic liminality; and (3) the period of reaggregation, or return to the mundane. In Turner's model, as in Woolf's novel, the symbolic liminality of social drama allows for the simultaneous expression or emergence of "a society's deepest values" and of "radical scepticism" about those values (*The Anthropology of Performance* [New York: PAJ Publications, 1987], 102). Woolf's ideas on classical drama and ritual in general were shaped by her reading of the Cambridge anthropologist Jane Harrison. For a study of Harrison's influence, see Patricia Maika, *Virginia Woolf's* Between the Acts *and Jane Harrison's Con/spiracy* (Ann Arbor: UMI Research, 1987), esp. 7–11 and 57–58.

75. Virginia helped Leonard assemble the research for *Empire and Commerce in Africa* (Phillips, *Virginia Woolf against Empire*, viii). Throughout the thirties, she remained actively involved in the work of the Hogarth Press, which was publishing key works of the decolonization movement, including C.L.R. James's *The Case for West Indian Self-Government* in 1933 and Leonard Barnes's *The Future of Colonies* in 1936 (Phillips, *Virginia Woolf against Empire*, xxxiv).

76. Woolf's most successful literary efforts, the novel *The Village in the Jungle* and the short fiction collected in *Stories of the East*, sharply undercut the glamour of British colonialism in Asia, dwelling on the disappointment that follows from blinkered, romantic investments in the exotic East. The stories anticipate Woolf's rational anti-imperialism of the 1920s and 1930s, illustrating that the English can govern by force, but can never fully grasp the nature of, their colonies. Imperial rule was, for Woolf, not so much politically unethical as utterly absurd.

77. Leonard Woolf, *Imperialism and Civilization* (New York: Harcourt, 1928), 20.

78. Leonard Woolf, *Barbarians Within and Without* (New York: Harcourt, 1939), 129.

79. *Diary of Virginia Woolf*, 5: 40.

80. For a more typical, darker reading of *Three Guineas*, emphasizing the insuperability of Woolf's doubts about the reform of patriarchy and imperialism, see Pamela Transue, *Virginia Woolf and the Politics of Style* (Albany: SUNY, 1986).

81. There are many small textual indicators of a larger antinarrative or repetitive logic—a feature singled out by J. Hillis Miller as central to this text (*Fiction and Repetition: Seven English Novels* [Cambridge: Harvard UP, 1982]). In the early conception of the novel, Woolf indicates an interest in repetition: "I saw the form of a new novel. Its [*sic*] to be first the statement of the theme: then the restatement: & so on: repeating the same story" (*Diary of Virginia Woolf*, 5: 114). Some of the novel's most memorable images, such as the snake circling a bloody toad in its mouth or the phonograph circling in the bushes, act as motifs of the narrative cycle or loop. Likewise, Isa responds to the pageant by wondering if the plot matters: "There was no need to puzzle out the plot. . . . Don't bother about the plot: the plot's nothing" (90–91). In many ways, these themes cut across the pageant and the frame narrative, seeming to collapse the difference between the two. The text invites a reading—Maria DiBattista is again exemplary here—of the creative-destructive dialectic as a feature of both pageant *and* novel. But the novel tends to locate the good version of English pastoral continuity in the public ritual of the pageant, whereas the flashes of human savagery tend to surface in the frame narrative.

82. Whereas both Eliot and Forster actually produced dramatic works, Woolf turned down the opportunity to do the same for the Rodmell Women's Institute, preferring to fictionalize her pageant-play. On the other hand, Woolf clearly thought of *Between the Acts* as an experiment in breaking up the traditional generic commitments of prose fiction; she wrote in 1938 that "Pointz Hall is to become in the end a play" (*Diary of Virginia Woolf*, 5: 139).

83. Many critics, including Judith Johnston, see this conclusion as a capitulation on Isa's part to the continuing cycle of patriarchal domination ("The Remediable Flaw").

84. There are some indications that Woolf ends by affirming the politics of privacy, and they have led many critics to see *Between the Acts* as, ultimately, an anticommunitarian novel. On this reading, any attempt to redefine or reclaim a national culture fails: the nation is irremediably corrupt, patriarchal, fragmented. Steve Ellis, for example, argues that the novel's turn toward Englishness ultimately yields the insight that the heart of England is either an absence or a dark and

barbaric presence (*The English Eliot: Design, Language and Landscape in Four Quartets* [London: Routledge, 1991], 86).

85. Patricia Laurence, "The Facts and Fugue of War: From *Three Guineas* to *Between the Acts*," in *Virginia Woolf and War*, ed. Mark Hussey (Syracuse: Syracuse UP, 1991), 228.

86. The struggle over authority, both social and artistic, is at the heart of the novel and most readings of it. Patricia K. Joplin has provided the most thorough account of Miss La Trobe's potentially authoritarian function. Joplin argues that the gramophone's mechanical, communal exhortations represent what Woolf would have seen as the dangers of mob culture and of a conformist call to unity via "the false transcendence of the state" ("The Authority of Illusion," 92). Michele Pridmore-Brown, too, reads the gramophone and the pageant as devices by which Woolf demonstrates the authoritarian dangers of "one-making." Pridmore-Brown suggests, however, that Woolf (using the same gramophone device) also disrupts authority and conformism by generating a kind of semantic "noise" around the pageant—a factor which symbolically safeguards each audience member's interpretative freedom ("1939–40: Of Virginia Woolf, Gramophones, and Fascism," *PMLA* 113 (May 1998): 408–21). While Joplin offers a convincing account of Woolf's radical skepticism about group behavior and Pridmore-Brown brings a useful and persuasive scientific vocabulary to the text, their arguments assimilate Woolf's politics back to the liberal protection of the individual without giving due weight to the novel's (wary) attempt to reinvent a safe form of group identity based on the resources of English folk tradition.

87. I refer here to Fredric Jameson, *The Political Unconscious: Narrative as a Socially Symbolic Act* (Ithaca: Cornell UP, 1981).

88. Woolf was reading Freud's *Group Psychology and the Analysis of the Ego* at the time and developing an interest in what DiBattista identifies as the "creative genius of the group in its use of language, particularly in the collective productions of folksong and folklore" (*Fables of Anon*, 220).

89. Brenda Silver, who prepared the two essays for publication in 1979 and contributed a useful critical introduction, notes that Woolf intended to present English literature as a "continuum" (introduction to " 'Anon' and 'The Reader': Virginia Woolf's Last Essays," *Twentieth Century Literature* 25 [1979]: 357). Both Silver and Hermione Lee observe a number of telling connections between the imagery of *Between the Acts* and *Reading at Random*, including, for instance, the figure of the pool/reservoir of culture (Lee, *Virginia Woolf*, 738).

90. I take Woolf's interest in primordial literary origins as one instance of a late modernist discourse of native or Anglo primitivism, defined against the derivative primitivism of colonial/modernist anthropology. In this connection, it is not incidental that Woolf *revised* her description of culture's primal scene, replacing the word "savages" with "huntsmen" (Silver, "Virginia Woolf's Last Essays," 402). To my ears, this emendation shifts the connotation away from ideals patterned on tribal others to ideals patterned on more familiar and local versions of the folk.

91. " 'Anon' and 'The Reader': Virginia Woolf's Last Essays," *Twentieth Century Literature* 25 (1979), 384–85; hereafter cited in the text as "Anon."

92. David McWhirter notes some of the resonances between late Woolf and late Eliot, including their shared appreciation of Elizabethan drama as a locus of

linguistic and formal wholeness (a neoclassical virtue) that capitulated neither to errant individualism nor to imposed orthodoxy ("The Novel, The Play, and The Book: *Between the Acts* and the Tragicomedy of History," *ELH* 60.3 [1993]: 790). McWhirter's point of emphasis is the important difference between Eliot's "ideological closure" and the radical relativizing effects of Woolf's parodic, Bakhtinian writing in *Between the Acts* (809–10). For my purposes, it is worth emphasizing the changing status of national culture as a concept/device that allows both Eliot and Woolf to mediate between genres, between concepts of individual and community, and perhaps most saliently, between local contingencies of history and deeper, vaster patterns of time.

93. *Diary of Virginia Woolf,* 5: 135.

94. In the last decade, Woolf scholarship has come increasingly to insist on a more public and political Woolf, and, perhaps not surprisingly, *Between the Acts* has been read more and read differently than it was twenty years ago. Although many readers continue to take the novel as a vexed recoil from group politics of any kind, a number of critics have recently observed that the novel's interest in national identity, though obviously ironized, is not fully rejected and indeed marks a kind of turn in Woolf's thinking. For example, Gillian Beer balances her reading of Woolf's elegiac and parodic stance toward her "island history" with a sensible recognition that the novel also values the persistence of the community's memory and cultural legacy (*Common Ground,* 170). James F. English provides an excellent account of the novel's contradictory relationship to nationalism, framed by a discussion of its comic exposure of the limits of communitarian logic (*Comic Transactions: Literature, Humor, and the Politics of Community in Twentieth-Century Britain* [Ithaca: Cornell UP, 1994], 120–27). Similarly, David McWhirter makes the case for the novel as a multigeneric tragicomedy designed to evade both the deep, tragic individualism that Woolf associates with Dostoyevsky and the comic, impersonal sense of community that Woolf associates with Austen ("The Novel, The Play, and The Book"). Rather than simply repeat the story of the novel's oscillating attraction/repulsion with regard to group politics, or argue for the novel's final choice between attraction and repulsion, these critics analyze Woolf's techniques for addressing the social dimension of art. Similarly, my reading does not attempt to determine *how much* value Woolf affixes to national belonging or group ritual, but to analyze the changing nature of those categories in the era of imperial retrenchment.

95. Moretti, *Modern Epic* (chap. 1, n. 105), 123–25.

96. *The Politics of Modernism,* (introduction, n. 7), 39–44.

97. "The Politics of the Possible," (chap. 1, n. 25), 182.

98. On this view, the modernist novel of consciousness takes the workings of perception, cognition, and imagination as features of an individual psyche, but conceives of that psyche in terms of universal human experience. In the Cambridge-centered intellectual sphere most relevant to Woolf, for example, G. E. Moore's *Principia Ethica* famously emphasizes the importance of attending to mental conditions and experiences. Moore's ethics linked the good mental state of the individual to the good condition of the universe, ignoring the intermediate and immediate demands of group identity.

99. In pursuing this line of reasoning about metropolitan perception and *Between the Acts*, I am extending Patrick McGee's basic contention that Woolf's fiction registers—at an unconscious level—the interdependence of imperial geopolitics and modernist aesthetics ("The Politics of Modernist Form; or, Who Rules *The Waves?*" *Modern Fiction Studies* 38.3 [1992]: 635). Raymond Williams has long since pointed out how tightly interwoven Bloomsbury critics of empire were with the power structure of the imperial ruling class ("The Bloomsbury Fraction," in *Problems in Materialism and Culture* [London: New Left Books, 1980]). Even as early as *The Voyage Out*, where the cultured Rachel Vinrace dimly acknowledges herself as the beneficiary of her father's overseas trading, Woolf herself thematizes the dependence of the civilized arts on imperial commerce. This relation takes on more complex form in *The Waves*, which has been read by Jane Marcus as an experimental text whose rendering of consciousness is shaped by an elegiac and critical representation of British colonialism, filtered through the absent center of Percival ("Britannia Rules *The Waves*," in *Decolonizing Tradition: New Views of Twentieth-Century "British" Literary Canons*, ed. Karen Lawrence [Urbana: U of Illinois P, 1992], 136–62). In a subtle rejoinder to Marcus, McGee insists that Woolf's virtuoso modernist characterization in *The Waves* depends—in a somewhat occulted or unconscious fashion—on the "ethnocentric mapping of the world into areas of light and areas of darkness" ("The Politics of Modernist Form," 645). *Between the Acts* offers, I think, an even more telling juncture of form and content in which the elegy for empire becomes an elegy for modernism. Noting rightly that Woolf's subjects are always in a sense doubly (and contradictorily) represented as both autonomous *and* culturally shaped, Tamar Katz proposes analyses of the "terms in which" Woolf presents that contradiction ("Modernism, Subjectivity, and Narrative Form: Abstraction in *The Waves*," *Narrative* 3.3 [1995]: 234). In that spirit, I argue that *Between the Acts* marks a relative shift in emphasis toward the culturally determined aspects of subjectivity and, further, that that shift is accompanied by the partial displacement of cosmopolitan subjectivity by national culture.

100. Powys, Eliot, and Woolf all stock their pageant texts with figures of vast or eternal perspective, figures whose purpose seems to be to assimilate local contingencies of space and time into wider geological, biological, and theological concepts. Because such concepts seem at times to overshadow the narrower historical and geographical frames of nationhood, critics of these writers have often tended to disavow or downplay the national or Anglocentric aspects of the texts in question. In each case, however, the text articulates its concept of cosmic or eternal or prehistorical time-space *through* (i.e., not simply in ironic counterpoint to) a specifically English set of conditions and traditions. In other words, even when anti- or supranational forces seem at one level to reveal the contingency of the nation's historical existence or the fraudulence of its associated traditions, the text's filtering of cultural meaning through the nation tends at another level to affirm its sociohistorical privilege and coherence.

101. As Christine Froula observes, Woolf increasingly sought to collapse the figure of the artist into her audience throughout the 1930s ("Modernism, Genetic Texts and Literary Authority in Virginia Woolf's Portraits of the Artist as the Audience," *Romanic Review* 86.3 [1995]: 525).

102. For readings of the novel as nascently postmodern, see McWhirter, "The Novel, The Play, and The Book"; and Jacqueline Buckman, "Virginia Woolf's *Between the Acts* and Some Problems of Periodization," *Durham University Journal*, July 1992, 279–89.

CHAPTER THREE

1. T. S. Eliot, *Notes towards the Definition of Culture* (1949), in *Christianity and Culture* (San Diego: Harcourt, 1977), 125; hereafter cited in the text as *NDC*.

2. Eliot described the essay as an "attempt to show that in many cases *no* interpretation of a rite could explain its origin. For the meaning of the series of acts is to the performers themselves an interpretation" (qtd. in James Longenbach, *Modernist Poetics of History: Pound, Eliot, and the Sense of the Past* [Princeton: Princeton UP, 1987], 165).

3. T. S. Eliot, *After Strange Gods: A Primer of Modern Heresy* (New York: Harcourt, 1933), 18. These published lectures record Eliot's most unapologetic statement of the value of territorial inertia and, in effect, racial solidarity: "The population should be homogeneous; where two or more cultures exist in the same place they are likely either to be fiercely self-conscious or both to become adulterate" (20).

4. The most thorough study of Eliot's anti-Semitism is Anthony Julius, *T. S. Eliot, Anti-Semitism, and Literary Form* (Cambridge: Cambridge UP, 1995). David Spurr has observed that Eliot tends to oppose Jews and "natives," with the former representing diasporic and *literary* values, the latter a redemptive set of primitive and *cultural* values ("Myths of Anthropology: Eliot, Joyce, Lévy-Bruhl," *PMLA* 109.2 [March 1994]: 273–77).

5. Leonard Woolf, *Imperialism and Civilization* (New York: Harcourt, 1928), 124.

6. Ibid., 142.

7. *Barbarians Within and Without* (chap. 1, n. 66), 129.

8. Ibid., 26–28.

9. *Selected Prose of T. S. Eliot*, ed. Frank Kermode (New York: Harcourt, 1975), 64; hereafter cited in the text as *SP*.

10. Milton, playing the bogeyman for Eliot, initiated the trajectory wherein poets cultivate "personal style" at the cost of common or classic style (*On Poetry and Poets* [London: Faber, 1957], 154). In a discussion of Eliot's relation to geographical contraction, it is probably worth noting that Eliot frequently generates a dichotomy between the bad infinities of romanticism and the good enclosures of classicism. Here, for example, Eliot associates the degraded Milton with images of "vast size, limitless space" (*On Poetry and Poets*, 156).

11. T. S. Eliot, *The Sacred Wood* (London: Methuen, 1950), 28.

12. Ibid., 32. David Trotter points out the significance of this review in his reading of *The Waste Land* as a late imperial/frontier poem ("Modernism and Empire" [chap. 1, n. 16]). Eliot's criticism of Wyndham's "type" captures his penchant for posing the metaphorical value of concentration and intensity against the metaphorical vice of expansion and dilation. For example, in *The Sacred Wood*, he criticizes Swinburne's tendency to reinforce emotion "not by intensifi-

cation, but by expansion" (147). For a discussion of the passage, see Sanford Schwartz, *The Matrix of Modernism: Pound, Eliot and Early Twentieth-Century Thought* (Princeton: Princeton UP, 1985), 163. Eliot applies these metaphors more and more often and with increasing literalness to problems of political geography in the 1930s and '40s.

13. Among the modernists, Eliot was the most forceful devotee of what Lucy McDiarmid calls "the myth of the seventeenth century" (*Saving Civilization: Yeats, Eliot, and Auden between the Wars* [Cambridge: Cambridge UP, 1984], 39–41). Seamus Deane has elegantly summarized the central role of this mythic "seventeenth-century Eden" in the canonical narratives of British imperialism, citing Eliot as one of its major exponents (introduction to *Nationalism, Colonialism and Literature* [Minneapolis: U of Minnesota P, 1990], 9). Deane does not, however, address the later Eliot's imaginative reversal of this paradigmatic narrative of decay. Once England entered a more obvious phase of contraction, Eliot mobilized the same historical myths in the service of a distinctively *postimperial* rhetoric of revival.

14. Michael North, *The Political Aesthetic of Yeats, Eliot and Pound* (Cambridge: Cambridge UP, 1991), 6–9. In an essay on Eliot and Lukács, North provides a detailed account of both divergences (especially in terms of a theory of social elites) and convergences, including the preference by both for restrained, classical form over varieties of romantic, subjective expression ("Eliot, Lukács, and the Politics of Modernism," in *T. S. Eliot: The Modernist in History*, ed. Ronald Bush [Cambridge: Cambridge UP, 1991], 172). In an earlier account of this relationship, Sanford Schwartz notes the common influence of Hegelian thought on Eliot (via Bradley) and Lukács (via Marx). Schwartz notes that both criticize the reification of modern minds—their lost capacity to conceptualize or represent wholes (*The Matrix of Modernism*, 162).

15. Georg Lukács, *The Theory of the Novel*, trans. Anna Bostock (Cambridge: MIT, 1971), 34.

16. The quotations appear in T. S. Eliot, "Religion without Humanism," in *Humanism and America*, ed. Norman Foerster (New York: Farrar and Rinehart, 1930), 112.

17. D. H. Lawrence, *Apocalypse* (London: Martin Secker, 1932), 97–98.

18. Frank Kermode, *The Sense of an Ending* (New York: Oxford UP, 1967), 47. To place Kermode's terms in a properly historical framework, it might be helpful to review the four models of time described by Johannes Fabian. The oldest model is traditional pagan time, based on seasonal and cyclical return. Judeo-Christian or eschatological time, which shapes history toward salvation, developed somewhat later. Next came what Fabian (citing Gusdorf) calls the "myth-history of reason," a temporal regime that begins with Enlightenment historicism and uses a kind of secularized Christian apparatus to shape time according to historical rationality. Finally, in the late nineteenth century, a fourth model of time emerges, in which the "myth-history of reason" gives way to a notion of linear mechanical time or history as a meaningless succession of events (*Time and the Other: How Anthropology Makes Its Object* [New York: Columbia UP, 1983], 2–21). It is that fourth form that I would describe as metropolitan standard time,

the time that corresponds to the modernist period and to the imperial, expansionist phase of capitalist development.

19. James Longenbach offers a nuanced reading of the modernist reaction to nineteenth-century linear and positivist models of history associated with Hegel and Comte (*Modernist Poetics of History*, 5–16).

20. David Trotter has pointed out that *The Waste Land*'s allusions to spatial and secular modes of exploration tend to complicate the model of a spiritual journey that is often applied to the poem ("Modernism and Empire," 146–47). Similarly, Hugh Kenner sees *The Waste Land* as an ironic echo of Virgil's *Aeneid*, a quest poem about the hero's journey to and discovery of a great imperial center (*A Sinking Island: The Modern English Writers* [New York: Knopf, 1988], 189–90).

21. Mary Butts, *Armed with Madness* (Kingston, N.Y.: McPherson, 1992), 121. For more on Butts and her place within an English, feminist, and countermodernist discourse, see Jane Garrity's *Step-daughters of England: British Women Modernists and the National Imaginary* (Manchester UP, 2003). Alison Light locates another set of women writers within a broadly conservative Anglocentrism of the interwar period. In a chapter on Jan Struther's *Mrs. Miniver* as an embodiment of feminine, domestic, conservative values in England, Light usefully notes that this strain of Anglocentrism is not politically conservative in a classic Tory sense, nor even nationalist, but national (*Forever England: Femininity, Literature and Conservatism between the Wars* [London: Routledge, 1991], 113–55).

22. The Oxford Christians are often written out of mainstream 1930s literary history as retiring crackpots not in step with major literary development, though Cunningham's more comprehensive history of the period redresses that omission. For more on Williams and Eliot, see Knowles, *A Purgatorial Flame* (Introduction, n. 29), 153–72.

23. T. S. Eliot, Introduction to Charles Williams, *All Hallow's Eve* (Grand Rapids: William B. Eerdmans, 1981), xvi.

24. Charles Williams, *Shadows of Ecstasy* (Grand Rapids: William B. Eerdmans, 1970), 169; hereafter cited in the text.

25. Fred Inglis, "Gentility and Powerlessness: Tolkien and the New Class," in *J.R.R. Tolkien: This Far Land*, ed. Robert Giddings (London: Vision Press, 1983), 33–35.

26. Gareth Knight, *The Magical World of the Inklings* (Longmead: Element Books, 1990), 13.

27. Jane Chance Nitzsche, *Tolkien's Art* (London: Macmillan, 1979), 1.

28. William Ready, *The Tolkien Relation* (Chicago: Henry Regnery, 1968), 8.

29. Knight, *Magical World*, 133.

30. Dobrée, "A Personal Reminiscence" (chap. 2, n. 34), 82.

31. T. S. Eliot, *The Idea of a Christian Society*, in *Christianity and Culture* (San Diego: Harcourt, 1977), 12; hereafter cited in the text as *ICS*.

32. In general during the 1930s, Eliot tends to turn imperial issues of the day back onto the question of saving England for and from itself. In a 1935 *Criterion* commentary, for instance, Eliot meditates on the discovery of a Papuan people, the Tari Furora, "lost in time" in New Guinea. He seconds the prevailing assumption, as represented by the *London Times*'s editorial voice, that European contact

will corrupt and ruin the Tari Furora. But in a turn typical of Eliot's thinking during this period, he uses the story to identify England's need to salvage its own civilization: "I am not horrified so much by the prospect of the future for the natives, black as that may be, as by the prospect of the future for *us*. For if we are so helpless in the hands of our 'civilization' that we admit our inability to prevent it from ruining Papuans, what hope have we of saving ourselves?" ("A Commentary," *Criterion* 15 [October 1935]: 66–67).

33. T. S. Eliot, "Building up the Christian World," *Listener* 7 (April 1932): 502.

34. T. S. Eliot, "A Commentary," *Criterion* 18 (October 1938): 59–60.

35. Lukács's critique of modernism is probably the locus classicus for the idea that modernist works provide formal unity to substitute for a lost social totality. In his view, modern literature makes "a desperate, purely artistic attempt to create, with the means of composition, structuring and organisation, a unity that is no longer organically given: a desperate attempt and a heroic failure. For unity can surely be achieved, but never a real totality" (*Theory of the Novel*, 53–55). *Theory of the Novel* anticipates both Eliot's cultural criticism and Woolf's story of Anon as an account of modernism's failure to make aesthetic unity and virtuosity compensate for a missing cultural totality.

36. Samuel Taylor Coleridge, *On the Constitution of the Church and State, According to the Idea of Each*, 4th ed. (London: Edward Moxon, 1852), xi.

37. Ibid., 26.

38. For more on Coleridge's influence on Eliot, particularly via the concept of the clerisy as an educated and faithful elite responsible for the transmission of a cultural endowment, see Roger Kojecky, *T. S. Eliot's Social Criticism* (New York: Farrar Straus and Giroux, 1972), 19–24. Because my argument centers on the British context and English applications of Eliot's thought, this sketch of its genealogy does not address key continental sources. For a full and persuasive treatment of the centrality of Charles Maurras and French conservative thought to Eliot's work over many decades, see Kenneth Asher, *T. S. Eliot and Ideology* (Cambridge: Cambridge UP, 1995). And of course, Herder and an entire German-romantic lineage stands behind Coleridge. In discussing Herder's relevance to later concepts of organic culture, Michael Gorra rightly notes that the ideal of authentic and spontaneous cultural unity is "possible only so long as a group remains isolated, homogeneous and small" (*After Empire* [introduction, n. 2], 76)—precisely the pre- and postimperial ideal that motivates Eliot's Anglocentrism.

39. Louis Menand, *Discovering Modernism: T. S. Eliot and His Context* (New York: Oxford UP, 1987), 161.

40. Homi K. Bhabha, *The Location of Culture* (London: Routledge, 1994), 142. Bhabha complicates Anderson's model by pointing out that national time is always double and disjunctive, split into the temporalities of a modern pluralist present and an archaic set of traditions. In *After Strange Gods*, Eliot makes his allegiance to the latter clear: "It is only a law of nature, that local patriotism, when it represents a distinct tradition and culture, takes precedence over a more abstract national patriotism" (21). For another occasion where Eliot seems to use the word "national" as a substitute or screen for "racial and local," see the 1943 essay "The Social Function of Poetry" (*On Poetry and Poets*, 18–19).

41. T. S. Eliot, "A Commentary," *Criterion* 17 (October 1937): 82.

42. Moreover, the essay anticipates the persistence of two key questions for U.K. national politics in the late twentieth century (and beyond): its proper relation to Europe and to Irish, Scottish, and Welsh nationalisms.

43. Eliot makes his position against hybrid and partial cultural transmission clear in a 1943 pamphlet opposing the union of the Indian Protestant churches. Naturally, Eliot fears a dilution of Anglican purity with forms of "minimal Christianity" that give "indefinite latitude" to "individual interpretation" of doctrine (*Reunion by Destruction: Reflections on a Scheme for Church Union in South India* [London: Pax House, 1943], 10). More to the point, Eliot insists on the value of cultural wholeness: any "union" must encompass a *whole culture*, not some mongrel collection of sects (21). Eliot takes cultural and religious wholeness as the only reliable basis for social order and—not incidentally—for psychic order (the "whole life of man"). As the Indian case reveals, Eliot believes that the right kind of religious totality or unity cannot be fostered except in settled, historically continuous nations. This conviction brings his attention back to the waste land that *can* be saved, England: "Between the 'missionary field' and the 'home field' there can be no radical difference—England was once a missionary field" (5).

44. Critics wary of ascribing nativist views to Eliot often seize on this portion of his writing to indicate a continuous commitment to Europe. Certainly Eliot did not wish for isolated culture, even when he advocated most forcefully for unified culture. But if we read even a bit below the surface of Eliot's own rhetoric, it becomes clear that the formulation of whatever cosmopolitanism remained to Eliot in the forties rested on a prior commitment to the integrity and unity (and, in fact, relative isolation and retrenchment) of a national culture.

45. Frank Kermode, *Modern Essays* (London: Fontana, 1971), 309.

46. At roughly the same time, F. R. Leavis was warning about the dangers of Americanism (particularly as disseminated by Hollywood films), and J. M. Keynes was urging "Death to Hollywood" (*CWK* 28: 371). The postwar fate of an artistically vital but commercially marginal British film industry certainly bore out these concerns.

47. Robert Crawford, *Devolving English Literature* (Oxford: Clarendon, 1992), 229.

48. T. S. Eliot, "Cultural Diversity and European Unity," *Review* 2.2 (1945): 64.

49. George Orwell, *The Orwell Reader* (San Diego: Harcourt, 1968), 250.

50. For other discussions of Eliot's slippage between normative and descriptive definitions of culture, see Asher, *T. S. Eliot and Ideology*, 93–94; and Terry Eagleton, "Eliot and a Common Culture," in *Eliot in Perspective: A Symposium*, ed. Graham Martin (London: Macmillan, 1970), 281–88.

51. It should come as no surprise to find the Celtic fringe playing the part of supplement or obverse to a discourse of Englishness. As Terence Hawkes has noted, the Celtic lurks below the surface not only of Arnoldian ideas about English culture but of Eliotic ones as well ("The Heimlich Manoeuvre," *Textual Practice* 8 [Summer 1994]: 309–11).

52. Many previous commentaries, perhaps most famously Raymond Williams's *Culture and Society*, make the basic differentiation between Eliot and Arnold: that Eliot's concept of culture (however elitist) was more anthropological,

Arnold's more aesthetic. Also, Arnold's belief in "culture" as an absolute value was for Eliot a secular-humanist heresy that did not take into account the necessity of religion's incarnation in culture. Finally, whereas Arnold imagined a cultural convergence at the top, Eliot holds increasingly to the sovereignty of local cultures.

53. Hugh MacDiarmid (C. M. Grieve), "English Ascendancy in British Literature," *Criterion* 10 (July 1931): 599–600.

54. Ibid., 608.

55. Ibid., 612.

56. Steve Ellis, *The English Eliot: Design, Language and Landscape in Four Quartets* (London: Routledge, 1991), 165. Like Donald Davie before him, Ellis argues against the Anglocentric reading of *Four Quartets*, pointing out that it is the poem's readers who have made it into an expression of national attachment (182). Like F. R. Leavis before *him*, David Gervais thinks that Eliot dissolves concrete Englishness into abstract ideals and that, as a result, the England of *Four Quartets* is merely "a state of mind" (*Literary Englands: Versions of "Englishness" in Modern Writing* [Cambridge: Cambridge UP, 1993], 137–43).

57. For more on the importance of allegory to Eliot's antiromanticism and to his theory of personality, see John Paul Riquelme, *Harmony of Dissonances: T. S. Eliot, Romanticism, and Imagination* (Baltimore: Johns Hopkins UP, 1991), 112–19. Riquelme's persuasive identification of *Four Quartets* as allegorical provides a useful formal basis for any historical approach to the poem (318–19). Riquelme emphasizes that Eliot's ideal society is merely a provisional point of reference; beyond it lies Eliot's true subject, which is always something deferred and negative. He thus reads *Four Quartets* as an allegory of "negativity" based on "the interminable movement of reading and writing" (114)—a more or less deconstructive view of the self-undoing of the poem's language that differs in emphasis from my interest in the poem's thematization of the cultural predicates for allegory. The first generation of readers often understood *Four Quartets* as a belated expression of doubts about lyric personae and lyric expression itself. More recent critics (including Riquelme) have tended to emphasize not so much the poet's agency as the poem's ability to activate the words themselves—again paradoxically—so as to reveal the erosion and leaching-away of meaning from language. My reading emphasizes the vexed agency neither of the poet nor of language but of culture itself, so that the author—and the authority—of the poem is a kind of national tradition. I propose this schema to clarify shifting and relative emphases, not absolute differences of interpretation.

58. Of course, like *The Waste Land*, *Four Quartets* includes elements from non-English sources. What matters is not so much the presence or absence of multicultural elements as their arrangement and the authority implied by their status as either autonomous (*The Waste Land*) or subordinate (*Four Quartets*) units of meaning.

59. The term chronotope comes from M. M. Bakhtin, who defines it as the "intrinsic connectedness of temporal and spatial relationships that are artistically expressed in literature" (*The Dialogic Imagination*, trans. Caryl Emerson and Michael Holquist [Austin: U of Texas P, 1981], 84). I use it simply and generally to refer to that interconnectedness in *Four Quartets* and not to signal a Bakhtinian method.

60. T. S. Eliot, *Four Quartets,* in *Collected Poems 1909–1962* (London: Faber, 1963), lines 1–5; hereafter cited in the text, using separate line counts for each of the four poems.

61. On the connection to Kipling's "They," see Lyndall Gordon, *Eliot's New Life* (New York: Farrar Straus Giroux, 1988), 46.

62. In the 1941 essay, Eliot seems to identify strongly with Kipling's late discovery of England as a charmed, alien landscape and with his returned-colonial impulse to root himself in the English soil, to "subdue himself to his surroundings" in Sussex. Eliot urges English readers to rediscover via Kipling all that is worthwhile and enchanted in their native land, describing in appreciative terms Kipling's evolution from an "imperial" to a "historical" imagination (*On Poetry and Poets,* 247). Eliot's views on Kipling reflect his own valuation of nation over empire: "In his later phase England and a particular corner of England become the centre of his vision. He is more concerned with . . . the core of empire; this core is something older, more natural and more permanent. But at the same time his vision takes a larger view, and he sees the Roman Empire and the place of England in it. The vision is almost that of an idea of empire laid up in heaven" (*On Poetry and Poets,* 245). Eliot emphasizes the fact that Kipling's move from imperialism into English localism is precisely what allows his vision to expand historically, and even beyond history into heaven. In a sense, Eliot's poetry evokes what the late Kipling (in his Sussex period) literalizes and narrativizes—just as it evokes what Charles Williams and J.R.R. Tolkien made into genre fiction.

63. In a certain sense, one might even say that, in *Four Quartets,* Eliot confronts an authentic historical (nonmythic) temporality for the first time. Michael Levenson suggests just this in arguing that the poem represents for Eliot "the beginning of history." In Levenson's view, Eliot's own aging plays an important part in forcing the encounter with real historical time in *Four Quartets* ("The End of Tradition and the Beginning of History," in *Words in Time: New Essays on Eliot's* Four Quartets, ed. Edward Lobb [Ann Arbor: U of Michigan P, 1993]).

64. Michael Levenson traces the shift in Eliot from *The Waste Land* to *Four Quartets* according to the progress from an aesthetics of plenitude or inclusion ("all") to an aesthetics of austerity or exclusion ("only") ("The End of Tradition," 167). This formal analysis makes particular sense when understood in the context of imperial contraction: the classical spareness of the later writing depends on the homogenous culture that Eliot envisions in the wake of empire and upon which he predicates *Four Quartets.*

65. Michael North's analysis of the process seems right to me: "The historicist principle of cultural specificity and unity has become an ahistorical, normative value" (*Political Aesthetic,* 88).

66. Grover Smith, *T. S. Eliot's Poetry and Plays: A Study in Sources and Meaning,* 2d ed. (Chicago: U of Chicago P, 1974), 268.

67. The emphasis on conjugal harmony here underscores the fact that Eliot's conservative vision of culture depends on the purging of unlicensed sexualities. It is framed and figured in terms of an orthodox and naturalized notion of heterosexual marriage, with order predicated on patriarchal authority. This comes as no surprise in a poet whose early work so regularly and so mercilessly presents its symptomatology of urban decay in terms of unregulated feminine desire and bad

sex, and whose master tropes for cultural dissolution are promiscuity and sterility (particularly as associated with women and with homosexuality—one has only to think of Lil's abortion or the sordid presentation of Mr. Eugenides in *The Waste Land*). It is worth noting that for Woolf, by contrast, the values associated with a resurgent insular and pastoral Englishness are antipatriarchal, based on her Outsider's allegory of imperialism as British patriarchy writ large across the globe. Even if, near the end, Woolf began to consider the possibility that the end of empire might recast English culture into its peaceable pastoral image, the harrowing oscillations of *Between the Acts*, with its queer dramaturge Miss LaTrobe, bear witness to Woolf's desperate reluctance to sacrifice gender and sexual dissidence for the comforts of national or communal belonging.

68. Eliot's later criticism on the devolution of English poetry tend to bring to the fore broad historical factors that remained largely tacit in his earlier, more purely literary accounts. His revisionary essay "Milton II," for instance, confesses to an earlier error in having traced the faultlines in modern poetry to Milton and Dryden themselves, rather than recognizing that the dissociation of sensibility was "a consequence of the same causes which brought about the Civil War"—those historical causes being too deep and tangled to identify or name (*SP* 266).

69. There is a well-established critical tradition, that reads *Four Quartets* as purgatorial, running from Northrop Frye (*T. S. Eliot* [Chicago: U of Chicago P, 1981]) to Sebastian Knowles (*A Purgatorial Flame* [Introduction, n. 30]). While my reading is essentially compatible with both, it emphasizes not so much the time of purgatory as the cultural/geographic assumptions that inform Eliot's coordination of purgatory *and* history.

70. Smith, *T. S. Eliot's Poetry and Plays*, 273.

71. Eliot, in other words, makes a virtue out of historical necessity by adumbrating the redemptive possibilities inherent in England's straitened circumstances of depression, war, and imperial decline. Edward Lobb reads "East Coker" as a series of meditations on the theme of transcending limitations by acknowledging them—a theme whose key emblem is the closed room or closed space ("Limitation and Transcendence in 'East Coker,' " in *Words in Time: New Essays on Eliot's "Four Quartets,"* ed. Lobb [Ann Arbor: U of Michigan P, 1993], 20–37). Lobb surveys several types of limitation, figured as enclosure, in the poem but does not mention the possibility that the informing context of an isolated or enclosed England stands as yet another form of limitation. Yet Lobb's argument can easily be extended in this way, for it is from within the acknowledged boundaries of a narrowly English culture that Eliot begins fully to articulate the possibility of communal redemption.

72. This recoding of "discovery" for domestic purposes directly echoes *The Rock* as discussed in chapter 2. The thematic shift from discovery to rebuilding in late modernism is summarized beautifully in a passage from Auden's *The Enchafed Flood*: "We live in a new age . . . in which the heroic image is not the nomad wandering through the desert . . . but the less exciting figure of the builder, who renews the ruined walls of the city" (qtd. in Lucy McDiarmid, *Saving Civilization*, 7). As McDiarmid notes, Eliot's project seems to shift subtly over the interwar years from saving "civilization" to saving "society" (124); it is precisely in such terms that we can see his reorientation from the imperial/cosmopolitan sphere to the narrower national sphere.

73. The snapshot imagist poem, such as Pound's famous and immediately relevant "In a station of the Metro," values the epiphanic moment in and for itself. But for Eliot in *Four Quartets*, the aesthetically perfected moment no longer suffices as the basis for a poetic practice: hence the poem's repeating and developing imagery. Simile gives way to simile, tropes are turned and returned, and moments are meaningful only as occasions to confront or encapsulate eternal time.

74. In this connection, Steve Ellis cites Eliot's approval of what he saw as "the gradual purging out of poetic ornament" in Yeats's late drama (*The English Eliot*, 9). As Helen Gardner notes, the figure of Yeats hovers like a watchful master over the entire poem, not just in the famous "compound ghost" section of "Little Gidding" (*The Composition of* Four Quartets [New York: Oxford UP, 1978], 65).

75. Smith, *T. S. Eliot's Poetry and Plays*, 255.

76. The notion of a "symbol perfected in death" clarifies the abstract and antiutopian nature of Eliot's cultural revivalism. Unlike many Celtic Revival intellectuals, for instance, Eliot did not aim to recover a specific trove of buried national texts, languages, legends. His revival defined, not an archive, but a spiritual stance toward that archive. This tricky fact makes reading Eliot as an Anglocentric antiquarian as implausible as denying his Anglocentrism altogether.

77. To put that another way, whereas symbols tend to arrogate aesthetic totality to themselves in a kind of perfection of form per se, allegory tends to seek completion extratextually, by reference backward to a cultural endowment that presupposes a shared tradition. As Walter Benjamin puts it: "it is as something incomplete and imperfect that objects stare out from the allegorical structure" (*The Origin of German Tragic Drama*, trans. John Osborne [London: NLB, 1977], 186). Given that Eliot's allegory is, in my reading, a more historically or diachronically organized mode than the ironic mythologies of *The Waste Land*, one could also invoke de Man's notion that allegory is the genre that best assimilates humanity's "authentically temporal destiny." To read the poem via de Man's revived notion of allegory is to emphasize its capacity to posit both identity with and difference from its own origins, so that it "establishes its language in the void of . . . temporal difference," all the while mining its language for historical and indeed eternal forms of temporal equivalence (Paul De Man, *Blindness and Insight: Essays in the Rhetoric of Contemporary Criticism* [Minneapolis: U of Minnesota P, 1983], 206–7). Even now, the prevailing critical tradition in Eliot studies would be to assimilate *Four Quartets* and indeed Eliot's oeuvre in general to the symbolist tradition. For a classic instance of that reading, see Murray Krieger, " 'A Waking Dream': The Symbolic Alternative to Allegory," in *Allegory, Myth and Symbol*, ed. Morton W. Bloomfield (Cambridge: Harvard UP, 1981), 9–10.

78. As Terry Eagleton rightly notes, the Eliot of the *Four Quartets* period no longer emphasizes poetry's ability to impose order on reality but, rather, focuses on what Eliot himself called "perception of an order *in* reality" (*Exiles and Émigrés* [New York: Schocken, 1970], 169).

79. Barthes uses the term to describe a mode of writing conditioned by the fact that the writer wishes to, but cannot, alter the "objective data which govern the consumption of literature" (Roland Barthes, *Writing Degree Zero*, trans. Annette Lavers and Colin Smith [New York: Hill and Wang, 1968], 15). As a result, the writer turns that wish back into the formal manipulation of language itself. The mode of writing in *Four Quartets*, in my view, brings Eliot toward, but not to, an

explicit and functional classicism, which is free, according to Barthes, to "suppose a collective consumption, akin to speech" (49).

80. In the Yeats essay mentioned above, Eliot himself distinguishes between two kinds of impersonality achieved by Yeats: an earlier kind based on stylistic effects and a later, more powerful kind based on his ability to make a "general symbol" out of particular experience. More to the point, Eliot associates Yeats's ability to attain the second kind with his abandonment of a kind of Anglicized and exoticizing relation to Ireland and his ability to become "more Irish" (*SP* 251–52). In other words, Eliot heroicizes Yeats's ability to abandon a cultured and cosmopolitan poetic practice in favor of the mature art that depends on implanting himself more fully in a coherent national culture. The path to impersonality is routed through the relationship to a culture or a people—a distinct sociocultural formation, as opposed, for example, to the old modernist universality based on the short circuit from psyche (one subject) to myth (all subjects).

81. This reading of the music of *Four Quartets* cuts against the grain of a more traditional view, in which the musical elements are among the most inward and obscure—a sign of symbolist self-referentiality rather than allegorical extroversion. For an example of that kind of reading, see Donald Davie, "Pound and Eliot: A Distinction," in *Eliot in Perspective: A Symposium*, ed. Graham Martin (London: Macmillan, 1970), 62–82.

82. Michael Gorra's *After Empire* concludes with a brief but suggestive reading of "Little Gidding" as a national poem and links Eliot's characteristic fragments of Englishness to Orwell's, concluding that Englishness was becoming the name for a culture that was "not merely insular but entirely self-referential." Gorra rightly points out that Eliot still manages to universalize from his English base especially by contrast, for example, with the more provincial "little Englandism" of Larkin (*After Empire*, 157–59). But Gorra's study does not address the fact that Eliot participated in a distinctly (though not exclusively) English shift in the provenance of universalism itself.

83. One of the important stories that Eliot's work on culture participates in is the nationalization of culture. *After Strange Gods* has seemed so objectionable because Eliot tends to insist there on the racial bases of social or cultural solidarity—a conceptual maneuver more sweeping in its effects than the text's repellent anti-Semitism. For more on Eliot's place in the development of (covertly) racialized concepts of culture, see Walter Benn Michaels, *Our America: Nativism, Modernism, and Pluralism* (Durham: Duke UP, 1995). Michaels, concentrating on the Eliot of the twenties, sees him keeping "nation" and "tradition" quite separate (102), but of course the later Eliot's thought creates an implicit but necessary identity between nation, tradition, and, ultimately, race.

CHAPTER FOUR

1. *Selected Essays of Hugh MacDiarmid* (Berkeley: U of California P, 1970), 67.

2. Or as Ioan Davies puts it: "If the 'English' had constructed an empire and a series of institutions with which to manage it, they had lost any sense of their own culture, except as archive" (*Cultural Studies and Beyond: Fragments of Empire* [London: Routledge, 1995], 177).

3. What emerges here is a powerful convergence between "metropolitan autoethnography" and "reverse ethnography," two terms that James Buzard has defined with superb precision in "Ethnography as Interruption" (Introduction, n. 20), 449.

4. The quoted phrase is from Hugo Radice, "The National Economy: A Keynesian Myth?" *Capital and Class* 22 (1984): 126.

5. Robert Skidelsky, *John Maynard Keynes: The Economist as Savior 1920–1937* (New York: Penguin, 1992), 317; hereafter cited in the text as *JMK*. By the time he published the *Tract* and the *Treatise*, Keynes had already begun to establish his reputation as an innovative writer and master stylist. Skidelsky notes that *The Economic Consequences of the Peace* (1919) elicited praise on purely literary grounds from a number of contemporary reviewers, including that connoisseur of style Lytton Strachey (*John Maynard Keynes: Hopes Betrayed 1883–1920* [New York: Penguin, 1983], 392).

6. See Simmel, "The Metropolis and Mental Life" (chap. 1, n. 45), 411.

7. Jennifer Wicke, "*Mrs. Dalloway* Goes to Market: Woolf, Keynes, and Modern Markets," *Novel* 28 (1994): 11.

8. If we view Keynes only as an innovative connoisseur of fluidity and play in the marketplace, we do not account for his later efforts to restore rational, solid order to the economy. Wicke's analysis, for example, beautifully captures a metropolitan moment of the 1920s in the work of Woolf and Keynes but does not extend to the next phase of modernist culture, in which Keynes's theoretical breakthroughs reflected a new state of affairs. The high metropolitan phase of British modernism corresponds to Keynes's most vigorous writing against the gold standard, providing a suggestive cross-Atlantic postscript to Walter Benn Michaels's thesis on the relation of the gold standard to literary naturalism (*The Gold Standard and the Logic of Naturalism* [Berkeley: U of California P, 1987]). Michaels's basic premise, that a given literary text does not so much approve or disapprove of economic systems as operate within their cultural logic, jibes with readings like Wicke's, in which modernist narrative assimilates the volatile market conditions between 1910 and 1930. According to Michaels, American naturalist writers of the late nineteenth century framed the problem of representation itself in terms set partly by the gold-standard debate, wherein one side favored more fixed, solid, or "real" representations. Keynes's main reformist point was that, in 1920s Britain, gold money no longer stood for objective, fixed relations between an object and its symbolic counterpart. In fact, he argued that the gold standard undergirded irrational economic conditions precisely insofar as it encouraged a perverse, outdated attachment to the idea of "real" money incarnated in metal. But, as I have suggested, both Keynesian and modernist representational style operated *within* the speculative, free-market logic of the gold-standard era. Within that logic, Keynesian and modernist writing tried to give a textual (but not social) organization to the dazzling stimuli and naturalist facts of the metropolis. In other words, from the point of view of form, it is more important that Keynes's 1920s writing was conditioned by the logic of gold than that it took an overtly antigold position. The high modernism of Keynes (and Woolf) is thus still *of* the gold-standard era, but (unlike naturalism) it coincides with its *final phase*. Along these lines, Patrick Brantlinger has recently suggested that Keynes's theorization of the

end of gold money coincides with cultural modernism and its general "crisis of representation" (*Fictions of State: Culture and Credit in Britain 1694–1994* [Ithaca: Cornell UP, 1996], 207). It is important to recognize, however, that modernism's "crisis of representation" unfolds, for the most part, back in the laissez-faire, gold-standard days. In fact, Keynes's most comprehensive theorization of postgold economics coincides not with high modernism itself but with its *end* in the late 1930s.

9. Piero V. Mini, *Keynes, Bloomsbury and* The General Theory (Hampshire, U.K.: Macmillan, 1991), 82–83.

10. Like his fellow member of old Bloomsbury Leonard Woolf, Keynes spent his formative political years struggling with the problems of imperial rule. During his tenure as a junior administrator at the India Office and afterward, Keynes recognized the gathering imperial twilight. By the 1930s, he was convinced that India (and other colonies) were evolving rapidly toward modernized and independent status—a process he thought it futile to resist. As Anand Chandavarkar reports, Keynes was "fully conversant with the sentiments of Indian political nationalism, particularly from his diligent readings of the Indian press" (*Keynes and India* [London: Macmillan, 1989], 136). In the years surrounding the composition of the *General Theory*, Keynes came to understand that a reorganization of British life must follow from the inevitable end of empire.

11. In making these arguments in favor of domestic consumption over foreign investment, Keynes echoes (and in a sense vindicates) the anti-imperialism of J. A. Hobson, who had suggested decades earlier that underconsumption was the "taproot of Imperialism" (*Imperialism*, [chap. 1, n. 6], 81).

12. Timothy Mitchell, "Fixing the Economy," *Cultural Studies* 12 (1998): 89.

13. Richard Adelstein, " 'The Nation as an Economic Unit': Keynes, Roosevelt, and the Managerial Ideal," *Journal of American History* 78.1 (1991): 171.

14. Mitchell, "Fixing the Economy," 90.

15. In an unpublished paper, Timothy Mitchell has suggestively located Malinowski's totalizing description of the Trobriand Islanders as having "an economy" within the larger epistemic shift crystallized by Keynesian economics. See "Origins and Limits of the Modern Idea of the Economy" (paper presented to the Seminar on Social Movements, University of Michigan, November 1995); 10. As a lifelong denizen of Cambridge, Keynes would certainly have known of contemporary developments in anthropology. Cambridge also made available another disciplinary resource for thinking about "primitive" economies as complex wholes: classics. During the 1920s, Keynes spent a great deal of time studying ancient currencies, especially Roman, Greek, and Babylonian. For the surviving fragments on those topics, including an unpublished piece entitled "The Origins of Money," see *CWK* 28: 223–94.

16. Perry Anderson, *English Questions* (London: Verso, 1992), 93.

17. In "Components of the National Culture" (1968), Anderson based his argument on the premature or stunted quality of bourgeois revolution in Britain. Reviewing that argument in 1990, Anderson himself acknowledges that it did not adequately account for the effects of imperialism on the "absent centre" of British intellectual life. Nor did it, by extension, account for the effects of imperial decline on an initial, midcentury phase of "retotalization" in the center. As a result, the

original argument tended not to recognize certain kinds of thinking about social totality that did, after all, emerge in postwar (Keynesian) Britain (*English Questions*, 195–208).

18. Anderson, *English Questions*, 78.

19. The piece was solicited by J. R. Ackerly for a larger project on art and the state across Europe, including the fascist states of Italy and Germany. In his letter of invitation to Keynes, Ackerly defines art as "painting, sculpture, architecture, and such new forms of art as, for instance, the pageantry of ceremony and festivity" (Ackerly to Keynes, 27 May 1936 [*CWK 28:* 335]).

20. It is perhaps not coincidental that Keynesian economics (with its neomercantilist leanings) harks back to cultural and economic ideals of preindustrial, preimperial England and specifically to the great mercantilist period, the Elizabethan age. Keynes, like Woolf and Eliot, associates the Elizabethan period with both the economic and cultural health of a distinctively English civilization. The fallen modernity of Eliot and Woolf, in which high aesthetics became an individualist, segregated sphere of activity, has its counterpart in the fallen modernity of Keynes, in which economics became an individualistic and specialized set of laissez-faire practices and rules.

21. Raymond Williams argues that the Bloomsbury Group, including Keynes, always returned to "the supreme value of the civilised individual," without "any alternative idea of a whole society" ("The Significance of 'Bloomsbury,' " in *Keynes and the Bloomsbury Group*, ed. Derek Crabtree and A. P. Thirlwall [London: Macmillan, 1980], 62). While it is true that neither Woolf nor Keynes ever fully broke with the privileged concept of the free individual, it is nonetheless worth tracking their relatively new and inventive attempts in the 1930s to address group identity and "macroanalysis" within a fundamentally liberal political culture.

22. As Skidelsky puts it, the early Keynes "was chiefly interested in asserting the claims of individual judgement against a social system of rules and conventions of 'correct behaviour.' " But the Keynes of the 1930s directed his attention "to the performance of economic systems. . . . In other words, he did come to believe that social structures were more organic than atomistic" (*JMK 87*). For a fuller and more technical economic discussion of Keynes's shift from atomistic to organic thinking, see R. J. Rotheim, "Organicism and the Role of the Individual in Keynes's Thought," in *John Maynard Keynes: Critical Assessments*, 2d ser., ed. John Cunningham Wood (London: Routledge, 1994), 7: 486–95.

23. Mitchell, "Fixing the Economy," 90.

24. Michael Szalay, "Wallace Stevens and the Invention of Social Security," *Modernism/ Modernity* 5.1 (1998): 49–74.

25. During the 1930s, Keynes was settling into the role of gentleman farmer at Tilton, in Sussex. Quentin Bell recalls that Keynes's urban nonconformism was leaching away into the soil at Tilton as "Maynard" developed a loving interest in "ancient traditions and ceremonies still observed," in "the customs, the conventions, and the glorious history of England" ("Reflections on Maynard Keynes," in *Keynes and the Bloomsbury Group*, ed. Derek Crabtree and A. P. Thirlwall [London: Macmillan, 1980], 79–81). Skidelsky, too, describes Keynes's turn to piggery experiments at Tilton as part of a general shift in sensibilities away from political radicalism and toward a rural English humanism. Moreover, Skidelsky

observes, the economic theories gave a "sophisticated rationale" to these new investments in native culture and agriculture (*JMK* 526–27).

26. Keynes's ideas about national self-sufficiency reappear in the *General Theory* in the section entitled "Notes on Mercantilism." There Keynes explicitly spurns the "unrealistic abstractions" of Ricardo (and Smith) in favor of Malthus and the mercantilists, who were more "concerned with the economic system as whole" (*CWK* 7: 335–40). Despite these neomercantilist affinities, Keynes remained wary about protectionism in the 1930s. I should also note that for Keynes the idea of a British national economy implied not insular but Commonwealth dimensions. Still, the thrust of Keynesian logic was toward a domestic definition of economic community, one that would be only loosely linked to the old colonial periphery.

27. Wicke, "*Mrs. Dalloway* Goes to Market," 11.

28. The crucial role of Keynes, then, is that his via media between economic individualism and state planning entailed an analogous compromise between national culture and state power. Indeed, Keynes, like his modernist contemporaries Eliot and Woolf, offers a crucial midcentury test case for the ability of a metropolitan intellectual to submit the rational freedom of cosmopolitanism to the relative restrictiveness of national tradition and, conversely, to carry the affective power of what Bruce Robbins calls "romantic localism" into the compromise formation of welfare-state cultural corporatism ("Actually Existing Cosmopolitanism," in *Cosmopolitics: Thinking and Feeling beyond the Nation*, ed. Pheng Cheah and Bruce Robbins [Minneapolis: U of Minnesota P, 1998], 3). Both Robbins and Pheng Cheah, in their introductory essays for *Cosmopolitics*, point out that the real challenge for cosmopolitanism is not to overcome its sporadically oppositional stance toward nationalism but to frame a productive, realistic, and dialectical relationship to the state—which is precisely, I think, where the case of Keynes is most instructive (Robbins, "Actually Existing Cosmopolitanism," 9; Cheah, "The Cosmopolitical—Today," in *Cosmopolitics*, 22).

29. Hugo Radice points out, for example, that the pursuit of Keynesian economic nationalism in Britain was "linked up . . . with national liberation struggles in the Third World" ("The National Economy," 112). The period of Keynesian thought's ascendancy, from the late 1930s to the late 1960s, covers not only the peak of fascist and communist power in Europe but also the rise of postwar welfare states and of new postcolonial nation-states. Taken together, these broad developments point to a relative interruption in the reign of international laissez-faire capitalism, framing the middle third of the century as a "Keynesian era," when national politics sought (and gained) some foothold against international capitalism. The same developments might also form the basis for a new description of the *cultural* interregnum between modernism and postmodernism.

30. Among the reflections or memoirs I have consulted and cited, see especially Raymond Williams, *Politics and Letters: Interviews with New Left Review* (London: New Left Books, 1979) and *Stuart Hall: Critical Dialogues in Cultural Studies*, ed. David Morley and Kuan-Hsing Chen (London: Routledge, 1996). There are now many critical accounts of Cultural Studies and the New Left in England; this chapter draws especially on the following: Davies, *Cultural Studies and Beyond*; Dennis Dworkin, *Cultural Marxism in Postwar Britain* (Durham: Duke

UP, 1997); Antony Easthope, *Literary into Cultural Studies* (London: Routledge, 1991); Francis Mulhern, *Culture/Metaculture* (London: Routledge, 2000); and Graeme Turner, *British Cultural Studies: An Introduction*, 2d ed. (London: Routledge, 1996). Of these, Davies's *Cultural Studies and Beyond* comes closest in emphasis to the argument in this section in that it considers the effect of imperial history and of uprooted colonial intellectuals on the original formation of Cultural Studies in England. But Davies also tends to consider the residual centrality, rather than the relative decline, of English power and, moreover, to emphasize the reception and reworking of Cultural Studies in Canada, Australia, and the United States. For more on the problem of the diffusion of Cultural Studies "from the Birmingham Centre outward," particularly to the ex-dominions, see Jon Stratton and Ien Ang, "On the Impossibility of a Global Cultural Studies," in *Stuart Hall: Critical Dialogues in Cultural Studies*, ed. Morley and Chen, 371.

31. Nairn, *The Break-up of Britain*, (Introduction, n. 15), 304.

32. Mulhern, *The Moment of "Scrutiny"* (London: New Left Books, 1979), 312.

33. Ibid., 76.

34. James English, in his study of English comedy, has offered a particularly useful critical trajectory from late modernism into postwar culturalism, noting the continuity between the modernist notion of a "disintegrative society held together by culture" and the idea, associated with Raymond Williams, of a "whole way of life" (*Comic Transactions* [chap. 2, n. 96], 114).

35. Williams certainly understood himself as opposing both conservative and liberal traditions of English cultural criticism: "I knew perfectly well who I was writing against: Eliot, Leavis and the whole of the cultural conservatism that had formed around them" (*Politics and Letters*, 112). It would be plausible, of course, to pose Williams against Leavis and Eliot in this way in order to pursue one kind of detailed political analysis, but I have instead emphasized the shared discourse of culturalism from right to left in order to make a different and perhaps broader kind of historical point.

36. Raymond Williams, *Culture and Society 1780–1950* (New York: Columbia UP, 1983), 193; hereafter cited in the text as *CS*.

37. Raymond Williams, *The Long Revolution* (Westport, Conn.: Greenwood Press, 1975), 101; hereafter cited in the text as *LR*.

38. Part of Williams's success as a literary scholar—in particular a student of drama—came from his anthropological insistence on aesthetics as the articulation and enactment of social values; his investment in public rituals rather than privatized texts marks out another crucial affinity with the later Eliot. As John Higgins points out, Eliot's ideas on modern drama—particularly his call for a "common system of belief"—were absorbed and revised by Williams into a somewhat more democratic and secular concept of "common language" (*Raymond Williams: Literature, Marxism and Cultural Materialism* [London: Routledge, 1999], 29). Higgins also stresses the crucial part played by dramatic form in the development of Williams's concept of the "structure of feeling." As Williams put it in 1954, the structure of feeling was a verbal pattern "adequate to communicate . . . the whole and unified life of man" (Higgins, *Raymond Williams*, 32). Just as Eliot saw in verse drama the possibility of attaining a newly collective and integrated aesthetic,

Williams saw in certain modern dramatic forms the possibility of a more public and unified set of artistic practices.

39. The point of tracing the anthropological turn across decades and political divides, from modernism to Cultural Studies, is not to discover (again) Williams's nativism (still less to argue for an implausibly populist T. S. Eliot). Christopher Prendergast rightly acknowledges that much of Williams's cultural analysis depended on a Gramscian notion that "progressive resources" can be found "within the national tradition," but defends Williams against the charge that he is "beset by a 'nativist' view of the national" and against "the generalized (and underinformed) image of Williams as caught up in regressive nostalgias for earlier social forms." Prendergast notes, for example, that Williams was highly suspicious of false national totalities in his work of the 1970s and 1980s. Moreover, Williams—unlike, say, Eliot—always accepted labor specialization and advanced technology as unavoidable features of the modern era ("Introduction: Groundings and Emergings," in *Cultural Materialism: On Raymond Williams*, ed. Prendergast [Minneapolis: U. of Minnesota P, 1995], 22–26).

40. Gilroy, *There Ain't No Black* (chap. 1, n. 103), 49.

41. As Francis Mulhern puts it, the "unself-conscious citation of 'England' meaning (or not meaning?) Britain or the United Kingdom" in Williams's early work "was a sign that in this as in matters of gender, the analysis of culture as one of classes remained abstract" (*The Present Lasts a Long Time: Essays in Cultural Politics* [Notre Dame: U of Notre Dame P, 1998], 131). Similarly, Iain Chambers observes that, despite their successful challenge to the high-cultural domain of Englishness, the radical historians of the fifties preserved the "moral economy" and "ethnic and gendered assumptions" associated with nativism (*Border Dialogues: Journeys in Postmodernity* [London: Routledge, 1990], 40).

42. *Politics and Letters*, 112.

43. Richard Hoggart, *The Uses of Literacy* (London: Penguin, 1992), 328; hereafter cited in the text as UL.

44. Stanley Aronowitz, "Between Criticsm and Ethnography: Raymond Williams and the Intervention of Cultural Studies," in *Cultural Materialism: On Raymond Williams*, ed. Prendergast, 325.

45. Qtd. in Dennis Dworkin, *Cultural Marxism in Postwar Britain* (Durham: Duke UP, 1997), 102.

46. Anderson, *English Questions*, 36.

47. Ibid., 54.

48. As Ioan Davies point out: "What is remarkable about the debates around Marxism and cultural studies in Britain was how much of the world's concerns were seen to have relevance for understanding the culture of the English" (*Cultural Studies and Beyond*, 3).

49. The framing of England as both "extraordinary pioneer" and "prototypical exemplar" in all the major narratives of modernity (democratization, industrialization, urbanization, empire building, secularization, decolonization, postindustrialism) corresponds, David Cannadine has observed, to the "Golden Age" of British historiography, from roughly the 1940s to the 1970s ("British History: Past, Present—and Future?" *Past & Present* 116 [1987]: 174–75). This was, of course, also the period of emergence for English Cultural Studies.

50. Raymond Williams, *The Country and the City* (New York: Oxford UP, 1973), 2.

51. E. P. Thompson, *The Making of the English Working Class* (New York: Vintage, 1966), 13.

52. Thus Thompson's major work is susceptible to critique—by Dipesh Chakrabarty, for instance—for offering both a particularized (English) *and* a universal (Marxist) narrative of working-class formation (Robert Gregg and Madhavi Kale, "The Empire and Mr. Thompson: The Making of Indian Princes and the English Working Class," *Economic and Political Weekly* 32.36 [1997]: 2283).

53. *Politics and Letters*, 72

54. "William Morris and the Moral Issues To-day," *Arena* 2.8 (1951): 29.

55. Gregg and Kale, "The Empire and Mr. Thompson," 2273–75

56. Gauri Viswanathan, "Raymond Williams and British Colonialism," in *Cultural Materialism: On Raymond Williams*, ed. Prendergast, 191.

57. Benita Parry, too, has pointed to the general absence of imperialism and colonized subjects in the "eurovision of the metropolitan left," citing Williams's early work as a crucial example ("Problems in Current Theories of Colonial Discourse," *Oxford Literary Review* 9 (1987): 51). For other views on the problem of empire/race in Williams's foundational work, see H. S. Mohapatra, "Residual or Emergent: Critiquing Raymond Williams's *The Country and the City*," *Journal of Contemporary Thought*, 1992, 23–35; Simon Gikandi, *Maps of Englishness* (New York: Columbia UP, 1996), xi; and Said, *Culture and Imperialism*, 82–84. And for an incisive commentary on the buried universalism within the apparent frank particularism of British Cultural Studies, see Stratton and Ang, "On the impossibility of a Global Cultural Studies," 379.

58. Paul Gilroy, *The Black Atlantic: Modernity and Double Consciousness* (Cambridge: Harvard UP, 1993), 3–18.

59. Gilroy makes the point that it is as inaccurate to think about class without including diasporic and transnational history as it would be to think about class without *national* history. He is no doubt right on this point, as he is about the legacy of Cultural Studies nativism lapsing, over time, into a "morbid celebration of England and Englishness" (*Black Atlantic*, 10). However, a corresponding danger has, I think, come alive in North American academic discourse dedicated to the trans- or postnational, which is a premature theoretical foreclosure on the historical importance of the nation. Although it has been important to develop working models of diasporic, syncretic, hybridized, and global cultural forms and formations, those models cannot simply displace analysis of the nation, of its territorial and ethnic variants, of its tacit claims to the epistemological privileges of totality, and of its explicit claims to the romance of deep belonging. On this broader point, see Timothy Brennan, *At Home in the World: Cosmopolitanism Now* (Cambridge: Harvard UP, 1997).

60. *Black Atlantic*, 2.

61. Stuart Hall, "New Ethnicities," in *Stuart Hall: Critical Dialogues*, ed. Morley and Chen, 447.

62. As Jon Stratton and Ien Ang put it: "If universalism is an unconscious parochialism, nationalism, at least in its radical, self-defensive mode, is a form of self-conscious parochialism" ("On the Impossibility of a Global Cultural studies," 380).

63. Stuart Hall, qtd. in Graeme Turner, *British Cultural Studies*, 51.

64. In "Culture is Ordinary," Williams presents himself as a Welsh European positioned at an angle to the dominant traditions of England and therefore, in a sense, positioned to both master and criticize them. As for Hall, he describes his relationship to England as that of the "familiar stranger" ("The Formation of a Diasporic Intellectual," in *Stuart Hall: Critical Dialogues*, ed. Morley and Chen, 490–92).

65. *Black Atlantic*, 10. See also Graeme Turner, who notes (but does not really examine) the coincidence of early black British writing and early Cultural Studies (*British Cultural Studies*, 227).

66. Davies, *Cultural Studies and Beyond*, 178.

67. The logic of cultural nationalism, unleashed for the purposes of redefining Englishness as an exclusive identity comes, in the end, to drive the devolution of other U.K. nations.

68. Kobena Mercer, *Welcome to the Jungle: New Positions in Black Cultural Studies* (New York: Routledge, 1994), 307.

69. Gilroy, *There Ain't No Black*, 59. Bill Schwarz, too, offers a critical reread-ing of "palpably conservative or racist manifestations of ethnic belonging in the 1950s and 1960s," arguing that the "frontiers of the empire, in their various forms, created the syntax for a particular style of domestic Englishness" and that "this was as true for the period of decolonisation as for earlier more manifestly imperial moments" ("Reveries of Race: The Closing of the Imperial Moment," in *Moments of Modernity: Reconstructing Britain 1945–1964*, ed. Becky Conekin, Frank Mort, and Chris Waters [London: Rivers Oram Press, 1999], 191).

70. The black presence in Britain was not new in the 1950s; there is now a rich body of scholarship dedicated to the longer history of black Britain and, more recently, to the problems raised by the persistence of an unwieldy term like "black British" to describe contemporary cultural production in the United Kingdom. For a compact survey of both issues, see Sarah Lawson Welsh, "(Un)belonging Citizens, Unmapped Territory: Black Immigration and British Identity in the Post-1945 Period," in *Not on Any Map: Essays on Postcoloniality and Cultural Na-tionalism*, ed. Stuart Murray (Devon: U. of Exeter P, 1997). In this chapter I use the term black British writing to describe an important historical phase in the emergence of a minority cultural formation. The term "black British" has now become outmoded, in large part because it fails to distinguish among several gen-erations of immigrants and citizens and among people from diverse locations in Africa, Asia, and the Caribbean.

71. Kathleen Paul, " 'British Subjects' and 'British Stock': Labour's Postwar Imperialism," *Journal of British Studies* 34 (April 1995): 276.

72. West Indian writers have captured the most attention (just as West Indian immigrants aboard the *Empire Windrush* in 1948 have tended to take center stage in most origin stories about multiethnic Britain), but there were mobile intellectu-als arriving from all over the old empire. Beyond Lamming and Selvon, the new wave of British Caribbean novelists in the 1950s included Jan Carew, Neville Dawes, Roger Mais, Edgar Mittelholzer, V. S. Naipaul, Vic Reid, and Andrew Salkey (not to mention C.L.R. James).

73. Sam Selvon, *Lonely Londoners* (Essex: Longman, 1956), 74; hereafter cited in the text as *LL*.

74. Clifford, *The Predicament of Culture* (chap. 1, n. 96), 92–97.

75. Kenneth Ramchand, introduction to *The Lonely Londoners*, 13.

76. Stuart Hall, "Lamming, Selvon and Some Trends in the West Indian Novel," *Bim* 6 (1955): 175.

77. George Lamming, *The Pleasures of Exile* (Ann Arbor: U of Michigan P, 1960), 38; hereafter cited in the text as *PE*.

78. George Lamming, *The Emigrants* (Ann Arbor: U of Michigan P, 1954), 107; hereafter cited in the text as *E*.

79. Frantz Fanon, *The Wretched of the Earth*, trans. Constance Farrington (New York: Grove, 1963), 39.

80. As Supriya Nair usefully reminds us, it is probably not accurate to think of Lamming's "Fanonian" elements as the result of direct influence, since Lamming and Fanon were in a stricter sense contemporaries, both responding theoretically and imaginatively to the same set of existential and colonial problems. See Nair, *Caliban's Curse: George Lamming and the Revisioning of History* (Ann Arbor: U of Michigan P, 1996), 146 n. 11.

81. Both Lamming and Selvon take pains to narrate the formation of the black intellectual within the web of a West Indian collectivity, in close relation to "the people." For more on the possibility of "Pan-Caribbean identity" in *The Emigrants*, see Simon Gikandi, *Writing in Limbo: Modernism and Caribbean Literature* (Ithaca: Cornell UP, 1992), 94–95. By contrast, we might point to the novels of V. S. Naipaul (*The Mimic Men*, for instance), in which the migrant protagonists and intellectuals seem to be formed by their existential estrangement from all forms of community. In this sense, Naipaul follows in the vein of the alienated cosmopolitan who does not accede to, but resists, the logic of the "cultural turn." Not coincidentally, he seems also to have bought into the myth of imperial decline in ways that echo the writers discussed in the conclusion.

82. It is of course also true, as noted in chapter 1, that the representation of England and its class structures according to the tropes of imperial science became conventional as early as the Victorian period. Nonetheless, the tropes and methods of reverse anthropology gain new historical and literary significance in the era of decolonization. It was in 1950, for example, that the French anthropologist Michel Leiris announced the possibility of a reversal of the anthropological gaze, with ethnographers from "colonized countries" coming to study "our ways of life" (*Brisées: Broken Branches*, trans. Lydia Davis [San Francisco: North Point, 1989], 128).

83. Doris Lessing, *In Pursuit of the English* (New York: Simon and Schuster, 1961), 12; hereafter cited in the text.

84. As James English has pointed out, Lessing's irony here turns on the instability of national and class signifiers, those sociological lodestars of the postwar New Left, into whose discourse Lessing introduces the complications of gender, race, and colonialism (*Comic Transactions*, 160–65).

85. For an alternative body of London writing from the late fifties, one might also consider the fiction and essays of Colin MacInnes, whose antiracism and genuine interest in the mixture of generational, sexual, and ethnic groups in post-

war London translate into a reportorial intensity approaching that of subcultural anthropology. Indeed, MacInnes's work has obvious resonances with the subcultures school that emerged out of the Cultural Studies project; moreover, MacInnes practiced his London ethnography with the mixed perspective of one whose family belonged to an English literary establishment but who was, like his cousin Rudyard Kipling, reared largely in the colonies—in MacInnes's case, Australia.

86. Dipesh Chakrabarty, *Provincializing Europe* (Princeton: Princeton UP, 2000), 36. Chaudhuri was not an émigré or expatriate intellectual; his time in England was always understood to be temporary and even touristic—a brief foray into direct observation funded by the BBC, who wanted to develop views of England from the ex-colonies. After the publication and success of his *Autobiography of an Unknown Indian* (1951), Chaudhuri was "widely regarded as a colonial Anglophile" (John Thieme, "Passages to England," in *Liminal Postmodernisms: the Postmodern, the (Post-)Colonial, and the (Post-)Feminist,* ed. Theo D'haen and Hans Bertens [Amsterdam: Rodopi, 1994], 61).

87. Nirad C. Chaudhuri, *A Passage to England* (New York: St. Martin's, 1959), 64; hereafter cited in the text.

88. *The English Auden,* ed. Edward Mendelson (London: Faber, 1977), 364.

89. *English Auden,* 180 and 186.

90. Cunningham, *British Writers of the Thirties,* 166–76.

91. *English Auden,* 222.

92. *English Auden,* 157–58.

93. Graham Greene, *The Confidential Agent* (New York: Viking, 1967), 3.

94. Mr. Muckerji recalls Kipling's Hurree Babu, an anglicized Bengali and autoethnographer who wishes to be a Fellow of the Royal Society. James Buzard's article on Mass-Observation (chap. 1, n. 92) first drew my attention to Mr. Muckerji.

95. *Confidential Agent,* 141–42.

96. Raymond Williams, *George Orwell* (New York: Columbia UP, 1971), 13.

97. George Orwell, *The Orwell Reader* (San Diego: Harcourt, 1968), 250.

98. Ibid., 270.

99. Ibid., 212.

100. Evelyn Waugh, *A Handful of Dust* (Boston: Little, Brown, 1962), 13.

101. Ibid., 209.

102. Francis Mulhern locates Leavisite thinking precisely in the historical transition from an "old imperial literary culture" to its " 'provincial' successor" (*The Present Lasts a Long Time,* 144–45).

103. Ibid., 137.

104. The second-order universalism that is (paradoxically) implicit in the anthropological turn stems from the fact that culturalism, in the words of Pheng Cheah, "presupposes the universal value of [local] autonomy and proposes to apply it to every particular group or collective unit" ("Given Culture: Rethinking Cosmopolitical Freedom in Transnationalism," in *Cosmopolitics: Thinking and Feeling beyond the Nation,* ed. Cheah and Bruce Robbins [Minneapolis: U of Minnesota P, 1998], 308).

105. To pose minor culture against minority culture in this way is to hark back to a particular historical moment in the definition of Englishness after empire.

In the decades since, a more contemporary definition of "minority culture" has displaced Leavis's construction of a straight, white, middle-class, male band of spiritual aristocrats attuned to the Great Tradition. In fact, "minority culture" might now be taken to refer, in the plural, to precisely those groups (nonwhite, nonmale, nonstraight, non-middle-class) whose claims to social difference and bids for political recognition have been vital areas of struggle and debate in the contemporary United Kingdom. This more contemporary version of "minority culture" politics is made all the more heated because it plays out in a nation still coming to terms with the legacies of its postimperial status as a "minor culture." Looking back on the first phase of the decolonization era now, it is of course striking that both the *Scrutiny* group and the early Cultural Studies intellectuals articulated their populist claims in terms that were equally likely to exclude race, gender, and sexuality from consideration. Similarly, many of the canonical literary groups of the midcentury, from the Auden circle to The Movement, were largely and sometimes by definition (e.g., the Angry Young Men) male. Despite the presence of women writers like Doris Lessing and Iris Murdoch, then, many of the intellectual and literary movements of the period (on both left and right), expressed their Anglocentrism in masculinist terms—and managed to code *both* high modernism and mass culture as feminized.

106. Lloyd, *Anomalous States*, 42.

107. It is part of the logic of postimperial introversion that cultural integrity is on sale in England for a domestic audience. But it is also the case, and an especially conspicuous one since the 1980s, that English Heritage has been consumed avidly in the United States, whether in the form of Merchant Ivory literariness or Raj nostalgia—or, indeed, in the form of the cultural authenticity upon which English Cultural Studies was originally predicated. Paul Gilroy hints at this academic and left-leaning form of historical consumption when he muses about "international enthusiasm for cultural studies" as a variant of (especially American) interest in England and Englishness (*Black Atlantic*, 5).

108. "Post-Traditional English Literature" (Introduction, n. 35), 436.

109. Seamus Heaney, *Preoccupations: Selected Prose 1968–1978* (London: Faber, 1980), 150–51.

INDEX

9 780691 115498